Agency and Answerability

Agency and Answerability

Selected Essays

GARY WATSON

CLARENDON PRESS · OXFORD

OXFORD

UNIVERSITY PRESS

Great Clarendon Street, Oxford OX2 6DP

Oxford University Press is a department of the University of Oxford.
It furthers the University's objective of excellence in research, scholarship,
and education by publishing worldwide in

Oxford New York

Auckland Bangkok Buenos Aires Cape Town Chennai
Dar es Salaam Delhi Hong Kong Istanbul Karachi Kolkata
Kuala Lumpur Madrid Melbourne Mexico City Mumbai Nairobi
São Paulo Shanghai Taipei Tokyo Toronto

Oxford is a registered trade mark of Oxford University Press
in the UK and in certain other countries

Published in the United States
by Oxford University Press Inc., New York

© in this volume Gary Watson 2004

The moral rights of the author have been asserted
Database right Oxford University Press (maker)

First published 2004

British Library Cataloguing in Publication Data
Data available

Library of Congress Cataloging in Publication Data
Data available

ISBN 0–19–927227–1
ISBN 0–19–927228–x (pbk.)

1 3 5 7 9 10 8 6 4 2

Typeset by Newgen Imaging Systems (P) Ltd., Chennai, India
Printed in Great Britain
on acid-free paper by
Biddles Ltd., King's Lynn, Norfolk

In memory of my mother, Bessie Turpin,
whose love remains

Sources

The essays in this volume originally appeared, in this order, in the following publications:

"Free Agency", *Journal of Philosophy*, 72/8 (April 24, 1975), 205–20.

"Skepticism about Weakness of Will", *Philosophical Review*, 86 (July 1977), 316–39.

"Free Action and Free Will", *Mind*, 96 (April 1987), 145–72.

"Responsibility and the Limits of Evil", in F. Schoeman (ed.), *Responsibility, Character, and the Emotions: New Essays in Moral Psychology* (Cambridge: Cambridge University Press, 1987), 256–86.

"Two Faces of Responsibility", *Philosophical Topics*, 24/2 (Fall 1996), 227–48.

"Disordered Appetites", in Jon Elster (ed.), *Addiction: Entries and Exits* (New York: Russell Sage Publications, 1999), 3–28.

"Excusing Addiction", *Law and Philosophy*, Volume 18, no. 6 (November 1999), 589–619.

"Soft Libertarianism and Hard Compatibilism", *Journal of Ethics*, 3, no. 4 (1999), 351–65.

"Reasons and Responsibility", *Ethics*, 111/1 (January 2001), 374–94.

"Volitional Necessities", in Sarah Buss and Lee Overton (eds.), *Contours of Agency* (Cambridge, Mass.: MIT Press, 2002), 129–59.

"The Work of the Will", in Sarah Stroud and Christine Tappolet (eds.), *Weakness of Will and Practical Irrationality* (Oxford University Press, 2003), 172–200.

Acknowledgments

I would like to thank Michael Bratman and Jay Wallace for encouraging me to collect these papers, and Peter Momtchiloff of Oxford University Press for his support of and patient assistance with the project. My colleagues and students in the Department of Philosophy at the University of California at Riverside have provided a most congenial and stimulating intellectual climate. I thank them as well. Finally, I am grateful to Matt Talbert. Despite his doubts about the practice of responsibility, he is responsible for the Index.

Contents

Introduction   1

PART I   FREEDOM, WILL, AND AGENCY

1. Free Agency   13
2. Skepticism about Weakness of Will   33
3. Disordered Appetites: Addiction, Compulsion,
    and Dependence   59
4. Volitional Necessities   88
5. The Work of the Will   123

PART II   AGENCY AND NECESSITY

6. Free Action and Free Will   161
7. Soft Libertarianism and Hard Compatibilism   197

PART III   RESPONSIBILITY AND
                ANSWERABILITY

8. Responsibility and the Limits of Evil: Variations
    on a Strawsonian Theme   219

9. Two Faces of Responsibility   260

10. Reasons and Responsibility   289

11. Excusing Addiction   318

Bibliography   351

Index   367

Introduction

This volume collects most of my publications on the interrelated topics of free will, agency, and responsibility. The essays are substantially unrevised. I do not stand by all of their central claims. They are, after all, mutually inconsistent. Some of the essays are dialectical developments of others; some involve a reconsideration and a change of mind or at least of emphasis. (I will characterize some of these tensions and changes very briefly below.) Inconclusive as they are, these essays certainly do not provide a sustained argument for a systematic resolution of the problems with which they wrestle. My hope is that, at least, they give us a better grasp of the issues.

The essays are grouped loosely by theme into three sections. The grouping is loose because most of the essays deal with more than one theme. As the title of the collection suggests, the essays are predominantly concerned with two intersecting questions: (1) What makes us agents—that is, individuals whose lives are attributable to them as something they (in part) conduct, not just as something that occurs?[1] (2) What makes us responsible to one another for how we

---

[1] There are weaker senses of 'agency' than the one we are after here. The spider moves its limbs in pursuit of the fly; its limbs do not just move on their own or from external stimulation. (See Harry Frankfurt, 'The Problem of Action', *American Philosophical Quarterly*, 1978.) It is notoriously difficult to articulate these distinctions, but one thing seems to me clear. The stronger sense cannot be understood merely by contrasting particular episodes of human limb movements with episodes of spider limb movements and asking what special conditions obtain at the moment. Agency in the stronger sense comes with living a life and therefore involves capacities of planning and self-reflection that spiders presumably lack. (For the importance of planning in connection with human agency, see Michael Bratman, *Intentions, Plans, and Practical Reason* (Cambridge, Mass.: Harvard University Press, 1987), and *idem*, *Faces of Intention* (Cambridge: Cambridge University Press, 1999).)

carry out our lives? The papers grouped together in Parts I and II focus by and large on the question of agency, whereas the question of responsibility is paramount in Part III.

My answer to both questions appeals to a single notion: the capacity for critical evaluation. We are agents because (and insofar as) we shape our lives by the exercise of normative intelligence; we are answerable to interpersonal norms of criticism because our lives are (in part) reflections of this capacity. That, at any rate, is the rough picture, which I first sketched in "Free Agency", Chapter 1. This picture raises problems both of interpretation and of substance. Let's call the capacity of critical evaluation "normative competence".[2] What does it involve? Normative competence admits of weaker and stronger interpretations. No doubt it involves the capacity to respond relevantly to reasons. But which reasons, and what counts as a relevant response? And what is it to have this capacity? "Free Agency" largely neglects these questions, but a number of the subsequent essays struggle with them in one form or another.

I

Let me briefly describe each group of papers. A persistent theme of the early essays (broached in Chapter 1 and pursued in the essays in Part I) is the ways in which human freedom can be diminished by an individual's own desires. In accordance with the picture just sketched, this loss of freedom is said to consist in the obstruction of the capacity to govern one's behavior by critical evaluation. But this explanation runs into trouble with weakness of will, where we fail to act as we think best. In practice, we treat these failures as more or less free. In going against our values, we act badly, so we are not just victims.

---

[2] Adopting Paul Benson's term: 'Freedom and Value', *Journal of Philosophy*, 84 (1987): 465–86. See also Susan Wolf, *Freedom within Reason* (Oxford: Oxford University Press, 1990).

This problem preoccupies me in Chapter 2, "Skepticism about Weakness of Will", where I question the common distinction between weakness of will, in which we give in to resistible temptation, and compulsion, in which we are unfree in virtue of overpowering or irresistible impulses. I argue that, because of obscurities in the idea of resistibility, we should think of the distinction between weakness and compulsion in a different way. Weak agents are distinguishable from victims of compulsion not because they are necessarily able to resist the impulses to which they are subject at the time but because their behavior displays a fault—a failure of self-control—in contrast to the compelled agent who is subject to motivational forces that even a person of exemplary self-control could not resist. This explanation involves a normative standard that does not commit us to the problematic judgment that at the time of action *akratic* agents must be subject to motivational forces that they are able to resist.

In these early discussions, I assumed that the notion of compulsion as irresistible desire was straightforward, and indeed was instantiated in some actual cases of addiction. Chapters 3 and 4 are suspicious of these assumptions. The idea that a desire could be an irresistible force, a sort of internal pressure that overpowers one's utmost efforts, seems deeply misleading, if not confused. To be subject to powerful desires is to find certain activities or objects intensely appealing (or revolting), rather than to be subject to pressures that no amount of effort on our part could counteract. As I put it in "Disordered Appetites", if desire enslaves, it does so "by appeal rather than brute force". Hence, the language of psychological or motivational compulsion must be understood very differently from that of interpersonal or external compulsion.[3] At most, it can indicate the presence of impulses so difficult to counteract that it would

[3] I am now inclined to think that "being captivated", or in some cases even "being possessed", are superior images to that of being compelled, which suggests something too external: that *you* aren't really involved, except as a bystander or victim. In states of captivation, it is not that you aren't into it, but that *you* are (temporarily) transformed (not displaced) by a superior power.

be unreasonable to expect even the strong-willed person to hold out. Desires are strong on this measure insofar as they have the power to compromise one's normative competence, one's capacity to respond appropriately to reasons.

I suggest in Chapter 3 that the threat to agency posed by addictions should be understood in these terms, rather than as sources of literally irresistible desire. Addictions (or at least central sorts of addiction) are in my view usefully construed as acquired appetites. Like their "natural" counterparts, addictions make us vulnerable to various kinds of practical irrationalities, and hence can compromise our freedom to one degree or another. Like other appetites, some addictions are relatively mild, others can nearly drive us crazy. This kind of vulnerability is not necessarily to be deplored, for it is also an inescapable feature of the kinds of attachments that give value to our lives (e.g. romantic or familial love). Addictions, too, can become part of the meaning of our lives, in the sense that their absence would be felt as a loss. (Our relation to our addictions is sometimes like an intensely captivating though ultimately destructive love affair. You know he's bad for you, but he has given you some of the most exciting moments of your life. And the prospect, more than the continued realization of such experiences, is what keeps you hooked.) If we take addictive attachments to be unfortunate, however, it is not (just) because addictions make us prone to loss of control but because of the nature and effects of the activities and experiences to which they dispose us. (I discuss issues of criminal responsibility for addictive behavior in Chapter 11.)

We have been concerned so far with the sense in which our agency can be diminished by our own desires. But some apparent constraints on the will do not seem to be constrictions of agency at all. In his defiance of political and religious authorities, Martin Luther declared, "I can do no other." However, in taking this stance, Luther was not a victim of his convictions. How then should we understand 'cannot' in such contexts? Does it mark a genuine necessity and constraint on Luther's will, or is it just a manner of speaking? Harry Frankfurt has taken this case to illustrate a sort of "volitional necessity" that does not involve weakness or a loss of self-control.[4] On the contrary, he argues, such incapacities are required if one is to have any "shape as a person" at all. Chapter 4 explores this claim and its implications for the interpretation of Frankfurt's philosophy of freedom and action.

Despite the frequency of the terms 'free will' and 'weakness of will' in these pages, the truth is that my work on free agency has largely ignored the phenomenon of the will. It assumed that legitimate questions about free will could readily be cast in terms of action, desire, or judgment. But it became increasingly clear to me that many of the classical concerns about freedom and agency were, after all, concerns about the will, conceived as the capacity that is exercised in the active formation of intention. Chapter 5, "The Work of the Will", tries to take the will seriously. Practical decision is the paradigm case. The first part of the chapter explores the relations between the will, so understood, and practical reason or judgment. The second part takes up decision in the realm of belief—that is, deciding that such and such is so. This phenomenon raises two questions. Since we decide *that* as well as *to*, should we speak of a doxastic will? Secondly, should we regard ourselves as active in the formation of our judgments as in the formation of our intentions? My answer to these two further questions is "no" and "yes", respectively. I see decisions in both realms as exercises of the capacity to assent to and be guided by relevant reasons. This capacity (once again a kind of normative competence) is central to what it is to be an epistemically and morally responsible being. Making up one's mind— "deciding that" and "deciding to"—is a basic and pervasive mode of activity in our theoretical and practical lives. Nevertheless, I argue that there is no straightforward analogue of the will in cognitive contexts. What follows from this, as I put it in Chapter 5, "is not that there is no cognitive agency, but that the boundaries between the active and the passive are not marked by the will".

[4] See e.g. 'The Importance of What We Care About', in Frankfurt's *The Importance of What We Care About: Philosophical Essays* (New York: Cambridge University Press, 1988).

II

The papers in Part I are concerned to understand the forms of "necessity" that lead us in our practical lives to worry about freedom: addiction, phobia, normative incapacitation. However, much of the history of the subject of free will has been shaped by a more abstract issue: the relation between freedom, agency, and causal determination. Even if our capacities to govern our lives by critical evaluation are unimpaired, many philosophers have argued, or at least suspected, that we are fully free or fully agents only if determinism is false. For unless determinism is false, we are subject systematically to necessity, and free agency is incompatible with necessity. Although this issue comes up here and there throughout this volume, the essays in Part II are my most sustained treatment of this subject.

Perhaps I can most usefully summarize my orientation to these questions by trying to explain briefly why I am not an incompatibilist. I state my position in these double-negative terms for several reasons. To say that one is a compatibilist (or incompatibilist for that matter) presumes that there is a coherent thesis of determinism with which one thinks that attributions of free agency are consistent (or not). This presumption seems to me very doubtful. I deny incompatibilism because there seems to me to be nothing in the fulfillment of the general aspirations of scientific explanation that threatens free agency. If the term 'compatibilist' suggests more than this negative thesis, if it suggests that compatibilism is a philosophical camp with a unified metaphysical/ethical outlook, it is an inapt name for my outlook. I find myself more deeply at odds with many compatibilists' agendas than with those of some libertarians. My opposition to incompatibilism is not motivated, for example, by the program of finding a place for agency in a causal reductionist conception of the world. I reject incompatibilism because it seems to me wrongheaded to suppose that the necessitation implied by some forms of scientific explanation has anything to do with the actual conditions that undermine freedom and responsibility.

As I suggest in Chapter 6, one might be troubled by causality in human affairs on two distinct grounds. The most familiar is that determinism appears to entail that no one can do or choose otherwise. A quite different worry, however, is that if our "actions" are just outcomes of the history of causal forces to which they are subject, they are not imputable to us as agents. The first version I call *modal incompatibilism*, because of its focus on possibility and necessity. The second version I call *explanatory incompatibilism*; if determinism is true, there seems to be no validity to the distinctive forms of explanation by which we attribute behavior to ourselves and one another.

Incompatibilism in either form has always seemed to me misguided, but I should say that of the two, the explanatory version seems to me to pose a deeper challenge. For it involves the more general philosophical task of fitting together a picture of ourselves as reason-responsive beings with our idea of nature as a system of meaningless forces, and we are not at all sure how to do that. It is indeed hard to see ourselves as products of nature, as I stress in Chapter 7, but the thought that indeterminacy will help is an illusion.

III

The idea of reasons responsiveness is central to our understanding of responsibility as well. This concept is the main subject of the essays in Part III. Discussions of responsibility tend to focus exclusively on the capacities of the individual. But responsibility is a triadic relationship: an individual (or group) is responsible *to* others *for* something. So it is equally important to understand what holding others responsible amounts to and to explore the basis of our standing to do this. These are of course complementary inquiries. Our understanding of the capacities of responsible agents must be controlled, at least implicitly, by our view of the conditions under which we are entitled to respond to others in the ways that constitute holding them responsible. A corollary of this point is that we lack a fully adequate understanding of responsible agency to the extent to which our authority to respond to others in this way is unexamined. This brings the topic of responsibility closer to some of the central topics of normative moral theory[5]—for example, the source of moral requirements, that is, of our authority to make demands of certain sorts on one another. Who are we to make such demands? (Skepticism about this notion of requirement is a less commonly discussed source of skepticism about the practice of responsibility.)

Responsibility, then, is a relationship in which we are entitled to make demands on one another and to respond in certain ways in case those demands are not met. Many philosophers have noticed and exploited the conceptual/etymological link between 'response' and 'responsibility': responsibility has to do at once with our capacity to respond appropriately to interpersonal requirements and with our entitlement to respond in certain ways to those who flout those norms. (Here I set aside the important case of holding oneself responsible.) Responsibility is in this way bound up with the ideas of answerability and accountability. Holding others responsible takes the form of requiring them to answer for their behavior, to give an account of themselves in light of their apparent violation of certain expectations, and, furthermore, to respond appropriately in case that account is unsatisfactory (by redress or apology, for instance). (The expectations in question need not be general moral require-ments; they could follow from particular commitments of a personal relationship.)

These connections support the idea that the capacity required for responsible agency is the capacity to respond to the standards to which we hold one another responsible. On the assumption that those standards imply reasons for acting (as well as choosing and

---

[5] For recent attempts to bring these subjects into contact, see R. Jay Wallace, *Responsibility and the Moral Sentiments* (Cambridge, Mass.: Harvard University Press, 1994), and T. M. Scanlon, *What We Owe to Each Other* (Cambridge, Mass.: Harvard University Press, 1998).

feeling) in certain ways, we can then conclude that responsible agency involves the capacity to respond to reasons. The difficult task is to give an adequate specification of this capacity. (I explore reasons-responsiveness in Chapter 10.)

To have this capacity is obviously not to exercise it well; otherwise, we couldn't be responsible for wrongful conduct. On the other hand, some of the evil in human action seems to bespeak a kind of insensitivity to certain moral reasons, at least of certain kinds. In what sense can a deeply cruel man, for example, respond to reasons of kindness? In practice we regard such a person as all the more blameworthy for his insensitivity. This seems to go against the idea we've been developing. Sensitivity to reasons, on a natural interpretation, requires moral sense; but anyone who thoroughly and systematically disregards fundamental moral reasons must be deficient in this regard. I explore some of these tensions in Chapter 8, "Responsibility and the Limits of Evil". As I put it there, "extreme evil [paradoxically] seems to disqualify us for blame".

But the notion of blame is elusive too. There is a sense of blame that doesn't impute anything more than causal responsibility, as when we blame the fuel pump for the poor performance of a car. We could make the same kind of judgment about a human being's conduct. Blaming, in this sense, just means finding fault, and finding fault doesn't imply responsibility. There is no appearance of paradox in blaming the evil character in this sense.

The idea of blameworthiness that is entailed by responsibility is stronger than this. And it might seem that the picture of freedom and responsibility that I advance in many of these essays can only justify something like this weaker sense of blame. Because our lives are reflections of the capacity for critical evaluation, the story goes, we are answerable to interpersonal norms of criticism. This story explains why human beings, who operate by critical reflection, can perform well or badly by standards not applicable to automobiles. These capacities provide the basis for certain aesthetic or aretaic judgments, perhaps, but that's not what (or all) we have in mind by moral blame. In this stronger sense of blame, our wrongdoing opens us up not just to certain kinds of appraisal but to adverse responses and treatments of various kinds—from hard feelings like resentment, to public condemnation, to imprisonment. To justify this stronger kind of reaction, according to this criticism, my picture needs to be supplemented by the condition that the cruel man could have avoided his becoming the bad actor he is. This kind of avoidability might well conflict with my claims about the irrelevance of causal determination.

I try to respond to this kind of worry in Chapter 9, where I distinguish two "faces" of responsibility: what I call 'attributability' and 'accountability'. Attributability has to do with the imputation of a deed to an individual as its author. This identifies a core notion of responsibility, I argue, that is involved when we make judgments about an individual's moral choices and how she has lived her life. The ways in which people conduct their lives and make their choices and form and dissolve their attachments are of deep interest to us as possible models of human achievement and failure. Aretaic judgments are not merely aesthetic, for they bear directly on how we are to conduct ourselves, what ends to adopt, and on what kind of agents to be. However, such judgments do not settle the question of how we should respond to people in view of their deeds: whether they deserve some kind of adverse reaction, and if so, what kind. This is the question of accountability. Accountability seems to involve the readiness to subject others to unwelcome treatment. *Prima facie* it is unfair to treat people adversely for failing to comply with demands unless they have had a reasonable opportunity to do so. So accountability raises special questions about the interpretation of avoidability that are not at issue from the aretaic perspective. This creates a foothold for incompatibilist doubts. Indeed, it is possible to be skeptical about the idea of accountability, on these or other grounds, without challenging the core notion of attributability.

Part I
Freedom, Will, and Agency

1   Free Agency

In this essay I discuss a distinction that is crucial to a correct account of free action and to an adequate conception of human motivation and responsibility.

I

According to one familiar conception of freedom, a person is free to the extent that he is able to do or get what he wants. To circumscribe a person's freedom is to contract the range of things he is able to do. I think that, suitably qualified, this account is correct, and that the chief and most interesting uses of the word 'free' can be explicated in its terms. But this general line has been resisted on a number of different grounds. One of the most important objections—and the one upon which I shall concentrate in this paper—is that this familiar view is too impoverished to handle talk of free actions and free will.

Frequently enough, we say, or are inclined to say, that a person is not in control of his own actions, that he is not a "free agent" with respect to them, even though his behavior is intentional. Possible examples of this sort of action include those which are explained by addictions, manias, and phobias of various sorts. But the concept of free action would seem to be pleonastic on the analysis of freedom in

I have profited from discussions with numerous friends, students, colleagues, and other audiences, on the material of this essay; I would like to thank them collectively. However, special thanks are due to Joel Feinberg, Harry Frankfurt, and Thomas Nagel.

terms of the ability to get what one wants. For if a person does something intentionally, then surely he was able at that time to do it. Hence, on this analysis, he was free to do it. The familiar account would not seem to allow for any further questions, as far as freedom is concerned, about the action. Accordingly, this account would seem to embody a conflation of free action and intentional action.

Philosophers who have defended some form of compatibilism have usually given this analysis of freedom, with the aim of showing that freedom and responsibility are not really incompatible with determinism. Some critics have rejected compatibilism precisely because of its association with this familiar account of freedom. For instance, Isaiah Berlin asks: if determinism is true,

. . . what reasons can you, in principle, adduce for attributing responsibility or applying moral rules to [people] which you would not think it reasonable to apply in the case of compulsive choosers—kleptomaniacs, dipsomaniacs, and the like?[1]

The idea is that the sense in which actions would be free in a deterministic world allows the actions of "compulsive choosers" to be free. To avoid this consequence, it is often suggested, we must adopt some sort of "contracausal" view of freedom.

Now, though compatibilists from Hobbes to J. J. C. Smart have given the relevant moral and psychological concepts an exceedingly crude treatment, this crudity is not inherent in compatibilism, nor does it result from the adoption of the conception of freedom in terms of the ability to get what one wants. For the difference between free and unfree actions—as we normally discern it—has nothing at all to do with the truth or falsity of determinism.

In the subsequent pages, I want to develop a distinction between wanting and valuing which will enable the familiar view of freedom to make sense of the notion of an unfree action. The contention will be that, in the case of actions that are unfree, the agent is unable to get what he most wants, *or values*, and this inability is due to his own

[1] *Four Essays on Liberty* (New York: Oxford, 1969), pp. xx–xxi.

"motivational system." In this case the obstruction to the action that he most wants to do is his own will. It is in this respect that the action is unfree: the agent is obstructed in and by the very performance of the action.

I do not conceive my remarks to be a defense of compatibilism. This point of view may be unacceptable for various reasons, some of which call into question the coherence of the concept of responsibility. But these reasons do not include the fact that compatibilism relies upon the conception of freedom in terms of the ability to get what one wants, nor must it conflate free action and intentional action. If compatibilism is to be shown to be wrong, its critics must go deeper.

II

What must be true of people if there is to be a significant notion of free action? Our talk of free action arises from the apparent fact that what a person most wants may not be what he is finally moved to get. It follows from this apparent fact that the extent to which one wants something is not determined solely by the *strength* of one's desires (or "motives") as measured by their effectiveness in action. One (perhaps trivial) measure of the strength of the desire or want is that the agent acts upon that desire or want (trivial, since it will be nonexplanatory to say that an agent acted upon that desire because it was the strongest). But, if what one most wants may not be what one most strongly wants, by this measure, then in what sense can it be true that one most wants it?[2]

To answer this question, one might begin by contrasting, at least in a crude way, a Humean with a Platonic conception of practical reasoning. The ancients distinguished between the rational and the

---

[2] I am going to use 'want' and 'desire' in the very inclusive sense now familiar in philosophy, whereby virtually any motivational factor that may figure in the explanation of intentional action is a want; 'desire' will be used mainly in connection with the appetites and passions.

irrational parts of the soul, between Reason and Appetite. Hume employed a superficially similar distinction. It is important to understand, however, that (for Plato at least) the rational part of the soul is not to be identified with what Hume called "Reason" and contradistinguished from the "Passions." On Hume's account, Reason is not a source of motivation, but a faculty of determining what is true and what is false, a faculty concerned solely with "matters of fact" and "relations among ideas." It is completely dumb on the question of what to do. Perhaps Hume could allow Reason this much practical voice: given an initial set of wants and beliefs about what is or is likely to be the case, particular desires are generated in the process. In other words, a Humean might allow Reason a crucial role in deliberation. But its essential role would not be to supply motivation—Reason is not that kind of thing—but rather to calculate, within a context of desires and ends, how to fulfill those desires and serve those ends. For Plato, however, the rational part of the soul is not some kind of inference mechanism. It is itself a source of motivation. In general form, the desires of Reason are desires for "the Good."

Perhaps the contrast can be illustrated by some elementary notions from decision theory. On the Bayesian model of deliberation, a preference scale is imposed upon various states of affairs contingent upon courses of action open to the agent. Each state of affairs can be assigned a numerical value (initial value) according to its place on the scale; given this assignment, and the probabilities that those states of affairs will obtain if the actions are performed, a final numerical value (expected desirability) can be assigned to the actions themselves. The rational agent performs the action with the highest expected desirability.

In these terms, on the Humean picture, Reason is the faculty that computes probabilities and expected desirabilities. Reason is in this sense neutral with respect to actions, for it can operate equally on any given assignment of initial values and probabilities—it has nothing whatsoever to say about the assignment of initial values. On the Platonic picture, however, the rational part of the soul itself determines what has *value* and how much, and thus is responsible for the original ranking of alternative states of affairs.

It may appear that the difference between these conceptions is merely a difference as to what is to be called "Reason" or "rational," and hence is not a substantive difference. In speaking of Reason, Hume has in mind a sharp contrast between what is wanted and what is thought to be the case. What contrast is implicit in the Platonic view that the ranking of alternative states of affairs is the task of the rational part of the soul?

The contrast here is not trivial; the difference in classificatory schemes reflects different views of human psychology. For one thing, in saying this (or what is tantamount to this) Plato was calling attention to the fact that it is one thing to think a state of affairs good, worthwhile, or worthy of promotion, and another simply to desire or want that state of affairs to obtain. Since the notion of value is tied to (cannot be understood independently of) those of the good and worthy, it is one thing to value (think good) a state of affairs and another to desire that it obtain. However, to think a thing good is at the same time to desire it (or its promotion). Reason is thus an original spring of action. It is because valuing is essentially related to thinking or *judging* good that it is appropriate to speak of the wants that are (or perhaps arise from) evaluations as belonging to, or originating in, the rational (that is, *judging*) part of the soul; values provide *reasons* for action. The contrast is with desires, whose objects may not be thought good and which are thus, in a natural sense, blind or irrational. Desires are mute on the question of what is good.[3]

Now it seems to me that—given the view of freedom as the ability to get what one wants—there can be a problem of free action only if the Platonic conception of the soul is (roughly) correct. The doctrine I shall

---

[3] To quote just one of many suggestive passages: "We must . . . observe that within each one of us there are two sorts of ruling or guiding principle that we follow. One is an innate desire for pleasure, the other an acquired judgment that aims at what is best. Sometimes these internal guides are in accord, sometimes at variance; now one gains the mastery, now the other. And when judgment guides us rationally toward

defend is Platonic in the sense that it involves a distinction between valuing and desiring which depends upon there being independent sources of motivation. No doubt Plato meant considerably more than this by his parts-of-the-soul doctrine; but he meant at least this. The Platonic conception provides an answer to the question I posed earlier (p. 15): in what sense can what one most wants differ from that which is the object of the strongest desire? The answer is that the phrase 'what one most wants' may mean either "the object of the strongest desire" or "what one most *values*." This phrase can be interpreted in terms of strength or in terms of ranking order or preference. The problem of free action arises because what one desires may not be what one values, and what one most values may not be what one is finally moved to get.[4]

The tacit identification of desiring or wanting with valuing is so common[5] that it is necessary to cite some examples of this distinction

what is best, and has the mastery, that mastery is called temperance, but when desire drags us irrationally toward pleasure, and has come to rule within us, the name given to that rule is wantonness" (*Phaedrus*, 237e–238e; Hackforth trans.).

For a fascinating discussion of Plato's parts-of-the-soul doctrine, see Terry Penner's "Thought and Desire in Plato," in Gregory Vlastos, ed., *Plato: A Collection of Critical Essays*, vol. II (New York: Anchor, 1971). As I see it (and here I have been influenced by Penner's article), the distinction I have attributed to Plato was meant by him to be a solution to the socratic problem of *akrasia*.

I would argue that this distinction, though necessary, is insufficient for the task, because it does not mark the difference between ("mere") incontinence or weakness of will and psychological compulsion. This difference requires a careful examination of the various things that might be meant in speaking of the strength of a desire. [See Chapter 2.]

[4] Here I shall not press the rational/nonrational contrast any further than this, though Plato would have wished to press it further. However, one important and anti-Humean implication of the minimal distinction is this: it is not the case that, if a person desires to do X, he therefore has (or even regards himself as having) a reason to do X.

[5] For example, I take my remarks to be incompatible with the characterization of value R. B. Perry gives in *General Theory of Value* (Cambridge, Mass.: Harvard, 1950). In ch. v, Perry writes: "This, then, we take to be the original source and constant feature of all value. That which is an object of interest is *eo ipso* invested with value." And 'interest' is characterized in the following way: ". . . liking and disliking, desire and aversion, will and refusal, or seeking and avoiding. It is to this all-pervasive characteristic of the motor-affective life, this *state, act, attitude or disposition of favor* of disfavor, to which we propose to give the name of 'interest'."

in order to illustrate how evaluation and desire may diverge. There seem to be two ways in which, in principle, a discrepancy may arise. First, it is possible that what one desires is not *to any degree* valued, held to be worthwhile, or thought good; one assigns *no* value whatever to the object of one's desire. Second, although one may indeed value what is desired, the strength of one's desire may not properly reflect the degree to which one values its object; that is, although the object of a desire is valuable, it may not be deemed the most valuable in the situation and yet one's desire for it may be stronger than the want for what is most valued.

The cases in which one in no way values what one desires are perhaps rare, but surely they exist. Consider the case of a woman who has a sudden urge to drown her bawling child in the bath; or the case of a squash player who, while suffering an ignominious defeat, desires to smash his opponent in the face with the racquet. It is just false that the mother values her child's being drowned or that the player values the injury and suffering of his opponent. But they desire these things nonetheless. They desire them in spite of themselves. It is not that they assign to these actions an initial value which is then outweighed by other considerations. These activities are not even represented by a positive entry, however small, on the initial "desirability matrix."

It may seem from these examples that this first and radical sort of divergence between desiring and valuing occurs only in the case of momentary and inexplicable urges or impulses. Yet I see no conclusive reason why a person could not be similarly estranged from a rather persistent and pervasive desire, and one that is explicable enough. Imagine a man who thinks his sexual inclinations are the work of the devil, that the very fact that he has sexual inclinations bespeaks his corrupt nature. This example is to be contrasted with that of the celibate who decides that the most fulfilling life for him will be one of abstinence. In this latter case, *one* of the things that receive consideration in the process of reaching his all-things-considered judgment is the value of sexual activity. There is something, from his point of view, to be said for sex, but there is more to be said in favor of celibacy. In contrast, the man who is estranged from his sexual inclinations does not acknowledge even a prima facie reason for sexual activity; that he is sexually inclined toward certain activities is not even *a* consideration. Another way of illustrating the difference is to say that, for the one man, forgoing sexual relationships constitutes a *loss*, even if negligible compared with the gains of celibacy; whereas from the standpoint of the other person, no loss is sustained at all.

Now, it must be admitted, any desire may provide the basis for a reason insofar as nonsatisfaction of the desire causes suffering and hinders the pursuit of ends of the agent. But it is important to notice that the reason generated in this way by a desire is a reason for *getting rid* of the desire, and one may get rid of a desire either by satisfying it or by eliminating it in some other manner (by tranquilizers, or cold showers). Hence this kind of reason differs importantly from the reasons based upon the evaluation of the activities or states of affairs in question. For, in the former case, attaining the object of desire is simply a means of eliminating discomfort or agitation, whereas in the latter case that attainment is the end itself. Normally, in the pursuit of the objects of our wants we are not attempting chiefly to relieve ourselves. We aim to satisfy, not just eliminate, desire.

Nevertheless, aside from transitory impulses, it may be that cases wherein nothing at all can be said in favor of the object of one's desire are rare. For it would seem that even the person who conceives his sexual desires to be essentially evil would have to admit that indulgence would be pleasurable, and surely that is something. (Perhaps not even this should be admitted. For indulgence may not yield pleasure at all in a context of anxiety. Furthermore, it is not obvious that pleasure is intrinsically good, independently of the worth of the pleasurable object.) In any case, the second sort of divergence between evaluation and desire remains: it is possible that, in a particular context, what one wants most strongly is not what one most values.

The distinction between valuing and desiring is not, it is crucial to see, a distinction among desires or wants according to their content.

That is to say, there is nothing in the specification of the objects of an agent's desires that singles out some wants as based upon that agent's values. The distinction in question has rather to do with the *source* of the want or with its role in the total "system" of the agent's desires and ends. It has to do with why the agent wants what he does.

Obviously, to identify a desire or want simply in terms of its content is not to identify its source(s). It does not follow from my wanting to eat that I am hungry. I may want to eat because I want to be well-nourished; or because I am hungry; or because eating is a pleasant activity. This single desire may have three independent sources. (These sources may not be altogether independent. It may be that eating is pleasurable only because I have appetites for food.) Some specifications of wants or desires—for instance, as cravings—pick out (at least roughly) the source of the motivation.

It is an essential feature of the appetites and the passions that they engender (or consist in) desires whose existence and persistence are independent of the person's judgment of the good. The appetite of hunger involves a desire to eat which has a source in physical needs and physiological states of the hungry organism. And emotions such as anger and fear partly consist in spontaneous inclinations to do various things—to attack or to flee the object of one's emotion, for example. It is intrinsic to the appetites and passions that appetitive and passionate beings can be motivated in spite of themselves. It is because desires such as these arise independently of the person's judgment and values that the ancients located the emotions and passions in the irrational part of the soul;[6] and it is because of this sort of independence that a conflict between valuing and desiring is possible.[7]

---

[6] Notice that most emotions differ from passions like lust in that they involve beliefs and some sort of valuation (cf. resentment). This may be the basis for Plato's positing a third part of the soul which is in a way partly rational—viz. *Thumos*.

[7] To be sure, one may attempt to cultivate or eliminate certain appetites and passions, so that the desires that result may be in this way dependent upon one's evaluations. Even so, the resulting desires will be such that they can persist independently of one's values. It is rather like jumping from an airplane.

These points may suggest an inordinately dualistic view according to which persons are split into inevitably alien, if not always antagonistic, halves. But this view does not follow from what has been said. As central as it is to human life, it is not often noted that some activities are valued only to the extent that they are objects of the appetites. This means that such activities would never be regarded as valuable constituents of one's life were it not for one's susceptibility to "blind" motivation—motivation independent of one's values. Sexual activity and eating are again examples. We may value the activity of eating to the degree that it provides nourishment. But we may also value it because it is an enjoyable activity, even though its having this status depends upon our appetites for food, our hunger. In the case of sex, in fact, if we were not erotic creatures, certain activities would not only lose their value to us, they might not even be physiologically possible.

These examples indicate, not that there is no distinction between desiring and valuing, but that the value placed upon certain activities depends upon their being the fulfillment of desires that arise and persist independently of what we value. So it is not that, when we value the activity of eating, we think there are reasons to eat no matter what other desires we have; rather, we value eating when food appeals to us; and, likewise, we value sexual relationships when we are aroused. Here an essential part of the *content* of our evaluation is that the activity in question be motivated by certain appetites. These activities may have value for us only insofar as they are appetitively motivated, even though to have these appetites is not *ipso facto* to value their objects.

Part of what it means to value some activities in this way is this: we judge that to cease to have such appetites is to lose something of worth. The judgment here is not merely that, if someone has these appetites, it is worthwhile (*ceteris paribus*) for him to indulge them. The judgment is rather that it is of value to have and (having them) to indulge these appetites. The former judgment does not account for the eunuch's loss or sorrow, whereas the latter does. And the latter judgment lies at the bottom of the discomfort one may feel when one envisages a situation in which, say, hunger is consistently eliminated and nourishment provided by insipid capsules.

It would be impossible for a non-erotic being or a person who lacked the appetite for food and drink fully to understand the value most of us attach to sex and to dining. Sexual activity must strike the non-erotic being as perfectly grotesque. (Perhaps that is why lust is sometimes said to be disgusting and sinful in the eyes of God.) Or consider an appetite that is in fact "unnatural" (i.e., acquired): the craving for tobacco. To a person who has never known the enticement of Lady Nicotine, what could be more incomprehensible than the filthy practice of consummating a fine meal by drawing into one's lungs the noxious fumes of a burning weed?

Thus, the relationship between evaluation and motivation is intricate. With respect to many of our activities, evaluation depends upon the possibility of our being moved to act independently of our judgment. So the distinction I have been pressing—that between desiring and valuing—does not commit one to an inevitable split between Reason and Appetite. Appetitively motivated activities may well constitute for a person the most worth-while aspects of his life.[8] But the distinction does commit us to the possibility of such a split. If there are sources of motivation independent of the agent's values, then it is possible that sometimes he is motivated to do things he does not deem worth doing. This possibility is the basis for the principal problem of free action: a person may be obstructed by his own will.

A related possibility that presents considerable problems for the understanding of free agency is this: some desires, when they arise, may "color" or influence what appear to be the agent's evaluations, but only temporarily. That is, when and only when he has the desire, is he inclined to think or say that what is desired or wanted is worth while or good. This possibility is to be distinguished from

[8] It is reported that H. G. Wells regarded the most important themes of his life to have been (1) the attainment of a World Society, and (2) sex.

another, according to which one thinks it worthwhile to eat when one is hungry or to engage in sexual activity when one is so inclined. For one may think this even on the occasions when the appetites are silent. The possibility I have in mind is rather that what one is disposed to say or judge is temporarily affected by the presence of the desire in such a way that, both before and after the "onslaught" of the desire, one judges that the desire's object is worth pursuing (in the circumstances) whether or not one has the desire. In this case one is likely, in a cool moment, to think it a matter for regret that one had been so influenced and to think that one should guard against desires that have this property. In other cases it may not be the desire itself that affects one's judgment, but the set of conditions in which those desires arise—e.g., the conditions induced by drugs or alcohol. (It is noteworthy that we say: "under the influence of alcohol.") Perhaps judgments made in such circumstances are often in some sense self-deceptive. In any event, this phenomenon raises problems about the identification of a person's values.

Despite our examples, it would be mistaken to conclude that the only desires that exhibit an independence of evaluation are appetitive or passionate desires. In Freudian terms, one may be as dissociated from the demands of the super-ego as from those of the id. One may be disinclined to move away from one's family, the thought of doing so being accompanied by compunction; and yet this disinclination may rest solely upon acculturation rather than upon a current judgment of what one is to do, reflecting perhaps an assessment of one's "duties" and interests. Or, taking another example, one may have been habituated to think that divorce is to be avoided in all cases, so that the aversion to divorce persists even though one sees no justification for maintaining one's marriage. In both of these cases, the attitude has its basis solely in acculturation and exists independently of the agent's judgment. For this reason, acculturated desires are irrational (better: nonrational) in the same sense as appetitive and passionate desires. In fact, despite the inhibitions acquired in the course of a puritan up-bringing, a person may deem the pursuit of sexual pleasure to be worthwhile, his judgment siding with the id rather than the super-ego. Acculturated attitudes may seem more akin to evaluation than to appetite in that they are often expressed in evaluative language ("divorce is wicked") and result in feelings of guilt when one's actions are not in conformity with them. But, since conflict is possible here, to want something as a result of acculturation is not thereby to value it, in the sense of 'to value' that we want to capture.

It is not easy to give a nontrivial account of the sense of 'to value' in question. In part, to value something is, in the appropriate circumstances, to want it, and to attribute a want for something to someone is to say that he is disposed to try to get it. So it will not be easy to draw this distinction in behavioral terms. Apparently the difference will have to do with the agent's attitude toward the various things he is disposed to try to get. We might say that an agent's values consist in those principles and ends which he—in a cool and non-self-deceptive moment—articulates as definitive of the good, fulfilling, and defensible life. That most people have articulate "conceptions of the good," coherent life-plans, *systems* of ends, and so on, is of course something of a fiction. Yet we all have more or less long-term aims and normative principles that we are willing to defend. It is such things as these that are to be identified with our values.

The valuational system of an agent is that set of considerations which, when combined with his factual beliefs (and probability estimates), yields judgments of the form: the thing for me to do in these circumstances, all things considered, is a. To ascribe free agency to a being presupposes it to be a being that makes judgments of this sort. To be this sort of being, one must assign values to alternative states of affairs, that is, rank them in terms of worth.

The motivational system of an agent is that set of considerations which move him to action. We identify his motivational system by identifying what motivates him. The possibility of unfree action consists in the fact that an agent's valuational system and motivational system may not completely coincide. Those systems harmonize to the extent that what determines the agent's all-things-considered judgments also determines his actions.

Now, to be sure, since to value is also to want, one's valuational and motivational systems must to a large extent overlap. If, in appropriate circumstances, one were never inclined to action by some alleged evaluation, the claim that that was indeed one's evaluation would be disconfirmed. Thus one's valuational system must have some (considerable) grip upon one's motivational system. The problem is that there are motivational factors other than valuational ones. The free agent has the capacity to translate his values into action; his actions flow from his evaluational system.

One's evaluational system may be said to constitute one's standpoint, the point of view from which one judges the world. The important feature of one's evaluational system is that one cannot coherently dissociate oneself from it *in its entirety*. For to dissociate oneself from the ends and principles that constitute one's evaluational system is to disclaim or repudiate them, and any ends and principles so disclaimed (self-deception aside) cease to be constitutive of one's valuational system. One can dissociate oneself from one set of ends and principles only from the standpoint of another such set that one does not disclaim. In short, one cannot dissociate oneself from all normative judgments without forfeiting all standpoints and therewith one's identity as an agent.

Of course, it does not follow from the fact that one must assume some standpoint that one must have only one, nor that one's standpoint is completely determinate. There may be ultimate conflicts, irresolvable tensions, and things about which one simply does not know what to do or say. Some of these possibilities point to problems about the unity of the person. Here the extreme case is pathological. I am inclined to think that when the split is severe enough, to have more than one standpoint is to have none.

This distinction between wanting and valuing requires far fuller explication than it has received so far. Perhaps the foregoing remarks have at least shown *that* the distinction exists and is important, and have hinted at its nature. This distinction is important to the adherent of the familiar view—that talk about free action and free agency can be understood in terms of the idea of being able to get what one wants—because it gives sense to the claim that in unfree actions the agents do not get what they really or most want. This distinction gives sense to the contrast between free action and intentional action. Admittedly, further argument is required to show that such unfree agents are *unable* to get what they want; but the initial step toward this end has been taken.

At this point, it will be profitable to consider briefly a doctrine that is in many respects like that which I have been developing. The contrast will, I think, clarify the claims that have been advanced in the preceding pages.

III

In an important and provocative article,[9] Harry Frankfurt has offered a description of what he takes to be the essential feature of "the concept of a person," a feature which, he alleges, is also basic to an understanding of "freedom of the will." This feature is the possession of higher-order volitions as well as first-order desires. Frankfurt construes the notion of a person's will as "the notion of an *effective* desire—one that moves (or will or would move) a person all the way to action" (14). Someone has a second-order volition, then, when he wants "a certain desire to be his will." (Frankfurt also considers the case of a second-order desire that is not a second-order volition, where one's desire is simply to have a certain desire and not to act upon it. For example, a man may be curious to know what it is like to be addicted to drugs; he thus desires to desire heroin, but he may not desire his desire for heroin to be effective, to be his will.

---

[9] "Freedom of the Will and the Concept of a Person," *Journal of Philosophy*, 68/1 (Jan. 14, 1971): 5–20; repr. in Frankfurt, 1988. All references are to the reprinted edition.

[c] In fact, Frankfurt's actual example is somewhat more special, for here the man's desire is not simply to have a desire for heroin: he wants to have a desire for heroin which has a certain source, i.e., is addictive. He wants to know what it is like to *crave* heroin.) Someone is a *wanton* if he has no second-order volitions. Finally, "it is only because a person has volitions of the second order that he is capable both of enjoying and of lacking freedom of the will" (19).

Frankfurt's thesis resembles the Platonic view we have been unfolding insofar as it focuses upon "the structure of a person's will" (6). I want to make a simple point about Frankfurt's paper: namely that the "structural" feature to which Frankfurt appeals is not the fundamental feature for either free agency or personhood; it is simply insufficient to the task he wants it to perform.

One job that Frankfurt wishes to do with the distinction between lower and higher orders of desire is to give an account of the sense in which some wants may be said to be more truly the agent's own than others (though in an obvious sense all are wants of the agent), the sense in which the agent "identifies" with one desire rather than another and the sense in which an agent may be unfree with respect to his own "will." This enterprise is similar to our own. But we can see that the notion of "higher-order volition" is not really the fundamental notion for these purposes, by raising the question: Can't one be a wanton, so to speak, with respect to one's second-order desires and volitions?

In a case of conflict, Frankfurt would have us believe that what it is to identify with some desire rather than another is to have a volition concerning the former which is of higher order than any concerning the latter. That the first desire is given a special status over the second is due to its having an n-order volition concerning it, whereas the second desire has at most an $(n - 1)$-order volition concerning it. But why does one necessarily care about one's higher-order volitions? Since second-order volitions are themselves simply desires, to add them to the context of conflict is just to increase the number of contenders; it is not to give a special place to any of those in contention.

The agent may not care which of the second-order desires win out. The same possibility arises at each higher order.

Quite aware of this difficulty, Frankfurt writes:

There is no theoretical limit to the length of the series of desires of higher and higher orders; nothing except common sense and, perhaps, a saving fatigue prevents an individual from obsessively refusing to identify himself with any of his desires until he forms a desire of the next higher order (21).

But he insists that

It is possible . . . to terminate such a series of acts [i.e., the formation of ever higher-order volitions] without cutting it off arbitrarily. When a person identifies himself *decisively* with one of his first-order desires, this commitment "resounds" throughout the potentially endless array of higher orders . . . The fact that his second-order volition to be moved by this desire is a decisive one means that there is no room for questions concerning the pertinence of volitions of higher orders . . . The decisiveness of the commitment he has made means that he has decided that no further question about his second-order volition, at any higher order, remains to be asked (21–2).

But either this reply is lame or it reveals that the notion of a higher-order volition is not the fundamental one. We wanted to know what prevents wantonness with regard to one's higher-order volitions. What gives these volitions any special relation to "oneself"? It is unhelpful to answer that one makes a "decisive commitment," where this just means that an interminable ascent to higher orders is not going to be permitted. This *is* arbitrary.

What this difficulty shows is that the notion of orders of desires or volitions does not do the work that Frankfurt wants it to do. It does not tell us why or how a particular want can have, among all of a person's "desires," the special property of being peculiarly his "own." There may be something to the notions of acts of identification and of decisive commitment, but these are in any case different notions from that of a second-(or *n*-)order desire. And if these are the crucial notions, it is unclear why these acts of identification cannot be

themselves of the first order—that is, identification with or commitment to courses of action (rather than with or to desires)—in which
case, no ascent is necessary, and the notion of higher-order volitions
becomes superfluous or at least secondary.

In fact, I think that such acts of "identification and commitment"
(if one goes for this way of speaking) are generally to courses of
action, that is, are first-order. Frankfurt's picture of practical judgment seems to be that of an agent with a given set of (first-order)
desires concerning which he then forms second-order volitions. But
this picture seems to be distorted. As I see it, agents frequently formulate values concerning alternatives they had not hitherto desired.
Initially, they do not (or need not usually) ask themselves which of
their desires they want to be effective in action; they ask themselves
which course of action is most worth pursuing. The initial practical
question is about courses of action and not about themselves.

Indeed, practical judgments are connected with "second-order
volitions." For the same considerations that constitute one's on-
balance reasons for doing some action, a, are reasons for wanting the
"desire" to do a to be effective in action, and for wanting contrary
desires to be ineffective. But in general, evaluations are prior and of
the first order. The first-order desires that result from practical judgments generate second-order volitions because they have this special
status; they do not have the special status that Frankfurt wants them
to have because there is a higher-order desire concerning them.

Therefore, Frankfurt's position resembles the Platonic conception
in its focus upon the structure of the "soul."[10] But the two views
draw their divisions differently; whereas Frankfurt divides the soul
into higher and lower orders of desire, the distinction for Plato—and
for my thesis—is among independent sources of motivation.[11]

---

[10] Frankfurt's idea of a wanton, suitably construed, can be put to further illuminating uses in moral psychology. It proves valuable, I think, in discussing the problematic phenomenon of psychopathy or sociopathy.

[11] Some very recent articles employ distinctions, for similar purposes, very like
Frankfurt's and my own. See, for example, Richard C. Jeffrey, "Preferences among

IV

In conclusion, it can now be seen that one worry that blocks the acceptance of the traditional view of freedom—and in turn, of compatibilism—is unfounded. To return to Berlin's question (p. 14 above), it is false that determinism entails that all our actions and choices have the same status as those of "compulsive choosers" such as "kleptomaniacs, dipsomaniacs, and the like." What is distinctive about such compulsive behavior, I would argue, is that the desires and emotions in question are more or less radically independent of the evaluational systems of these agents. The compulsive character of a kleptomaniac's thievery has nothing at all to do with determinism. (His desires to steal may arise quite randomly.) Rather, it is because his desires express themselves independently of his evaluational judgments that we tend to think of his actions as unfree. [For more on this theme, see Chapters 2 and 3.]

The truth, of course, is that God (traditionally conceived) is the only free agent, *sans phrase*. In the case of God, who is omnipotent and omniscient, there can be no disparity between valuational and motivational systems. The dependence of motivation upon evaluation is total, for there is but a single source of motivation: his presumably benign judgments.[12] In the case of the Brutes, as well, motivation has a single source: appetite and (perhaps) passion. The Brutes (or so we normally think) have no evaluational system. But human beings are only more or less free agents, typically less. They are free agents only in some respects. With regard to the appetites and passions, it is plain that in some situations the motivational systems of human beings exhibit an independence from their values which is inconsistent with free agency; that is to say, people are

---

Preferences," *Journal of Philosophy*, 71/13 (July 18, 1974): 377–91. In "Freedom and Desire," *Philosophical Review*, 83/1 (January 1974): 32–54, Wright Neely appeals to higher-order desires.

[12] God could not act *akratically*. In this respect, Socrates thought people were distinguishable from such a being only by ignorance and limited power.

sometimes moved by their appetites and passions in conflict with their practical judgments.[13]

As Nietzsche said (probably with a rather different point in mind): "Man's belly is the reason why man does not easily take himself for a god."[14]

---

[13] This possibility is a definitive feature of appetitive and passionate wants.

[14] *Beyond Good and Evil*, section 141.

2 Skepticism about Weakness of Will

Two kinds of skepticism

Although it occurs with deplorable frequency, weakness of will has seemed to many philosophers hard to understand. The motivation of weak behavior[1] is generally familiar and intelligible enough: the desire to remain in bed, or the desire for another drink are ordinary examples. Nevertheless, our common ways of describing and explaining this phenomenon have been thought to involve serious difficulties. These descriptions and explanations can, upon reflection, seem incoherent.

Accordingly, weakness of will has given rise to various forms of skepticism. The most notorious form is socratism, which denies the possibility of such behavior. Another form of skepticism admits its possibility but casts doubt upon a complex of distinctions and moral attitudes involved in the common view. Briefly, it argues that no one who acts contrary to his or her better judgment does so freely, that weakness of will cannot be significantly distinguished from psychological compulsion,[2] and that therefore certain moral distinctions implicit in the common view cannot be justified.

Many people have contributed to my thinking on this topic. I am especially grateful to Robert Audi, Charles Kahn, Ruth Mattern, the editors of the *Philosophical Review*, and Michael Slote.

[1] Weakness of will occurs only if one knowingly does something contrary to one's better judgment. We will see that this condition does not distinguish between weakness and compulsion.

[2] I shall assume throughout that if someone is psychologically compelled to do something, he or she is unable to refrain from doing it (though not necessarily

My concern in this paper will be to explore and develop a version of nonsocratic skepticism. In my view, socratism is incorrect, but like Socrates, I think that the common understanding of weakness of will raises serious problems. Contrary to socratism, it is possible for a person knowingly to act contrary to his or her better judgment. But this description does not exhaust the common view of weakness. Also implicit in this view is the belief that actions which are contrary to one's better judgment are free in the sense that the agent could have done otherwise. The grounds for skepticism about this belief will be my theme.[3]

To clear the way and to introduce some important distinctions, it will be helpful to begin with a discussion of socratic skepticism. Then I will set out what I take to be the crucial elements in the common account of weakness, and consider the apparent emptiness of that account as an explanatory model; it is said that one takes the drink *because* one's will is weak, for example, and this explanation is supposed to contrast with the compulsive case in which one takes the drink because one's desire is too strong. Finally, I will discuss and compare the merits of an alternative way of drawing the distinction between weakness and compulsion.

Socrates and Davidson

A brief look at Donald Davidson's essay, "How is Weakness of the Will Possible?",[4] will help us to isolate the errors of socratism. His

conversely). The compulsive's motivation is literally irresistible. This concept is discussed further on pp. 41ff. [For doubts about this, see Chapter 3 in this volume.]

[3] In the socratic dialogues of Plato, the view that Socrates denies is often formulated as the view that people often, *freely and voluntarily*, act contrary to their better judgments. This position will be rejected by both forms of skepticism. But the focus of Socrates' arguments is the weaker proposition that one can knowingly act contrary to one's better judgment. Hence I call "socratic" only this version of skepticism.

[4] In *Moral Concepts*, edited by Joel Feinberg, Oxford University Press, 1970. [Reprinted in Davidson, 1980. References are to this latter volume.]

paper is worth considering because, among other reasons, it contains an excellent formulation of some principles which have caused much of the traditional philosophical trouble. Although I believe his own solution to have difficulties of its own, I wish rather to examine the way in which he generates the problem.

Davidson sees the problem of "incontinence" as arising from the apparent incompatibility between two principles which connect judgment, motivation, and action, and the belief that incontinence (possibly) exists. He characterizes incontinence in this way:

In doing x an agent acts incontinently if and only if: (a) the agent does x intentionally; (b) the agent believes there is an alternate action y open to him; and (c) the agent judges that, all things considered, it would be better to do y than to do x (p. 22).

The principles with which the belief in the existence of incontinence is at odds are these:

P1. If an agent wants to do x more than he wants to do y and he believes himself free to do either x or y, then he will intentionally do x if he does either x or y intentionally.

P2. If an agent judges that it would be better to do x than to do y, then he wants to do x more than he wants to do y (p. 23).

As Davidson says, P1 connects "wanting" with "acting intentionally," whereas P2 connects "judging better" with "wanting." He insists that the tension cannot be alleviated by modifying these principles to make them both true and consistent with the belief in incontinence—not that P1 and P2 are crystal clear and unambiguous as they stand: but "the problem will survive new wording, refinement, and elimination of ambiguity" (p. 24).

Since Davidson accepts these principles and believes incontinence exists, he must deny that these principles logically conflict with this belief. The main burden of his paper is to show how we may accept them and still maintain weakness to be possible. The first point to notice, then, is that with the appropriate addition of the phrase "all things considered" to P2, the principles and the belief in incontinence clearly are contradictory. The incontinent are supposed to act against their all-things-considered judgments; but *P*2 is stated in terms of judgment *simpliciter*. It is this apparent difference that Davidson exploits. What he thinks happens in incontinence (so defined) is that one acts contrary to one's all-things-considered judgment; but in so acting one acts in accordance with one's "unconditional" or "unqualified" judgment, or with one's judgment *simpliciter* (pp. 38–40).

Several questions arise about Davidson's position. First, is the distinction between a judgment all-things-considered and an unqualified or unconditional judgment sound? It might well be supposed that an all-things-considered judgment is precisely an unqualified judgment made on the basis of all considerations thought relevant by the agent. Second, even if this distinction were made out, is there not equally good reason to think that people act contrary to their unqualified or unconditional judgments, as there is to think that people act contrary to their all-things-considered judgments? Davidson's theses entail that this is impossible. Third, are *P*1 and *P*2 true?

Davidson's remarks on practical reasoning are certainly novel and interesting; but it is this last question that will concern me here, for the problem lies with these socratic principles. Aside from the fact that *P*1 and *P*2 lead to a denial of what intuitively seems to exist, there are strong general reasons for rejecting them. To see this, recall the reasoning in Plato's *Protagoras* which led Socrates (or the early Plato) to deny the possibility of *akrasia*. In this work, Socrates denied the common account, according to which agents may knowingly fail to do what they believe best in the situation, because they yield to temptation, or short-term pleasure, or are overcome by appetite. Socrates denied this account because he believed that human beings always most desire, and hence pursue, what is (thought to be) best (compare *P*1 and *P*2). On this supposition, in acting weakly they would have to be pursuing what they believe to be best, believing it not to be best.

Instead, Socrates insisted that what is called weakness of will (*akrasia*) is really a species of ignorance. The weak agent suffers from a kind of evaluational illusion, very like an optical illusion—the nearer, more immediate good looks the greater. The so-called weak agent lacks the art of measurement, the art of correctly weighing nearer and farther goods, and to have this art is to have knowledge of good and evil. (Hence the thesis that virtue is a kind of knowledge, to which I shall return.)

Despite the ingenuity of this appeal to evaluational illusions (which I think in fact occur), the later Plato came to see this matter differently. He came to realize that we are generally susceptible to motivation which is independent, in strength and origin, of our judgments concerning how it is best to act. Plato's distinction between the rational and nonrational parts of the soul may be taken as a distinction between sources of motivation. The rational part of the soul is the source of evaluations—judgments as to the value or worth of a particular course of action or state of affairs. The nonrational part of the soul is the source of such desires as arise from the appetites and emotions. These desires are blind in the sense that they do not depend fundamentally upon the agent's view of the good. Since these sources of motivation differ, they may conflict, and in certain cases, the desires of the nonrational soul may motivate the agent contrary to his or her "desires" for the good. In some such way, Plato tried to account for motivational conflict and for the possibility of both self-mastery and its opposite.[5]

On the basis of this distinction, then, Plato rejected Socrates' (or his own earlier) view that a person's desires are always desires for the "good" and that what a person most desires is what is (thought) best. Elementary as these points are, they suffice to show the possibility of

[5] I develop this distinction, and apply it to the concept of free action, in "Free Agency", *Journal of Philosophy*, April 24, 1975 [Ch. 1 in this volume].

An interpretative point: Plato appears to have held that the distinction between knowledge and belief is relevant in some way I fail to appreciate. Hence he may still have denied the possibility of acting contrary to one's *knowledge*.

weakness of will. The desires of hunger and sex, the desires of anger and fear, do not depend upon one's assessment of the value of doing what one is thereby inclined to do. But if such desires exist, as they surely do, then it is possible that they are strong enough to motivate one contrary to one's judgment of what is best; it is possible that one's evaluations and desires diverge in certain cases in such a way that one is led to do things which one does not think worth doing, or as much worth doing as some available option. Hence socratism is false. There are no good theoretical grounds for denying *akrasia*.

To bring these points to bear on Davidson's principles: let us distinguish two senses of "wants more" or "wants most," an evaluational sense and motivational sense.[6] In the first sense, if one wants to do x more than one wants to do y, one *prefers x to y* or ranks x higher than y on some scale of values or "desirability matrix." In the second sense, if one wants to do x more than y, one is more strongly motivated to do x than to do y. Thus, P2 may be true if understood in the language of evaluation, but false if understood in the language of motivation; whereas P1 is true if understood in the language of motivation, but false if understood in the language of evaluation. If a person judges x to be better than y, then he or she values x more than y. But as we have seen, it does not follow that the agent's desire or want for x, rather than for y, will motivate the agent to act (if either does). But this must follow if P1 and P2 are jointly to have the consequences that Davidson accepts. There is no univocal interpretation of the key phrases of P1 and P2 on which these principles turn out to be true, or even very plausible.

Thus, even though Davidson wishes to allow the existence of "incontinence," in these principles we encounter the socratic viewpoint

[6] The distinction between the language of motivation and the language of evaluation is clearly drawn by G. Santas, in "Plato's *Protagoras*, and Explanations of Weakness", *The Philosophical Review*, 1966. His discussion of weakness is one of the best that I know of. In insisting upon this distinction, I do not wish to assert a semantical ambiguity of "want." The point is rather that there are different, and noncoincident criteria for whether someone wants to do one thing *more than* another.

SKEPTICISM ABOUT WEAKNESS OF WILL · 39

once again. It is important to note in addition that the above principles also rule out the possibility of being compulsively motivated to
act contrary to one's practical judgment. Once we are disabused of
the idea that the strength of one's desire is necessarily proportional
to the degree to which one values its object, there is conceptual room
for compulsion as well as weakness.[7] The real problem, as we shall see,
is not to admit but to distinguish them. But first it will be instructive
to look at some related distortions implicit in the socratic theory of
virtue.

Self-control and the socratic theory of virtue

Consider the virtue of courage, and how this virtue is misconceived
by the socratic view. Courage is a virtue which it is in the interest of
everyone to have, and is in this respect like continence. Now for
Socrates, courage is, as it should be, the virtue which applies to situations of danger. But for him it applies in the following eccentric way:
courage is the knowledge of what is really dangerous or not. Since
Socrates thought that the only danger is evil, or doing evil, all that it
takes to possess the virtue of courage, and to act courageously in
appropriate circumstances, is the knowledge of what is good and
evil. (This is the keystone of his doctrine of the unity of the virtues:
each virtue is a special case of wisdom (knowledge of good and evil)
applied to particular contexts: courage is wisdom about danger,
temperance is wisdom about what is really pleasant, justice is wisdom
applied to social relationships and statecraft, and so on. If you have
wisdom in general, then you will have the other virtues, and if you
lack one of these, you will lack wisdom). Hence the coward is one who

---

[7] The existence of weakness of will, or generally the divergence between evaluation
and motivation, reveals one kind of limitation on decision theory, conceived as an
explanatory theory of behavior. Decision theory will be correct only on the assumption
(often unjustified) of "continence." Explaining weak action will require a different
branch of psychology.

has a false view of what is really dangerous. The courageous person is one who is able to distinguish apparent from real dangers.

But surely courage is not like this. Courage is the capacity to deal with one's fear in contexts where one is thereby spontaneously inclined to actions which are contrary to one's view of what should be done. The virtue of courage has a role only because we are not as Socrates says we are; it is needed because of the irrational part of the soul, because our inclinations do not always harmonize with our judgments of the good. Socrates thinks that the courageous person's virtue is that he or she sees there is nothing really to fear, whereas the coward is benighted about this. But the truth appears to be that courage is needed precisely where there *is* something to fear, but where this emotion would lead one to act contrary to one's better judgment.

Courage is thus a special type of self-control; it is self-control in situations of personal danger. Consequently, self-control has a broader application than to pleasure and temptation. If human psychology were as Socrates assumes, such a virtue would have no use. Self-control is a virtue only for beings who are susceptible to motivation which is in potential conflict with their judgments of what is good to pursue; only to beings like ourselves who have appetites and emotions which may incline them contrary to their better judgments.[8]

[8] The appetites and emotions are not the only sources of such motivation. Perhaps appetites (like hunger, thirst, sex) may be distinguished from emotions (like anger, fear, resentment) in that the latter essentially involve beliefs (that something is dangerous, that one has been wronged, that another is obstructing one), whereas appetites do not. But the following examples do not seem to fit clearly into either category—the inclinations arising from pain, the inclination to excrete, the inclination to sleep (arising from sleepiness)—and these surely belong to the "nonrational" part of the soul. Why isn't sleepiness, like hunger, an appetite?

Let me hasten to add that, as Ruth Mattern has pointed out to me, self-control should not be conceived as a unified capacity, such that if one has it in one area, one will have it in all areas. A person may be "soft" with respect to pain, but never yield to temptation, or one may be perfectly courageous, but continually give in to the desire to drink.

In passing, it is worth noting that possessing the capacity to make one's practical judgments effective in action is generally in the interest of every being with some sort of view of how to live, and does not presuppose a particularly austere or "rationalistic" ethic. Even those who favor spontaneity and propose to follow their inclinations should want the virtue of self-control. To use an example of Thomas Nagel,[9] even those who favor a spontaneous life will want to be able to resist the sudden urge to join the Marine Corps—or more generally, to resist those inclinations the satisfaction of which would render them unable to act impulsively in the future.

As I see it, then, the virtue of self-control is the capacity to counteract recalcitrant motivation, that is, motivation which is contrary to one's better judgment. It is this virtue that the weak agent lacks, or at least fails to exercise; and for this virtue, knowledge in the ordinary sense is clearly insufficient. Now both compulsion and weakness of will involve a failure of self-control. In the next section, I want to consider some common ways of distinguishing these types of failure.

Weakness and compulsion

Suppose that a particular woman intentionally takes a drink. To provide an evaluative context, suppose also that we think she ought not to have another because she will then be unfit to fulfill some of her obligations. Preanalytically, most of us would insist on the possibility and significance of the following three descriptions of the case: (1) the reckless or self-indulgent case; (2) the weak case; and (3) the compulsive case. In (1), the woman knows what she is doing but accepts the consequences. Her choice is to get drunk or risk getting drunk. She acts in accordance with her judgment. In (2) the woman knowingly takes the drink contrary to her (conscious) better judgment; the

---

[9] In *The Possibility of Altruism*, Oxford, The Clarendon Press, 1970.

explanation for this lack of self-control is that she is weak-willed. In (3), she knowingly takes the drink contrary to her better judgment, but she is a victim of a compulsive (irresistible) desire to drink.

These variations reveal the leading features of the common conception of weakness. On this model, the weak drinker is like the compulsive drinker in that she acts contrary to her better judgment,[10] but she is like the reckless drinker in that she is able to resist the drink. Accordingly, she is placed morally somewhere "in between" the others. Since she acted contrary to her judgment, she is not, like the reckless drinker, just morally "bad"—her values and judgment are not in question. But unlike the compulsive, she is not a victim of irresistible desires. She shares with the reckless the ability to resist, and for this reason we hold her responsible.

The common account, then, insists that the weak person has, but fails to exercise, the capacity of self-control. It is this requirement that nonsocratic skepticism challenges. Before posing the challenge, I will illustrate and clarify the concept of motivational compulsion, and then raise some preliminary difficulties in distinguishing it from weakness. Subsequently, I will argue that this common way of making the distinction is untenable, and will propose an alternative way that does not rest upon this requirement.

The notion of psychological or motivational compulsion is probably an extension of the ordinary notion of interpersonal compulsion, in which one person is forced by another to act "against his will." Although psychological compulsion may not be widely recognized in ordinary life, I think that the concepts of mania, phobia, and addiction imply its possibility.[11] I shall assume that when an action is literally compelled motivationally, the agent is motivated by a desire (or

---

[10] Acting contrary to one's better judgment is not, however, a necessary condition of compulsion; one's desire might be compulsive and happen to accord with one's judgment.

[11] See the leading psychological study, *Fears and Phobias* [Academic Press, 1969] by Isaac Marks. In his discussion of "obsessive-compulsive" neuroses, Freud also speaks of being unable to resist certain "impulses".

"impulse" or "inclination") that he or she is unable to resist. In illustration, a man might have a dread fear of spiders or rats so overwhelmingly strong that, even when it is urgently important for him to do so, he is literally unable to handle one. Or a starving woman may be driven by her hunger to do such acts as she would rather die than perform. Or a drug addict, because of his or her unconquerable craving for the drug, may be unable (at least over a span of time) to refuse the opportunity to obtain and consume some heroin.

It is not true that manic and phobic actions are necessarily compulsive; the motivations may raise the cost of alternative actions prohibitively, and thus "coerce" rather than compel. If I give in to my fear of flying, recognizing all the while that this fear is baseless, it does not follow that I was compelled to remain grounded. It may rather be that the difficulties and anxieties involved in my overcoming my admittedly irrational fear make doing so too costly. (Nor would this be a case of weakness of will; here I act on my judgment that flying is not worth the suffering.) However, there may be circumstances in which I am unable to overcome my phobia, even when it is practically urgent for me to fly. Nevertheless, even though manic or phobic desires do not necessarily compel, they are potentially compulsive in that their strength is to a large degree independent of the person's will. [For further discussion, see Chapter 3 of this volume.]

In what follows, I wish to exclude from consideration cases of unconscious or "semi-conscious" or self-deceptive actions. Where one deceives oneself about what is best, or about one's situation of action, one does not act contrary to one's better judgment, but rather in accordance with one's self-deceptive judgment. Or perhaps in such cases, it is radically unclear what the real judgment is. Self-deception is itself philosophically troublesome, and as a matter of fact many actions we call weak may involve self-deception of some sort. But no philosophical reasons drive us to redescribe the phenomenon in this way, and certainly the common view insists on the possibility of "clear-headed" action contrary to better judgment. Furthermore, the problems raised by weakness of will differ distinctively from the problems raised by self-deception. The former problem is how a judgment can fail to lead to appropriate action. The latter problem concerns the way in which beliefs and judgments can be influenced by desires. Consequently, I will restrict my attention to actions involving failures of the former kind.[12]

Preliminary difficulties

It is important to emphasize that "weakness of will," in ordinary usage, purports to be an explanatory concept; weakness of will is not just any sort of action contrary to the agent's judgment. To identify behavior in this way is to offer a minimal kind of explanation: one acts contrary to one's better judgment *because* one is weak; one *yields* to temptation, *allows* oneself to give in to appetite, and so forth.

Now the force of this explanation is quite unclear, especially if it is supposed to contrast with an explanation in terms of compulsion. For the present, the problem of distinguishing weakness from compulsion may be expressed in the following way. In those examples given earlier, what is most striking, and leads naturally to the invocation of the notion of compulsion, is that the agents' actual motivation is independent of any conception that they have of the worth of their actions. Their motivation is in this way "alien" to them. In some significant sense, they seem motivated contrary to their own wills. Clearly, the "will" here cannot be the *strongest* motive; for compulsives do not act contrary to their strongest motive. They act contrary to their

[12] On a larger view, this distinction may prove to be superficial. If, as I suggest, self-control or strength of will is the capacity to ensure that one's practical judgment is effective in action, then presumably it would be part of this capacity to maintain clarity of judgment in the face of temptation. In a significant sense, one's practical judgment is ineffective in self-deceptive action, and one can yield to bad reasoning as well as directly to temptation. But I shall adhere in the text to this characterization of weakness as action contrary to one's conscious and immediate practical judgment, both for simplicity and because this case is conceptually most problematic for my concerns.

judgments of the worth of their actions. It is plausible, then, to identify the "will" with practical judgment. This suggests that the mark of a compulsive desire is its capacity to motivate the agent contrary to practical judgment. But it follows that the weak agent acts contrary to his or her judgment in exactly the same sense, and therefore acts under compulsion.

This consequence is admittedly counterintuitive. Surely if it is plausible in some circumstances to say that a starving person is unable to resist taking the bread, that in general compulsives are driven ineluctably to acts beyond their control, it is quite implausible to say this of the well-nourished who capitulate to their fondness for bagels.

Similarly, we are inclined to contrast weakness and compulsion like so: in the case of compulsive acts, it is not so much that the will is too weak as that the contrary motivation is too strong; whereas, in weakness of will properly so-called, it is not that the contrary motivation is too strong, but that the will is too weak.

There is, I think, something correct in this contrast; but the following difficulty remains. This talk of strength of desires is obscure enough, but insofar as it has meaning, there does not appear to be any way of judging the strength of desires except as they result in action. For why is it said that the compulsive's desires are too strong? Isn't it just because these agents are motivated contrary to their wills? Isn't the only relatively clear measure of strength of desires the tendency of those desires to express themselves independently of the agent's will? If this is so, the desires which motivate the weak contrary to their judgments are "too strong" as well, and explanations of weakness and compulsion come to the same thing. We are left again with the conclusion that weakness is a case of compulsion.[13]

---

[13] A few remarks on internalism may be in order here. I am supposing, as I think we ordinarily do, that when one acts weakly, one wants to some degree to do what one judges best. Weakness of will is marked by conflict and regret. However, this supposition does not entail a commitment to a general internalist view that a person necessarily wants what he or she judges best. (Note that even this general view is

We have seen why socratism is to be rejected, but a real problem remains. If a sufficient condition of compulsive motivation is that the motivation be contrary to the agent's practical judgment, then weakness of will is a species of compulsion. And if compulsive behavior is involuntary and unfree, weak behavior is involuntary and unfree. In any case, weakness and compulsion are on a par. The intuition that the agent's will is too weak, whereas in the other case, the contrary motivation is too strong, appears to rest on an illusion.

One way to avoid this conclusion—that all weak actions are compulsive—would be to argue that no actions are compulsive, since no desires are irresistible. One philosopher who is skeptical about the idea of an irresistible desire is Joel Feinberg. "There is much obscurity in the notion of the strength of a desire," Feinberg writes, but he thinks several points are clear:

The first is that strictly speaking no impulse is irresistible; for every case of giving in to a desire, I would argue, it will be true that, if the person had tried harder he would have resisted it successfully. . . . Nevertheless, it does make sense to say that some desires are stronger than others and that some have an intensity and power that are felt as overwhelming.[14]

Feinberg's confidence on these points puzzles me. One may well be dubious in practice about particular pleas of irresistibility. And,

a weaker internalism than Davidson's P2.) For even if it is possible not at all to want what one judges best, it would be a distortion to describe such a case as weakness of will. For such an externalist agent would have a strong and undivided will—and what he or she lacked certainly would not be self-control. I think one trouble with Davidson's discussion (op. cit.) is that it leaves untouched the way in which weakness of will is supposed to involve weakness; "incontinence" turns out to be a "surd" noncompliance with the "principle of continence," and hence is construed as merely practical irrationality. (Compare Nietzsche's remark: "When the mind is made up, the ear is deaf to even the best arguments. This is the sign of a strong character. In other words, an occasional will to stupidity." [Beyond Good and Evil, sec. 107] Consider also an Andy Capp cartoon I recently saw. On his way to the local pub, Andy encounters his priest, who asks him, "Have you no self-control?" He replies, "Yes, Father, I have, but I will not be a slave to it.")

[14] "What is So Special about Mental Illness?", in Doing and Deserving, Princeton University Press, 1970, pp. 282–3. [I reconsider this passage in Chapter 3.]

if one is in the dark about the notion of strength, one may well have blanket doubts about such claims. But if it is granted that desires may be *hard* to resist, on what grounds can it be denied that sometimes desires may be *too* hard to resist? Why must the feeling that some desires are overwhelmingly "intense and powerful" be mistaken? What puzzles me is how the possibility of irresistible desires can be rejected a priori unless the notion of strength here is altogether empty.

Not only do many psychologists assume this possibility, the common view of weakness seems committed to it as well. For it insists that the weak person has but does not exercise the capacity to resist. This insistence presupposes the intelligibility of lacking this capacity. In any case, even if it is true, as Feinberg believes, that in all cases, "if the person had tried harder, he would have resisted," this does not show that no desires are irresistible. For a person may be unable to try harder and for this reason be unable to resist.

Therefore, it seems unjustified to hold that no desires are too strong for an agent to resist. In fact, we very frequently compare the strengths of desires, both when they are those of a particular individual at a given time, and when the desires belong to different persons or the same person at different times. (*P*'s desire to lounge in bed is stronger than his desire to keep appointments; *Q* has stronger sexual desires than most, or than she herself had when she was fifteen.) It is not clear what criteria we invoke in such comparisons, but two obvious criteria are clearly unhelpful. Motivational efficacy will not do because on this measure any desire which motivates would thereby be the strongest.[15] And this measure would not allow for significant interpersonal comparisons. Nor, once again, will independence

---

[15] This needs some qualification. The motivational efficacy of desire could be understood counterfactually. For example, it may be that a woman is motivated by her thirst rather than her hunger, even though the latter is stronger than the former in this sense: if she had thought she could satisfy her hunger, that desire rather than her thirst would have motivated her. But the statement in the text seems to hold for *competing* desires, where two desires are competing if the agent believes it is now possible to satisfy either but not both. I owe this notion of a competing desire to Robert Audi.

of the agent's will or better judgment do, for then the desires of the weak and the compulsive will be equally strong.

Strength and resistibility

It might help at this point to return to my earlier description of self-control as the capacity to resist recalcitrant desires; such desires are strong to the extent to which they *need* to be resisted. For again, not all actual desires which one does not in the end act upon are therefore resisted. To resist cannot simply be to refrain from acting upon some desire one has. As Aristotle observed (*Nicomachean Ethics,* 1152a1 ff.), there is a difference between the "continent" and the "temperate" person which rests upon the notion of strength. For both types, "choice" regulates action—both act upon their evaluations— but while the temperate person has moderate appetites, the continent person acts rightly *despite* strong contrary inclinations. A person's desires are moderate to the degree to which they do not require resistance.

The important point is that practical conflict may assume both a decision-theoretic and a psychological form. When the conflict takes the first form, it arises from the question of what to do. But motivational conflicts may persist after this question is settled. Here the strength of desires is revealed and the need for resistance emerges. The temperate are less susceptible than others to this motivational conflict. Their souls are harmonious. The continent are so susceptible, but manage to resist. The weak fail.

Why then do the continent manage successfully to resist, whereas the weak do not? The answer cannot be that the weak are subject to stronger desires than the continent, for this would not explain why they are weaker; nor would it enable us to distinguish weakness from compulsion. The proposal I now wish to entertain is the following. The weak and the strong may be subject to desires of exactly the same strength. What makes the former weak is that they give in to desires which the possession of the normal degree of self-control would enable them to resist. In contrast, compulsive desires are such that the normal capacities of resistance are or would be insufficient to enable the agent to resist. This fact about compulsive desires is what gives substance to the claim that they are too strong. The fact that weak agents' desires would be controlled by the exercise of the normal capacities of resistance gives point to the claim that these agents are weak.

Something like this distinction is suggested by a passage of Aristotle. He remarks that the difference between weakness and what we have called compulsion might depend on the fact that the desires which defeat the weak person are such that most people could have resisted:

> . . . if a man is defeated by violent and excessive pleasures or pains, there is nothing wonderful in that; indeed we are ready to pardon him if he has resisted [is overcome while offering resistance—Ostwald] . . . But it is surprising if a man is defeated by and cannot resist pleasures and pains which most men can hold out against, when this is not due to heredity and disease . . . (*Nicomachean Ethics*, 1150*b*7 ff., Ross trans.).

This way of expressing the point is unfortunate; for it may suggest that desires are like barbells which most people can or cannot lift. Whatever the ontological status of desires, it does not seem intelligible to say of an inclination that a particular person has on a particular occasion, that most others would be able to hold out against that very inclination. It makes better sense to ask not whether other people could have resisted that particular motivation—but whether the individual would have been able to hold out had he or she possessed and exercised the kinds of capacity of self-control normally possessed by others, or whether persons of normal self-control would resist similar desires of the same strength. Such a counterfactual is no doubt formidable to establish, but at least it is intelligible. I suggest that when we believe it, or something like it, to be true of people who do not resist, we think them weak (the fault is with them, not with the opposing desires); when we believe that they could not have resisted even so, then we think of them as victims of compulsion (the fault is not with them, but rather their desires are too strong). (Perhaps this way of looking at the matter also presupposes that we believe weak persons both could and should possess and exercise those skills—otherwise it would not be their *fault*.) In this manner, we can distinguish among "temperance" and "continence" (in Aristotle's sense), weakness and compulsion. And we can avoid saying either that no desires are irresistible or that weakness is a case of compulsion.

In summary, then, there are capacities and skills of resistance which are generally acquired in the normal course of socialization and practice, and which we hold one another responsible for acquiring and maintaining. Weak agents fall short of standards of "reasonable and normal" self-control (for which we hold them responsible), whereas compulsive agents are motivated by desires which they could not resist even if they met those standards. That is why we focus on the weakness of the agent in the one case (it is the agent's fault), but on the power of the contrary motivation in the compulsive case. And this view allows explanations in terms of weakness of will to be significantly different from explanations in terms of compulsion. In the case of weakness, one acts contrary to one's better judgment *because one has failed* to meet standards of reasonable or normal self-control; whereas, this explanation does not hold of compulsive behavior.

Let us now note some of the implications of this proposal. One obvious point is that, on this account, a desire is compulsive (irresistible) or not only relative to certain norms of self-control; only relative to the capacities of the normal person, and this probably means the typical adult in our society. It may be true, for example, that having undergone from childhood an intensive program of discipline, such as yoga, would have enabled a person to resist certain desires now. But this fact would not incline us at all to withdraw the claim that the individual was suffering from compulsive desires.

Hence the fact that one would be a weak person in a community of yogis does not mean that one would not be compulsive among us. (It does not follow from this account, however, that weak agents are those with less self-control than most others in their society *in fact* have. Weakness is relative to expectations and norms, and it is conceivable that a whole community could fall short of these.)

The relativity of this viewpoint may conflict with our ordinary view of weakness; perhaps prior to reflection we think that a desire is either resistible or it isn't. Even so, it seems to me that this relativity is a desirable feature of the present account. We could define an absolute concept of compulsion in something like the following manner: an agent is motivated by a compulsive desire if *no* degree of training and discipline would have enabled him or her to resist. But it is an open question whether *any* desires are compulsive on this definition, and it does not seem to apply in the right way to the cases we think of as compulsive. Relativity is in any case a feature of the concept of weakness in general—for example, the concept of physical weakness. The possible existence of races of creatures who could lift 500-pound weights, or of training programs which would enable most of us to do so, would not mean that those of us who cannot lift this weight were physically weak.[16]

This doctrine accords fairly closely with typical moral attitudes toward weakness as well. In contrast to "bad characters," we do not criticize weak agents for their principles or values but for their failure to develop or maintain the capacities necessary to make those values effective in action. The appropriate blaming attitudes toward the weak, by themselves and others, are shame and (if one goes in for this sort of thing) contempt, not guilt and indignation. For the fault is not injustice, but lack of control. And since they have (or may have) the right values, they are as much an object of pity as reproach—from

[16] Note, however, that on this account I could easily be mistaken about whether my action was weak or compulsive, because I could be mistaken about what the relevant standards were. Indeed, in the absence of shared expectations and norms the distinction might come to lose its force altogether.

any point of view, *especially their own*,[17] they are in a bad way. Since shame characteristically involves falling short of shared standards of excellence in conduct, shame will often be appropriate in the case of weakness in a way in which it will not be for compulsion.[18]

The proposed account versus the common account

The proposed account entails that the desires of weak agents are resistible in the sense that had they developed and maintained certain normal capacities of self-control, they would have resisted them. And to the degree to which we judge such agents blameworthy and responsible for their weak behavior, we believe they could and should have developed and maintained these capacities. So the weak must be constitutionally capable of meeting these standards. But these implications are consistent with their being unable at the time of action to resist. Hence, this account differs significantly from the common one. On the latter the ability to resist at the time of action is a distinguishing feature of weakness.

Morally, the proposed account likens weakness to negligence in its emphasis on the point that blameworthiness does not require that one be able to resist or that weak behavior be fully under voluntary control. For negligence is a paradigm case of blameworthy but

[17] For one's "point of view" includes preeminently the values which determine one's better judgment.

[18] To say that there is generally a moral contrast between weak and compulsive behavior is neither to deny that a compulsive may sometimes be blameworthy, nor to imply that a weak person always is. Just as compulsive agents may sometimes be responsible and blameworthy for having allowed themselves to become or remain compulsive, so the failure of the weak agent might be excusable, as Aristotle intimates, if it were due to "disease." Perhaps we would not or should not classify such a person as weak of will; we would not call a person negligent who was subnormally careless due to disease. If so, weakness of will differs in this respect from physical weakness, which carries no implication of responsibility.

nonvoluntary behavior. Engrossed in an interesting conversation, a man forgets to look both ways at the intersection and therefore collides with another vehicle. He does not do so voluntarily, or even intentionally, and yet we may judge him blameworthy for failing to meet standards (or the "duty") of reasonable care. (To be sure, the man is engaged in numerous voluntary actions at the time of the collision, but colliding, for which he is blamed, is not among them.) Could he have remembered? It is not at all clear that he could have. Remembering is not in this case even an action. What we believe is that he should have remembered to look and because of this, that he falls short of standards of reasonable care. The accident is explained by his fault (just as weak behavior is explained by the agent's fault).[19]

Perhaps to think him blameworthy we must also believe that he could have been or become the kind of person who exercises reasonable care. But these beliefs do not entail that he was able, at the time of action, to avoid the accident. On the proposed account, the case of weak behavior is quite parallel. The weak person may be seen as negligent for failing to acquire the relevant capacities. And like the standard of normal self-control, the standard of reasonable care (and thus what counts as negligence) is relative to social norms and particular contexts. Moreover, like the weak person in the above example, the negligent person is not criticized for his values and judgments (he is not bad or unjust) but for failing to ensure that his behavior is informed by, and conforms to, those values and judgments. (However, unlike the negligent person, but like the compulsive, the weak person does of course act intentionally.[20])

---

[19] I do not suppose that the phenomenon of negligence is well understood; it poses some hard questions for the theory of responsibility. I would claim, however, that weakness resembles negligence in this respect, that both are nonvoluntary behavior thought to be open to blame. The important point is that the responsibility of weak agents is no more (or less) problematic than the responsibility of negligent agents.

[20] Some may wish to deny that compulsive behavior is, or can be, intentional if it is not free. This denial seems to me unjustified. For one thing, on leading views of intentionality, both compulsive and weak action will count as intentional. Both the

Therefore, the fact that on the proposed account weak agents may be no more able at the time of action to conform their behavior to their judgments than compulsives does not rob the distinction between weakness and compulsion of its moral significance. That distinction can be significantly drawn without requiring ability. I shall now argue that, furthermore, there are strong reasons for doubting that this requirement can be satisfied, and thus for rejecting this central feature of the common account. By the common account, the culpability of the drinker in our earlier example is located not in her failure to develop or maintain the normal capacity of resistance, but in her failure to exercise the capacity she possesses. The challenge to this account is to find a pertinent explanation of this failure.

Generally, people fail to perform some action for a combination of the following kinds of reason: (a) they are unaware of the action as an option; (b) they do not want or choose to do it; or (c) they are unable to do it. Given awareness, nonperformance indicates lack of "power" or lack of "will" or both.[21] This is why inquiries into capacities and knowledge are relevant in contexts of moral appraisal. For instance, if you know that the curtains are burning, and you are able to extinguish the fire, I infer from your nonperformance that you did not want or choose to put the fire out. I thereby learn something important about your values and priorities. On the other hand, of course, if you did not choose to let the curtains burn, or did not even do it knowingly, you would not necessarily be exculpated, for your action or omission may be explained by your culpable ignorance or

compulsive and the weak person act on a "primary reason" (in Davidson's [1980b] sense: "Actions, Reasons, and Causes", *Journal of Philosophy*, 1963.) Their behavior is consciously motivated; hence both may have "practical knowledge" and be able to answer a certain kind of question "Why?" (See E. Anscombe, *Intention*.) More decisively, compulsive and weak behavior both involve at least a minimal form of practical reasoning: the person with a dread fear of spiders may reason about how best to escape, a weak person about how best to obtain some cigarettes. To deny intentionality here is unjustifiably to conflate intentional with free action.

[21] This theme is pursued in Chapter 2 of Stuart Hampshire's *Freedom of the Individual*.

carelessness. Generally, then, culpable failures or omissions are explained either by lack of choice, or by culpable lack of care, knowledge, or ability.

The proposed account fits weakness into a scheme of this kind. Weak agents fail or neglect to meet certain standards of self-control, and their culpability does not require choice or ability at the time of action. The explanation of the weak agent's failure to act upon practical judgment involves attributing this failure to another culpable failure to develop or maintain the relevant capacities.

The challenge to the common account is to provide a similarly pertinent explanation of the weak person's failure. This failure is due neither to lack of knowledge nor, putatively, to lack of ability or negligence. To return to the case of the weak drinker, the woman judges that she should resist and therefore, by her own lights, has sufficient reason for exercising her alleged capacity. What might explain her not doing so?

There seem to me only two possible explanations. (1) She *chooses* not to. (2) Her *effort* to resist is culpably insufficient. Both of these explanations will be found inadequate.

(1) First, the notion of choice (and also decision) seems to me to involve the notion of applying one's values to the perceived practical options. (Aristotle is close when he speaks of choice as desire in accordance with deliberation.) In this sense, it is of course generally true that one may choose not to exercise some capacity that one has. But the capacity of self-control is special in this respect. For the capacity of self-control involves the capacity to counteract and resist the strength of desires which are contrary to what one has chosen or judged best to do. The weak drinker's failure to resist her desire to drink is a failure to implement her choice not to drink. To choose not to implement this choice would be to change her original judgment, and the case would no longer be a case of failure to implement judgment. Therefore, the weak agent's failure to resist the drink cannot intelligibly be explained by her choice.

Equally important, even if it made sense to explain her failure in this way, doing so would result in the moral assimilation of the weak case to the reckless case. The common account rightly wishes to distinguish these, but the difference would collapse if both involved choice.

(2) Second, it might be supposed that the drinker's failure is to be explained by her culpably insufficient *effort*. Sometimes we attribute a person's failure, not to absence of ability or choice, but to lack of sufficient effort.[22] I may try and fail to throw a coin across the Schuylkill River even when I wanted very much to do so and was able to do so. The explanation may be that I misjudged either the amount of effort required or the distance across. Or in a basketball game, my failure to make a jump-shot from the free-throw line might be explained by insufficient concentration rather than lack of capability or will. Using "effort" to include both physical exertion and psychological factors such as concentration and "keeping one's head," in both cases, we may suppose, I not only would have succeeded with greater effort, but could have made the requisite effort.

Perhaps weakness of will is commonly viewed as involving insufficient effort. In order to help here, an explanation of this kind must be conjoined with the assumption that the weak person is able to make the requisite effort to resist. For obviously, if effort of a certain kind and degree is necessary to successful resistance, it will be true that the drinker is able to resist only if she has the capacity to make an effort of that kind and degree to resist. Our focus is thus shifted to her failure of effort, and everything now turns on why she does not make *it*. But it is far from clear what explanation is forthcoming.

The explanation cannot be that making the effort is not thought to be worth it. For once again, implicit in the judgment that it is best not to drink is the judgment that it is best to resist contrary desires. If the drinker really judges that it is not worth that much effort, she either changes her mind or originally only made a conditional judgment of the form: it is best not to drink unless not doing so requires too much effort.

---

[22] I owe my appreciation of this point to the editors of *The Philosophical Review*.

The explanation cannot be that she misjudged the amount of effort required. I may have underestimated how much exertion would be required to throw the coin across the Schuylkill, or how much concentration was necessary to make the basket. But it is not clear what the analogue to this in the case of resisting a drink would be. And even if misjudgment were involved, that would be a different fault from weakness of will.

So we do not seem to have a pertinent explanation of why the weak drinker fails to exert adequate effort. No doubt her failure has something to do with the relative strengths of her desires to resist and to drink. But *this* is not enough for the common account, since it is consistent with her being unable to make the effort. Inasmuch as she has the same good reasons for making the effort to resist as for not drinking, we need an explanation which makes it clear that she is able to resist. For even if some (further) effort would enable her to resist, the desire to drink may generate desires not to make this effort (in the way that desires frequently cause other desires for the means to their fulfillment) and these may be irresistibly strong.

Given her strong motive for making an effort (namely, her considered practical judgment), and in the absence of a special explanation for her not making it (such as "I didn't think it was worth it", or "I didn't think it was necessary"), we are entitled to be skeptical about the common view, and to conclude that the person was unable to resist.

Conclusion

Socrates found the common conception of weakness of will to be confused. However, his reasons for rejecting that account are unsound. They deny the morally and psychologically important complexity of human motivation, and in particular the potential divergence between certain kinds of desire and judgments of the good. This divergence is what makes room for the virtue of self-control and, obversely, the vice of weakness of will.

Just the same, I have offered doubts of a nonsocratic sort about the common account of weakness. To take seriously the possibility of acting contrary to one's better judgment is at the same time to raise problems about the distinction between weakness and compulsion. I have argued that the common view, according to which the differentiating feature is that the weak are able to conform their behavior to their practical judgments, is unjustified. Instead, I have proposed that weakness of will involves the failure to develop certain normal capacities of self-control, whereas compulsion involves desires which even the possession of such capacities would not enable one to resist.

3   Disordered Appetites: Addiction, Compulsion, and Dependence

In both popular and technical discussion, addictive behavior is said to be in some sense *out of control*. However, this description does not distinguish addiction from various forms of moral weakness. The excessive indulgence of appetites, for example, gluttony and promiscuity, are excesses for which we still hold one another responsible. The loss of control in addiction seems different: Addiction appears to be a source of compulsive desire, desire too strong for the agent to resist.[1]

The World Health Organization expresses this view in its 1969 definition of "dependence" (a term that replaced the use of "addiction" in its earlier declarations). Dependence is defined as

a state, psychic and sometimes also physical, resulting from the interaction between a living organism and a drug, characterized by behavioral and other responses that always include a compulsion to take the drug on a continuous or periodic basis in order to experience its psychic effects, and

This paper was prepared for a conference on addiction at the Russell Sage Foundation in June 1997. I am grateful to the other participants in the conference for comments, especially to my commentator on that occasion, Michael Bratman. I also thank Jon Elster for convening and moderating the conference as well as for his insightful work on virtually all aspects of this topic. This chapter has also benefited from discussions with Teresa Chandler, Michael Hudson, Sara Lundquist, and audiences at various colloquia.

[1] In the scattered allusions to addiction in my own writing, I have certainly tended, uncritically, to take it as exemplary of motivational compulsion. [See Chapters 1 and 2 in this volume.]

sometimes to avoid the discomfort of its absence. (Grinspoon and Bakular 1976, 177)

Nonetheless, talk of compulsion remains controversial among theorists and practitioners as well as among nonprofessionals in their dealings with addictive behavior.[2] In part, the controversy is due to moral ambivalence. If addiction is compulsive, then addicts might be absolved from responsibility. To some, this implication is a necessary step to a more humane policy ("Addicts need help, not blame"). Others find this way of thinking morally evasive—indeed, countertherapeutic. Moreover, thinking of addiction in this way encourages a dangerous paternalistic public policy.[3]

The controversy about compulsion is also conceptual. It is far from clear how the notion of motivational compulsion is to be analyzed. The moral and conceptual concerns interact with one another. Insofar as talk of compulsion is ill defined, it is liable to abuse. As Grinspoon and Bakular (1976, 191) skeptically put it, "What we know so far is only that sometimes some people intensely desire to consume certain substances called psychoactive drugs." They suspected that

words like *compulsion, craving,* and *overpowering need,* that are used to explicate *dependence* in the WHO definitions, apply just as often to love of chocolate cake, or for that matter to love of another human being, as to desire to take the drug; or else they are merely scare rhetoric to incite punitive campaigns. (Grinspoon and Bakular 1976, 186)

---

[2] The authors of later editions of *Diagnostic and Statistical Manual of Mental Disorders* of the American Psychiatric Association depart from the second edition by dropping the reference to the "compelling desire to use a substance" in the definition of dependency. This change was apparently prompted by the goal of appealing only to "patterns of pathological use that can be objectively quantified." This goal does not prevent the third and fourth editions from using the "ability to cut down or stop use" as a criterion. See Kuehule and Spitzer (1992, 22–3).

[3] The list of skeptics includes Fingarette (1988); Grinspoon and Bakular (1976); and Peele (1985). Peele insists that "people are not passive victims of the addictive urges or cues that occur in their bodies or in their lives; they select not only the settings in which to live nonaddicted lives but also the reactions they have to the urges they experience to return to their addictions. The methods they use are in keeping with their values and the people they see themselves as having become" (191).

With the recent appearance of twelve-step programs not only for food and relationship junkies but also for those hooked on debt or on the internet, perhaps these words have lost some of their rhetorical force. Still, the caveat is well taken; we should remain wary of the tendency to conflate devotion and addiction, temptation and compulsion.

My focus in this essay is mainly on the conceptual issues, though I touch on some normative questions at the end. I have two main aims. First, I want to explore some of the analytical difficulties arising from talk of motivational compulsion. Second, I try to propose an account of addiction that avoids problematic notions of compulsion and clarifies some of the differences between addictions and other forms of dependency.

Motivational Compulsion

The kind of compulsion under consideration here is *intrapersonal*; you, or your behavior, is in some sense compelled by your own desires. Let's consider how this notion is related to the interpersonal paradigm.

When the bouncer compels you to leave the room by literally picking you up and tossing you into the alley, the movement of your body is explained by another's purposes, rather than your own. In interpersonal compulsion, one is subject to the intentions of someone else. This is not enough to constitute compulsion, however. Suppose you allow someone to move your arm along the table. To be a case of compulsion, the explanation must entail your inability to resist.[4] A third feature is typically present as well: As in the case of the bouncer, you are guided by the other's aims not only independently

---

[4] In the bouncer case, we should distinguish two possible moments of resistance. Perhaps you could have resisted the efforts to throw you out. Once thrown, however, you are powerless to counteract the forces that move you. This distinction has a possible counterpart in the case of addiction. It may be within one's power to resist taking the drug up to a certain point but not beyond it. So one might be responsible for getting to that point and, therefore, for allowing oneself to reach the point of powerlessness.

of your will but *against* it.[5] When that condition is in place, you are moved, helplessly, by someone else's desires, contrary to your own.[6]

The question about "motivational compulsion" (as I call it) is this: Could I have a relation to (some of) my own desires that is sufficiently parallel to my relation to the bouncer's intentions to warrant nonmetaphorical talk of compulsion?

One phenomenon that leads us to take the notion of intrapersonal compulsion seriously is a certain kind of motivational conflict. Just as the bouncer can force you out of the room contrary to your will, so your appetites and impulses might lead you where you do not "really" want to be. This form of conflict reflects a kind of duality that is analogous to the two-person case. Here the opposition is not between you and another but between you—that is, your evaluative judgment—and your other desires. Here, the "other" is your own motivation. This kind of conflict presents an issue of self-control rather than deliberation because here insubordinate desires are *to be resisted*. In these circumstances, their claims lack authority.[7]

---

[5] What seems crucial here is independence rather than actual conflict. To continue with the parallel, just as the bouncer might compel me to go exactly where I want to be (perhaps even in the same manner), an impulse might have an overpowering force without actually going against the agent's aims. In both the interpersonal and intrapersonal cases, actual conflict is a manifestation, but not a criterion, of independence. This is what Frankfurt (1971 [1988]) has in mind by "willing addicts," whose compulsive desires to take the drug agree with their critical evaluations. Frankfurt would not agree, by the way, that in these cases the individuals' agency is entirely undermined. If the behavior is performed not only because it is compulsive but also because of their critical evaluation, then the actors are responsible for what they do.

[6] This formulation is based on examples of forced movement. Of course, someone might *prevent* you from moving, instead. The bouncer might immobilize you by pinning you to the ground. We could take intrapersonal compulsion to comprise both cases, as well. This would be to treat agoraphobic panic, say, as an irresistible aversion to leaving the house. I doubt that this is the best approach to these cases, but this question is not central to the purposes of this chapter.

[7] Plato was concerned with these issues in *The Republic*, where he comments on the case of Leontius, who

became aware of dead bodies that lay at the place of public execution, at the same time felt a desire to see them and a repugnance and aversion, and . . . for a time

Doubts about Compulsion as Irresistibility

Does this sort of duality warrant serious talk of motivational compulsion? A strong case can be made for a negative answer to this question. Consider Joel Feinberg's claim about the notion of irresistible desire:

Strictly speaking no impulse is irresistible; for every case of giving in to a desire . . . it will be true that, if the person had tried harder, he would have resisted it successfully. The psychological situation is never—or hardly ever—like that of the man who hangs from a windowsill by his fingernails until the sheer physical force of gravity rips his nails off and sends him plummeting to the ground, or like that of the man who dives from a sinking ship in the middle of the ocean and swims until he is exhausted and then drowns. Human endurance puts a severe limit on how long one can stay afloat in an ocean; but there is no comparable limit to our ability to resist temptation. (Feinberg 1970, 282–83)[8]

Now we do speak of some recalcitrant desires being stronger than others and of some being very hard to resist. Unless we call into question the notion of strength of desire altogether, on what grounds can we deny that some desires are so strong that they are *too* hard to

he resisted and veiled his head, but overpowered in despite of all by his desire, with wide staring eyes he rushed up to the corpses and cried, There, ye wretches, take your fill of the fine spectacle! (439e–40a)

The sources of desires, Plato concludes, are multiple. Appetites per se are desires, for food and drink, not for good food or good drink (438–9). The hunger for french fries is one thing; the concern to eat what is good for me to eat is another. The latter has its source in the agent's evaluative judgment; the former arises from appetite. Judgments of the good belong to reason:

[S]ome men sometimes though thirsty refuse to drink . . . Is it not that there is a something in the soul that bids them drink and a something that forbids, a different something that masters that which bids? . . . And is it not the fact that that which inhibits such actions arises when it arises from the calculations of reason?

[439e, following. The foregoing translations are Paul Shorey's (Hamilton and Cairns 1989).] For a searching discussion of Plato's doctrine see Terry Penner (Vlastos 1971, 96–118).

[8] I discussed this passage less appreciatively in Chapter 2 of this volume.

resist, quite beyond the limits of one's capacities?[9] Would this denial mean that we are all endowed with unlimited willpower? If so, the capacity to resist temptation would surely be extraordinary among human powers.

Feinberg appeals in this passage to a conditional criterion of resistibility: If one had tried harder, then one would have resisted. The adequacy of this test is suspect because it does not address whether one *could* have tried harder, in which case one may still not have been able to resist. Still, it seems right to say that failure to satisfy Feinberg's criterion is a sufficient condition of *ir*resistibility. If one's utmost efforts do not prevail, surely one is up against an irresistible force. Feinberg's insight is that this negative test has no clear application in the motivational case, for circumstances of temptation necessarily involve motivational conflict, which precludes wholehearted effort.[10]

To satisfy the wholehearted attempt criterion, a desire would have to be an internal pressure that might be opposed, successfully or not, with all one's might—as one might attempt to counter the gravitational force of a slab of stone. This conception of desire, however, is of questionable coherence. Perhaps examples that come close to this are the felt stress of a full bladder, the urge to release one's breath after holding it for a while, or to ejaculate. Significantly, each of these cases involves material in tubes or sacs under pressure. These pressures can be felt in extreme cases as nearly unconquerable hydraulic forces inextricable from desire.

---

[9] "For months, Rafael Ramos [a recovering heroin addict] lived in fear of catching a glimpse of bare arms, his own or someone else's. Whenever he did, he remembers, he would be seized by a nearly unbearable urge to find a drug-filled syringe" (Nash 1997, 72). Would it not be strange if there were motivational forces that were nearly unbearable but none unqualifiedly so?

[10] The parallel point holds for inability. As Hampshire (1965) says: "When we definitely, and without qualification or conflict, want to do something at a particular moment, sincerely make the attempt in normal conditions, and yet fail, we know as surely as we can ever know that at that moment we could not do it" (3). This criterion is central to our attributions of powers, but it does not give us a handle on the notion of motivational inability, since the antecedent conditions are never, in those cases, satisfied.

Perhaps one could so transcend the pain and discomfort caused by such pressure that one could be described as wholeheartedly resisting these forces (successfully or not). In this case, if it is intelligible, one would have succeeded in externalizing the desire, thereby transmuting it from a source of attraction or temptation into a physical tension. To be defeated in this case would no more be a misdirection of the will than would be the failure of the wholehearted attempt to resist the force of the boulder. Yielding to pressure would not in this instance be voluntary movement.[11] If this example as described makes sense at all, however, it is hardly the typical case in which we tend to speak of compulsive desire.

The circumstance described would certainly not be one of temptation. Recalcitrant cravings for nicotine or heroin are not like internal tensions, sometimes mounting to a breaking point. The circumstances of the seriously unwilling addict seem rather more like those of the exhausted climber. The discomfort both inclines one to give up the project and leads one not (in the end) to resist the desire to do so. Unlike external obstacles (or internal pressures), motivational obstacles work in part not by defeating one's best efforts but by diverting one from effective resistance. One's behavior remains in these cases in an important sense voluntary.

That is the crucial difference between the mass of the boulder and the motivational force of a desire. The mass of the boulder can overpower me by bypassing my will, whereas desire cannot. Being overpowered by the hunk of stone means that full, unconflicted use of one's powers is insufficient to resist its force. Being defeated by a desire means that one's capacities to resist are not unconflictedly employed. Hence, one who is defeated by appetite is more like a collaborationist than an unsuccessful freedom fighter. This explains

---

[11] In his critical discussion of the idea that free will (as distinct from free action) might be compromised by compulsive desire, Albritton (1985) remarks that compulsive sexual desire would have to be "like being thrown into bed." However, then "there's no unfreedom of will in it. You haven't in the relevant sense *done* anything" (420). For a discussion of Albritton, see Hoffman (1995) and Watson (1995).

why it can feel especially shameful; to one degree or another, it seems to compromise one's integrity. A parallel point holds for addictions. For self-reflexive beings, the ambivalence of addiction is built into its mechanism: It enslaves by appeal, rather than by brute force.

Thus Feinberg's doubts about irresistibility call attention to a conceptual point about desire rather than to an awesome volitional power of human beings. It is not that there are certain forces that, remarkably, are no match for human determination; rather, we do not stand to our desires as to slabs of stone. For this reason, desires cannot be said to be irresistible by the same criterion, and perhaps in the same sense, as forces of nature. The corollary for the concept of motivational ability is this: In Feinberg's words again, that "there is no . . . limit to our ability to resist temptation" that is comparable to the limits of our physical capacities: not, again, because of an unusual omnipotence in this region of life, but because ability means something quite different in the motivational case.

To sum up: Feinberg's observations point to an important disanalogy between the interpersonal and intrapersonal notions of compulsion. The forces that defeat us in motivational compulsion do so not by opposing our wills but by directing them. Does this disanalogy mean that talk of motivational irresistibility is hyperbole or that putative cases of compulsion are after all cases of weakness? Or can we make sense of the phenomena in some other way?

Resistibility as Reasons Responsiveness

A number of philosophers have proposed to identify the capacity for self-control with sensitivity to countervailing reasons. John Fischer, who analyzes motivational compulsion in terms of the absence of "guidance control,"[12] applies this idea to addiction in the

---

[12] "An agent exhibits guidance control of an action insofar as the mechanism that actually issues in the action is reasons-responsive" (Fischer 1994, 163). See also Fischer 1987; Fischer and Ravizza 1991. [See Chapter 10, this volume, for a fuller treatment of Fischer's and Ravizza's conception of reasons-responsiveness.]

following passage:

When a [drug addict] acts from a literally irresistible urge, he is undergoing a kind of physical process that is not reasons responsive, and it is this lack of reasons responsiveness of the actual physical process that rules out guidance control and moral responsibility. (Fischer 1994, 174)

Jonathan Glover's notion of unalterable intention is basically the same idea:

The test for self-control, which differentiates between my intention and that of the alcoholic, is that my intention can be altered by providing reasons that give me a sufficiently strong motive, while his can only be altered, if at all, by some form of manipulation such as behavior therapy or drugs.[13]

"Where we have evidence of an unalterable intention of this kind," Glover goes on to say, "it is reasonable to say that the person who acts on it cannot help what he does" (Glover 1970, 99; for a related analysis, see Gert and Duggan 1979).

One difficulty here is that the susceptibility to counterincentives might not be responsiveness to them qua reasons. If motivated behavior can be insensitive to reasons, as compulsion must be on this view, then it is no good appealing to susceptibility to countermotivation as a criterion of control unless that motivation would be operating in a reason-responsive manner rather than compulsively. One's response to what is in fact a reason might not be an instance of sensitivity to reasons.[14] That my desire to shoot up would be overpowered

[13] But, suppose that the agent's intentions are alterable by self-administered behavior modification therapy and that the agent knows how to do this. (I suppress here some worries about the coherence of putting some of Glover's points in terms of intention.)

[14] What is more, such accounts must block the possibility that the circumstance of the counterfactual incentive (even when that incentive operates rationally) somehow renders one responsive to reasons (by somehow bringing one to one's senses, as it were). My criticisms show that the capacity for reasons responsiveness cannot be understood purely dispositionally. Fischer (1994, 164–8) would try to provide for this and some of the worries in the text by appealing to a requirement that the actual

by my dread of punishment (or of rats) might only prove that I am doubly enslaved.[15] Freedom cannot be understood as subjection to countervailing compulsions.[16]

This point parallels the objection to the "cop at your shoulder" standard sometimes invoked in discussions of criminal responsibility. That the accused would have resisted if they had had that kind of incentive is supposed to show that they possessed powers of self-restraint sufficient for legal responsibility. Similarly, if you knew your drug taking was subject to immediate punishment, then you would have had a certain kind of reason to abstain. If that knowledge would have led you to abstain, then you are at least minimally responsive to reasons.[17] My objection is that the counterfactual incentive might be compulsive as well.

Although this objection helps itself to an unexplained notion of compulsion, it is valuable, nonetheless. If we can make sense of

mechanism that issues in the action be held fixed in the counterfactual situation. The operation of the counterfactual incentive would show that one's action is actually reasons responsive only if the same mechanism is at work in the actual and counterfactual circumstances. This idea meets the requirement, formally, but I am skeptical about the possibility of filling out its content in a satisfactory way.

[15] Consider the possibility of an individual with competing addictions; that is, sources of potentially incompatible compulsive desires. The only thing that will lead me not to take a drink, suppose, is the belief that drinking now would require me to forgo heroin for a long while. Or perhaps I would resist taking the heroin only if the supply were guarded by rats, to which I am highly phobic.

[16] Taken as a sufficient condition, Feinberg's (1970) test is open to a similar objection. If I tried harder, I would resist. Perhaps the presence of a counterincentive would *enable* me to try harder than I could in its absence. If my capacity to try were in some way impaired in certain contexts of temptation, my susceptibility to deterrent incentives under certain circumstances would not show that the desire is under my control (here and now). There is some plausibility to the idea that addictions tend to have this effect; I return to this point later.

[17] In terms of learning theory, of course, all aversive consequences are tantamount to punishment. So the restriction by the "cop at one's shoulder" standard to this one counterincentive seems arbitrary. If this standard reflects a deterrent or regulative conception of criminal law, however, the restriction is intelligible. If you are susceptible to the prospect of deterrence by legal threats, then it makes sense to subject you to them. [See Chapter 11 for a fuller discussion of criminal responsibility for addiction.]

motivational compulsion at all, then susceptibility to different motivation does not prove voluntary control. Hence, no serious test of compulsion in terms of susceptibility to counterincentives will work. Perhaps these worries can be met by suitable refinements. Another, even more obvious, concern comes to the fore in Glover's discussion: to avoid conflating incapacity and incontinence. How is unalterability to be distinguished from weakness of will?[18]

Here is Glover's suggestion:

If, like the alcoholic or drug addict, he is not open to persuasion by himself or by other people, then he does have a psychological incapacity. Yet, if a reasonable amount of persuasion would alter his intentions, but he himself chooses to avert his attention from the reasons in question, his is then a case of moral weakness without psychological incapacity. (Glover 1970, 100)

It is not clear why Glover is so confident that those we call addicts do *not* "choose to avert their attention from reasons." The philosophical worry, however, is that the appeal to such a choice returns us to our starting point. For the choice to avert one's attention is itself not reasons responsive. If it is not on that account unalterable, then self-control is not just a matter of reasons responsiveness. If the choice not to be responsive to reasons is noncompulsive, as it must be if Glover is to distinguish weakness from addiction, then we must supplement sensitivity to reasons with an independent notion of control. We are left in the end, then, with an unanalyzed appeal to what is in the agent's power and, hence, with the question: Is it within the agent's power to resist the temptation to go against reason?

The appeal to choice suggests a further complication. An intention might be unalterable because it expresses a determination to close off further consideration. Such resolution might be a kind of strength, if

[18] Glover (1970) points out two different ways in which an intention might be unalterable: It is independent of reasons one takes to be sufficient, or one would see contrary considerations to be sufficient if one were to "reason properly, or were not in some way deluded" (100). My worry concerns the first way. The second kind of unresponsiveness to reasons might well involve an incapacity, but it is not a case of irresistible desire.

not a virtue, or it might just be stubbornness—but it should not count as compulsive. (Nor, indeed, as weakness of will.)

Fischer distinguishes incontinence from incapacity by defining guidance control in terms of *weak responsiveness*: In contrast to the compulsive agent, the weak-willed agent is sensitive to *at least some* sufficient reasons to do otherwise. But, I doubt that any clearly intentional behavior fails to meet this condition. Certainly, the paradigm cases of severe and desperate addictions are not literally irresistible in this sense. Few if any addicts are beyond the reach of one counterincentive or another.[19]

The case of Ben Sanderson, the drunken character in the film *Leaving Las Vegas,* might be instructive here. Initially, Sanderson might strike one as an example of someone whose alcoholic behavior is unalterable, but this example is complicated. What is unwavering here, if anything, is not Sanderson's intention to drink *simpliciter* but his mission to drink himself to death to escape a shattered existence. Much of the dramatic tension in the film centers on the question whether the loving ministrations of Sera, the prostitute, will call him back to life. In the end, they do not; but it is not clear that nothing could have deflected him from his suicidal course: for example, that he would have been unmoved by a vivid and immediate threat to kill his children (for whom he appears still to have some attachment) unless he remained in the detox center for three months.

Of course, Sanderson's determination reflects not stubbornness but despair. He cannot see a way to go on with his life. (This might remain so even if he had pulled himself together for a bit to save his child.) The problem is not that his intention to put an end to his life

---

[19] James (1950, 2: 543) quotes a report "of a man who, while under treatment for inebriety, during four weeks secretly drank the alcohol from six jars containing morbid specimens. On asking him why he committed this loathsome act, he replied, 'Sir, it is as impossible for me to control this diseased appetite as it is for me to control the pulsations of my heart.'" James also tells us of a "dipsomaniac" who claimed, "Were a keg of rum in one corner of a room and were a cannon constantly discharging balls between me and it, I could not refrain from passing before that cannon in order to get the rum." I remain skeptical. (I thank George Loewenstein for this reference.)

is unalterable but that he sees no reason to alter it. He can see no future for himself that makes sense. This might indeed point to a sense in which Sanderson is motivationally disabled; but the incapacity here is not the incapacity to resist desire but to care.

Compulsion and Disruption

I suspect, then, that no reasons responsiveness theory will by itself provide a satisfactory account of motivational compulsion or enable us to preserve a plausible and significant distinction between compulsive and weak-willed behavior. (I discuss this distinction in Watson 1977 [Chapter 2 in this volume].) Nothing in these criticisms shows that the relevant notion of control cannot be identified with the *capacity* for sensitivity to reasons (or normative competence). They do show, however, that this capacity cannot be understood solely in terms of susceptibility to counterincentives.

Just the same, the idea that addiction involves a diminishment of the sensitivity to reasons has a good deal of plausibility. Characteristically, addicts have difficulty in bringing reason effectively to bear on their choices in a certain region of deliberation, at least under some circumstances. We will do well, I think, to abandon the interpersonal model, which features the power of addictive desire to defeat our best efforts and, instead, to understand the relevant notion of compulsion in terms of the tendency of certain incentives to impair our capacity to make those efforts. We are not so much overpowered by brute force as seduced.

One feature of desires experienced as compulsive is their power to capture one's attention. It is in this sense that we speak of a musical rhythm, or a literary plot, as compelling. This quality is generally desirable in a tune or drama but can be quite unwanted in other contexts. Desires can be more or less compelling in this sense. One measure of the strength of desires is their capacity to claim one's consciousness, direct one's fantasies, break one's concentration on other things. One finds it difficult to keep one's mind on one's work because one keeps thinking of one's lover, or of the chocolate cake in the pantry, or of the cigarettes at the market. The objects of these desires tend to demand or dominate one's attention, despite oneself.

These desires are sources of a good deal of "noise"—like a party next door. The clamor of appetite directs one's attention to its object as something to be enjoyed. This feature of desire, it seems to me, accounts both for the potential irrationality and the power of desires we experience as compulsive. The efforts involved in various techniques of resistance require a focus (or redirection) of consciousness that is hard to achieve in the midst of much appetitive noise. Again, this is the source of what might be called the predicament of self-control. Techniques of self-control often work by maintaining one's focus against such distractions, and yet employing those resources already takes an amount of focus that tends to dissolve precisely when it is needed.[20] This fragmentation of consciousness is one of the familiar elements of practical irrationality (Elster 1999a).

Understood in this way, compelling desires are often implicated in a kind of impairment of normative competence.[21] This impairment admits of degrees and does not entail complete incapacity. I am inclined to see the distinction between weakness and compulsion as a normative one: Roughly, individuals we describe as weakly giving into temptation are those who reasonably could be expected to have resisted or to have developed the capacities to resist. This view locates compulsion toward one end of a continuum that includes weakness of will; those at this end of the continuum are subject to such strong

[20] Consider the remarks of a former heavy drinker: "It seems to me that a person needs to have it within himself, be strong enough to handle his own problems . . . You have got to have some inner strength, some of your own strength in resources that you can call up in yourself" (Peele 1985, 194).

[21] For this term, see Wolf (1990, 129). In Wolf's terms, the addict's will is less intelligent than it would be in the absence of addiction. Addictions can impair normative competence not only by distorting probabilistic judgment or instrumental rationality, but also by affecting our sense of our fundamental values and projects—what we find meaningful in life.

desires that it is unreasonable to expect even a strong-willed person to hold out.[22]

I do not have the space to develop and assess this proposal here. I am sure it is unsatisfactory as it stands, but it does have some appeal. The concept it identifies is an important one, and makes sense of many of our practical concerns. Compulsive behavior tends to disrupt one's life in ways that are very difficult to control without help. It is this characteristic that elicits sympathy. It is this characteristic that is of interest to the therapeutic community. (Indeed, this is what *creates* that community.)

The overall effect of this proposal is to give up on the understanding of addictive compulsions as forms of necessitation. Anyway, addictions are not necessarily compulsive, even in the proposed sense. Some addictive conditions are relatively mild; others are terribly difficult to break; but if enough is at stake in someone's life, it might not be unreasonable to expect, or indeed demand, that she (genuinely seek help to) overcome the problem.

Addiction and Dependency

I have, among other things, been presenting some grounds for dissatisfaction with talk about motivational compulsion, understood on

---

[22] A normative account is developed in Greenspan (1986). Her discussion focuses on those who are subjected to aversive behavioral control (such as the character Alex in Anthony Burgess's *Clockwork Orange*). The victim of compulsion is "unfree because he is faced with a kind of threat, like a robbery victim coerced at gunpoint, with intense discomfort as his only option to compliance. This means that the actions he is compelled to take will be reasonable—reasonable in the light of an *un*reasonable threat" (Greenspan 1986, 196). In Chapter 2 of this volume, I suggest a normative account of a different kind. Whereas Greenspan suggests that we can account for compulsion without assuming that the compulsive cannot do otherwise, I argue there that we can account for the difference between compulsion and weakness without assuming that the weak agent *can* at the time do otherwise. The idea is that weakness is the manifestation of a vice; someone is a victim of compulsion if she is subject to motivation that even a person of exemplary self-control could not resist. My discussion there presumes (though it does not require) what I have been questioning here: that motivational compulsion in the sense of irresistibility makes sense.

the model of irresistible desire. Although addiction is commonly described (if not always strictly defined) in these terms, we need not be skeptical about the concept itself. For the crucial notion here, I suggest, is the idea of an *acquired appetite*. It is this notion that explains the stereotypical or symptomatic characteristics of addiction, including its association with compulsion. I develop this idea in what follows.

It is important to distinguish three levels of dependency. The first level I call *physical dependency*. Very roughly, individuals are physically or chemically dependent on some substance if consuming that substance has made them prone to suffer withdrawal symptoms—discomfort, agitation, restlessness, illness—when deprived of the substance for a period of time and, usually, to find the ingestion of the substance highly pleasurable.

Whether or not physical dependency is necessary for addiction, it is clearly not sufficient. Imagine you have been given morphine for pain control while in the hospital.[23] Suppose upon withdrawal you have no idea of the cause of your malaise. Although you no doubt desire relief, you have no desire, overpowering or not, to take the drug. Once you learn the cause of your discontent, probably you will come to want, and want badly, some morphine (or anything else) to avoid the discomfort. Clearly, *this* instrumental desire for the drug would not be the craving that is constitutive of addiction. One could have this sort of desire for morphine without ever having ingested the stuff—to relieve a toothache, say. So a desire for the drug (overwhelming or not) that is motivated by the discomfort resulting from this physical dependency is not on that account addictive.[24]

[23] This example, and the point it supports, come from Seeburger (1993, 46): "Hospital patients who are given morphine or other narcotics for relief from pain can develop tolerance and can show withdrawal symptoms, once the administration of the drug is discontinued. Nevertheless, they rarely become addicted. Most have no difficulty getting off the drug and are often grateful to be able to do so."

[24] Portenoy and Payne (1997) insist upon a distinction between physical dependence and addiction. What they mean by physical dependence is roughly what I mean, but they define addiction as a condition in which one is unable to abstain: "Use of the

When infants are said to be born addicted, what must be meant is a condition of narcotic dependence that does not involve cravings or addictive behavior. To call this addiction without qualification seems to me misleading, since it need not involve addictive craving and corresponding patterns of behavior. Nor need it involve the propensity to irrational thought and desire.

To be addicted, in the sense in which infants and those who become aware of their chemically dependent states cannot (yet) be, involves a dependency of a further kind. It requires a history of behavior that forges a cognitive link and a motivational link between that kind of substance and behavior and pleasure and relief. The fact that behavior of a certain kind (drug-taking behavior) has certain effects (dependent on the individual's chemical dependency) generates a periodic craving. The physical dependency increases one's tendency to be (more or less intensely) rewarded by the behavior and to be more or less acutely uncomfortable without this substance (or behavior). These withdrawal symptoms might secondarily reinforce behavior that leads to ingestion of the substance. Only then does one acquire, not only a dependency on but an *appetite* for the substance or behavior in question.[25]

term 'addiction' to describe patients who are merely physically dependent reinforces the stigma associated with opioid therapy and should be abandoned. If the clinician wishes to describe a patient who is believed to have the capacity for abstinence, the term physical dependency must be used" (564). Since my second level of dependency, which I consider to be addiction proper, need not involve this inability, Portenoy and Payne are marking a different distinction.

[25] Spelling out these cognitive and motivational links is complicated. One of the complications concerns the relation between the object of one's appetite and what one is addicted to. Rats and people become addicted to cocaine. Should we say that a rat or a person craves or wants cocaine even if it or she has no conception of that substance? (I am grateful to John Christman for raising this issue with me.) Suppose you have a completely false belief about the object of your appetite. Suppose you are regularly but unknowingly exposed to certain addictive "fumes" when and only when at a certain villa in Italy. When you are away for a while, you find yourself "craving" another visit; when you return you are deeply gratified, and you find that you need to return more frequently, for longer visits. You might imagine that you have developed an attachment to the place. You are in fact addicted to the "gas"; what is your appetite for? (I am indebted to Lee Overton for suggesting to me an example like this.)

This further condition is sometimes satisfied by nonhuman animals. In experimental conditions, rats can become chemically dependent on opiates and stimulants. They learn to do various things to get more. They thereby acquire something structurally similar to their natural needs for water and food. They come to enjoy taking in opiates as they do food. When they are deprived of these things, they are distressed.

Since nonhuman animals lack a capacity for critical evaluation, they are not even prima facie candidates for either motivational compulsion or weakness. Addictions may move them contrary to their own good but not contrary to their own conceptions of the good. Nevertheless, when their addictive behavior displaces their natural appetites, they suffer from what might be called an appetitive impairment.

To become addicted is to acquire an appetite, an appetite that, typically, is caused and sustained by the regular ingestion of certain substances. To acquire an appetite is to acquire a felt need, a source of pleasure and pain, that has a periodic motivational force that is independent of one's capacity for critical judgment. Hence, for creatures with such a capacity, to acquire an appetite is to become vulnerable to temptation.

Appetites involve positive and negative inclinations. We are naturally hooked on food and drink. When I am hungry, I typically become more or less uncomfortable. That is distracting. I desire to various degrees to relieve this discomfort, but that is not all. More positively, the distinction between the edible and the nonedible in my environment becomes highly salient to me. Depending on experience, certain sorts of food are especially alluring and their consumption intensely enjoyable. It can be more or less difficult to resist eating, or seeking, food, primarily because it becomes more or less difficult to keep my mind off the subject. We do not call these ordinary food dependencies addictions. Indeed, lack of interest in food or drink after a period of abstinence is a sign of disordered appetite.

An addiction is a nonnatural or acquired appetite. The ingestion of nicotine or caffeine can induce a periodic craving for these substances. Although addictions tend to be in some measure compelling, in the sense we discussed earlier, nothing in this conception implies straightaway that the addicted person is subject to cravings that are irresistible.[26] When temporary abstinence is the result of a deliberate, wholehearted plan (say, for the observance of a religious holiday), smokers often get by without much difficulty—just as some people fast for quite a while without being subject to great temptation. The strategies and techniques of self-control are similar for natural and nonnatural appetites.

Nor does the conception of addiction as acquired appetite imply that this condition is necessarily harmful, all things considered. Certain addictions can be regulated without interference with a person's physical or mental health or with productive social relations.[27] Opiate dependency can be a reasonable price to pay for control of acute or chronic pain.[28] Just the same, acquiring appetites is a hazardous business. Natural appetites are grounded in natural needs, and the health of an animal depends in general upon their satisfaction. We tend to do poorly when our natural appetites are suppressed or disordered. Insofar as addictions exhibit the phenomenon of tolerance (which, apparently, not all of them do), the appetites in which

[26] This is contrary to Halikas et al. (1997, 85), who define craving as "an irresistible urge to use a substance that compels drug-seeking behavior."

[27] This is the goal of methadone maintenance programs. Apparently, when properly administered, these have had considerable worldwide success in countering the adverse effects of heroin addiction. Nevertheless, as a matter of public policy, they have been controversial in the United States partly because they are thought merely to replace one addiction with another (Lowinson et al. 1997a; Kreek and Reisinger 1997).

[28] Portenoy and Payne (1997) observe that physical dependency as a result of prolonged use of opiates in programs of pain management does not reliably lead to addiction. "A reasonable hypothesis is that addiction results from the interaction between the reinforcing properties of opioid drugs and any number of characteristics . . . - specific to the individual . . . such as the capacity for euphoria from an opioid and psychopathy" (582).

they consist are more difficult to regulate and tend toward an unhealthy insatiability.

As we have seen, addictions involve a tendency to various kinds of irrationality—but so do the appetites generally. There may be nothing distinctive about addictions in this respect; hunger, thirst, and sexual attraction create similar liabilities. On the other hand, possibly certain addictions are linked to special or especially serious distortions of judgment and reasoning. For all I know, certain addictive substances have distinctive effects on parts of the brain that govern cognitive functions.[29] If deprivation of food or water, for example, were shown not to have similar effects, then that would support the idea that (some) addictions made us especially liable to distortions of rationality.[30] For my purposes, it suffices to note our general susceptibilities as appetitive beings.

One advantage of characterizing addiction primarily in terms of its effects on rationality rather than in terms of irresistibility is that this conception readily makes sense of the idea of mild addictions, for the disorder it identifies has different degrees and dimensions. Caffeine addiction rarely if ever leads to fundamental changes in personality or to severe distortions in practical thought. Even here, there are familiar distortions—for example, a professor who risks being late to lecture in order to stop by the espresso stand on the way to class. ("It will just take a minute.") Note that one might do this for pastry, as well, without having what some call a food disorder.

---

[29] Of course, extreme intake of alcohol (or speed or LSD) can induce psychosis and cause brain damage. So can eating lead paint or, for that matter, I suppose, a great deal of carrot juice.

[30] It is important to distinguish the effects on rationality of the dependency itself from the more direct effects of the ingestion of certain addictive substances. As dependencies, all addictions create liabilities to irrationalities when one is deprived (or threatened with deprivation) of the substance. Addictive substances differ, however, in their intoxicating properties. Being "high" may itself diminish rationality. I suspect these differences are linked to the different capacities of substances to lead to what I call existential dependency; some of these impairments of consciousness are precisely what one comes to "need." (Here, I am indebted to discussion with Susan Neiman.)

On this view, again, addictions are continuous with ordinary appetites, such as one's craving for croissants (to go with that latte).

Further Questions

The conception of addictions as acquired appetites raises difficult questions about both of its constitutive concepts. What should be comprised under the heading of appetite? How exactly can we distinguish between appetites that are acquired and those that are original? Here, I can only touch on these issues.

I have been working with a paradigm list of natural appetites—hunger, thirst, and sex—but I have no precise account of the criteria of membership. The natural appetites have to do with what is needed for the health or flourishing of the individual, I said, but sexual appetite is anomalous in a number of respects. Sexual attraction often exhibits a periodic appetitive structure, tied to hormonal activity; but unlike nutrition, sexual activity is not required for the survival of the individual. To be sure, many of us find abstinence distressing, but this effect depends somewhat on individual circumstance, age, and culture. As difficult as it may be for others to understand, some physically normal individuals manage to flourish in celibacy.

Moreover, unlike hunger and thirst, sexual appetite is fulfilled by behavior without the ingestion of substances into the body. To be sure, natural reproduction in human beings occurs by the literal incorporation of certain substances into the body of female sexual partners. This brings out a deep biological parallel with the other appetites.[31] For evolutionary reasons, human beings tend periodically to find specific activities more or less intensely pleasurable and to be discomfited by their frustration. Nonetheless, a significant contrast with hunger and thirst remains. The satisfactions and fulfillment of sexual desire, and the discomfort resulting from nonfulfillment, have

---

[31] Here, I am indebted to discussions with Michael Hudson.

nothing to do with the ingestion of substances. If so, and if addictions are acquired appetites, then there is room for the possibility of acquired behavioral appetites, as many people think. In any case, beyond (male?) adolescence, sexual desire is connected only loosely with appetitive periodicity. It has much richer emotional and interpersonal content than hunger and thirst.[32] Erotic responsiveness is often evoked by the perceived sexual interest of others in us. This would be an unexpected feature of the other appetites: as though I were aroused to hunger by the recognition of the desire of the blueberry muffin to be eaten by me.

Furthermore, not all natural needs for substances are appetitive. Oxygen is essential to individual survival; we feel extreme discomfort when deprived of it for even a moment or two; and a felt need to breathe exhibits a (very short) periodic structure. Why, then, is the need to breathe not appetitive?[33]

This question deserves a fuller treatment than I can give it here. The answer, I think, is connected with the fact that breathing is an automatic response, controlled by the autonomic nervous system. Appetites, acquired and unacquired, are sustained by reward.[34]

[32] I am grateful to Sharon Lloyd for emphasizing this point.

[33] The desire to sleep (from sleepiness) is periodic and naturally connected with the individual's health. Why isn't it appetitive? (See Watson 1977 [Ch. 2]; I am grateful to Laurie Piper for pressing this question on me again.) I do not have an adequate answer. My hunch is that this desire does not constitute a craving that arises from and is focused on voluntary behavior in the relevant way—but this is too obscurely put for me to have much confidence in it.

[34] Ainslie (1998) summarizes neurophysiological work since the 1950s in this way: Researchers "have found that most or all recreational substances . . . exert their rewarding effect by stimulating dopamine release in one small part of the midbrain, the nucleus accumbens, which is the same site where normal rewards like food and sex occur" (16). That both addictions and appetites involve in some way a subsystem of the brain's dopamine system is supported by Gardner and Lowinson (1993). According to them, "more than three decades of neuroanatomical, neurochemical, neuropharmacological, neurophysiological, and neurobehavioural studies have converged to indicate that brain stimulation reward is largely mediated by a portion of the mesotelencephalic dopamine system of the ventral limbic forebrain" (360). This reward system "is strongly implicated in the pleasures produced by natural rewards

In contrast, I suppose, the desire to breathe and the discomfort of not breathing do not involve the brain's reward system in the same way, but I am not sure how to incorporate these observations into a satisfactory definition of the appetitive.

These are questions about what an appetite is. Another set of issues concerns the contrast between acquired and original appetites. I said earlier that we are naturally hooked on food and drink, but of course what is edible and drinkable (or sexually appealing) is largely a cultural matter. The appetites are not just for indeterminate food or drink or physical contact. What an individual who is hungry or thirsty or sexually aroused thereby desires depends upon specific training and experience. One wants this or that culturally available form of satisfaction.

In one sense, then, all appetites are acquired. Beyond early infancy, the ways we satisfy our appetites are virtually always mediated by acculturated tastes. On the other hand, addictions are in a sense perfectly natural. Our constitution is such that many of us are prone to become physically dependent when exposed to certain substances (or activities?) and to acquire appetitive desires for these. The idea that natural appetites (in contrast to addictions) are unacquired has to be interpreted in a way that is consistent with these truths.

Nevertheless, I think the distinction marks a real difference. Its defense depends on the fact that the social construction of the appetites takes place on a biological foundation of culturally independent needs. This point certainly requires careful formulation and development. Until then, a certain amount of caution, if not skepticism is admittedly in order.

Dependence and Attachment

Addiction often involves what some writers call *existential dependence* (Seeburger 1993); that is, the development of an identity to

(for example, food and sex)." See also Gardner (1997); Gold and Miller (1997) note that dopamine "antagonists block the rewarding effects of food and water just as they block the self-administration of stimulants such as cocaine" (174).

which the addictive practices are crucial. In this way, devotion to the relevant behavior becomes bound up with the meaning of one's life. Pete Hamill (1994) describes his relation to drinking in this way:

I had entered the drinking life. Drinking was part of being a man. Drinking was an integral part of sexuality, easing entrance to its dark and mysterious treasure chambers. Drinking was the sacramental binder of friendships. Drinking was the reward for work, fuel for celebration, the consolation for death or defeat. Drinking gave one strength, confidence, ease, laughter; it made me believe that dreams really could come true. (146–7)

Breaking the addiction thus requires fashioning a new sense of what one's life is about. Herbert Fingarette (1988) emphasizes this kind of dependence as a feature of alcoholism (though he scrupulously avoids the language of addiction):

For a heavy drinker to make a major change in his drinking patterns requires a reconstruction of his way of life. The drinker must learn over time to see the world in different terms, to cultivate new values and interests, to find or create new physical or social settings, to develop new relationships, to devise new ways of behaving in those new relationships and settings. (110)

Existential dependency is surely one of the most disturbing features of paradigmatic addictions. One's existence might come to be more or less centered around the satisfaction of this appetite, in such a way that one's sense of what is most important in (one's) life is defined by one's addiction, and life without it would seem significantly diminished in meaning. This explains what is often so demeaning about that condition: One becomes *devoted* to what is unworthy of devotion.[35] Still, I see no reason to think that addictive appetites are necessarily bound up with a distinctive way of life.[36] Existential

---

[35] Seeburger (1993, 50–1) endorses William Burroughs's remark that "junk is not a kick. It is a way of life. . . . You become a narcotics addict because you do not have strong motivations in any other directions." Addiction either supplants whatever had provided meaning to the individual before, or it supplies meaning to an otherwise empty life.

[36] If being addicted to alcohol means having acquired an appetite in virtue of one's chemical dependency, and if being an alcoholic means coming to center the meaning

dependence is a matter of degree. Acquired appetites (like natural ones) might lead to such dependence but they need not to any notable extent. We should not be misled by sensational examples into thinking of this level as a feature of all addiction.[37] It is rarely if ever reached by those who are hooked on caffeine or even nicotine. (But, consider the remarkable example of the literary critic, Mikhail Bakhtin, who reportedly used up the only copy of his book manuscript for cigarette paper.)

For something to be bound up importantly in my way of life, I need not see myself as strictly unable to do without it. It is enough that its absence would leave, as we say, a very big hole. Individuals in this third stage of dependency have an especially difficult time changing. In the extreme case, I might find another form of life unthinkable—I cannot imagine my life without it.[38]

It is useful to see this stage of dependence as involving *attachment* to one's addiction. Life without one's addiction presents itself to one as a grave loss. The prospect of a change is at least daunting, sometimes even terrifying. The sense that one otherwise lacks the resources to cope with everyday life might induce panic. In extreme cases, this sense might amount to an attachment disorder.

Dependence and Autonomy

The difficulties presented by addictive dependency are not necessarily different in kind or degree from other dependencies that we would not want to count as addictions. Attachments that are central

of one's life around the consumption of alcohol, then we ought to distinguish alcoholism from alcohol addiction *simpliciter*. More generally, we should distinguish being addicted to this or that from *being an addict*.

[37] Elster (1999*b*) refers to this kind of dependency as "crowding out." Elster rightly rejects it as a necessary condition of addiction.

[38] This, again, is a different form of motivational incapacity from irresistible desire. This is an instance of what Frankfurt calls volitional necessity; see "Rationality and the Unthinkable" in Frankfurt (1988). [And see Chapter 4 in this volume.]

to human flourishing make us vulnerable to losses of a similar magnitude.[39] It is not just a question of wanted versus unwanted addictions. Unwise attachments are not on that account addictions.

Existential dependence is not necessarily regrettable. Most of our lives are structured around the appetites in one way or another. They and their expression tend to be dear to us. The pains and perplexities of this devotion sometimes tempt us to ideals of detachment; but on reflection our appetitive lives matter to most of us in ways that we do not regret.

The same goes for attachment to acquired appetites. As we have seen, some people can manage their addictions. Addiction is in principle compatible with temperance.[40] We cannot dismiss a regulated devotion to tobacco or drink as demeaning or enslaving just on the grounds that it involves dependence. That would presuppose an ideal of self-mastery that would condemn much of what we value in human life.

Let me press this point a bit further. I am told that it is possible for a well-supplied heroin addict to live an otherwise healthy and productive life. (It appears to be otherwise with cocaine and amphetamines.) In any case, imagine that this is so for a certain severely addictive substance, S, and that in a certain culture, otherwise similar to ours, the use of S is not only tolerated but respected as highly spiritually beneficial. This culture regards the dependency on this substance, which is to say, the vulnerability to various kinds of

---

[39] Seeburger (1993) ignores this point: "What counts in addiction is that one relates to something, whether a substance, a process, a relationship, or whatever, in such a way that one experiences oneself as unable to do without it" (58–9). So much for grand passion (for Vronsky and Anna Karenina) as well as the ideals and attachments of everyday life.

[40] Or at least with continence, which Aristotle distinguishes from virtue proper (*Nicomachean Ethics*, 1152). If addictive cravings are inherently sources of temptation, then addiction is incompatible with the virtue of temperance, as Aristotle conceives it. That would sharply distinguish addictive appetites from natural ones, for the virtuous woman or man will, in Aristotle's picture, have and enjoy the natural appetites. My claim is that a virtuous person could have the same relation to his or her acquired appetites.

diminished self-control, as a small price to pay for the enrichment of human life provided by S. Fortunately, S is easily obtainable, perhaps even subsidized by the society for religious reasons.

This fantasy makes it clear that the moral significance of an individual's volitional vulnerability depends not only on individual responsibility and the limits of human endurance but also on judgments about the meaning and value of the behavior and relationships that they make possible. In our imagined society, both the use of and dependency on S are regarded as entirely fitting and normal, on a par with the appetites for food and drink. The unfortunate minority who cannot tolerate S are thought to be missing something. To become addicted to S is not thereby to infringe any social or legal norms of self-control. The content of such norms is not determined by an abstract standard of self-control but by a sense of what is worth pursuing in human life. The threat of being deprived of one's S is here on a par with the prospect of imminent starvation.

The assessment of addiction as a form of slavery depends as much on norms regarding the value of addictive dependencies as from concerns about self-control per se. We tend to see them as demeaning or destructive rather than as possible sources of worthwhile human activity. For this reason, we tend to expect people to avoid those conditions and see the plight created by those conditions as the individual's own fault.

I know of no substance in our culture that has the role of S exactly, but there are instructive examples of parallel acquired dependencies which we encourage and honor. I have in mind the various relationship attachments exemplified by parenting or being in love. Like addictions, to be attached in these ways is to be vulnerable to diminished control of certain kinds.

I am not arguing that addictions of any kind should be valued in the way we value the attachments just mentioned. Perhaps we are right as a culture to disrespect addiction. That deserves a separate discussion. My point is that these forms of dependency cannot be disparaged *solely* on the grounds that they diminish self-control, that is, simply because they *are* dependencies. Addictions must be shown in some further way to reduce the value of human experience or agency. Obviously, countless lives have been ruined by devotion to drugs. On the other hand, addictive substances help many of us to endure what would otherwise be rather bleak prospects.

Conclusion

The concepts of appetite and of addiction are both highly indeterminate. Therefore, any proposed analysis is perforce somewhat regimentary. It would be wrongheaded, then, to object that those who would speak of curiosity as an appetite for learning or of obsessions with chess or music as addictions are misusing the terms. Similarly, those who define the term "addiction" as involving uncontrollable impulses or self-destructive behavior can find a lot of support in both popular and technical discussions. The issue for us is theoretical: What regimentation is most illuminating? Even the answer to this question is partly relative to purposes. It is quite natural for the therapeutic community to work with a normative conception according to which the addicted individual is one who needs help, but these broader and normative conceptions seem to me to obscure connections and differences among the phenomena that the conception of addiction as acquired appetite highlights. This narrower conception enables us to see structural similarities between the clear cases of addiction and natural appetites.[41] These similarities illuminate the connection of addiction with various forms of irrationality (and in extreme cases motivational impairment) and suggest common neurophysical processes.[42]

---

[41] The closest relative of this account that I have found in the empirical literature is Loewenstein's (1999) visceral theory. Loewenstein identifies addictions with conditional cravings. Like the proposed account, this view emphasizes the similarities between addictions and appetites and other visceral factors. Loewenstein also emphasizes the importance of cue conditioning for craving. I am not clear enough about the author's conception of craving to venture a more detailed comparison and contrast here.

[42] Elster (1999b) critically discusses accounts of addiction that focus on "phenomenological similarities rather than causal commonalities."

By itself, this conception leaves it open whether and to what extent addiction is a bad thing in particular cases. That seems to me desirable. The issues raised by addiction are not sharply distinct from the issues raised by the appetites in general. In part, these concern our notorious troubles in dealing well with the pleasures of life. Addictions dispose us to be led on and distracted by pleasure, as though it were our master. In extreme cases, they can even corrupt our sense of what evil is, but they can also figure as part of the meaning of a life well enough lived, at least compared to the alternatives. In this respect, too, addictions lie on a continuum with the other appetites.

4   Volitional Necessities

I. Introduction

My aim, ultimately, is to investigate what Harry Frankfurt calls *volitional necessity*:

> If a person who is constrained by volitional necessity is for that reason unable to pursue a certain course of action, the explanation is not that he is in any straightforward way too weak to overcome the constraint. That sort of explanation can account for the experience of an addict, who dissociates himself from the addiction constraining him but who is unsuccessful in his attempt to oppose his own energies to the impetus of his habit. A person who is constrained by volitional necessity, however, is in a situation that differs significantly from that one. Unlike the addict, he does not accede to the constraining force because he lacks sufficient strength of will to defeat it. He accedes to it because he is *unwilling* to oppose it and because, furthermore, his unwillingness is *itself* something which he is unwilling to alter.[1]

I want to express my gratitude to Sarah Buss and Lee Overton for organizing the conference for which this essay was first prepared, and to the conference participants for the extraordinarily high level of philosophical intelligence and good spirits they brought to the occasion. I am also grateful to Sarah and Lee for their painstaking editorial work on the volume in which this chapter originally appeared. In preparing the final draft, I have profited enormously from their efforts. The comments of Michael Bratman, John Fischer, Paul Hoffman, and Jennifer Rosner have also helped me a great deal. Finally, I want to thank Harry Frankfurt for opening up and shaping this philosophical territory in the first place; without him, we are unlikely to have gone there at all.

[1] Harry Frankfurt, "The Importance of What We Care About," in *The Importance of What We Care About: Philosophical Essays* (New York: Cambridge University

The topic Frankfurt opens up here is profoundly difficult. One difficulty has to do with "necessity." What does it mean to speak of volition being *necessitated* in this way? Another hard question concerns "volition." How are we to understand that which is necessitated? These questions, and especially the second, take us to the heart of Frankfurt's philosophy of agency.

Any satisfactory constructive (that is, non-skeptical) treatment of volitional necessity must distinguish it both from inability to act and from other ways in which the "will" might be constrained. As a preliminary, then, I shall contrast the sorts of impairment involved in addictions and phobias with a more basic notion of inability to act. Then I turn to the task of distinguishing such impairments from volitional necessity. In the end, I find that Frankfurt's discussion of this phenomenon exposes a theoretical tension between two conceptions of volition.

II. *Inability to Act*

Donald Davidson's characterization of this concept is a useful starting point. He suggests the following analysis of "what a man can do":

A can do *x* intentionally (under the description *d*) means that if *A* has desires and beliefs that rationalize *x* (under *d*), then *A* does *x*.[2]

Davidson's point, I take it, is that the basic concept of what someone can do is given by a certain kind of dependency relation between the individual's concerns or reasons and his or her behavior. Roughly, I can do what I will succeed in doing if I want to do that, rather than

Press, 1988), 87. As far as I know, Frankfurt is the first to take up this topic. Bernard Williams singles out a similar range of phenomena. See his "Moral Incapacity," in *Making Sense of Humanity* (Cambridge, England: Cambridge University Press, 1995). I compare Williams' treatment of the topic with Frankfurt's below.

[2] Donald Davidson, "Freedom to Act," in *Essays on Actions and Events* (New York: Oxford University Press, 1980), 73. All subsequent page references to Davidson in the text will be to this essay.

another thing. As Davidson puts it, ". . . what an agent does do intentionally is what he is free to [that is, can] do *and* has adequate reasons for doing" (74). If I did something intentionally, it follows that my doing what I did depended on my "desires" and beliefs, and hence, in the sense just defined, that I could at that time do (in his language "was free to do") what I did.[3]

Almost everyone agrees by now that this basic concept, in all its variants, leaves untouched many important issues about freedom and incapacity. Davidson himself hastens to add: "I do not want to suggest that the nature of an agent's beliefs and desires, and the question how he acquired them, are irrelevant to how free he, or his actions, are. But these questions are on a different and more sophisticated level from that of our present discussion" (73). These more "sophisticated" questions arise, among other sources, from reflections on ways in which an individual's capacity to choose (or form intentions, or try) might be impaired. We can signal this need for refinement by amending the basic notion accordingly: what we can do is what depends on the exercise of our unimpaired capacity for choice.

Before we consider some of these refinements, I want to underscore the centrality of this basic concept to the way we think about human action. One fundamental contrast marked by this basic concept is a distinction between will and power; it is one thing to be unwilling to do something, quite another to be unable. Consider

---

[3] Now there are importantly different variants on this type of conditional account. In place of the notion of a desire/belief pair, for example, one could speak instead of the formation of intentions so to act (as I would prefer). For the purposes of this discussion, these questions won't matter much. Notice two points about this notion. It satisfies standard modal principles by preserving inferences of the form 'if S Xs, then S can X' (where 'X' is a description under which the agent acts intentionally). Notice also that since Davidson identifies reasons with desire/belief pairs, to act intentionally is on his account to act on a reason. It follows, in this minimal sense, that if someone can do otherwise, she is "responsive to reasons." This idea figures in the discussion below.

Clara, who lies cozily in bed. Though she has no reason or inclination to arise, she is perfectly able to do so. In attributing abilities in this way, we bracket questions about the agent's actual desires and reasons, focusing instead on what is open to her, whatever those reasons might be.

For many purposes, for instance, prediction or control, this distinction seems irrelevant. We might as effectively ensure that Clara remains in her room by making her comfortable as by chaining her to the bedposts. Either way, we've removed a necessary condition of her exit; in this sense it is not possible that she will in these circumstances arise.

But from the (overlapping) standpoints of responsibility and agency, the distinction is vital. If Clara doesn't turn up at the office, her colleagues and students will be inconvenienced anyway. Yet it might well matter to them whether she stayed at home for her own (good or bad) reasons, or whether she was prevented from coming. Furthermore, this distinction frames each individual's view of his or her prospective behavior. In thinking about what to do (for example, as I consider whether to arise), I am of course not trying to predict my future but determine it; I am trying to determine which of what I take to be my (feasible) options I shall take. To discover that I am paralyzed is to realize that certain options do not in fact exist. It is crucial to this standpoint of deliberation, then, to distinguish what I am able to do (what my options are) from what I shall do. The point is to determine the latter in view of the former. And the relevant notion of an "option" from this standpoint is roughly this: my options are those courses of action whose realization depends on what I determine to do—on my decision, choice, or intention (as the case may be). To learn that something is not an option, not within my capacity in this sense, is to learn that it does not stand in this relation to my choice.

Thus, the distinction between what does and does not depend on my will is central both to interpersonal concerns of responsibility and to first-personal concerns about agency and deliberation.[4] What others might want to know is whether Clara's absence is due to factors independent of her will, or whether she would have come if she had chosen. They want to know whether the absence was her choice. This distinction is salient as well in her question about whether to get out of bed, which presupposes that whether she arises depends on what she decides—that is, that getting up is among her options. When this dependency relation obtains, it follows that certain things are in one important sense under her control; they are, as we say, up to her.

We can sum up the point so far in this way. Our conception of human ability relies on a distinction between the *performance conditions* and the *enabling conditions* of an action. Roughly put, the latter are a proper subset of the former. From the standpoint of theoretical explanation and prediction, the fact that Clara has no intention of getting up this morning is on a par with any other *sine qua non* concerning the conditions of her limbs and muscles and central nervous system. From that point of view, the ordinary notion of ability to act seems arbitrary and uninteresting, as though one were to insist that the coffee in my cup can boil here and now, in the cool environment of my study, because it *would* boil if it were heated up. A possible way of speaking, I suppose, but rather pointless.

In contrast, it is crucial to our practical lives to distinguish some necessary conditions from others. Intending to get up is a condition of the performance but not of the ability. We can ask sensibly whether it is possible for certain behavior to occur in the absence of

---

[4] In her book, *Freedom and Responsibility* (Princeton: Princeton University Press, 1999), Hilary Bok shows the importance of distinguishing the kind of possibility that is central to many theoretical contexts (which she calls possibility *tout court*) from that which is important to deliberative concerns. Philosophers who are inclined to look at the notion of ability to act from a theoretical point of view will say that the idea of what an individual would do if she intended or tried yields at most a notion of what an individual *could* do under certain conditions, which is of course not at all the same as what an individual can do under actual conditions. This is, again, a possible way of speaking, but for understandable reasons it is not of much use in deliberative contexts.

certain conditions—whether it is possible that Clara arises here and now, given that her legs have been removed or immobilized, or given that she doesn't intend to do so. Presumably not. Again, in the same sense, it is not possible that my coffee will boil in the present atmosphere of my study. But it would show confusion about the meaning and role of the ordinary notion of ability to say of lounging Clara that she can't get out of bed just because one of the conditions of her doing so is absent—namely her intending to get up.[5] The will to get out of bed is a performance condition, not an enabling condition.

III. Disabilities of the Will

The limits of this concept for understanding human freedom come to the fore when something goes wrong with the will. Suppose Clara were instead afflicted with the pathological depression or anxiety depicted in the following autobiographical report by Andrew Solomon:

> I ran home shaking and went to bed, but I did not sleep, and *could not get up* the following day. I wanted to call people to cancel birthday plans, but I *couldn't.* . . . I knew that for years I had taken a shower every day. Hoping that someone else could open the bathroom door, I would, with all the force in my body, sit up; turn and put my feet on the floor, and then feel so incapacitated and frightened that I would roll over and lie face down. I would cry again, weeping because the fact that I *could not do it* seemed so idiotic to me.[6]

This passage describes what it is natural to call a *volitional disability* or *impairment*, in this case, an incapacity to will to get out of bed

---

[5] This is a major theme of Stuart Hampshire's *Freedom of the Individual* (New York: Harper and Row, 1965).

[6] Andrew Solomon, "Anatomy of Melancholy," *The New Yorker* (January 12, 1998), 46–58 (my emphasis). The sentence before the ellipsis is from p. 46; the rest of the quotation comes from p. 49.

(as distinct from an incapacity to get out of bed as and when one wills). I won't undertake a systematic discussion of phobias and similar phenomena here. But I must make a few observations in preparation for the discussion of what Frankfurt has in mind by volitional necessity.

To begin with, it is perhaps not obvious that we need to invoke a notion of volitional incapacity at all to understand a case like Solomon's. After all, Solomon struggles hard to sit up in an effort to get out of bed; he sees and responds to reasons to arise. But his fear overcomes him. His fear is an obstacle to his efforts to carry out his intentions. It prevents him from carrying out his will. So this is just incapacity in the basic sense, it seems. The problem is not with his will but with the relation between his will and his actions. He is as effectively disabled by his fear as he would be by literal paralysis of the limbs. Nothing in the basic concept requires the obstacle to be physical.

This analysis seems wrong. It doesn't deal with cases in which the individual is too terrified even to try. But even where the agent does struggle, as in this case, the phobia works not by conquering his fullest, wholehearted efforts, but by leading him to abandon his intentions. This is an important contrast with a case of literal paralysis. Suppose that Clara attempts to arise, only to discover that she has been paralyzed by a stroke. She struggles mightily but to no avail. Although Paralyzed Clara's agency is ineffective in this respect, her basic agency remains intact. In contrast, Solomon (to say the least) is in serious conflict. He is ineffective in carrying out his intentions because his agency is undermined by his melancholy. In contrast to Paralyzed Clara, his problem is not that he can't get out of bed *simpliciter* but that he can't get himself to do so. Part of what makes his plight so horrible is that his integrity as an agent is compromised.

It might be thought that phobias impair *judgment*, rather than will. No doubt this kind of impairment is common. But that doesn't seem to be all that's going on in the scene Solomon describes, or in numerous others. Quite apart from being unable to see clearly what is to be done, or to do as he wills, he is sometimes unable to commit himself to implementing his judgments or prior intentions. Of course, it is not easy always to distinguish impairments of judgment from impairments of will; they are often combined and are equally vexing to practical reason. Furthermore, phobias can "handicap" without fully incapacitating. Disabilities come in degrees. If I have a phobia of dogs, I might walk far out of my way to avoid certain neighborhoods. This choice might reflect the perfectly reasonable judgment that exposing myself to the objects of my dread is just not worth it. I might even form the intention and make an effort to walk that way, as exposure therapy,[7] and then decide, in the end, perfectly rationally (and non*akratically*) that my efforts are not worth the agony.

It is worth noting two distinct kinds of reasons that I might express by saying "I fear the dogs." The first is simply the consideration that I might get bitten; (non-phobic) fear, like (well-functioning) emotions in general, registers an independently existing (at least apparent) reason. But, independently of its content, anxiety as such can also give rise to a reason. To be apprehensive of dog bites in this way means that I will be able to go into that neighborhood only at the cost of extreme distress, which may make it reasonable for me to avoid the area, quite apart from the probability of my sustaining the dreaded injury. The prospect of unfriendly dogs and my fear of dogs both work as obstacles or constraints by threatening the costs, respectively, of dog bite or dread of dog bite. The latter is a distinctive consideration, which can figure as a reason in the formation of one's intentions. This can be so, even though one takes one's fear to be unreasonable and experiences it as a constraint.

What is crucial to our topic is fear's effect as a volitional impediment, not just as a rational constraint of either of these kinds. This effect

---

[7] Exposure therapy can backfire. Isaac Marks tells the sad story of a woman with a dread of flying who "was put on her test flight from Tel Aviv to Paris only to find that it was hijacked to Entebbe." *Fears, Phobias, and Rituals* (New York: Oxford University Press, 1987), 391.

emerges when one decides that the costs are worth it. Here one has counted and overruled whatever reasons the anxiety itself (as distinct from the considerations expressed by its content) provided. The dread remains, and must be dealt with, not just as a potential cost of the action but as something that might defeat one's agency by leading one to abandon the intention to pay the price.

There appears to be a difference between being unable to bring oneself to act and simply giving up in the face of great difficulty, but the distinction is obscure. To fail in one's wholehearted and persistent efforts might seem to be as decisive a test of inability to act, there and then, as we ever have.[8] But this criterion doesn't apply very clearly in cases of volitional incapacity, in which the individual is torn by conflict. In these cases, it will almost always be true that the individual is led to give up his attempts. This point of course does not demonstrate that the person is not incapacitated; but it makes the concept of volitional ability rather darker than the basic concept of ability to act.[9] Perhaps "necessity" here is really a matter of degree; we speak of incapacity to emphasize the magnitude of the difficulty.

---

[8] As Hampshire puts it: "When we definitely, and without qualification or conflict, want to do something at a particular moment, sincerely make the attempt in normal conditions, and yet fail, we know as surely as we can ever know, that at that moment we could not do it." Hampshire, Freedom of the Individual, 3. It is often hard to know, of course, whether the antecedent conditions have been fulfilled. But even when we think they have been, we do not infer inability from single failures. Paul Hoffman has reminded me that failures of execution in complicated performances often do not lead us to conclude that we were unable to do the thing then and there, especially if we have succeeded (or go on to succeed) in similar circumstances. Athletes frequently say, "We could have won that game," without implying that their effort or concentration was faulty. This judgment seems to rest on the assessment that they had the opportunity and the requisite skill to win. So the issue is more complicated than Hampshire's criterion would have it.

[9] The contrast should not be drawn too starkly. To persist in physically demanding tasks takes not only muscular strength and coordinational skills but the capacity to deal with pain, tedium, discomfort, discouragement and hence with the desire to quit. Tests of physical strength are typically, in part, tests of will. (Much of the drama of athletics turns on this.) So obstacles to physical feats almost always include motivational resistance as well.

The distinction seems to be in part normative, to mark the point at which we think it is unreasonable to expect someone to hold out.[10]

One point is reasonably clear, however: the fact that one might in different circumstances be brought to do the thing to which one is averse is not sufficient to show that one is after all capable of doing it. Otherwise, there would be few if any volitional incapacities of the kind in question. For as Isaac Marks notes, when the house is burning down, agoraphobics always find the wherewithal to "temporarily overcome their phobias and venture forth. Once the emergency subsides, the phobia reappears in pristine form."[11] As Marks also notes, the observation that the phobic is virtually always susceptible to counterincentives underlies a good deal of skepticism about assertions of phobic incapacity. Family and friends are inclined to see the individual's inactivity as "the result of mere laziness, lack of willpower, or a way of getting out of awkward situations . . ." (344–5).

Marks rejects this skepticism: "It is very hard for agoraphobics to muster their energies in such a way that every minor shopping trip is treated like a house on fire. Not only agoraphobics but everybody performs unexpected feats in an acute crisis, but it would be unrealistic to demand such feats of everybody as a routine . . ."[12] The skeptical reaction is based, I think, on the thought that the counter-incentives to which the phobic is susceptible work solely by changing the structure of her reasons.[13] Since she would get out of bed

[10] In his article, Solomon moves easily from talk of inability/incapacity to the language of "difficulty." He compares his efforts here to an earlier experience as a skydiver, noting that it had been "easier to climb along a strut toward the tip of a plane's wing against an eighty-mile-an-hour wind at five thousand feet than it was to get out of bed those days." Solomon, "Anatomy of Melancholy," 49. This move is natural because there is no precise line between "that would be too difficult to do" and "that would be beyond my capacity." We distinguish them only for practical purposes.

[11] Marks, *Fears, Phobias, and Rituals*, 344.

[12] Note the normative criterion to which Marks appeals here.

[13] For a development of the idea that the lack of control exhibited in phobias and compulsions can be understood in terms of the lack of reasons-responsiveness, see John Fischer and Mark Rivizza, *Responsibility and Control* (New York: Cambridge University Press, 1997): "When an agent acts from a literally irresistible urge, he is

in these other circumstances, her failure to leave the house in the actual situation is a function of her relative judgment about what is worthwhile under the circumstances. But, as we've insisted, the presence or absence of perceived reasons for action is part of the performance conditions, not the enabling conditions, of an action. So the skeptic sees the case of the so-called phobic as more like that of Cozy Clara—a reflection of the individual's peculiar priorities, not capacities.[14]

This reasoning fails to attend sufficiently to the distinction between incentives and reasons. Implicit in our discussion of psychological obstacles is the point that the motivational force of a consideration is not necessarily in proportion to its rational force. This is a familiar point from the experience of everyday aversions—say, to eating a plate of maggots, or to use Bernard Williams's example, roast rat.[15] You might not be able to overcome your repugnance even in response to a credible offer that in your judgment made doing so

undergoing a kind of physical process that is not reasons-responsive, and it is this lack of reasons-responsiveness of the actual physical process that rules out guidance control and moral responsibility" (48). Insofar as reasons-responsiveness is understood just in terms of susceptibility to counterincentives, this criterion is inadequate, as the examples below show. Fischer and Ravizza do not explicitly discuss the kinds of examples I have raised, but they do consider in general terms cases in which an "agent somehow gets considerably more energy or focus if he is presented with a *strong* reason to do otherwise . . ." (74). They would say, presumably, that the susceptibility to certain counterincentives changes the mechanism in the kinds of cases I have in mind. The theory is that the "actual mechanism" that motivates the action must be reasons-responsive. In our example, the "mechanism" that operates to keep the man inside the house before the alarm goes off (the phobia) is not the same mechanism as that which is operating in the emergency (the fear of fire). My worry is that this claim is either *ad hoc*, or trivializes the thesis by including in the identity conditions for mechanisms the kind of reason to which the process is responsive—a worry which the authors themselves acknowledge.

[14] The skepticism about the phobic is bolstered by the strangeness of the fear, in contrast to the more familiar and "natural" aversion to eating what is conceived as filthy or putrid.

[15] Bernard Williams, "Moral Incapacity," 49. These examples remind us that volitional incapacities are not necessarily disabilities, but part of the equipment of a healthy creature.

well worth it—say for rather a large sum of money which you badly need. But you might manage to do so with a gun at your (or your child's) head. It is not just that the threat to you or to your child presents you with a stronger reason (though it does); its capacity to counter the aversion, I suggest, depends upon the nature of the incentive it creates. It gives you the strength to overcome the initial aversion.[16]

The strength of a consideration *qua* inducement is thus distinguishable from its strength *qua* reason. This distinction comes out more clearly in the case of the phobic in the house afire. It might well be that the reasons he has to leave the house in general, namely to pursue his career, or support his children, or have a self-respecting life, are in his view as strong, or stronger, *qua* reasons, than those created by the immediate danger of the fire; he may see his housebound existence as scarcely worth preserving.[17] But only the latter is sufficient to move him. It does so, I think, not (just, if at all) by giving rise to weightier reasons but by in effect creating counteraversions. In contrast to Cozy Clara, the presence of these incentives is not only part of the performance conditions but *enables* him to

[16] The fact that a phobic could get on the plane with a companion doesn't show that she can get on without one—anymore than the fact that she could move the boulder with the aid of another implies that she could move it by herself. Of course there are interesting differences. Her companion comforts her, giving her confidence that she can make it without calamity; her companion's help supports her agency.

[17] We shouldn't forget how ruinous real agoraphobia can be. The following cases are not untypical of the malady. "Finding myself in the midst of a large gathering would inspire a feeling of terror [which] . . . could be relieved in but one way—by getting away from the spot as soon as possible. Acting on this impulse . . . I have left churches, theatres, even funerals, simply because of an utter inability to control myself to stay. . . . This malady . . . has throttled all ambition, and killed all personal pride, spoiled every pleasure. . . . [O]ver this the will seems to have no control." Marks, *Fears, Phobias, and Rituals*, 325–6. Joy Melville tells of an American woman who "hid for two days at Heathrow Airport, rather than catch her flight to New York. When she was questioned by a police officer, she confessed to being too afraid to fly. She was allowed to stay another night at Heathrow and, next day, got as far as boarding a plane—but officials decided she was unfit to travel and she was taken to hospital." Joy Melville, *Phobias and Obsessions* (London: George Allen & Unwin Ltd., 1977), 53.

get out of bed, either by overcoming or even entirely eliminating (albeit temporarily) his dread.

To sum up, I have contrasted three cases. The fact that there is no chance that Cozy Clara will get up, given her present incentives, is no reason to say she can't. It is not as though her overwhelming lack of interest in leaving her comfortable environment renders her impotent. In contrast, Paralyzed Clara is incapable of getting out of bed; her behavior is not dependent on her will. The third case is Agoraphobic Clara, who, like Solomon, displays a volitional impairment; she is incapable of willing in certain ways.

IV. Volitional Necessity: Some Interpretations

So far I have been discussing a basic sense of ability according to which one's options are identified by what depends upon one's unimpaired will. A central feature of this notion is that ability is identified independently of the presence or absence of an agent's reasons or concerns. Both Frankfurt and Bernard Williams argue that Martin Luther's "I can do no other" asserts a kind of necessity that is importantly different from what we have considered so far: it is at once a genuine incapacity and yet in no way compromises one's agency or self-control. How are we to understand this kind of necessity?

As we will see, Frankfurt's and Williams's views differ subtly and significantly. But their initial characterizations of the phenomenon are roughly similar. "A moral incapacity," Williams says, is an incapacity "with which the agent is identified."[18] Similarly, Frankfurt remarks that volitional necessity is not "the same thing as simply

---

[18] Bernard Williams, "Moral Incapacity," 54. All parenthetical page references to Williams in the text will be to this essay.

being overwhelmingly averse. . . . In addition, the aversion has his endorsement; and it constrains his conduct so effectively precisely because of this."[19]

Or as he puts it in a later essay, "the effectiveness of the person's incapacity derives from the fact that the person considers that incapacity to be important to him."[20] For both philosophers, then, the necessity is somehow dependent on the agent's identifications or sense of what is important.

How are we to understand this? I begin by considering some alternative proposals regarding Luther cases. I will then return to Williams's and Frankfurt's remarks.

KANE'S PROPOSAL

Robert Kane suggests one way to reconcile necessity, responsibility and agency in Luther cases. "If we have no hesitation in saying that he was responsible for the final affirmation ['Here I stand'],"
Kane proposes, "it is because we believe that [Luther] was responsible through many past choices and actions for making himself into the kind of man he then was."[21] However, this proposal fails to capture the way in which Luther cases appear to involve a form of

---

[19] Harry Frankfurt, "Rationality and the Unthinkable," in *The Importance of What We Care About* (New York: Cambridge University Press, 1988), 182.

[20] Harry Frankfurt, "On the Necessity of Ideals," in *Necessity, Volition, and Love* (New York: Cambridge University Press, 1999), 111–12. Of course, we should not understand this to mean that moral incapacities or volitional necessities are just welcome aversions or compulsions. (Otherwise, Frankfurt's example of the happy addict ["Freedom of the Will and the Concept of a Person," in *The Importance of What We Care About*] would perforce be a case of volitional necessity.) Most of us unequivocally affirm our deep revulsion to eating maggots, even if we can imagine circumstances in which we would see good reason to counter it. The crucial difference is that the incapacity or necessity is not here mediated by an ethical conception (in Williams's terms) or, as Frankfurt wants to say, by a conception of what matters to one. I say more about this below.

[21] Robert Kane, *The Significance of Free Will* (New York: Oxford University Press, 1996), 39–40.

necessitation that is in itself fully voluntary. In describing the relationship as one for which the agent is only ancestrally responsible, Kane would assimilate Luther cases to those in which we treat addicts as responsible for having become addicted. This derivative relationship fails to bring out the sense in which acting under volitional necessity is supposed to be in itself an instance of free and responsible agency.

NORMATIVE NECESSITY

A natural alternative is to take cases like Luther's to be instances of practical or normative necessity.[22] We say the following sort of thing everyday: "I can't come to the meeting; I must look after the baby," or "I can't sleep with you; I'm engaged." The necessity in question is just the requirement of practical reasons. It is impossible for me to come to the meeting (sleep with you) and also take care of my child (remain faithful to my engagement). This kind of necessity is also asserted in first-personal retrospective judgments. "I couldn't turn in the paper on time; my car broke down." In practice the statement would be meant elliptically: "I couldn't turn the paper in on time without . . . ," where the ellipsis is filled in by specifying alternatives (stealing a car, hiring a helicopter) that would be prohibitively immoral or costly but not physically out of reach. Of course, such talk is often insincere or hyperbolic.[23] But it is sometimes entirely apt.

Is this a plausible understanding of Luther cases? Here Williams makes an important observation. Assertions of genuine incapacities should answer to the principle that "can't" implies "doesn't," and this appears to distinguish them from normative necessity as construed so far. Consider the bank official who "simply can't" let one into the

[22] Rogers Albritton understands these cases in this way in "Freedom of Will, and Freedom of Action," Presidential address delivered in 1985 to the Pacific Division APA, in *Proceedings and Addresses of the American Philosophical Association* (1985); reprinted in Gary Watson (ed.), *Free Will*, 2nd edn. (Oxford: Oxford University Press, 2003).

[23] A familiar kind of "bullshit," on Frankfurt's analysis; see his "On Bullshit," in *The Importance of What We Care About*.

bank because it has just closed. This assertion of normative necessity is not refuted by his subsequently being browbeaten or bribed into doing so.

This point is related to another. According to Williams and Frankfurt, the "I can't" in Luther cases is not merely a judgment about normative priorities, as it seems to be on the normative interpretation, but a conclusion about *oneself*, a personal judgment. As Williams puts it (somewhat elusively), such a judgment "can present itself to the agent at once as a decision, and as a discovery."[24] Normative necessity asserts not a real incapacity but a relation among norms or reasons. This leaves out what is most interesting in Luther cases.[25]

There is more to be said on behalf of the normative interpretation. Assertions of normative impossibility are not equivalent to some statement, N, say, that my going to the meeting is inconsistent with my parental duties. By itself, N doesn't preclude the inference: "Therefore, I'll have to neglect the baby." N fails to capture the fact that I, like Luther, was *taking a stand*. Statements of normative necessity assert not only an inconsistency between certain courses of action and certain considerations but also express a commitment to certain normative priorities. These two features can be seen in the two ways in which statements of normative necessity are open to challenge. One might challenge N ("Why don't you bring the child?") or dispute the commitment of normative priority ("The meeting is just too important for you to miss"). In either of these cases, one would be challenging my stand. Furthermore, the second feature brings statements of normative necessity into conformity with the principle, *"can't"* implies *"doesn't,"* after all. "I can't but I will" suffers from the same kind of performative infelicity as "I hereby commit myself to Xing but I won't X." Taking a stand forecloses certain options, and in this sense rules out acting otherwise.

---

[24] Williams, "Moral Incapacity," 52.
[25] For all we've said, of course, either this interpretation or Kane's proposal might be just the right thing to say about the historical example of Luther, in which case Luther's case might not be what I am calling a Luther case.

Still, on this reading, talk of necessity could be dropped without loss of meaning. One might have thought "I can do no other" purported to give a kind of backing to or elaboration of "Here I stand." On the normative interpretation, "I can do no other" adds nothing that was not already implicit in the latter. This brings out a crucial difference between (mere) normative necessity and what Williams and Frankfurt have in mind. The necessity they mean to identify attaches to the stand taken by the agent. Perhaps the officious security guard is quite correct to say that allowing customers into the building after closing hours exceeds his rightful authority—that he can't, consistently with the commitments of his office, permit us to enter the building. The question of moral or volitional necessity is the further question of whether or not he can abandon his commitments or endorse his exceeding his authority in this way.

DENNETT'S PROPOSAL

Both of the proposals we have considered so far fail to bring out what strikes Frankfurt and Williams as philosophically interesting in Luther's stand: the way in which agency and necessity are combined. However, they fail in converse ways. Kane's proposal gives agency too derivative a position, whereas normative necessity by itself is not a personal incapacity.

Daniel Dennett's remarks on Luther cases seem more promising. "[W]hen I say I cannot do otherwise I mean I cannot because I see so clearly what the situation is and because my rational control faculty is *not* impaired. It is too obvious what to do; reason dictates it; I would have to be mad to do otherwise, and since I happen not to be mad, I cannot do otherwise."[26] This remark seems closer to combining agency and incapacity in just the right way, since it attaches necessity precisely to the deliberative faculties in which agency is exercised.

[26] Daniel Dennett, *Elbow Room* (Cambridge, Mass.: MIT Press, 1984), 133.

Nonetheless, it falls short of providing what Williams and Frankfurt are after. For the incapacity Dennett identifies is not the necessity that is expressed in deliberative conclusions. This proposal interprets judgments of moral impossibility from a non-deliberative point of view. The "cannot do otherwise" here is a judgment *about* someone's (perhaps one's own) deliberative faculties, rather than a first-personal deliverance of them. This interpretation therefore fails to make sense of Williams' idea that the "I cannot" at once reports an incapacity and expresses a "decision."

Once judgments of necessity are read in this external way, it is hard to avoid a slippery slope leading to the general conclusion that we are unable to do anything for which we lack a reason or incentive.[27] Thus, by parallel reasoning:

(1) To do otherwise, I would have to have a reason or incentive to do otherwise.

(2) I don't happen to have such a reason or incentive.

(3) Therefore, I can't do otherwise.

Here again, (3), the conclusion asserting necessity, is not the deliberative judgment; premise (2) is. Perhaps there is some useful sense in which the absence of reasons implies that a reasonable person can't do (or believe) otherwise in circumstances in which she is faced with no counter-reasons. But that is not the sense under investigation here. Our enterprise is to understand the notion of impossibility that agents invoke in cases like Luther's but not in Cozy Clara's. To construe moral or volitional incapacity in the foregoing terms is to

---

[27] Peter van Inwagen willingly makes this slide; he argues that an "agent cannot do anything other than the thing that seems to him to be clearly the only sensible thing." Peter van Inwagen, "When is the Will Free?" in *Agents, Causes, and Events*, ed. Timothy O'Connor (New York: Oxford University Press, 1995), 232. By the same reasoning: ". . . if a person has done A, and if he wanted very much to do A, and if he had no desires whatever that inclined him toward not doing A, then he was unable not to do A; not doing A was simply not within his power" (230). For a critical discussion, see John Martin Fischer and Mark Ravizza, "When the Will is Free," in *Agents, Causes, and Events*.

collapse the difference. From the comfort of her covers, Clara might now appropriately declare: "Here I lie: I can do no other."

Dennett's interpretation, then, shifts the necessity from a deliberative to an explanatory perspective.[28] It is from the deliberative perspective that the situations of Luther and of Clara are different. From the explanatory perspective, they are arguably in the same position. Neither will act otherwise unless a certain kind of reason is available. In the circumstances, there is no such reason, nor is it up to them whether such a reason obtains, or whether they are reasons-sensitive beings. (Compare belief.) This gives an intelligible sense in which neither could in the circumstances do otherwise. But this is not quite what Frankfurt and Williams have in mind.

V. Unthinkability and Deliberative Necessity

I want to try to clarify some of these points by means of an example from Jane Austen's *Pride and Prejudice*. In this novel, Mr. Collins makes a proposal of marriage to Elizabeth Bennett. Elizabeth replies as follows: "I am very sensible of the honour of your proposals, but it is impossible for me to do otherwise than decline them."[29] The necessity here is not, as it were, blind or brute; it is grounded in Elizabeth's ideals of marriage. Miss Bennett is a woman for whom a precondition of marriage is mutual love and respect, which could not

---

[28] The distinction here is importantly different from the one we stressed in the first section of the paper. In contrast to the explanatory perspective I had in mind there, Dennett's explanation here is in an important sense normative, in that it involves judgments on the part of the *observer* about what it is rational for the agent to do under the circumstances. That, together with the proposition that the agent *is* rational, yields the conclusion in question.

[29] *The Oxford Illustrated Jane Austen*, 3rd edn., ed. R. W. Chapman (Oxford: Oxford University Press, 1932–54), vol. 2, 107. All page references to *Pride and Prejudice* are to this edition.

be satisfied in a relation to the ridiculously self-satisfied Mr. Collins. "You could not make *me* happy," she bluntly informs him, "and I am convinced that I am the last woman in the world who would make *you* so" (107). Hence, she reiterates, marriage in this situation is " absolutely impossible. My feelings in every respect forbid it" (109).

By contrast, Elizabeth's friend and neighbor, Charlotte Lucas, has less romantic notions. While "marriage had always been her object," Charlotte conceives of this state less as a union of mutual love than as "an honourable provision for well educated young women of small fortune," a "preservative from want" (122–3). When Charlotte finds herself next in line for Mr. Collins' attentions, she accepts his proposal "solely from the pure and disinterested desire of an establishment." This development seems to her, "at the age of twenty-seven, without having ever been handsome," a piece of good fortune.

This example brings out a number of points. First, Elizabeth's case (like Luther's, we may suppose) involves a certain kind of *unthinkability*. Unthinkability here is not of course a kind of cognitive deficit. Elizabeth is indeed forced by Collins' proposal to have thoughts about a certain proposition. The unthinkability of accepting the proposal consists in its being "out of the question," in its being altogether off the deliberative screen. To have ideals and principles is to be committed to not taking certain considerations seriously as reasons in certain contexts.[30] The structure of reasons that excludes certain considerations from practical force can itself have evolved from deliberation. At an earlier stage, the deliberative conclusion that such and such was impossible might have decisively placed certain considerations beyond the pale. In some cases, though, it might be less deliberate than that. One might discover that one just can't take certain proposals seriously—not just that one cannot give

---

[30] For helpful remarks on the ways in which reasons are structured and silenced by principles and intentions, see T. M. Scanlon, *What We Owe to One Another* (Cambridge, Mass.: Harvard University Press, 1998), 50–5.

a lot of weight to a certain consideration but that one cannot take them as counting at all.[31]

So judgments of impossibility of this kind are often deliberative starting points rather than conclusions; they indicate the boundaries of the space of reasons in which deliberation takes place. In either case such judgments involve normative reflection about the structure of reasons and what is eligible for deliberation. To say a proposal is impossible is to give it a certain status: it means that it is not eligible for consideration. This defines a narrower sense of option from that given by the basic concept of what a person can do—only some among the courses of action whose realization depend on the agent's choice are what we might call *deliberative* options. Accepting Collins' offer is an option in the broader, non-normative sense, but not in the narrower sense.[32] Let us call this deliberative necessity.

Deliberative necessity is distinct from both mere normative necessity and from the necessity identified by Dennett—that is, the impossibility of acting contrary to the weightiest reasons, given that one is a rational agent. Given her feelings, Elizabeth cannot be attracted to Collins. Given her ideals, she cannot see marrying Collins as in any way worthwhile. So she is just as incapable of marrying Collins as she is of believing it to be raining as she stands open-eyed in the bright sunshine. But the assertion of moral or volitional necessity is not just the assertion of a constraint on one's deliberative judgments (due, say, to the limits imposed by one's

---

[31] Here I have profited from comments by Sarah Buss.

[32] That marrying Collins is, as Elizabeth says, "absolutely impossible" doesn't entail that there are no conceivable circumstances in which she would marry Collins without changing her ideals. We may imagine that if her family depended on it to remain out of the poor house, or if it were necessary to save the life of her sister, Jane, then she could have resigned herself to such a dismal union. The impossibility in question here depends on the structure of reasons in which Elizabeth finds herself. What she cannot do is to "sacrifice every better feeling to worldly advantage." That's what the marriage to Collins would mean in the actual circumstances. In the imagined circumstances, she would have faced a different choice. Marrying Collins would then have meant something else: devotion to her family, say.

nature as a rational being) but part of the content of those judgments. Elizabeth's "feelings forbid it"; that is part of what they *say*, not just what they do. The recognition of the impossibility of giving practical force to certain considerations and hence as taking them as grounds for action is itself a discrimination of ethical sensibility. In this way, we can understand how moral incapacity can combine the features alleged by Williams: "I can't" can be at once a decision and a report of an incapacity.

Contrast Elizabeth with Cozy Clara. For Clara, getting out of bed is an option in both senses. It is not out of the question; it just doesn't come up. She may judge, "I have no reason to arise, and plenty of reasons to remain in bed." If her reason-recognitional faculties are intact, she can't, in the sense identified by Dennett, rouse herself. But if so, they do not constrain her by rendering the proposal to get up deliberatively impossible.[33]

Notice, as well, that deliberative necessity seems fully compatible with agency and responsibility. According to Elizabeth, to be unable to accept Collins's proposal is a mark of good character. She is astonished by, and disapproving of, her friend's capacity to set aside her "better feeling":

She had always felt that Charlotte's opinion of matrimony was not exactly like her own, but she could not have supposed it possible that when called into action, she would have sacrificed every better feeling to worldly advantage. Charlotte the wife of Mr. Collins, was a most humiliating picture!—And to the pang of a friend disgracing herself and sunk in her esteem, was added the distressing conviction that it was impossible for that friend to be tolerably happy in the lot she had chosen.[34]

Finally, we can see the difference between deliberative necessity and "overwhelming aversion" by imagining a variation on Charlotte's

[33] Conceivably, Clara's ideals might be such that to force herself out of bed whimsically or capriciously would violate her sense of who she is; her "feelings" might forbid it. But I am supposing that, as for most of us, this matter is of no real importance to her.   [34] Austen, *Pride and Prejudice*, 125.

case. Being fully aware of "the stupidity with which [Collins] is favoured by nature" (122), Charlotte might well have found herself so repelled in the end that she was unable, regretfully, to take advantage of her best opportunity for security. That would have been a case of psychological, not deliberative necessity. In contrast to Elizabeth's, her aversion would not have been constituted by her sense of what was most appropriate, important, or best; rather, it would have prevented her from enacting that sense.

VI. Williams and Frankfurt: A Comparison

This account of deliberative necessity seems a plausible answer to the first question we posed at the beginning: how should we distinguish the kind of necessity involved in what Frankfurt and Williams (respectively) call volitional or moral impossibility? So far, however, I have been ignoring important differences in their positions. These differences bear on the second question: how should we understand that which is necessitated? In Frankfurt's case, this is the question: how should we understand the relevant notion of volition?

MORAL INCAPACITY AND VOLITIONAL NECESSITY

Despite Williams's title, neither philosopher is concerned with an agent's relation to *moral* considerations specifically. Clearly Williams has in mind at least the broader category he elsewhere calls "ethical." Even so, the phrase "ethical incapacity" describes a narrower range of cases than Frankfurt is concerned with. The contrast here is subtle and complex, but significant.

For Williams, the "I can't" of Luther cases expresses a deliberative conclusion, where deliberation is concerned with considerations of "the good, the useful, the obligatory, and so on . . ."[35] A deliberative conclusion is thus a conclusion about what it is best to do (however broadly construed). On Frankfurt's view, however, such conclusions may not express a judgment about what is best at all. They may express a determination of one's *will*, from which Frankfurt takes pains to distinguish not only the appetitive, the emotional, and the cognitive, but also the evaluative or choiceworthy.[36] In particular, the first-personal recognition of volitional necessity does not imply the judgment that doing otherwise would be a worse thing to do. A person might be "unable to bring himself to pursue a certain course of action even if he were to recognize it as best."[37] For instance, Frankfurt imagines a mother who believes it would be best to give up her child for adoption, but who finds that she cannot will or endorse what is required by her sincere evaluation. (I'll return to this case later.)

EVALUATION AND VOLITION

At the same time, throughout his writings on the subject, Frankfurt links the volitional attitudes essential to human agency to what he calls an evaluative capacity. A distinguishing feature of a wanton, we are told, is that "he is not concerned with the *desirability* of his desires themselves."[38] Personhood is said to involve "the capacity for

---

[35] Williams, "Moral Incapacity," 48. Of course, they express more than this, as we saw in the discussion of so-called normative necessity; they are also conclusions about oneself. Significantly, for Williams, all deliberation is in some sense about oneself, not, trivially, in that it concerns what it is best for one to do, but in that such questions are always somehow about one's "underlying dispositions" (52). This difficult idea is central to the account in Bernard Williams, "Internal and External Reasons," in *Moral Luck* (Cambridge: Cambridge University Press, 1981).

[36] See, among other places, Frankfurt, "On the Necessity of Ideals," 110. Perhaps the present difference reflects Frankfurt's rejection of the kind of internalism referred to in the previous note.

[37] Frankfurt, "Rationality and the Unthinkable," 184.

[38] Frankfurt, "Freedom of the Will and the Concept of a Person," 17 (my emphasis).

reflective evaluation that is manifested in the formation of second-order desires."[39]

To be a person entails *evaluative* attitudes (not necessarily based on moral considerations) toward oneself. A person is a creature prepared to endorse or repudiate the motives from which he acts and to organize the preferences and priorities by which his choices are ordered. He is disposed to consider whether what attracts him is actually important to him.[40]

The issue of what to endorse is, then, an evaluative issue.[41] It is an issue about what is important or matters to one, or what one cares about. But this is not the same question as what is most choiceworthy. The former is an essentially volitional and personal question; the latter is not.

Perhaps this blunts the contrast with Williams a bit. Since the task of deliberation is to decide what to do, to make up one's mind, to determine what's important to one, the "I can't" of volitional necessity is indeed a deliberative conclusion for Frankfurt as well.[42] That task is not necessarily completed when one arrives at a firm belief about what is best to do. Nonetheless, an important difference remains. For Williams, moral incapacities depend upon, and express, the agent's ethical conception of the alternatives. Frankfurt's volitional necessities would take this ethical form, if an individual's volitional nature were bound up with the ethical; but they need not

[39] Frankfurt, "Freedom of the Will and the Concept of a Person," 12.

[40] Frankfurt, "On the Necessity of Ideals," 113–14 (my emphasis). Personhood involves "the capacity for reflective evaluation that is manifested in the formation of second-order desires." Frankfurt, "Freedom of the Will and the Concept of a Person," 12. See also Frankfurt, "The Faintest Passion," in *Necessity, Volition and Love*, 103, n. 14. "To be a person, as distinct from simply a human organism, requires a complex volitional structure involving reflective self-evaluation."

[41] Early on, it is true, Frankfurt's notion of evaluation was extremely thin; higher-order volitions "express evaluations only in the sense that they are preferences." Frankfurt, "Freedom of the Person and the Concept of a Person," 19, n. 6. But the talk of evaluation assumes more substance in later work, once the notion of caring is in the foreground.

[42] See Harry Frankfurt, "Identification and Wholeheartedness," in *The Importance of What We Care About*, 174–5.

be, he thinks. For a conclusion about what is important to one is not for Frankfurt equivalent to a judgment about what is choiceworthy.[43] This difference can be put in terms of the notion of reasons. "To understand moral incapacity," Williams says, "we have to consider . . . the way in which the incapacity is connected with the agent's reasons" (50): " 'I can't' recognizes an incapacity in the light of deliberative reasons" (53). One cannot do otherwise because one cannot take certain considerations as reasons to do otherwise. In contrast, the possible disconnection between identification and judgments of what is best means that, for Frankfurt, volitional necessity might involve the discovery that one's identifications are less than rational.[44] So the attitude in which such an incapacity consists need not be reasons-sensitive.[45]

IDENTIFICATION

This last contrast reflects a crucial difference about the nature of "identification." Williams tells us that an individual cannot coherently set out to remove or overcome his moral incapacity

because a fundamental way in which a moral incapacity expresses itself is in the refusal to undertake any such project. A moral incapacity in the sense under discussion is one with which the agent is identified. Of course an agent may come to see a moral incapacity of his as something with which he is no longer identified, and try to overcome it. But so soon as this is his state of mind . . . then he has lost the moral incapacity. . . . [I]t is no longer a moral incapacity, but rather one that is merely psychological.[46]

[43] Frankfurt, "On the Necessity of Ideals," 112.

[44] Frankfurt, "Rationality and the Unthinkable," 184.

[45] If, following Michael Bratman, "Identification, Decision, and Treating as a Reason," *Philosophical Topics*, 24 (1996): 1–18, we link deliberation or decision and reasons by construing the upshot of deliberation as a commitment to take or exclude certain considerations as reason giving, then volitional necessity can be described as a condition in which one finds that one cannot take R as a reason even though one might judge that R supports the best course of action—that is, that R is a conclusive reason.

[46] Williams, "Moral Incapacity," 54.

For Williams, to oppose one's own identifications is to cease to have them. Frankfurt thinks otherwise:

[I]t is surely open to someone for whom an action is unthinkable to alter his own will in such a way that the action becomes thinkable for him. The fact that a person cannot bring himself to perform an action does not entail that he cannot bring himself to act with the intention of changing that fact.[47]

To "take steps to alter one's volitional capacities"[48] is to take steps to alter what one identifies with.

This last difference, especially, raises important questions about Frankfurt's notion of the volitional. What is the nature of the opposition that is exhibited in struggles to bring oneself to act otherwise? What does it teach us about identification and agency?

VII. Identification, Endorsement and Caring

If volitional activity consisted in the formation of highest-order volitions, as Frankfurt preferred to say in his earlier work, then volitional necessity would be the inability to form one's highest-order volitions in any other way.[49] But to characterize the motivational standpoint of those who struggle against their own volitional capacities requires a more complex picture of what volitional activity consists in. And it is not clear how the more complex account is to be filled in, for the prospect of such struggles brings out some tensions in Frankfurt's treatment of the subject.

At one point, for example, Frankfurt argues that volitional necessity delineates the province of one's will.

---

[47] Frankfurt, "Rationality and the Unthinkable," 187.   [48] Ibid. 187.

[49] The mere absence of alternative possibilities is not sufficient for volitional necessity, however. The thesis that higher-order necessity is compatible with agency and responsibility is defended in the early essays by appealing to cases of "overdetermination." These are not cases of volitional necessity, I take it, because the source of the impossibility is exogenous.

To the extent that a person is constrained by volitional necessities, there are certain things that he can't help willing or that he cannot bring himself to do. . . . [T]he essential nature of a person consists in what he must will. The boundaries of his will define his shape as a person.[50]

This remark would make sense if Frankfurt were in agreement with Williams about identification, or if volitional necessity were confined to unthinkability in the strict sense. In view of his remarks on cases of volitional struggles, as we might call them, the passage is in fact very puzzling. If the effort to overcome what turns out to be volitional necessity is an effort to work against the limits of one's will, one's opposition to that necessity exhibits a source of agency that is independent of those confines. On what ground can the struggle be mounted?

Take Frankfurt's case of the woman who believes that giving up her child would be best overall. By her unsuccessful attempt to overcome her deep attachment,[51] she discovers the limits of what she can, in one sense, will. Yet in this endeavor she is not a witness, but active on behalf of her sense of what is best. Now a "person is active when it is by his own will that he does what he does, even when his will is not itself within the scope of his voluntary control."[52] So her will must be engaged in volitional opposition, too, and the necessity exhibited in her failure to bring herself to give up the child cannot completely define the bounds of the mother's volitional capacities— nor, *a fortiori*, what Frankfurt calls her "shape as a person."[53]

---

[50] Frankfurt, "On the Necessity of Ideals," 114.

[51] In contrast to the man who undertook to transform his attitudes toward eating flesh, what the woman opposes here is not the love itself but that to which the love inclines her.

[52] Frankfurt, "The Importance of What We Care About," 88. Although Frankfurt does not say "only when," this follows if we read the remark as a definition rather than as a statement of sufficient conditions.

[53] Frankfurt, "On the Necessity of Ideals," 114. Note that the case of the mother does not fit Frankfurt's characterization of volitional necessity in the passage we quoted at the beginning of this essay. Unlike the addict, the person under volitional necessity is said not to "accede to the constraining force because he lacks sufficient strength of will to defeat it. He accedes to it because he is *unwilling* to oppose it and because, furthermore, his unwillingness is *itself* something which he is unwilling to

The source of these tensions lies, I think, in the divergent ways in which Frankfurt characterizes the distinction between volitional necessity and other kinds of incapacity. As we've seen, one criterion is that "the aversion has [one's] endorsement . . . and . . . constrains [one's] conduct so effectively precisely because of this."[54] Here what one can will is shown by what one can *endorse*. Frankfurt also tells us that in volitional necessity, "the effectiveness of the person's incapacity derives from the fact that the person considers that incapacity to be important to him."[55] On this second criterion, a mere aversion is one whose motivational force does not depend on one's sense of what's important. These criteria, which we may call the endorsement and the caring criteria, respectively, can and do come apart in many struggles of the kind that Frankfurt discusses.

This divergence is especially conspicuous in cases in which one not only attempts to overcome what one cares about in a particular situation but also undertakes the longer-term project of modifying or eliminating one's identifications. Frankfurt imagines someone who cannot bring himself to consume human flesh but finds himself regularly in circumstances in which this inability proves to be "inimical to his interests."[56] Such a person "might take steps to alter his volitional capacities so as to be capable of doing what he now finds unthinkable."[57] How is this example to be distinguished from a case of mere revulsion? On the endorsement criterion, the cases seem indistinguishable. In view of his sustained campaign against it, it makes no sense to say that the aversion any longer has the man's endorsement. What one endorses is a matter of what one stands behind, what one commits oneself to. To take on the project of extinguishing the aversion *is* to repudiate it, and to repudiate the

---

alter." Frankfurt, "The Importance of What We Care About," 87. This is a plausible description of unthinkability, perhaps, but not of cases of volitional struggle. The woman *is* in a plain sense willing to oppose her attachment, and she does so because she is willing.

[54] Frankfurt, "Rationality and the Unthinkable," 182.
[55] Frankfurt, "On the Necessity of Ideals," 111–12.
[56] Frankfurt, "Rationality and the Unthinkable," 187.   [57] Ibid.

aversion is to withdraw one's endorsement. Higher-order endorsement logically constrains lower-order endorsement.

The logic of caring is different. What one cares about is measured by how much one is "invested" in or bound up with something, by one's sense of loss or diminishment upon not realizing or achieving the object of one's care. The man's endorsement of the transformation does not negate the fact that it continues to matter to him not to be "cannibalistic." The foregoing characterizations of volitional necessity, then, are not equivalent; one might not endorse everything that means something to one. Contrary simultaneous endorsements by the same individual cancel out one another, but not so with what one cares about. A person under volitional necessity "may care about something even though he wishes that he didn't, and despite strenuous efforts to stop."[58] The man's aversion to eating human flesh is distinguishable from an overwhelming aversion only on the caring criterion.

There are, correspondingly, two distinct notions of identification: identification as endorsement and identification as what one cares about.[59] Both notions pick out something naturally called "identification." On both conceptions, furthermore, volitional necessity contrasts with "mere overwhelming aversion." In struggling against what one cares about, one is indeed in a contest with (part of) oneself, not just with what appears as an alien force.[60] Nevertheless, the

[58] Frankfurt, "On Caring," in *Necessity, Volition and Love*, 161–2.

[59] Bratman's notion of identification as committing oneself to take certain considerations as reasons fits (and can perhaps be seen as an analysis of) the endorsement, rather than the caring, conception.

[60] As addictive desire can sometimes do. That is not to say that people don't commonly care about their addictions. If I am unable to resist the addictive desires I affirm, as in Frankfurt's case of the happy addict, that is not necessarily a case of volitional necessity, for the force of the desire might be independent of my endorsement or of my sense of what is important to do or be. Yet being addicted might be incorporated into my sense of importance in such a way that it is that sense, and not just the chemically rooted motivational dependency, against which I am struggling. If I am an unhappy addict, I might deplore not only my addictive tendencies, but also my attachment to my addiction. Then I would be struggling against myself in a different sense. (I discuss the idea of attachment to one's addictions in "Disordered Appetites: Addiction, Compulsion, and Dependence," in *Addiction: Entries and Exits*, ed. Jon Elster [Russell Sage Foundation, 1999], 3–28 [Ch. 3, this volume].)

difference between these conceptions explains the contrast we noted above between Williams's and Frankfurt's positions. Williams's position follows the logic of endorsement rather than caring.[61] A plausible explanation of why undertaking to alter one's concerns precludes identification with them is that it rescinds, or presupposes the withdrawal of, one's endorsement. In contrast, what Frankfurt has in mind in cases of volitional struggles is the endeavor to go against what one cares about.[62]

When an agent opposes her own sense of what is important in this way, must that opposition be prompted by something else she cares about? Or can endorsement, and hence agency, have another

[61] So does the notion of identification that Frankfurt tended to employ in his earlier essays: "It makes no sense to ask whether someone identifies himself with his identification of himself, unless this is intended simply as asking whether his identification is wholehearted or complete." Frankfurt, "Three Concepts of Free Action," in *The Importance of What We Care About*, 54. This is, importantly, not true on the caring conception. Endorsement "'resounds' throughout the potentially endless array of higher orders," as Frankfurt famously puts it in his first formulation of these issues ("Freedom of the Will and the Concept of a Person," 21) because endorsement implies commitment all the way up. Perhaps caring has a hierarchical structure as well. If friendship with you really means anything to me (in contrast to my taste for spicy foods), I cannot be entirely unconcerned about ceasing to care about you. But the hierarchical structure of endorsement is importantly different, it seems to me, in virtue of its connection with commitments and reasons. (Here I am indebted to a discussion with the participants of the Stanford Workshop on Moral Responsibility, especially Michael Bratman and Jennifer Rosner.) I return to this point briefly at the end.

[62] The idea of volitional struggle as opposition to one's own identifications appears to be ruled out by the doctrine of "The Faintest Passion," according to which identification "is constituted . . . by an endorsing higher-order desire with which the person is satisfied" (105), where "satisfaction" entails "an absence of restlessness or resistance" (103). On the satisfaction criterion, neither that against which one struggles, nor that on behalf of which one struggles could be said to reveal what one identifies with. Perhaps we should take "The Faintest Passion" to be defining *complete* or *full* identification. Elsewhere, Frankfurt speaks of ambivalent agents as "*in part* opposed to a motivational tendency with which they are also *in part* identified" (my emphases). Frankfurt, "Autonomy, Necessity, and Love," in *Necessity, Volition and Love*, 137–8. Thus, cases of volitional struggle would be instances of conflicting partial identifications. And this in turn could be a matter either of contrary caring, or of a divergence between caring and endorsement.

provenance? Now, Frankfurt does in fact allow that we can be active on behalf of what we don't care about:

We often devote our time and effort and other resources to the pursuit of goals that we desire to attain because we are convinced of their intrinsic value but that we do not really consider to be of any importance to us. . . . There is no incoherence in appraising something as intrinsically valuable, and pursuing it actively as a final end that is worth having in itself, and yet not caring about it.[63]

So one can be prompted to pursue something valuable even though the value in question is of no importance to one. However, Frankfurt's own illustration is the enjoyment of inconsequential pleasures, where nothing much is at stake; enjoying oneself here neither realizes nor conflicts with anything one takes to be important. This passage leaves it open whether one can actively counter something of great significance to one just because of the perception of the "intrinsic value" of doing so.

Consider again the case of the unfortunate mother. How are we to characterize the motivational standpoint of someone who struggles against her own concerns in this way? This question is quite independent of the issue of necessity; it arises equally in cases that fall short of that, cases of severe volitional difficulty in which the individual succeeds in her struggle.[64] Imagine that the woman manages, despite her attachment, to give up her child for adoption. Her effort manifests an identification with the standpoint of what is best. Must this mean that she *cares*, in the end, more about conforming to that

---

[63] Frankfurt, "On Caring," 159.

[64] To see the distance between Frankfurt's early treatment of freedom of the will and his later account of volitional necessity, it is instructive to notice that the earlier hierarchical treatment would imply that the mother did not act with freedom of the will. For her endorsement of the project of giving up her child is a higher-order desire to which her first-order will does not conform. Frankfurt does not want to say that volitional necessity is a violation of free will, however. Perhaps he thinks that there is an even higher-order volition in support of her keeping the child, but that seems strained in this case. Instead, he may think that this highest-level endorsement does not amount to a volition.

standpoint than about maintaining her relationship? If we insist that it must, then we are clearly not *grounding* identification, and hence agency, in caring, but rather using identification in the sense of endorsement as a criterion of what is most important to her. Her agency is exercised in the privileging of some of her concerns over others. Perhaps this stance entails that doing what's best overall is more important to her than following her heart. But if we say that, we are taking her volitional activity to be fundamentally a matter of what she stands for or endorses, rather than what she cares about in some independent sense.

To be sure, a crucial feature of this case is that the woman's love is at war with itself. It comprises both her need for the relationship and her desire for the well-being of her child. She will in a way be betraying her love in any case. So it would be misleading to portray the case as one in which she makes a personal sacrifice for merely impersonal considerations. She is after all acting out of concern for *her* child. Just the same, there is something to that portrayal, as we can see by comparing the original case to the scenario in which she succeeds in her struggle. It is unlikely, for example, that the outcome of her failure to give up the child, as in the original example, would be as personally devastating as the outcome in the modified case. What she has to live with differs significantly in the two scenarios. She might or might not feel guilty in the original case, but she will not feel alienated or broken in the way it would be natural for her to feel in the second case. In that scenario, she is likely to feel empty, just "going through the motions." For a source of meaning will have been removed from her everyday experience. Just the same, she may do all this tearfully but in a sense resolutely and without regret, not because that would be too mild a description of her reaction but because that would be the wrong description. For she is doing, we may suppose, what she sees clearly to be the right thing, in a way unequivocally, though perhaps, since her heart's not in it, not exactly wholeheartedly.

The divergence between endorsement and caring raises the question: how important, in the end, *is* what we care about? Or, better, how important is the notion of what we care about to understanding human agency? Whatever the answer to this question may be, the divergence also suggests an important difference in the two cases with respect to the issue of agency. Although the outcome in the first scenario might be easier for her to live with, there is an important sense in which it involves a failure—one to which she might resign herself, but a failure just the same. In deliberately violating her attachment, as in the second case, she indeed does injury to herself. But in an important sense, her agency has not been damaged or defeated, since the outcome is an upshot of her endorsement. This means that she authorizes the outcome in a way in which she would not have in the first case. So the idea of endorsement seems more central to agency than is the idea of what we care about.

To invoke another elusive notion, we might say that while the woman's "integrity" is compromised in either case, the difference between endorsement and caring reveals two dimensions of integrity. When caring comes apart from endorsement in this way, it still remains integral to what one's life is about, but its reason-giving status is altered. As shattering as the triumph of her efforts might be, the second outcome leaves her with a kind of volitional or authorial integrity that is not achieved in the other case. Her privileging of her conviction about what is best for the child over her needs for the relationship imposes a coherent deliberative structure among her ends and concerns. This kind of order is unavailable to her in the other scenario.

Whether this achievement is enough to help her to carry on is another question entirely. The mother loses in either case, and I am not making any claims about the relative value of volitional integrity in comparison to preserving her attachments. My claim is just that the losses are significantly different. One loss involves a defeat of agency in a way in which the other does not. This conclusion doesn't imply that what one cares about in Frankfurt's sense is less important to one's "identity" than what one endorses. Rather, what follows is that one's identity is not just a matter of one's agency.

VIII. Conclusion

A satisfactory description of volitional struggle requires a distinction among three motivational structures. First, there are the sources of motivation whose force is independent of one's endorsement or of what one cares about.[65] Second, there is what one cares about, is attached to, finds meaningful, the loss of which tends to be felt acutely. Third, there is what one endorses as an end, project, or principle— what one commits oneself to, stands for and behind. The relations among these structures are complex; they are largely overlapping but distinct. Even if we only endorsed projects that independently mattered to us, we would have to take a position (make a deliberative commitment) regarding the ordering of our various concerns.

Each of these structures is a possible source of necessity. The first structure raises questions about irresistible desires and overwhelming aversions. Frankfurt's discussion of volitional struggle brings to light two further locations for motivational necessity. Perhaps I am unable to bring myself to give up something because it means too much to me; that is one thing that Frankfurt calls volitional necessity. In such a case, I might then undertake to bypass or transform what I care about. That further undertaking would be an exercise of agency, an authorization of the project of overcoming. The stances that I take with respect to my sense of what matters might themselves be subject to necessity. Perhaps I am unable to do anything but undertake to oppose my own concerns in certain ways. That could be the situation of the mother who cannot bring herself to give up her child because that relationship is too important to her. At the same time, it may be, she cannot do otherwise than attempt to bring herself to give it up—because, for instance, she thinks it is best to do so. In that case, on Frankfurt's criteria, she is subject to two levels of volitional necessity at once.

---

[65] These are part of the self, so to speak, only so long as they behave in ways that are harmonious with the others. Insofar as they don't, they are estranged in an important sense. See Frankfurt, "Identification and Externality," in *The Importance of What We Care About*.

5   The Work of the Will

Not so long ago, talking about the will aroused widespread suspicion in English-speaking philosophy. Brain O'Shaughnessy was going against the grain in 1980 when he declared his belief 'in the existence of the contentious psychological phenomenon, the will', which he took to be 'a *sui generis* psychological phenomenal something whose existence philosophers have in recent years tended to deny' (O'Shaughnessy 1980: i. 30). For reasons that are not fully clear to me, the concept is nowadays taken more seriously. This shift does seem to be correlated with two other (independent but overlapping) trends in which a notion of the will tends to be featured: with a developing sympathy for one or another Kantian account of agency, and with the revival of libertarian theories of freedom. However, there are influential discussions of the will that don't represent either of these movements, notably Harry Frankfurt's and Brian O'Shaughnessy's.[1]

This revival is not always signalled by the use of the term 'will'. Some writers speak mainly of decisions or choices.[2] Thomas Pink

The first version of this chapter was presented at the conference Weakness of Will and Varieties of Practical Irrationality, Montreal, May 2001. I learned a lot from the participants, and especially from David Owens's commentary, on that occasion. Subsequent presentations and drafts have benefited from comments by Lilli Alanen, Richard Arneson, Sarah Buss, Pamela Hieronymi, Paul Hoffman, Bryan Lee, Sara Lundquist, Gideon Yaffe, Andrew Youpa, Linda Zagzebski, and participants in the Agency Dissertation Workshop at Riverside. Finally, I am most grateful to Sarah Stroud and Christine Tappolet for organizing the Montreal conference, and for their editorial work on this essay.

[1] Whether these are discussions of the same concept of the 'will' is another question.

[2] I shall mostly speak of deciding rather than of choosing. There are, however, revealing differences between 'decision' and 'choice' that will become important later.

explicitly equates the will with the capacity to decide: 'We . . . believe ourselves to have a *will*—a capacity for decision-making or intention formation' (Pink 1996: 16). What matters is not of course the terminology but the thought that the corresponding phenomenon is a primary locus of human agency.[3] This thought is also developed in some recent work by R. Jay Wallace:

By volition here I mean a kind of motivational state that, by contrast with . . . given desires . . . are [*sic*] directly under the control of the agent. Familiar examples of volitional states in this sense are intentions, choices, and decisions . . . intentions, choices, and decisions are things we do, primitive examples of the phenomenon of agency itself. . . . This line . . . marks a distinction of fundamental importance, the line between the passive and the active in our psychological lives.

(Wallace 1999: 636–7)

It is this idea of decision as an especially central, if not unique, case of agency that is the subject matter of this chapter.[4] Although I will try to respond to a few objections along the way, for the most part I will proceed on the assumption that the idea is correct. I shall be pursuing two sets of questions about the will, understood as the capacity to decide. In Section I, I ask: is the will the same thing as practical reason or judgement? If not, how are they related? Section II is concerned with decisions in the realm of belief. For instance, after studying the matter, I conclude—that is, come to believe—that creationism ('creation science') is false. The earth is much, much

---

[3] As we will see, however, one of the philosophers whose name is linked with philosophical renewal of interest in the will—Brian O'Shaughnessy—denies that decision itself has these features.

[4] The idea of the will in question here is not to be confused with the notion of will as 'will-power'. As Robert Roberts points out, we often use the term 'will' to pick out 'a family of capacities for resisting adverse inclinations' (Roberts 1984: 227). These capacities are 'skills of self-management', as Roberts puts it (238). This notion is less basic than the capacity to form decisions, as we can see by noting that one can decide to exercise one's will-power or not. For another discussion of will-power, see Richard Holton, 'How is Strength of Will Possible?' in Stroud and Tappolet 2003: ch. 2.

older than 7,000 years. Should we take such decisions (decisions *that* as distinct from decisions *to*) to be instances of our agency as well? If so, should we speak, too, of a doxastic will? As we shall see at the end, these two sets of questions are connected.

There is some dispute about the extension of the term 'deciding', so I should say a few words by way of clarification. We ordinarily restrict the term to contexts in which there is prior uncertainty and an attempt to make up one's mind by deliberation.[5] The active phenomenon that I am concerned with, however, need not involve such doubt or deliberation. Perhaps the following case will illustrate what I am after. Suppose I am walking along a residential street when I notice, across the way, a frail, elderly person struggling to pull a very heavy piece of luggage up a steep set of stairs. Noticing his need, I put down my packages and cross the street to offer my assistance. In this case, I am not in a state of uncertainty that requires resolution by deliberation. The thing to do is clear at once. So on the aforementioned criteria, this is not strictly a case of deciding what to do. But it does exhibit the activity that concerns me. What matters for my purposes is not whether we call this deciding; what matters is the active phenomenon that also occurs in explicit deciding, namely, adopting and forming an intention, in other words the settling on this course of action. In this example, I claim, without the need for prior deliberation, I form or adopt an intention to help, and this is itself an instance of agency.[6]

---

[5] Cf. O'Shaughnessy: 'Thus, decidings form a sub-class of comings-to-intend. Namely: the class of those comings-to-intend events that resolve a state of uncertainty over what to do' (O'Shaughnessy 1980: ii. 297).

[6] I do not suppose that talk of decisions assumes an awareness of discrete episodes of intention formation, any more than talk of perceptions and thoughts does. We could also say that (implicitly) I judged that lending a hand was more important than proceeding with my business, though nothing like that 'crossed my mind'. I agree with Larry Wright: 'Most of the judgements we make in the course of our lives we reach without deliberating on them at all. The stream of life is filled with learnings and decidings that we do not even pick out of the smooth flow as articulated episodes, much less as the objects of deliberation. Usually, it is only after the fact, and for particular purposes, that we break out the thoughts or decisions . . . ' (Wright 1995: 567).

It might be objected that in this case there is no need to distinguish any such special prior activity. Perhaps my agency consists solely in my *attempting* to help in some way, say, by my giving him a hand. No doubt in some cases it will be artificial to distinguish adopting the intention to *x* and *x*ing (or attempting to *x*). But in my example, and in many others, the distinction seems real. Prior to actually helping, or offering to help, I do certain things, such as setting down what I am carrying and crossing the street, in preparation to help, and therefore with that intention. Preparing to help is not yet attempting to do so. The distinction is especially clear where there is a significant time lag—if, for example, I form the intention to help once I deliver my packages down the street. So I am not claiming (or denying) that all instances of intentional bodily movement are preceded by intention formation. Nor am I claiming (or denying) that all intention acquisition is active. (I assume that there are ways of acquiring intentions besides *adopting* them.[7]) What matters for the purposes of my investigation is that: (1) adopting intentions in the way just illustrated is an ubiquitous instance of agency, namely a case of setting oneself to act in a certain way, whether or not there was prior uncertainty or an immediate attempt; and (2) the sort of activity illustrated here is especially central to what it is to be a rational agent, so that a human being who never engaged in such activity would be an agent only in a very truncated sense.[8]

I

DELIBERATING AND DECIDING

With these points in mind, then, I will focus on deciding in what follows, since that is a clear, if not unique, case of the phenomenon.

---

[7] This issue is explored in Mele 2000.

[8] Although the active formation of intention is not typically preceded by deliberation, I do think that such agency presupposes the general capacity for deliberation, so that there could not be a creature without practical reason who decided in this way. I think the active status of the phenomenon under consideration has to do with its sensitivity to reasons, which depends on the capacity for critical reflection. I return to this briefly at the end.

My first question, as I vaguely posed it, was about the relation of deciding to practical reason.

Practical reasoning, in the sense of deliberation, is a species of normative reasoning about action. It is characterized not just by its content—what should be done by certain agents, including oneself, under certain circumstances—but by its aim.[9] Practical deliberation, as I think of it, is *reasoning about what is best (or satisfactory) to do with a view to making up one's mind about what to do.*[10] This connects practical reasoning with *decision* because it connects it with making up one's mind. If we identify the will with deciding to act, then we can say that practical reasoning is reasoning about what to do with a view to determining one's will.[11] One's aim in deliberation is to make a commitment to a course of action by making a judgement about what is best (or good enough) to do.[12] This commitment—the adoption of an intention—is the conceptual terminus of reason when it's directed to action.

Although nothing crucial to my aims in this chapter depends on it, I shall assume in what follows that judgements about what is best can be true or false. If theoretical deliberation is concerned to arrive at true beliefs, it follows that (quite apart from the empirical premises upon which it relies) practical deliberation involves theoretical reasoning. This implication doesn't render practical reason a kind of theoretical reasoning, since true belief is not its ultimate end. Rather, these forms of reasoning necessarily intersect (on this so-called cognitivist view). One could avoid this conclusion, without abandoning the assumption, simply by excluding beliefs about choiceworthiness from the province of theoretical reason.

[9] Contrast a discussion of the general conditions under which going to war is justified with the question of whether to go to war. Both involve practical reason, but only the latter is deliberative. (Of course the former might be part of the latter.)

[10] Compare Richard Moran: 'The aim and conclusion [of deliberation] is the binding of oneself to a certain course of action (or proposition) . . . ' (Moran 2000: 95).

[11] We could also say that practical reasoning is reasoning about what is most choiceworthy with a view to choosing.

[12] Cf. David Velleman: 'the object of theoretical reasoning is to arrive at true belief' (Velleman 1996: 180).

But this stipulation would have no philosophical purpose, as far as I can tell. Such judgements are not usefully to be contrasted with something called theoretical or 'factual' judgements, unless these terms are given an artificially limited sense.[13]

Notice that, when things go as intended, practical deliberation involves making up my mind *twice*. Making up my mind about what is best to do is coming to a judgement: deciding *that* such and such is the thing to do.[14] Making up my mind about what to do is forming an intention: deciding *to* do such and such. (Adapting T. M. Scanlon's useful terminology, we might call these 'assessing' and 'opting', respectively; Scanlon 2002: 169–70.) Both moments of resolution are part of the enterprise of practical deliberation. Although they typically coincide, these are importantly distinct forms of commitment. The distinction manifests itself in at least two familiar ways: first, when we fail to reach a decision about what is best to do because the reasons are unclear or indeterminate but we still must decide to do *x* or to do *y*; and, secondly, when we fail to follow our decision about what is best.

Suppose I receive an offer of an attractive faculty position in another part of the country, away from my birthplace and extended family. One of three things might occur. Perhaps, after reflection, I arrive at a definite conclusion (say, that it is best to decline the offer) and so decide to do so. Or I might be unable to decide what's best, because the considerations on both sides seem equally compelling or perhaps incommensurable. Still, I must decide what to do, if only by default. Or, I might conclude, unequivocally, that I should

---

[13] For a discussion and brief defence of this view, see Scanlon 1998: 55–64. Although David Owens agrees that practical judgements are true or false, he denies that they are beliefs or comings to believe; see Owens 2000: 110 ff.

[14] I assume, too, that in the contexts that we have in mind, judging that *p* is coming to believe that *p*. Thus just as 'decision to' is an intention-forming process, 'deciding that' is a belief-forming process. But the relation of judging to believing is probably more complicated than this. See Cohen 1989.

decline, say. Even though I have made up my mind on the normative question, I might remain unsettled about what to do. It is plausible to say that what is in evidence in the second and third cases is the distinction between practical judgement and will.[15]

TWO CONCEPTIONS OF AGENCY

Contrast two conceptions of how human agency is oriented towards practical reason or the good. What I shall call *internalist* conceptions of agency regard the will (in so far as they make use of this concept) as having some kind of necessary connection or concern with the good or the choiceworthy. (Here the classical statement is the opening line of Aristotle's *Nicomachean Ethics*: 'Every craft and every investigation, and likewise every action and decision, seems to aim at some good'; Aristotle, *Nicomachean Ethics* (1985 edn.), 1094ᵃ1.) Internalists take the link between intention and the good to be analogous to the connection of belief with truth. Just as no attitude that wasn't to some extent regulated by truth-relevant considerations could be the attitude of belief, so nothing could count as intending (or willing) if it were totally unguided by the good. Externalists deny any such connection of intention to the good. On their view, the will comes most prominently into play once the question of what is good to do is settled.

The contrast, to put it very crudely, is between the Greeks and the Christians.[16] On the Greek view, the human 'capacity' to oppose the good is a liability (rather than a power) we should work to overcome.

---

[15] Since, according to me, judgement is a form of decision, why shouldn't we speak of it as an exercise of will? This is part of the second set of questions distinguished in my opening remarks. I venture an answer to this question towards the end.

[16] Crudely (to mention only one reason) because obviously there are Christian thinkers on both sides of this issue. But it is a generalization worth making because the question becomes a preoccupation in Christian thought. (I suspect that a certain conception of sin requires externalism.)

It is an imperfection that limits our powers rather than underwriting our agency. For Aristotle, there are three (or four) characters whose behaviour has different relations to the good: the virtuous, the vicious, and the incontinent (or continent). In much modern philosophy, another type comes to the fore, he who would challenge the good. (I don't say that this type was beyond the ken of Greek philosophy.) On all accounts, this capacity indeed makes us liable to evil, but the modern tendency is to see that liability as a necessary condition of self-governance. This is only a tendency, however. As heirs of both traditions, most of us feel the tension between them, and find both conceptions, unadorned, deeply problematic in their own ways. My aim is not to adjudicate this large issue here, but to investigate whether the idea of the will can have a prominent place only in externalist accounts. But some development of this issue will be necessary to set up the later discussion of 'cognitive agency'.

A rather pure contemporary version of internalism about agency (though without the language of 'will') is defended by Sarah Buss, who argues that

if we ever do anything intentionally, then evaluative beliefs must play a direct, independent motivating role in our behaviour. . . . We do nothing intentionally to achieve [our] ends unless we act as we do because we accept certain practical norms; our actions are not self-directed unless they reflect our beliefs about how it is rational, or appropriate, or right, or good, or desirable, or acceptable to behave.

(Buss 1999: 400–1)[17]

Rogers Albritton defends the opposing view:

But having to do a thing [in that one has compelling reasons to do it] does not settle magically the question whether to *do* it or not. Reasons, of whatever species, can't close that question. It's a question of a different

---

[17] Christine Korsgaard is an internalist who explicitly appeals to volition. The analogue of belief, Korsgaard claims, is 'volition or choice', and willing is a normative commitment. See Korsgaard 1996, 1997. For a formulation of a Kantian version of internalism, see Herman 2002.

genre, and is not relative to any system of reasons. It isn't for *reasons*, in the end, that we act for reasons.

(Albritton 1985: 248)[18]

For the externalist, it is the difference between these questions that indicates the work of the will: to determine whether to comply with the outcome of normative reflection. Unlike practical judgement, or belief in general, volitional commitment is not, in R. Jay Wallace's phrase, 'an essentially normative stance'.[19] Accordingly, it is not necessarily guided by the norms of practical reason.

Externalism must be true, Wallace argues, if we are to make sense of our capacity for self-determination. Further, he thinks that this view of intention is supported by reflection on Moore's Paradox. Wallace observes that 'I believe that p, but p is not true' is paradoxical in a way that 'I intend to x, but $x$ing is not choiceworthy' is not. In the first case, the endorsements expressed in the two conjuncts cancel one another out in such a way that it seems impossible coherently to attribute either of these attitudes to me. This does not seem to be so in the second case. This shows that whereas the capacity to form beliefs must be regulated by truth-relevant norms, the capacity to form intentions is not constrained by the norms of choiceworthiness.[20] Thus, Wallace accepts internalism for belief but not for intention.

On this account, the internalists' mistake is to conflate these two types of commitment. Hence the notorious difficulty of understanding akrasia (and all that). They can allow, in various ways, for the possibility of knowingly behaving contrary to practical judgement, but the problem is to account for our sense that such counter-normative

---

[18] Robert Kane emphasizes the difference between these two questions as well. See Kane 1996: 21.

[19] See Wallace 2001. (My treatment of the issues in this chapter is much indebted to this essay.) After citing Albritton's discussion approvingly, Wallace writes, 'The question of what action we are going to perform is not necessarily answered by our having determined to our own satisfaction what it would be best to do' (Wallace 2001: 11).

[20] For an alternative view of practical versions of Moore's Paradox, see Moran 2000, esp. ch. 2.

conduct[21] is voluntary or an exercise of agency at all.[22] If the will follows normative commitment, then an individual cannot willingly go against practical judgement. On Aristotle's account of akrasia, for example, it is hard to see why the akratic individual acts voluntarily as distinct from having her agency hijacked or bypassed by the brute forces of desire.[23] What is missing, it seems, is the idea of the akratic individual consenting to or forming the intention to depart from practical reason. What is missing, in other words, is the very idea of the will.

This leads to a second complaint. The objection is not just that the internalist conception of the will seems inadequate for an understanding of the agency that is displayed in akrasia (and the like); the point is that this inadequacy is due precisely to the absence of any notion of the will distinct from practical judgement. So the fact that we *have* a concept of the will at all, a distinction between deciding to and deciding that, is implicitly a rebuke to the internalist picture. (See Appendix 1.)

The primary appeal of externalism, then, is just the failure of internalism to make sense of counter-normative agency. But I don't think we can be happy with this view, either. The idea that the question 'What shall I do?' is always left open by practical reason[24] threatens to sever the notions of choice and choiceworthiness in an

---

[21] By this phrase, I refer to conduct that is in the ordinary sense weak-willed, as well as choices made in indifference to or defiance of what the agent takes to be best, if these are possible.

[22] I do not say that the only recourse for internalists is flat denial of weakness of will. Indeed, quite a lot has been said along these lines to accommodate common sense. But to remain internalist, the account will have to imply that in akrasia we are less fully agents than otherwise.

[23] This implication—that the akratic's agency is overcome or compromised— would not entail that the individual could not be held responsible for this failure, in so far as it was a failure of character.

[24] It might be tempting to construe the open question in this way: 'What kind of self shall I be? A self that responds to such-and-such considerations or to others?' This doesn't provide the 'shall' with a non-normative sense, however; it just poses the deliberative question at a different level. Kane seems to construe the question in this way in the case of akratic struggles: '*qua* agent and practical reasoner, she has the general purpose of resolving the conflict in one way or the other and thereby deciding (for the present at least) what sort of person she wants to be—which of her internal

incoherent way.[25] If making up one's mind what to do is not 'an essentially normative stance', is just different in this way from making up one's mind about what is best to do, then there would seem to be no more than a contingent connection between these two moments of resolution. But then agency would be located, as O'Shaughnessy says, 'in the motion of the will, understood as an explanatory ultimate' (O'Shaughnessy 1980: ii. 341). It would make sense to suppose that such commitments could become unhinged from reasons in a quite general way.[26] Absurdly, it would then seem a wonder why we ever bothered about the good at all.

Something is wrong with the externalist picture. What requires explanation is disregarding the good, not seeking it. This point blunts the force of Wallace's claim about Moore's Paradox. Believing something one regards as false is indeed less coherent than intending to pursue what one takes to be the inferior option. Just the same, 'I *never* intend to do what I decide is best to do' *is* incoherent. The externalist owes us an explanation of why the global case makes no sense, if intending has no internal connection to what is choiceworthy.[27]

Moreover, for the same reasons, externalism is problematic even where we would expect to find it most helpful: in its treatment

points of view . . . she wishes to have prevail' (Kane 1996: 139). Kane speaks of such moments as occasions 'when agents are torn between conflicting visions of what they should become' (Kane 1996: 130). If the question about what kind of person to be is a normative question, then in the cases we are discussing it has already been settled. If it's a volitional question, what is its content?

[25] David Velleman proposes a mixed externalist position. He objects to the conception of an agent 'as being capable of intentional action—and hence as being an agent—only by virtue of being a pursuer of value' (Velleman 1992: 99). But in contrast to Albritton and Wallace, Velleman *is* an internalist regarding the connection of agency with *reason(s)*. He manages this unusual juxtaposition, of course, by disconnecting reason from value.

[26] For reasons indicated in the previous note, Velleman would object to this way of putting it, since he thinks reasons don't necessarily come from value. Note also that in going against practical judgement one might still be responding to the specific (prima facie or *pro tanto*) considerations that favour this sub-optimal choice.

[27] Wallace writes: 'In practice, of course, cases of non-normative choice are the exception rather than the rule' (Wallace 2001: 14). But why 'of course'?

of weakness of will. The internalists' problem is to make sense of weakness as genuine agency. In contrast, externalists have trouble explaining what is, after all, *weak* in akratic behaviour. In weakness of will, properly so-called, one goes against the grain of one's own commitments, and this is an appropriate description only if practical judgement constitutes a commitment *to act*.[28] On the externalist view, however, going against reason must always come down to a choice among possible commitments. Externalism is therefore in danger of conflating weakness and 'radical choice'.

For these reasons, neither (unqualified) internalism nor (unqualified) externalism is satisfactory. The truth must lie somewhere in between. An adequate view must provide for a 'non-contingent' connection between normative and volitional commitment and at the same time make sense of the possibility of sometimes deliberately opting for the lesser good. Obviously, the issue is too undeveloped and complex to adjudicate here. My main concern is with a much narrower but still significant question. Does the notion of the will have a distinctive role only in views that want to make room for counter-normative assertions of agency?

THE EXECUTIVE FUNCTION OF THE WILL

A positive answer to this question would predict that internalist philosophies of action have no use for the concept of will except as another name for practical judgement. But that would be wrong. (See Appendix 2.) For as noted at the end of the section 'Deliberating and Deciding', the distinction between practical judgement and will is not motivated exclusively by the need to account for counter-normative agency. The distinction is also revealed in circumstances of normative uncertainty or indeterminacy. In these contexts, the question 'What shall I do?' is clearly different from the question

---

[28] For an understanding of weakness of will as irresolution with respect to one's volitional commitments, rather than as going against one's normative judgements, see Holton 1999 and Holton *op. cit.*

'What should I do?' The issue here is not 'Shall I comply with my judgement?' but 'What shall I do in view of the fact that the reasons, all things considered, are not decisive?' Here there is a need for volitional commitment that can and should be recognized by the most robust version of internalism. This is sometimes called the 'executive' function of the will.[29] (See Appendix 3.)

Even when reason is not entirely silent, uncertain, or indeterminate, the will has constructive work to do. Judgement may leave open the constitutive or instrumental means to responding to certain reasons. Moreover, as many writers have stressed (including Thomas Pink and especially Michael Bratman[30]), practical commitment has a planning and coordinational role that is needed for coherent action over time.[31] In this way, decisions might be in the service of rational agency even when they are not carrying out substantive demands or recommendations (at whatever level of generality). They might be said in these contexts to be constrained by the formal aims of practical reason. Furthermore, as Bratman emphasizes, adopting intentions to serve this planning role then gives us reasons for additional intentions and actions.

[29] 'A decision', Thomas Pink says, 'is a second-order executive action—an action by which we ensure that we subsequently perform the first-order actions which, as deliberators, we have judged it desirable to perform' (Pink 1996: 5). For the bearing of Kant's distinction between *Wille* and *Willkür* on this idea of an executive function, see Appendix 3.

[30] See Bratman 1987. As David Owens puts it, following Bratman and Pink, the function of intention 'is simply to perpetuate the motivational force of practical judgement over time' (Owens 2000: 105).

[31] Frankfurt proposes a similar view: 'a function of decision is to integrate the person both dynamically and statically. Dynamically insofar as it provides . . . for coherence and unity of purpose over time; statically, insofar as it establishes . . . a reflexive or hierarchical structure by which one person's identity may be in part constituted' (Frankfurt 1987: 175). This identity-constituting function can be seen as serving the interests of reason, since without it one lacks any standpoint as a practical reasoner. Nonetheless, Frankfurt, here and especially in later work, rejects the idea that the function of reason is to enable one to act well—that, he says, is the business of deliberation (Frankfurt 1987: 174).

The political image here is suggestive. The will comes into play on an internalist view only when intention is not completely scripted in advance by reasons. 'Deciding to' typically involves shaping priorities among a structure of reasons and thereby giving certain considerations a special reason-giving force.[32] And this is precisely what is required for a substantive executive role: that the executive have latitude for its own operation within a legislative framework to which it is subordinate. On the other hand, the will would not be carrying out practical reason if it went against its mandates. When intention fails to be guided by judgement, it fails to operate in its executive capacity—it fails to operate *as* a will. For the internalist, intentional activity that is not under judgemental control is not an exercise of agential control, or of full-blooded agency.[33]

Recall the comparison of will and belief. For the internalist, the will is like belief in this respect: just as total indifference to truth is not compatible with belief, so nothing that operated indifferently to the aims of practical reason could count as the operation of the will. Externalists insist on a sharp disanalogy here. They agree that the function of the will is executive, if this is taken in a strictly normative sense. Trivially, we misuse our volitional powers when we form intentions that flout practical norms. But the capacity for misuse is not a defect in those powers themselves; on the contrary, it is integral to them.[34] In contrast, externalists think, the capacity to violate

---

[32] See Michael Bratman's discussion of decision as 'treating something as a reason' in Bratman 1996.

[33] Cf. David Owens: 'the mere fact that something is produced by my will, that my will motivates it, does not put me in control of it. I am in control of it only when my judgement as to whether it ought to be produced at will can determine whether it is produced at will. I am in control of the products of my will when the will itself is under my reflective control' (Owens 2000: 80).

[34] Wallace argues that the capacity for rational self-guidance necessarily contains the potential for self-alienation, because it requires a capacity of motivational transcendence that can be turned against the disposition to be guided by normative conclusions (Wallace 2001: 10). This argument might show that our capacity for rational action is contingent upon certain skills that also make us liable to practical irrationality. But it doesn't follow, as Wallace seems to think, that when these enabling capacities are

the norms of theoretical reason constitutes an imperfection in our cognitive faculties as such.

DELIBERATION IN THE SERVICE OF INTENTION

I have been contrasting two ways of thinking of the relation between practical judgement and the will. Before I turn to the second set of questions about agency and belief, I want to note an important qualification to my characterization of deliberation. I have been assuming that the aim of deliberative practical reason is to make up one's mind on the basis of one's determination of which available option is best. The question I have just been exploring is whether the idea of a power to make up one's mind that is distinct from normative assessment has a role only in an externalist theory. My answer is 'no'. But this description of deliberation is surely idealized. Counter-normative conduct often involves deliberation as well. So, it might be objected, practical reasoning is no more 'internally connected' to the good than the will is.

This observation reminds us to beware of linking practical reasoning too tightly with unconditional judgements about what is best to do, but it doesn't show that deliberation is not always concerned with what it is good to do. Perhaps I have akratically resolved to have an affair, or to take up (or continue) smoking, or to steal some morphine from a pharmacy to quiet my addiction. I will sometimes, and perhaps typically, engage in practical reasoning in executing these aims. And these deliberations needn't be purely strategic. For example, in the most obvious kind of case, I might carry out my sub-optimal intention to smoke in a way that mitigates its destructive effects (e.g. 'low tar' tobacco). In a more interesting kind of case, I might seek (perhaps self-deceptively) to be unfaithful in a way that is less rather than more disrespectful to my spouse, or choose ways of stealing the drugs that

misused their manifestations are themselves instances of self-determination. They are at most, as he himself puts it, 'hazardous by-products' of the contingent conditions of self-determination.

minimize the risk to others' lives and property. In these ways, I employ genuinely normative, sometimes even moral, thought in the pursuit of unworthy aims.[35] Intending to do the forbidden thing need not mean kicking over all the moral traces. In some cases, normative constraints might lead me to give up my akratic project altogether. We are often trying to act as well as possible given our defective aims, treating those ends as part of the background scene, as though they were someone else's or those of ourselves in the past.[36]

There is a need in the theory of moral reasoning for an analogue to John Rawls's distinction in political philosophy between 'full' and 'partial' compliance theory. From the moral point of view, there can be better and worse ways, right and wrong forms of carrying out impermissible maxims, just as there can be just and unjust ways of responding to injustices. In Kantian terms, for example, obviously I can be responsive to hypothetical imperatives in the employment of maxims that violate the categorical imperative. But distinctively moral judgement could also be involved in the execution of a maxim that I know to be non-universalizable. The reasoning involved here would be conditional upon my having adopted that maxim, but it would not be strictly hypothetical in Kant's sense. Of course I should abandon my adulterous project, but given that I am not going to, there is room for reasoning about which sub-maxims are permissible (taking the project as fixed).

In sum, akratic commitments are not just a matter of bypassing or rejecting one's evaluative capacities and judgements. Those capacities

[35] See Wallace 2001 for an insightful discussion of the role of 'instrumental rationality' in akratic action. My point here is that the reasoning in question need not be just instrumental.

[36] Cf. O'Shaughnessy 1980: ii. 342: ' . . . there are ways of relating to the past that are "in bad faith". Thus a man can relate to his previous decisions as to the decrees of an authority he dare not question. Thereby he places his present self in subjection, as to a destiny, to a tyrannical past self. Now this is a loss of freedom—akin to the compulsions of the obsessional—and rationality. For the "authentic" and rational relation to one's past decisions is that they are perpetually open to review. . . . In short, something between uncertainty and fate, viz., *commitment.*'

and judgements are often engaged in that counter-normative conduct. What follows, though, is not that deliberation can proceed in indifference to the good, but that this concern can be qualified and compromised in the ways just indicated. I am not saying that all deliberation in the service of objectionable ends is *morally* mitigating in this way. Using the hypothetical imperative without any concession to the moral point of view, or even to prudence, is still a restricted kind of deliberation, and hence a restricted kind of concern for reasons. Deliberation remains an inherently normative process.

II

DECIDING AS AN ACTIVE PHENOMENON

Judging, making up our minds what to think, is something for which we are, in principle, responsible—something we freely do, as opposed to something that merely happens in our lives. . . . This freedom, exemplified in responsible acts of judging, is essentially a matter of being answerable to criticism in the light of rationally relevant considerations. So the realm of freedom, at least the realm of the freedom of judging, can be identified with the space of reasons.

(John McDowell)

Belief and other attitudes [unlike the sensations] . . . are stances of the person to which the demand for justification is internal. And the demand for justification internal to attitudes involves a sense of agency and authority that is fundamentally different from the various forms of direction or control one may be able to exercise over some mind or another.

(Richard Moran)

I turn at last to the second set of questions I posed in the beginning. Should we regard 'doxastic' decisions—our making up our minds what to believe on a certain matter—to be instances of agency, as I (with Wallace and some others) have assumed volitional commitments to be? If so, should we speak of the will in this domain?[37]

I won't attempt anything like a sustained defence of my initial assumption that practical decision, 'deciding to', is an active phenomenon. In the rest of the chapter, I will be concerned mainly with whether there is any good reason to deny the same status to doxastic commitments. Thus my case in what follows is more or less an *ad hominem* to those who agree with this assumption but refuse to admit doxastic agency. If you insist on David Owens's definition of activity as 'events subject to the will, events whose justification lies in how desirable their occurrence would be' (Owens 2000: 85), you will dismiss the possibility of this sort of agency from the start.[38] But it is important to note that this definition precludes not only doxastic agency, but the agency of practical decisions as well. For in general the decision or intention to x is justified by the choiceworthiness of xing, not by the independent desirability of so deciding or intending.[39] So anyone who regards volitional commitments as instances of activity will need another understanding of the basic idea. My question is whether doxastic commitments are active in the very same sense. As far as I can see, they are.[40]

Unfortunately, it is beyond my powers to say anything very helpful here, but I should try to say something about the basic notion, as I understand it. I think that both 'deciding that' and 'deciding to', assessings and optings, are exercises of agency because they are forms of *assenting or rejecting*. The idea of agency seems to me bound up with the sense in which these are instances of practical or cognitive

---

[37] As Descartes does. See App. 2.

[38] Not that Owens himself dismisses the possibility by definition. His book is a sustained argument for this conclusion.

[39] As Owens himself emphasizes (Owens 2000: 81–2). So does Pink (1996, *passim*).

[40] I hasten to make the same qualification I made about practical decision. I am not saying that all belief acquisition is an instance of forming a belief or making a judgement; therefore I am not saying that all believing is active.

commitment. We are answerable for our decisions because they are attributable to us in these ways.

Before we take up the specifically doxastic case, it is crucial for my purposes to distinguish deciding as a basic form of activity from trying. If 'deciding to' is an activity, it is peculiar in some respects because of its relation to intentionality. My deliberation about whether to accept the offer of employment is of course intentional, guided by the aim of making up my mind on the question of whether to go. However, it cannot target its specific terminus; I cannot aim to make up my mind, specifically, to decline. For, typically anyway,[41] to aim to commit myself to *x*ing, with a view to following through on that commitment, I must already intend to *x* and hence must already have made up my mind on the matter.[42]

If I understand him correctly, Brian O'Shaughnessy is led by these features of decision to conclude that deciding (as distinct from deliberating) is not intentional[43] and so is not an instance of activity. Deliberation is intentional activity, on his view, because it consists in trying to make up one's mind. But the culmination of this activity— deciding to decline the offer—is not.[44] For O'Shaughnessy, deciding signals the activity of the will only to the extent to which it is the termination of the activity of trying, namely trying to make up

[41] Typically. But there are circumstances, for example, of irresolution, in which I might set out to bring about a state of conviction on my part. Thanks to Pamela Hieronymi and Dana Nelkin for pressing me on this point. Hieronymi discusses some of the subtleties of this issue in 'Controlling Attitudes' (unpub. ms).

[42] There is a performative or behavioural sense in which deciding is not opaque in this way. A judge can decide in favour of the plaintiff, intending in advance to do just that. That is because 'decide in favour of' denotes here a public declaration of some kind. In the sense under consideration in this chapter, if she is to intend to find in favour of the plaintiff, the judge must already have decided so to find.

[43] Hugh McCann disagrees: 'It is impossible to make a decision without intending to decide, and without intending to decide exactly as we do' (McCann 1986: 142).

[44] He puts it this way: in deliberation, 'an active procedure, that . . . falls essentially under [the description] "trying to decide whether to do" and inessentially under "deciding what to do", is followed by an essentially inactive event of "deciding to do"' (O'Shaughnessy 1980: ii. 300).

one's mind.[45] If trying were the root of all activity, then that would be a reason for denying that decisions of any kind are instances of agency.

Someone who shared O'Shaughnessy's view that trying is the basic form of intentional activity might insist that decidings to act should still be called active and intentional in virtue of being the realizations of the attempt to settle on a course of action.[46] Whether or not this is a plausible thing to say,[47] I do not think that the active character of forming intentions is just derivative in this way from the activity of trying to decide. These are, in my view, distinct modes of agency.[48] As I said at the beginning, on many occasions (indeed, typically) we form intentions without attempting to make up our minds to act. In these cases, what O'Shaughnessy says of (what he calls) 'willing'—that it is 'something such that its happening *in* one is never its happening *to* one'— seems clearly to apply (O'Shaughnessy 1980: ii. 345). Like tryings, my deciding to decline the offer or my forming the intention to help the man with his luggage do not 'just happen' to me along the way, in the way that receiving the offer or encountering a man in need do; they are (more or less) intelligent responses that I make as I move around in the world. Practical commitment, to use

[45] O'Shaughnessy thinks that decision is always subsequent to uncertainty but that it needn't result from an attempt to make up one's mind. So decision needn't even be the upshot of activity. He thinks 'a man can go to bed undecided and wake to a state of decision . . . All that may be required is that the mental dust should settle. In any case, that practical uncertainty should give way to practical commitment' (O'Shaughnessy 1980: ii. 301). For criticisms of O'Shaughnessy on this point, see Magill 1997: 92.

[46] Mele's view is something like this, but he doesn't emphasize trying. He proposes that 'practical decidings are intentional actions' in virtue of being 'produced' by 'an intention to decide what to do' (Mele 2000: 93).

[47] O'Shaughnessy thinks it is not (O'Shaughnessy 1980: i. 299). The relation of deciding to decline the offer to deliberating about whether to decline, he suggests, is analogous to the relation between finding and seeking.

[48] See Pink 1996 for a very helpful discussion of O'Shaughnessy's views, and for defence of the claim that trying and deciding are distinct forms of agency.

O'Shaughnessy's term,[49] is just as much an 'essentially active phenomenon' as trying. It is an exercise of agency not because it is an instance or product of trying but because, as I said, it is a case of *assenting or rejecting.*

COGNITIVE AGENCY

The same seems to me to be true of 'cognitive' commitments.[50] Philosophers resist this idea because they think that in the realm of belief we don't have the necessary kind of *control*. Recall Jay Wallace's view:

> By volition here I mean a kind of motivational state that, by contrast with . . . given desires . . . are [sic] directly under the control of the agent. Familiar examples of volitional states in this sense are intentions, choices, and decisions. . . . intentions, choices, and decisions are things we do, primitive examples of the phenomenon of agency itself. . . . This line . . . marks a distinction of fundamental importance, the line between the passive and the active in our psychological lives.

(Wallace 1999: 636–7)

[49] This way of characterizing intentions raises questions about non-reflective creatures. O'Shaughnessy certainly thinks they have intentions, but calling these states 'commitments' doesn't ring true. It might be thought that 'prior' intentions are commitments and that the other animals do not have these. However, if the concept of intention applies to animals at all, the occurrence of preparatory activity on their part seems to require the attribution of prior intentions. If the dog is digging the hole in order to bury the bone, and if one thinks that the dog both digs the hole and buries the bone intentionally, what grounds would one have for denying that it digs the hole with the intention of burying the bone? Alternatively, as I am inclined to think, perhaps it is appropriate to speak of intentions as practical commitments only in case the creature has *formed* those intentions, as distinct from acquiring them in other ways. In that case, we could allow for prior intentions in non-reflective beings without attributing practical commitments to them. I would want to make a parallel claim about cognitive commitments.

[50] Unsurprisingly, O'Shaughnessy disagrees: 'Believing is in itself essentially inactive' (O'Shaughnessy 1980: i. 28). So does Bernard Williams, who agrees 'with Hume against Descartes that belief is an essentially passive phenomenon' (Williams 1978: 177).

Does a criterion of direct control mark 'decidings to' as active in a way in which judgements (practical or otherwise) cannot be?

To begin with, no one denies that we have at least *indirect* control of our beliefs in so far as it is up to us to undertake to gather or evaluate evidence. When I conclude, after weighing the evidence, that the Earth is more than 5,000 years old, my belief comes about as a result of my intentional activities. The dispute is whether we have a form of control or agency with respect to judgement or belief that is not derivative in this way. John Heil thinks not. We select our 'belief-generating procedures', he says, but we don't select our beliefs. 'We believe, not because on reflection a certain thing seems worthy of belief, seems epistemically *valuable*, but because in reflecting we become vulnerable in certain ways to beliefs of certain sorts.' In this respect, Heil concludes, 'We are largely *at the mercy* of our belief-forming equipment' (Heil 1983: 358). David Owens agrees. 'In the end, it is the world that determines what I believe, not me.' Once we decide to attend to the evidence, he supposes, 'the evidence takes over and I lose control' (Owens 2000: 12).

This sounds scary, as though I am a bystander to the "output" of my epistemic constitution. I think that Heil and Owens draw here a false contrast. Doxastic control is not opposed to being determined, in accordance with some 'belief-relevant norms',[51] by the 'world'. On the contrary, that is what such control amounts to. Our cognitive lives would be out of control to the extent to which we were incapable of responding to norms of coherence and relevant evidence, that is, were not normatively competent in this way.

To be sure, often, as we say, I 'can't help' making certain judgements given the reasons available to me. When I stand in the garden, eyes open, I can't just choose whether or not to believe that the sun is shining, although I might have been able to avoid encountering the overwhelming evidence in the first place. This lack of choice is not to be deplored. Everyone admits that judgement must answer to

---

[51] I borrow this phrase from Pettit and Smith 1996.

evidence or reason in a way that is not true of practical commitment. I cannot, transparently, form the judgement that 'creation science' is true merely because I suppose that its truth, or believing in its truth, would serve my ends or would be otherwise desirable.[52] Yet that is possible, with transparency, in at least some if not all cases of forming intentions to act. Nothing that was subject to my particular ends in this way could count as 'belief'. Again, this means that some version of internalism must hold in the case of cognitive agency.

This contrast might seem to entail straight away that beliefs couldn't be under your 'direct control'. And yet the point about the irresistibility of certain reasons holds for practical decision as well. Just as I am powerless to believe that the Earth came into existence just a few thousand years ago, given what else I know, in the very same sense, it seems to me, I am powerless to form the intention to lop off my leg, given my other (non-destructive) doxastic and practical commitments. Do I have the power to adopt the intention to do what seems to me pointless or crazy? Perhaps in some sense I do. But I doubt that it is a sense that is *both* inapplicable to the formation of judgements and clearly a condition of agency.

If agency is exercised by assent to propositions or courses of action, then the relevant notion of control is the notion that is appropriate to the mode of assent in question. So I don't concede that the absence of a certain kind of dependency on your ends that often obtains in the case of intentions means that, in the case of our cognitive commitments, we lack control in the relevant sense. Again, such dependency, if systematic and thoroughgoing, would undercut the capacity for

---

[52] But compare this exchange between Charles Ryder and Sebastian Flyte in Waugh 1945/1967: 83:

'But my dear Sebastian, you can't seriously *believe* it all.'
'Can't I?'
'I mean about Christmas and the star and the three kings and the ox and the ass.'
'Oh yes, I believe that. It's a lovely idea.'
'But you can't *believe* things because they're a lovely idea.'
'But I *do*. That's how I believe.'

judgement, so it can hardly be part of the pertinent notion of cognitive agency. Nor do I concede that our beliefs are things that happen to us, are mere effects upon us of the world.

Is there a Doxastic Will?

So far I have been speaking in favour of cognitive agency, but what about the related question I raised earlier: if doxastic commitments are instances of activity, should they be regarded as exercises of the will? There are good reasons, prima facie, to deny the consequent. In common speech, we don't naturally speak of 'voluntariness' outside the practical realm.[53] Doesn't this suggest the fundamental asymmetry I have been (perhaps stubbornly) resisting? In accordance with the etymology of the word, ordinary language suggests that there is no use for the notion of the will beyond that realm. This tells against cognitive agency, it might be argued, since where there is no will, there is no agency.

Perhaps, though, this fact about ordinary language is philosophically superficial. Notice, for one thing, that we don't speak of forming intentions voluntarily or involuntarily either. Something is voluntary, it seems, when it is appropriately related to intention.[54] So this observation can't be the basis for any special contrast of belief with intention. More significantly, judgement generally has some of the central features that Aristotle, for example, associates with the

---

[53] For good discussions of 'the voluntariness of belief', consult Code 1987 and Zagzebski 1996: 61–73.

[54] An alternative explanation of the oddity of speaking of intentions as voluntary might be that they couldn't fail to be voluntary. Hugh McCann thinks intentions are 'essentially voluntary'. 'Volition [which includes for McCann forming intentions] can be voluntary in the way water can be wet—that is, essentially, in a way that does not require some means as explanation' (McCann 1974: 92). The idea is that water isn't wet in the same sense that the streets are wet; that is, it isn't covered with water. Rather water is wetting, productive of wetness; it is what makes things wet. In this sense, I would agree that intending is voluntary: it is the (or a) source of voluntariness.

voluntary.[55] I don't know what views Aristotle had about the status of belief. But he suggests in book 3 of the *Nicomachean Ethics* that not only actions but also feelings and 'decisions' (in his special sense of deliberative desires) are voluntary. We don't speak this way in common English, but the core feature of Aristotle's idea applies here as well: the 'origin', or 'moving principle', is in us.[56] Far from being 'at the mercy' of those faculties, coming to believe (or intend) is attributable to me as its author because (and if) it is related in the right way to my adjudicative (and executive) capacities. In this sense, we can (and do) say that my beliefs are 'up to me': they are subject (potentially at least) to my decision-making powers, my normative competence.[57] What is up to me in this sense is what I am (potentially) responsible for. What is up to me[58] is what falls within the range of my responsibilities.

All the same, I think there is an insight embodied in ordinary usage. As we have seen, there are two grounds for distinguishing between the will and judgement. One is the need, emphasized by externalists, to account for counter-normative exercises of agency.

[55] Thanks to Barbara Herman for emphasizing to me the relevance of Aristotle's treatment of the voluntary.

[56] Consider the following paradigm of involuntary reactions: 'Facing [Oakland A's batter] Johnny Damon in the first inning, [the Seattle Mariner pitcher John] Halama stuck his bare hand up and deflected Damon's comebacker. "I keep telling myself not to do that," Halama said, "but it's just a reaction. I say I am not going to do it, and wind up doing it." (Jim Street, MLB.com, 11 Apr. 2001). The origin of movement is not, in the relevant sense, in Halama. To adapt Heil's remark, Halama is at the mercy of his intention-forming equipment. Something like this can happen in the cognitive realm as well. Unreflective cognitive reactions can go against one's reflective judgements (though not as transparently). I keep telling myself that the fact that seven heads in a row have come up doesn't increase the probability of tails on the next flip, but I wind up expecting tails anyway. Perhaps we shouldn't think of this expectation as a belief, exactly—perhaps just a 'hunch'. But a parallel qualification seems equally apt in the case of intention.

[57] For a helpful discussion of attributability, responsibility, and being up to us, see Scanlon 1998: 18–22 and ch. 6; 2002.

[58] An explicitly normative application of this phrase is apparent in 'it was [or will be] up to you to see to it that the doors are locked'.

This ground can have no application to belief, since it is agreed by virtually everyone that one can believe only under the guise of truth. The other ground is that we need a notion of the will as distinct from judgement where there is executive work to do. And there is work of this kind only because practical judgement doesn't fully determine practical commitment. That's why there is a further question, 'What shall I do?', to which the adoption of an intention is an answer. And this answer is often tantamount to giving certain considerations reason-giving force that they otherwise wouldn't have.[59] For practical purposes, then, we need a capacity for commitment that is distinct from judgement.[60] The non-practical case looks different, however. Once I have assessed the evidence, it seems, there can be no remaining question about what to believe, no place for an epistemic 'opting' that goes beyond the relevant assessment.[61]

But we must be careful to distinguish assessing the evidence regarding p from believing that p. This distinction complicates our issue. My assessment of the evidence may not always yield conviction, either because of theoretical akrasia,[62] or, more importantly for our purposes, because the evidence is not decisive. Consider the moderate form of voluntarism defended by William James in 'The Will to Believe' (James 1896). James considers cases in which theoretical reason doesn't and perhaps can't decisively favour p or not-p. In some of these cases, he thinks, it is not unreasonable to be influenced by non-epistemic considerations, for example, regarding the kind of life to which believing that p might contribute. The issue between James and W. K. Clifford is precisely over whether our assessment of the evidence always settles the question of what *to*

---

[59] Again, see Bratman's discussion of decision as 'treating something as a reason' in Bratman 1996.   [60] Owens 2000 is very helpful on this topic.

[61] It is revealing that 'choose' is a rough synonym for 'decide' in 'deciding to', but not in 'deciding that'. Choosing is 'opting', not 'assessing'.

[62] For discussions of theoretical akrasia, see Hurley 1989, Scanlon 1998, and Wallace 2001.

believe (Clifford 1866). If James is right, there is latitude for 'opting' in the cognitive realm as well, precisely where theoretical reasons run out.

It is an important question here whether the will to believe in these cases is indeed a will to *believe*, as distinct from a determination to live as if one believed *p* were true, or to accept *p* as true for the purposes of improving one's life.[63] Certainly, this is contestable. Unlike extreme voluntarism, though, we can't dismiss James's position out of hand. Someone who sincerely utters, 'I believe *p*, though not-*p* is equally supported by the evidence', might or might not be irresponsible, as Clifford urges. But unlike 'I believe *p*, but *p* isn't true', the utterance is not Moore-paradoxical. Indeed, the debate between James and Clifford—whether such believing could be reasonable—presumes that the endorsement of this conjunction of attitudes can be coherently attributable to someone.

Thus, our initial explanation of why there is no cognitive version of the will—namely, that there is no occasion for doxastic commitment that goes beyond the epistemic reasons—was flawed. Even so, a fundamental disanalogy remains. Intending and acting in the face of uncertainty or indeterminacy can serve the ends of practical reason. But believing (as distinct from some weaker form of acceptance) on insufficient evidence cannot serve the ends of theoretical reason. Hence, in the kind of case on which James focuses, doxastic commitment is merely an instrumentally valuable result of the operation of practical reason, rather than a cognitive form of the will. This conclusion should lead us not to reject cognitive agency but to question the idea that where there is no will, we are inactive.[64]

---

[63] Michael Bratman distinguishes belief from acceptance in Bratman 1992. See also Cohen 1989.

[64] Joseph Raz also defends the thesis that we are active in believing even though we don't (in any straightforward sense) believe voluntarily (Raz 1999). Linda Zagzebski (2001) thinks that an individual's epistemic achievements are 'up to her', though not voluntary.

AGENCY AND RESPONSIBILITY

My case for cognitive agency has relied a good deal on the thought that we are as responsible for the judgements we make as for the intentions we form. In both cases I am open to normative appraisal and answerable for my commitments. It makes sense to press me on my reasons, and to say of me, 'You should have reached a different conclusion (formed a different intention).' But some philosophers, for example, David Owens, deny the assumption that responsibility requires agency or control in any sense.[65] I find this denial extremely puzzling, because responsibility for particular attitudes seems to me to require a kind of attributability that is sufficient for agency of the kind I have been at pains to articulate. When, in the passage quoted earlier, Owens insists that 'it is the world that determines what I believe, not me', he is making a claim about control, but that claim would equally deny my responsibility. If the world, or my cognitive equipment, *and not I*, determines what I believe, then it is inapt to attribute the outcome to me, to credit or fault me for these attitudes.

Not surprisingly, the disagreement here turns on what kind of control is required for agency. Since Owens thinks we don't have that kind of control, and yet agrees that we are responsible for our epistemic commitments, he thinks responsibility does not presuppose agency. I think that Owens is wrong about agency but right about responsibility. I have nothing more to say in support of this position here. But I would like to conclude this part of the chapter with a slight concession to those who think that Owens is right about agency but wrong about responsibility.[66] I have stressed important

---

[65] This is one of the targets of Owens 2000; see esp. chs. 1 and 8.

[66] Linda Zagzebski (1996: 68) notes the 'dependency of our responsibility for our acts on our responsibility for the beliefs providing our reasons for acting', an observation she attributes to Edmund Pincoffs. Some might be tempted to see this responsibility as reducible to responsibility for earlier evidence-gathering, and hence as reducible to (or traceable to) act-responsibility. But that seems just to push the question back to the individual's responsibility for her earlier beliefs relevant to the evidence-gathering decisions.

parallels between epistemic and practical responsibility. But there are striking differences as well, differences that might lead some to deny that we are directly responsible for our beliefs in the same sense in which we are responsible for our conduct. Both epistemic and moral responsibility involve a kind of accountability. But there are dimensions of moral accountability for intention that have no counterpart in the epistemic case. We can put this by saying that we have notions of culpability and guilt that don't apply to responsibility for belief. There is no such thing as epistemic guilt, really— just various forms of fault. The notions I have in mind are thought to ground various reactive attitudes, blame, and other hard treatment of the culprit. Now the kinds of capacity for responsiveness to reasons to which I have alluded here account for the possibility of various sorts of normative criticism, but they hardly ground the thought that the agent deserves to be subject to retributive sanctions in virtue of her rational shortcomings. It might be supposed, then, that accountability of this further kind makes sense only if we have a kind of control—volitional control, perhaps—that goes beyond the kind of reasons-responsiveness that is involved in belief (something called free will). Indeed, it is common to suppose that what is required is just the capacity for counter-normative agency.

My concession, then, is that there might be dimensions of responsibility that have no epistemic counterpart because there is a kind of control over conduct that is absent in the cognitive realm. I said that this was a *slight* concession for two reasons. First, I don't in fact see how this further, counter-normative form of control is supposed to ground the retributive practices in any case. But obviously this is a larger question than I can take on here. Secondly, to deny that we are 'really' responsible in the cognitive realm on the foregoing grounds is to overlook the multidimensional character of responsibility. Even if there are valid forms of calling people to account that require different kinds of control from those we could have over our beliefs, it remains true that some significant facets of responsibility apply to us equally as epistemic and as moral beings.

CONCLUSION

The two main topics of this chapter—the issue of cognitive agency and the dispute between internalists and externalists—are linked in an important way. Externalism about practical decision is at odds with the idea that there is distinctively doxastic activity.[67] As we have seen, suitably qualified, internalism about the cognitive realm is uncontroversial. This means that belief is an attitude that is constituted in part by its subjection to norms of relevant evidence. It is controlled by considerations of truth. But, as we have seen, externalism about practical decision rests on the thought that, if intention stands to goodness as belief stands to truth, there is no place here for control or (hence) for agency. What opens up the possibility of agency, according to this idea, is precisely that intention is not a 'normative stance'; if it were, it would be controlled by the good (or by the individual's 'normative equipment') rather than by the agent. As Wallace says, the 'normative aspect of believing . . . is connected with the further fact that there are clear limits, of a conceptual nature, on the possibility of believing at will' (Wallace 2001: 10). If I can adopt a certain attitude 'at will', the attitude in question can't be an 'essentially normative stance'; it can't be part of what it is to be that attitude that it be regulated by certain norms. For those regulatory limits would be limits on agency. On the other hand, those who allow for agency or control in the doxastic realm are apt to do so on the basis of an understanding of control as normative competence. Given this understanding, the case for thinking that something different in kind is necessary for intention and action seems less than compelling.

I have found no convincing reasons to think that adopting intentions and making judgements belong on different sides of a line dividing our agency from what merely happens to us. The capacity to assent to

---

[67] I don't say that these are strictly contradictory. Rather, the natural lines of thought supporting each position are opposed to one another.

and be guided by relevant reasons is central to what it is to be an epistemically and morally responsible being, and this normative competence involves a fundamental kind of agency. Making up one's mind—'deciding that' or 'deciding to'—is a basic mode of activity that pervades our theoretical and practical lives. Nevertheless, I have argued, there is no straightforward analogue of the will in cognitive contexts. What follows from this, in my view, is not that there is no cognitive agency, but that the boundaries between the active and the passive are not marked by the will.

APPENDIX 1. ARISTOTLE AND THE WILL

The idea that the will plays no role in internalist philosophies of mind is arguably borne out by Aristotle's work. Many readers are led to conclude that Aristotle lacks the concept of will precisely because they don't find in his philosophy an unambiguous acknowledgement of counter-normative agency. Although 'prohairesis' is usually translated as 'choice' (or less often 'decision'), Aristotle glosses it as 'desiring in accordance with the good as the result of deliberation'. So akratic behaviour is plainly not an exercise of 'choice' in this sense. This problem is part of what worried Elizabeth Anscombe regarding 'prohairesis':

> At any rate, 'choice' cannot do all the work Aristotle wants to make it do. The uncontrolled man who has further intentions in doing what he does, whose actions are deliberate, although the deliberation is in the interests of a desire which conflicts with what he regards as doing well—to describe his action we need a concept (our 'intention') having to do with will or appetition.
>
> (Anscombe 1965: 150)

According to Terence Irwin, the Greeks are often thought to lack a notion of the will because they worked with a belief–desire model of behaviour that appears to treat 'agents as passive subjects of their desires, and in doing so they seem to leave out an important aspect of their agency'. Of course, this is just the externalist thought that without the will you don't have agency at all, but only motivational states like desires and beliefs that lead to action without the need for an agent. However, Irwin argues that

> it would be both a historical and philosophical mistake . . . to claim that Greek philosophers lack a concept of the will, if we simply mean that they are not voluntarists,[68] for the debate between voluntarism and intellectualism[69] is a debate between two views of the will among disputants who share a concept of the will.
>
> (Irwin 1992: 468)

Irwin himself suggests a way of characterizing the will in a way that is neutral between internalist and externalist conceptions, such that Aristotle and 'voluntarists' have different views about the nature of the will, and not different concepts. What is common, Irwin suggests, is the idea of something that performs the regulative function of critical reflection on our desires in order to adjudicate among them. This general concept is sufficient to imply agency, Irwin thinks, because it implies rational control. So we are agents because we are capable of rational choice among different desires in so far as we are capable of deliberating about them 'in the light of our views of the overall good, and capable of choice in accordance with the result of this deliberation' (Irwin 1992: 467).

This rebuts the charge that an internalist conception can't account for agency, but it doesn't suffice to provide a notion of the will as something distinct from judgement. For what plays the adjudicating role here is practical reason, not *prohairesis*. (For further historical discussion, see Kahn 1985 and Normore 1998.)

APPENDIX 2. DESCARTES AND INTERNALISM

Descartes defines the will as 'the ability to do or not do something (that is, to affirm or deny, to pursue or avoid)' (Meditation IV, in Descartes 1641c/1984: ii. 40). Two points are especially noteworthy in his treatment: it has definite internalist tendencies, and it applies to intellectual judgement and intention alike. His conception appears to be to some extent internalist, for it is in the nature of the will to be drawn to the good: 'The will of a thinking being is borne, willingly indeed and freely (*for that is of the essence of*

---

[68] In my terms, roughly, externalists.   [69] In my terms, roughly, internalists.

will), but none the less infallibly, towards the good that it clearly knows' (Descartes 1641*a*/1967: ii. 56, my emphasis). In the following passage from Descartes 1649 (Article 177), Descartes even suggests that the normative orientation of the will doesn't depend on clear and distinct perception (on what one *knows*): 'For if we were wholly certain that what we are doing is bad, we would refrain from doing it, since the will tends only towards objects that have some semblance of goodness' (Descartes 1649/1984: i. 392). Note, however, that the idea that we are drawn only to courses of action that bear the 'semblance' of good is consistent with a moderate form of internalism, for it allows for the possibility of willing akrasia. That we are attracted only to options *qua* good doesn't entail that we can't be attracted to an option we take to be *less* good than an alternative.

Descartes explicitly rejects the 'indifference' to reason that is implied by strong externalism: 'In order to be free, there is no need for me to be inclined both ways; on the contrary, the more I incline in one direction— either because I clearly understand that reasons of truth and goodness point that way, or because of a divinely produced disposition of my inmost thoughts—the freer is my choice' (Meditation IV, in Descartes 1641*c*/1984: ii. 40). Indifference, he says, 'does not belong to the essence of human freedom, since not only are we free when our ignorance of the right renders us indifferent, but we are also free—indeed, at our freest— when a clear perception impels us to pursue some object' (Descartes 1641*b*/1984: ii. 292). For Descartes, only God's will is 'indifferent', for his will is the source of the true and the good and hence is not guided by them. 'Thus the supreme indifference to be found in God is the supreme indication of his omnipotence' (Descartes 1641*b*/1984: ii. 292). It is not far off, then, to characterize acts of the externalist will as God-like, if we conjoin that view with a Cartesian conception of God.[70] The freedom of finite beings, in contrast, requires responsiveness to norms that are not of their own creation:

> But as for man, since he finds that the nature of all goodness and truth
> is already determined by God, and his will cannot tend towards

---

[70] It is this idea of the will that O'Shaughnessy ridicules when he writes of those who 'conceive of self-determination as akin to the whims of a Deity responsible to nothing. . . . But that would banish intelligibility from all action'; O'Shaughnessy 1980: ii. 341.

anything else, it is evident that he will embrace what is good and true all the more willingly and hence more freely, in proportion as he sees it more clearly. . . . Hence the indifference which belongs to human freedom is very different from that which belongs to divine freedom.

(Descartes 1641b/1984: ii. 292)

It is noteworthy that, at least in the first edition of the *Essay Concerning Human Understanding*, Locke takes the same line on God's freedom as Descartes here takes on human freedom: 'God himself cannot choose what is not good; the Freedom of the Almighty hinders not his being determined by what is best' (Locke 1690/1975: II. xxi. 49). For an illuminating recent treatment of Locke on freedom, see Yaffe 2000.

There are passages that create difficulties for this internalist interpretation. For example (and I'm sure there are others), in a letter to Mesland in 1645 Descartes says this: 'when a very evident reason moves us in one direction, although morally speaking we can hardly move in the contrary direction, absolutely speaking we can'.[71] This remark suggests that the constraints on willing against the good are merely normative.

There is a question, finally, about what makes Descartes's will a unified capacity, as Bernard Williams takes it to be: 'the operation of the will is the same, whether one is concerned with reasons of "the true" or of "the good" ' (Williams 1978: 169). The power to assent to proposals to believe or act might be said to be a general capacity with two sub-capacities or sub-functions, depending on whether it is concerned with the issue of the true or the good.[72] But suppose someone said that vision and hearing were functions or sub-capacities of a general capacity of sense-perception. That would seem artificial. Is it any less so in the case of the double function of Descartes's will? Alternatively, unity might result from an intellectualist construal of the good. Exercises of the will are *always* affirmations or denials; the 'practical' will involves affirmations of ideas with practical content, that is, ideas about the good. (I am not suggesting that this is Descartes's own view.) But then the problem is to see what such affirmations have to do with *intention*.

---

[71] Quoted in Youpa 2002; I have learned a lot from Youpa's discussion of Descartes.

[72] Here I am indebted to communications with Paul Hoffman.

APPENDIX 3. KANT AND INTERNALISM

Is Kant an internalist or externalist? As usual, he is difficult to put into conventional categories. Initially, one might be inclined to see his distinction between *Wille* and *Willkür* as marking a familiar externalist distinction between practical reason and volition. In the following passage, though, Kant speaks with the internalists, but, of course, the distinction between 'phenomenon' and 'noumenon' significantly complicates the exegesis:

> But freedom of choice [*Willkür*] cannot be defined—as some have tried to define it—as the capacity to make a choice for or against the law (*libertas indifferentiae*), even though choice as a *phenomenon* provides frequent examples of this in experience. . . . Only freedom in relation to the internal lawgiving of reason is really a capacity; the possibility of deviating from it is an incapacity. How can that capacity [namely, freedom] be defined by this incapacity?
>
> (Kant 1797/1991, Ak. vi. 226–7)

Kant's distinction between *Wille* and *Willkür* is suggestive in connection with the idea of the executive will. According to Henry Allison, 'Kant uses the terms *Wille* and *Willkür* to characterize respectively the legislative and executive functions of a unified faculty of volition, which he likewise refers to as *Wille*' (Allison 1990: 129). Allison says that this distinction identifies a 'duality within unity' (Allison 1990: 130). It is in these terms, he suggests, that the idea of autonomy (understood as the will's giving laws to and for itself) must be construed, 'since this is just a matter of *Wille* giving the law to, or being the law for, *Willkür*. Strictly speaking it is only *Wille* in the broad sense that has the property of autonomy, since it is only *Wille* in this sense that can be characterized as a law to itself' (Allison 1990: 131). The duality is clear, but I'm not sure why the unity is anything more than nominal. The claim seems rather like saying of the master–servant pair that *it* is self-determining.

For an internalist discussion of the Kantian conception of the will, see Herman 2002.

Part II
Agency and Necessity

6 Free Action and Free Will

I Self-determination

(i) Two features of freedom

One old-fashioned way of classifying conceptions of free agency is to distinguish between 'liberty of indifference' and 'liberty of spontaneity'. This classification is unobjectionable as a way of bringing out importantly different emphases in different writers. It is seriously misleading, however, if it is meant to isolate competing conceptions of freedom. For what these two labels signify are interpretations of two different features of freedom that must be captured in any reasonable conception—namely, self-determination (or autonomy) and the availability of alternative possibilities. Any adequate notion of free agency must provide for possibility and autonomy in *some* sense, and, in my view, the traditional conceptions that are still taken seriously were meant to do so.[1]

---

[1] Bernard Williams [1985] says that classical compatibilism opposed freedom to constraint, not to necessity. This is misleading. Of course, compatibilism holds that freedom is not opposed to necessity in the sense in which determinism implies necessity. And Hobbes [1648/1969] in particular took pains to stress this. But that does not mean that freedom does not conflict with necessity in any sense. Locke [1690/1975] did oppose freedom (but not voluntary action) to necessity: 'Wherever . . . the power to act or forbear according to the direction of thought [that is, liberty] [is wanting], there necessity takes place' (II. 21. 13).

I confine my remarks in this essay to the 'moderns'. One could argue that these two features of freedom were present in a rudimentary form in Aristotle's discussion of the voluntary in *Nicomachean Ethics*, III. 5. There he thinks of the voluntary as that which has its origin 'in' the agent, in contrast to acting under constraint 'to which the person contributes nothing'. ('A human being originates his own actions . . . as he

In its own way, even classical compatibilism made room, or tried to make room, for both. Its basic tenet, that freedom is dependence of action upon the will, provides a way of interpreting both features. Alternative possibilities are to be identified relatively and counter-factually, by what is possible relative to the subject's will. And the relevant dependency relation defines the relevant notion of self-determination; the self *is* the will. Hence self-determination is determination by the will.[2]

The real dispute, then and now, is not whether freedom is to be understood exclusively in terms of one feature rather than another. The dispute is over the interpretation of and relations among them. Compatibilism has been criticized from the start for its charac-terization of both self-determination and alternative possibilities. Typically, libertarians[3] focus their attention upon the compatibilist

---

fathers his own children', 1113b18.) But the voluntary also involves a kind of dual power: ' . . . when acting is up to us, so is not acting' (1113b6), that may bring in the element of alternative possibility. Though he had much to say about necessity, Aristotle did not have a developed notion of determinism or of freedom, perhaps because he did not face the kind of threat that seemed to be posed by modern science. (For a libertarian reading of Aristotle, see Sorabji [1983], and a reply by Fine [1981].) The medievals, on the other hand, were provoked to worry about freedom mainly by the problem of divine foreknowledge.

[2] Locke's [1690/1975] concern to provide for a notion of self-determination is explicit: ' . . . every man is put under a necessity, by his constitution as an intelligent being, to be determined in willing by his own thought and judgment what is best for him to do, else he would be under the determination of some other than himself, which is want of liberty' (II. 21. 48). It is also implicit in Hobbes: 'Liberty is the absence of all the impediments to action that are not contained in the nature and intrinsical quality of the agent' ([1649/1969] p. 67). What is 'intrinsical' to the self cannot be an impediment to the self, and action determined thereby is self-determined.

[3] To oppose compatibilism to libertarianism is somewhat terminologically inapt. We need a term that stands to 'compatibilism' as 'libertarianism' stands to 'incompatibilism'. To indicate what I take to be the basic inspiration of compatibilism, the idea that freedom can be characterized in terms of (potential) changes (deterministic or not) in natural objects, I would propose 'naturalism'—except that term is already used in so many different senses. Libertarians might well protest that this proposal insinuates that there is something *un*natural about libertarian freedom. Then again, before the term became established usage, 'naturalists' might have protested that 'libertarianism' insinuates that its detractors do not believe in liberty.

treatment of the latter, although their criticisms bear upon the other feature as well. On the other hand, while contemporary versions of compatibilism differ from their predecessors in the details of their treatment of alternative possibilities, these treatments usually exhibit the classical structure. Their chief quarrel with older versions concerns the other element; they charge the classical accounts with inadequate conceptions of self-determination. Their own version of self-determination then dictates the details of their version of alternative possibilities. That which figures, in their account of self-determination, as the factor on which free agency depends (desire or preference in the classical versions, something more complex on later accounts) is that relative to which alternative possibilities are to be defined.

On a libertarian account, the structual relations among these elements is not as straightforward. Historically, I think, the main inspiration of libertarianism is an understanding of self-determination that is incompatible with determinism; roughly, determinism means determination by something other than the self, and hence heteronomy. This construal of autonomy thus dictates an indeterministic interpretation of alternative possibilities. Libertarianism can also *begin* with an interpretation of alternative possibilities that is incompatible with the kind of necessitation implied by determinism. In either case, the central problem for libertarianism has been that its interpretation of the features do not cohere with one another—for example, that its interpretation of alternative possibilities (freedom of indifference, if you like) threatens to preclude the satisfaction of the condition of self-determination. For if, in a given case, you might have acted otherwise, given all the facts obtaining at the time, including all the facts about yourself, there seems to be no room for the idea that *you* made the difference, for the idea of self-determination. Hence the problematic appeal to a special kind of agent-causation, that both must and cannot be a feature of the world.[4] The problem

---

[4] Kant 1788/1956, *inter alia*, was, of course, very much alive to these problems. But Kant was not an agent-causation theorist in the sense of Chisholm and Richard Taylor.

for libertarianism, then, is to provide a coherent interpretation of these conditions taken together.

I want to approach the contemporary literature by asking how different views of free agency unite the two features of freedom in a single conception. I shall begin by discussing contemporary compatibilist accounts of self-determination.

(ii) Self-determination and hierarchical motivation

Classical compatibilists conceived of free agency in terms of external impediments to the subject's 'will'. One prominent problem with classical work is its neglect of more 'internal' impediments. This neglect is due in part to the thinness of the notion of will. However much one's behaviour may depend on one's will—conceived as one's effective desire or preference—one's behaviour may still seem against, or at least independent of, one's will in a more important sense. Compulsive and addictive behaviour is hardly an instance of autonomy.

The most prevalent current response to this sort of problem is to appeal to hierarchical motivation. The most influential essay of this sort is by Harry Frankfurt (see Frankfurt [1971]). Frankfurt stresses that the problem of freedom of will is after all a problem about the *will*, whereas classical compatibilism succeeds only in discussing problems about free action. The problem of freedom of will arises only for beings of a certain motivational complexity, who are

(See Part III, below.) Agent-causation is thought of as a form of causation *in nature*. For Kant, the problem is that we are committed to an account of nature in which there is no room for agent-causation. Like the compatibilists, he thought that freedom is compatible with nature as a deterministic system of events and changes. Like libertarians, he thought that freedom cannot be characterized in terms of deterministic changes among natural objects. That is, he rejected 'naturalism' (in the sense of note 3) as a 'wretched subterfuge', giving us merely the 'freedom of a turnspit'. Hence the antinomy requires us to think of ourselves as beings who transcend nature.

That it is not determinism as such that is threatening to free agency, but something else, 'mechanism', or 'objectivism' or (in another sense) 'naturalism', see Nagel [1986] and C. Taylor [1985]; also Albritton [1985] and Watson ([1982b], Introduction). I regret that I haven't time to explore this question further here.

capable of caring about what desires move them to action. Second-order volitions, as Frankfurt calls them, are desires that particular first-order desires be effective in action (be one's will, in Frankfurt's technical sense). Freedom of will, then, is freedom 'to will what [one] wants to will, or to have the will [one] wants' (ibid., p. 20). Freedom of will is exercised 'in securing the conformity of [one's] will to [one's] second-order volitions' (ibid., p. 20).

It is easy to see how the hierarchical account can be used to enrich classical compatibilism's construal of self-determination. The self is to be understood in terms of higher-order volitions; freedom is construed in terms of a dependency relation between one's first-order desires and one's higher-order volitions. Alternative possibilities are then defined relative to higher-order volitions. As before, the account of alternative possibilities falls out of the account of self-determination.

(That is not to say that the satisfaction of the latter condition entails the satisfaction of the former, but only that there is a general connection. In a case of 'over-determination' of one's first-order desire, both by one's higher-order volition and by, say, a severe compulsion or phobia, the connection will not hold. That desire (to take the drugs) would be one's will even if one had a contrary higher-order volition, and even if it were not compulsive. In this kind of case, Frankfurt thinks the agent is morally responsible even though she could not have done otherwise. She acts freely even though she could not have been otherwise motivated.)[5]

---

[5] See Frankfurt [1969]; and also van Inwagen [1978a], and Fischer [1982], for critical discussions.

I should say Frankfurt's own attitude toward compatibilism is not exactly clear. The condition that a person be 'free either to make that desire his will or to make some other first-order desire his will instead' can be read in a way that is not captured by the dependency analysis, and he nowhere explicitly says that that analysis is sufficient as well as necessary for free will. And he also says that it is a 'vexed question' what it means to say that someone 'could have done otherwise than to constitute his will as he did' ([1971], p. 24), suggesting that the dependency analysis is not sufficient. He does say that his conception of free will 'appears to be neutral with regard to the problem of determinism' (p. 95), but it is not clear whether he means 'neutral with regard to determinism' or 'neutral with regard to the question of whether

Hierarchical accounts do a better job with compulsion and phobias than do the classical conceptions; but, as accounts of self-determination, they remain seriously defective in at least two ways.[6] The first problem concerns the source of one's higher-order volitions. For all this account tells us, the person's higher-order preference may be the result of brainwashing, or severe conditioning of the kind which is plainly incompatible with autonomy. This is of course a standard problem for compatibilism and the hierarchical version merely moves it up a level. I shall return to it later.

The second deficiency is less obvious; it concerns the notion of 'identification' that is at work in Frankfurt's theory. This notion is relevant to freedom in the following way. Something can be intelligibly seen as an impediment only if it is seen as in some way external to the self; 'externality' does not mean outside the body. The Hobbesean account can be extended this far, but it thinks of desire as delineating the bounds of the self, thereby overlooking the fact that desire can itself be seen as impedimental. This fact requires a richer conception of the self than classical compatibilism provides.

Hierarchical accounts can be understood as responses to this problem. The boundaries of the self are not coterminous with desire, but are drawn by higher-order volitions. What it is to regard a desire as external is to have a contrary higher-order volition concerning it. When one's conduct is dominated by this standpoint, one has true self-determination. But just as it is possible to regard one's appetites as external, so it is possible to regard a given higher-order volition.

determinism is compatible with free will'. For he goes on to consider 'the proposition that it is determined, ineluctably and by forces beyond their control, that certain people have free will, and others do not' (ibid., p. 25). But the question of compatibilism is not whether the possession of free will can be determined but whether its exercise can. His discussion of Chisholm, however, does seem to express an allegiance to compatibilism. In any case, it is not clear that Frankfurt is a 'conditionalist' in the sense discussed in Part II below.

[6] See Dworkin [1970], Holstrom [1977], Lehrer [1980], Neely [1974], Shatz [1986], Thalberg [1978], and D. Zimmerman [1981], [1980] for various formulations and criticisms of hierarchical accounts.

This may not be thought to be a problem, because a higher-order volition can be so regarded, it might be said, only from the standpoint of a yet higher-order volition. It is the highest-order volition that is decisive.

The problem with this response is not that there is a regressive ascent up the hierarchy, or that people are not that complex, but simply that higher-order volitions are just, after all, desires, and nothing about their level gives them any special authority with respect to externality. If they have that authority they are *given* it by something else. To have significance, the hierarchy must be grounded in something else that precludes externality.

(iii) Identification and evaluation

In the past, I believed that the notion of an evaluational standpoint could do this job; that the hierarchy must be grounded in the subject's evaluations, or conception of the good, and this notion would suffice to define the relevant (necessarily internal) standpoint. To be alienated from one's conduct or desires is to see them as unworthy or in some other way bad. What gives the appeal to higher-order volitions whatever plausibility it has is that higher-order volitions characteristically are grounded in one's conception of a worthwhile way to live. When and only when higher-order volitions are so grounded are they any more than mere desires.

To dissociate oneself from the ends and principles that constitute one's evaluational system is to disclaim or repudiate them, and any ends and principles so disclaimed (self-deception aside) cease to be constitutive of one's evaluational system. One can dissociate oneself from one set of ends or principles only from the standpoint of another such set that one does not disclaim. (Watson [this volume, Ch. 1])

The explanatorily prior notion, then, is that of evaluation, rather than higher-order desire. Only evaluations can give one *reasons* to oppose first-order desires, and when and only when agents' behaviour expresses their evaluations are they sources and 'authors' of (because they 'authorized') their behaviour.[7]

In 'Free Agency' [Chapter 1 in this volume] I wished to reject a Humean conception of desire, reason, and evaluation that was common to the hierarchical view and classical compatibilism: valuing cannot be reduced to desiring (at any level). While I still wish to maintain a non-Humean view, it now seems to me that the picture presented there is altogether too rationalistic. For one thing, it conflates valuing with judging good. Notoriously, judging good has no invariable connection with motivation, and one can fail to 'identify' with one's evaluational judgements. One can in an important sense fail to value what one judges valuable. But even if this conflation is rectified by construing valuing as caring about something because (in as much as) it is deemed to be valuable, what one values in a particular case may not be sanctioned by a more general evaluational standpoint that one would be prepared to accept. When it comes right down to it, I might fully 'embrace' a course of action I do not judge best; it may not be thought best, but is fun, or thrilling; one loves doing it, and it's too bad it's not also the best thing to do, but one goes for it without compunction. Perhaps in such a case one must see this thrilling thing as good, must value it; but, again, one needn't see it as expressing or even conforming to a general standpoint one would be prepared to defend. One may think it is after all rather

---

[7] Frankfurt identifies higher-order volitions with evaluations in [1971], p. 19, n. 6. Thus he may be seen there as accepting the evaluational account of identification and offering a particular analysis of evaluation.

In [1975], Frankfurt writes: 'As for a person's second-order volitions themselves, it is impossible for him to be a passive bystander to them . . . They *constitute* his activity—i.e. his being active rather than passive—and the question of whether or not he identifies himself with them cannot arise. It makes no sense to ask whether someone identifies himself with his identification of himself . . . ' (p. 54). My view, then, is this. If second-order volitions are just desires with the specified content, this is a false account of identification. If they are not, if they are such desires plus something else, then the hierarchical account has not after all given us an account of identification; moreover, there is no reason to think that such identification is necessarily higher-order.

mindless, or vulgar, or demeaning, but when it comes down to it, one is not (as) interested in that.

Call such cases, if you like, perverse cases. The point is that perverse cases are plainly neither cases of compulsion nor weakness of will.[8] There is no estrangement here. One's will is fully behind what one does.[9] Of course, a person's evaluational system might be defined just in terms of what that person does, without regret, when it comes right down to it, but that would be to give up on the explanation of identification by evaluation. Just as the hierarchical account ends up presupposing rather than explaining the notion of identification, evaluation would now do no explanatory work.

We are left with a rather elusive notion of identification and thereby an elusive notion of self-determination.[10] The picture of identification as some kind of brute self-assertion seems totally unsatisfactory, but I have no idea what an illuminating account might be.[11]

---

[8] I recognized this point in Watson [1977] [Ch. 2, this volume], p. 327, n. 3, but I failed to face up to the difficulties it creates for the dichotomy implicit in 'Free Agency' [Ch. 1, this volume]: that either one's actions express one's evaluational system or they do not express the 'self'.

[9] A further difficulty that must be faced concerns the interpretation of intentional action in cases of compulsion and weakness of will. To ensure that such agents are correctly said to be acting contrary to their wills, one has to say that they do not 'endorse' their own actions. But to the extent to which this is so, it may be harder to see the behaviour in question as intentional at all. It begins to look like a case of automatism in which the agent's will is bypassed altogether. In what sense is it intentional? If one views intentions as Davidson sees them (see [1980d]), as evaluations, the problem is particularly acute. For then the agent will be acting in accordance with her or his judgement of what is most desirable. Combining the evaluational account of intention with the endorsement view results in a case of split mind, or will, something that looks very different from weakness of will. (One problem with Davidson's treatment of 'incontinence' in [1980c] is that it counts the perverse case as weakness of will.) See Bratman [1985] for discussion of Davidson on intention.

[10] See Piper [1985] for an interesting discussion of this issue.

[11] Perhaps a look at the notion of identification as it figures in psychoanalytic writing would be helpful; although my cursory reading of the literature suggests that the notion there is in need of much explanation as well.

(iv) Brave New World cases

Difficulties with the concept of identification are everyone's problem; they have no particular bearing on the issue of compatibilism. But the other, more conspicuous problem we noted with hierarchical accounts does seem to reveal an inherent difficulty for the entire spectrum of compatibilist theories. Again, this is the problem of the origins of one's 'will', however that is to be understood. These theories say nothing to rule out the possibility that one's evaluations, or higher-order volitions (or brute acts of identification) are merely the products of conditioning, manipulation, or brainwashing. The conditions of free agency suggested by these theories could be satisfied by citizens of the Brave New World. While these theories may have made some headway with the problems of compulsions and the like, the problems posed by these cases require a different treatment altogether. Despite significant differences among them, I shall, for the sake of brevity, call these Brave New World cases.

One question is whether further conditions can be placed on free agency that will plausibly explain Brave New World cases and also be acceptable to compatibilism. On one natural diagnosis of the problem, those further conditions clearly will not be. What is threatening in Brave New World cases, it appears, is that the citizens have no control over their 'identifications'. And they have no control over this because those are caused by conditions over which they have no control. But that is universally so if determinism is true.

Two responses to such cases can be found in the literature. One response is to locate the problem in the interpersonal features of the cases, features which are not, of course, involved in all deterministic explanations. What is crucial to the cases, it is said, is that the individuals are manipulated and coerced. The incompatibilist's mistake is to confuse causation with constraint. As A. J. Ayer puts it, 'It is not when my action has any cause at all, but only when it has a special sort of cause that it is reckoned not to be free.'[12] And here what is special is causation by human agents.

<hr />

[12] Ayer [1982], p. 21.

So we have two explanations of the cases: (a) they involve deterministic explanations of the individual's choices, decisions or values; (b) they involve causation by other agents or institutions. Explanation (b) is surely a poor one. In the case of external constraints, we don't think that human origin is relevant in itself. My freedom to dance is equally impaired whether my legs are paralysed by organic disease or shackled by human hands.[13] What needs explanation is that the Brave New World individuals are impaired in certain ways. It is a mistake to think that it matters whether this impairment has a natural or human origin. In fact, since compatibilists are committed to the possibility that completely deterministic processes are compatible with unimpaired free agency, they are committed to the irrelevance of this distinction. For conceivably any such process could be initiated by a human or super-human agent.

For some philosophers, this commitment is sufficient to refute compatibilism. For what it amounts to, they suppose, is accepting the possibility that free agents are under the control of a 'demonic neurologist'.

Consider the frequently discussed case of the demonic neurologist who directly manipulates a person's brain to induce all his desires, beliefs, and decisions. (Fischer [1982], p. 37.)

But it is crucial to ask what is being imagined here, and whether the shock to our intuitions is not induced by irrelevant features of the case. Does it matter how the 'demonic neurologist' goes about his business? We should reflect on Daniel Dennett's parody of this example:

Consider the infrequently discussed case of the eloquent philosopher who indirectly manipulates a person's brain by bombarding his ears with words of ravishing clarity and a host of persuasively presented reasons, thereby inducing all his desires, beliefs and decisions.

Or:

the delightful case of the well-informed truthful oracle who indirectly manipulates a person's brain by bombarding his ears with lucid and accurate warnings, made all the more irresistible by the citation of all

---

[13] This point is well made by Kane [1985].

the evidence in their favor and a frank account of the entire evidence-gathering operation. (Dennett [1984], p. 64.)

Dennett's point suggests the second compatibilist response. The subjects in the Brave New World cases lack freedom not because their decisions can be deterministically explained, nor because they are caused by human agents, but because their evaluational and volitional and other cognitive faculties have been impaired in certain ways. The crucial thing about their situation is that they are incapable of effectively envisaging or seeing the significance of certain alternatives, of reflecting on themselves and on the origins of their motivations, of comprehending or responding to relevant theoretical and evaluational criteria.[14]

The theme of reflective evaluation has been particularly stressed in the writings of Stuart Hampshire.[15] To some extent, we do have the capacity to stand back from our attachments and decisions, and to reconsider them in view of a fuller knowledge of their causes and influences. This is not to be pictured merely as ascending a hierarchy, of affirming the last order of desire. The reflective standpoint extends horizontally as well as vertically, to see what can be sustained in the light of fuller information. Certain information, of the kind familiar to psychoanalytic theory, or of the kind that is conspicuous to observers in Brave New World cases, debunks our ordinary understanding of ourselves, or implies certain impairments of practical thought and desire.

These points are relevant to freedom because they are relevant to self-determination and control. It is part of our idea of autonomy that the fundamental determinants of our behaviour are ones that we could endorse without delusion. Furthermore, reflective evaluation is not a

---

[14] For some relevant discussion, see Dworkin [1976], Gert and Duggan [1979], Glover [1970], Greenspan [1978], and Young [1979, 1980].

[15] 'It is this power [of reflection] to which men are referring . . . when they speak of the kind of freedom which only human beings . . . enjoy, and which they can still develop and exploit' (Hampshire [1983b], p. 81). See also Hampshire [1959] and [1983c].

practically idle standpoint, but bears upon control. The exercise of this capacity can affect the determinants of one's behaviour. For the recognition that some attachment is anchored in anxiety, say, can alter its motivational efficacy and affect the character of one's identifications.

The compatibilists' thesis, then, is that there is no reason to suppose that the presence of delusion or impairment of this sort is implied by deterministic explanations as such. On this point they seem to be right. They also hold of course that deterministic explanations entail nothing else that conflicts with freedom. Whether they are right about this is the topic of Part II.

II Alternative possibilities

. . . judge then what a pretty kind of liberty it is which is maintained by T. H., such a liberty as is in little children before they have the use of reason, before they can consult or deliberate of any thing. Is this not a childish liberty; and such a liberty as is in brute beasts? (Bishop Bramhall [1962], p. 43.)

Hobbes, Locke, Hume, Moore, Schlick, Ayer, Stevenson, and a host of others have done what can be done, or ought ever to have been needed, to remove the confusions that can make determinism seem to frustrate freedom. (Davidson [1980b], p. 63.)

(v) The ambiguity of 'can'

The discussion of the last section was devoted to the following reasoning: our views about Brave New World cases, and the like, commit us to criteria for freedom that could not be satisfied in a deterministic world. Because it focuses upon our intuitions about particular cases, this might be called a 'bottom-up' argument for incompatibilism. Whatever the plausibility of this bottom-up argument, top-down arguments —which deduce incompatibilism from general principles presented as self-evident—have seemed to many very compelling. These arguments have centred on the interpretation of the condition of alternative possibilities. In this part, I shall review these arguments.

As I noted earlier, the compatibilist treatment of alternative possibilities usually is a consequence of its view of self-determination. Once autonomy is characterized in terms of the notion of the relevant notion of the self (and this is refined to meet the Brave New World cases), then alternative possibilities are defined by what is dependent on the self, that is, upon the will. The result is some kind of conditional account of 'can'.[16]

Two points about such accounts are obvious from the outset. First, compatibilism will insist that there are different notions of possibility (or different senses of 'possibility'), and that the notion picked out by a conditional account is the one relevant to free agency. The second point is that a conditional analysis cannot (without vicious regress) be applied to the relevant notion of 'will', so that in an important sense, no compatibilist account of 'free *will*' can be given. I will turn to the second point later on.

If determinism is true, then clearly, in some sense, there are no alternative possibilities. Relative to the laws of nature and antecedent conditions, it is not possible that one does anything but what one does. Compatibilists must dismiss this sense as irrelevant to free agency, and often they claim that incompatibilist arguments trade on ambiguities of 'can' or 'possible'.

Some philosophers regard these claims to ambiguity as *ad hoc*, as having no force independent of some programme to make determinism safe for human freedom. But this claim should be acknowledged from the start. Conditionalists take themselves to be giving an account of such ordinary contexts as 'S is able to walk out of the room'. Such a sentence might indeed be true even though there is no possibility that S will do so. For example, suppose S has no interest, concern, or reason to walk out of the room. In that case, it may well

---

[16] Not all compatibilists are conditionalists. See Lehrer [1966a] and [1982]: he apparently changes his mind in [1980], and Davidson [1980b].

be true that there is no possibility that S will do so, even though S is perfectly able to do so. This point does not of course support a conditional analysis, but it does permit us to ask whether the sense in which determinism entails the absence of alternative possibilities is a sense that is relevant to the interpretation of such sentences.

Furthermore, the example shows that the ordinary notion of ability is in some way relative to attributions of desire or will. It is simply a misuse of 'able to' to say: 'S is unable to leave the room because he doesn't want to (or has no reason to).' This gives some initial plausibility to the idea that attributions of abilities and powers of action are independent of attributions of 'will'.[17]

One can be drawn to a conditional analysis, not out of adherence to a programme, but because it can seem to accommodate these points. Further, the notion picked out by a conditional analysis is arguably of considerable practical and ethical interest. If to learn about what someone is able to do is to learn about what depends upon the person's will, then to learn that someone was able to do what was left undone will be to learn something about the person's actual will.

(vi) The consequence argument

Before turning to some criticisms of conditional analyses, I want to consider what seems to be the most powerful, top-down argument for incompatibilism. For it has been said that this argument is sound even if conditionalism is correct. This argument is well put by Peter van Inwagen:

If determinism is true, then our acts are the consequences of the laws of nature and events in the remote past. But it is not up to us what went on before we were born, and neither is it up to us what the laws of nature are. Therefore, the consequences of these things (including our present acts) are not up to us. (Van Inwagen [1983], p. 16.)

The Consequence Argument, as van Inwagen calls it, can be formulated in terms of 'able to' in the following way. Suppose you are

---

[17] See Chapter 1 of Hampshire [1965].

moving your left hand at the moment. If determinism is true, that your hand is moving (M) is entailed by the laws of nature (L) together with a statement of the conditions of nature prior to your existence (P). You are unable to change the past; you are unable to break the laws of nature; therefore you are unable (and never have been able) to avoid the fact that your hand is moving at the moment.

It will be convenient to set out the premises in this way.

(1) $(L \& P) \rightarrow M$
(2) If $((L \& P) \rightarrow M)$, and you can falsify 'M', then you can falsify '$(L \& P)$'
(3) You cannot falsify 'L'
(4) You cannot falsify 'P'
(5) Therefore you cannot falsify 'M'

From this it clearly follows that you are unable to refrain from moving your hand.[18]

This argument is superior to traditional top-down arguments in several respects. Traditional formulations often rely upon the identification of determinism with the doctrine that every event or state of affairs is caused by some set of antecedent events or states of affairs. But it is not obvious that causation itself involves the kind of necessitation that is required for incompatibilism. Ayer, for example, thinks of causation in terms of 'invariable factual correlation' ([1982] p. 22). The argument for incompatibilism cannot even get started with this conception of determinism, since nothing will follow from such correlations about what is possible. The same goes for formulations in terms of complete (in principle) predictability. There is no reason to think we can't (rather than simply don't) falsify invariable factual correlations or true predictions. In the present argument, this defect is remedied by the notion of a law of nature. This notion is admittedly poorly understood, but whatever else is true of laws of nature, propositions

---

[18] For recent formulations of the Consequence Argument, see Ginet [1966], [1980], and [1983], and Lamb [1977]; and also van Inwagen [1982].

which laws express (unlike mere correlations) are not accessible to human agency. The same goes for propositions about the past.

Secondly, for the same reason, the present argument seems to obviate disputes about the conditional analysis; for even on that account, it seems (or had *better* seem), you are able neither to break a law of nature nor to alter the past.

Thirdly, the present argument makes minimal assumptions about the scope of determinism. All that it requires is *physical determinism*. It should thus disturb those philosophers who are inclined to say that physical determinism has nothing to do with freedom because it has nothing to do with action.[19] Even if laws of nature have nothing to say about people moving their hands, as distinct from hands moving, the conclusion of this argument, generalized, is that we are powerless with regard to any facts involving the movements of our bodies. Surely the room left for freedom would be distressingly small.

Nonetheless, recent work has cast serious doubt on the soundness of this type of argument. It has been argued by David Lewis and others that the alleged consequences of physical determinism—that one is able to refrain from moving one's hand only if one is able either to falsify laws of nature or true propositions about the past—is susceptible to both a stronger and a weaker reading, and that, as Lewis puts it, 'it is the strong version that is incredible and the weak version that is the consequence' ([1981] p. 113).[20]

What is incredible is that you can do something that falsifies a law of nature, or that causes a law of nature to be falsified; or that you can initiate a causal sequence that alters the past. But these are not consequences of physical determinism together with the premise that you are able to refrain from M. What is a consequence is the weaker claim that you are able to do something such that, if you did it, some

---

[19] For example, Melden [1961] and Kenny [1976]; see Warnock [1963] on this point.

[20] Lewis [1981] confines his own critique to the claim about laws. In addition to Lewis, my presentation depends also on Fischer [1983] and [1986]; see also Foley [1979] and Lehrer [1980].

proposition expressed by an actual law of nature, or by a description of the actual past, would be falsified.

Let's say that an event falsifies a proposition, p, just in case, necessarily, if that event occurs, p is false.

The strong version of being able to falsify a proposition, then, is this: S is able to falsify p if and only if S is able to do something such that, if S does it, p is falsified either by S's act or by something caused by S's act.

The weak version is this: S is able to falsify p just in case S is able to do something such that if S did it, p would be falsified.

Premise (2) is obviously true on the weak version. If $p \rightarrow q$, then anything I do that is sufficient to falsify q will be sufficient to falsify p. Thus if I am able to do something that falsifies q, I am able to do something that falsifies p. But this does not entail that I have incredible causal powers. It implies only that certain (non-causal, 'backtracking') counterfactuals are true, such that in the 'world' in which I refrained from moving my hand, the set of propositions expressed by 'L & P' would be different. In *that* world, you do not violate a law of nature or affect the past.

If (2) is read in the strong way, what reason is there to suppose it true? On a conditional analysis of 'can', where the conditionals are understood causally, (2) will not be true. For suppose that if you were to will to refrain from moving your hand, your hand would, as a consequence, remain still. The fact that the movement of your hand is so dependent does not entail that L or P, or the entailment relation expressed in (1), is causally dependent on your will. The evaluation of the consequence argument is after all not independent of issues about conditionalism.

It may be urged that if (2) is not true on a conditional analysis, then so much the worse for that account. Nonetheless, on the strong reading, it can hardly be said that (2) is self-evident, as it would be on the weak reading. Therefore, there is room for the reasonable suspicion that the argument trades on these different readings. Further, some recent work offers general reasons for doubting principles of the type that (2) instantiates.[21]

[21] See Slote [1982].

(vii) Objections to the conditional analysis:
(a) Lehrer's argument

Let us turn to criticisms of the conditional analyses themselves. In the current literature, one finds two general types of criticism. The first type is, as far as I know, new. It is due to Keith Lehrer [1966a]. It seems to me unsound. The second type captures objections that have long been made against such analyses, and, though it is inconclusive, it succeeds in raising deep issues about the notion of free will. I begin with the first.

A conditional analysis has the form:

(1) If C, then S will M.

Lehrer claims that, for any such analysis, the following will be logically possible:

(2) If not-C, then S cannot M.

This claim is based on the consideration that (1) is meant to be a causal conditional, and causes are logically independent of effects. But suppose:

(3) C does not obtain.
Then: (4) S cannot M.
So (1) cannot entail: (5) S can M.

G. E. M. Anscombe agrees with Lehrer. Alvin Goldman and Donald Davidson disagree. Goldman [1970] argues that if Lehrer's reasoning were sound, no dispositional analysis of solubility could be correct. Since it is not obvious that such analyses are correct, this point is inconclusive. Davidson says:

The correct response to Lehrer is simply that if one analyses solubility by a causal conditional, one can't consistently allow that what causes dissolving is also a necessary condition of solubility, since in that case the only soluble things would be dissolved.[22]

---

[22] Davidson [1980b], note to p. 70.

That is: if one analyses abilities in this way, all abilities would be exercised. But does that tell against the analysis or against the admission of (2)? Lehrer would say the former.

Lehrer illustrates his contention in this way.

Suppose that unknown to myself, a small object has been implanted in my brain, and that when the button is pushed by a demonic being who implanted this object, I become temporarily paralyzed and unable to act. My not choosing to perform an act might cause the button to be pushed and thereby render me unable to act. ([1982], p. 44.)

One of Anscombe's examples is this: 'They will let you be burnt on your husband's funeral pyre, but only if you choose' ([1981c], p. 168). In the same vein, we might imagine a 'demonic being' who secretly locks all your doors whenever you are not trying to open them, but unlocks them the moment before you make an attempt.

These examples should arouse our suspicions about the argument. Such a demonic being (hereafter DB) may succeed in falsifying your beliefs that certain necessary conditions of your prospective conduct are present. But if DB supposes that he has thereby deluded you about your abilities to move your hand (or open the door), the illusion is his. There is no constraint here at all.

It is natural to suppose that my ability to move my hand depends upon the presence of certain neural connections, N. Clearly N may fail to obtain even when it is true that if I willed to move my hand, I would do so (intentionally). For DB might destroy or reconstitute those connections depending on what I will. Lehrer's point can be put in this way: if there are internal physical conditions necessary for the ability to move my hand (as there surely are), then it is logically possible for those conditions to be absent when the conditional statement is true. Thus the truth of this statement is not sufficient for the ability.

But I claim that no condition that is dependent in this way upon the will could be a necessary condition of the ability to move my hand. Is this *a priori* physiology? When N is absent, we may suppose, the hand is *paralysed*. To say that I am able to move my hand while

N is absent is to say that I am able to move my hand while paralysed! My claim is that the notion of paralysis cannot be understood independently of what reliably depends on the will. Although my moving my hand is causally dependent on N, where the presence of N is reliably ensured by my willing to move my hand, its absence is not a necessary condition of my ability. What is necessary for my ability is that N depend on my will.

Nor is it the case that during the time N does not obtain, I am unable to move my hand. For throughout that interval, it is true that whether or not N obtains depends upon my will. To be sure: it can't be the case that (I move my hand and N not obtain). And that is one reading of 'I can't move my hand while N does not obtain'. But that is not the 'can't' of 'is able to', as we have already seen; furthermore, on that reading, the inference to step (4) is fallacious.

My objection to the argument is not due to a question-begging assumption of the correctness of conditionalism, but to a considera-tion of examples. Suppose my ability to call up the local pizza parlour depends (as it surely does) upon the existence of certain telephone circuits (TC). Suppose that DB is a telephone technician, who has access not only to my phone lines but to my mind, and destroys TC whenever I don't choose to call, but restores it immediately when-ever I do. Surely, it might be thought, I am unable to phone the parlour while TC is destroyed. To think otherwise is to think I can make phone calls when the equipment doesn't work!

In both cases, it is clear that, rather than disabling me, DB has mere-ly added a causal complexity to my ability. (Of course, he *could* have disabled me by not restoring TC (or N), but he didn't. That fact that I am in his control in this way may be a cause for resentment—he has no business playing around with my neural or telephone connections—but if he doesn't exercise that control, he doesn't disable me.)

It is worth asking (see Dennett [1984]) what role is played by the assumption that the interfering agent is *demonic*. Imagine instead a guardian angel (GA). The phone company has deactivated TC because I haven't paid my bill. GA activates TC only when I wish to phone out.

The facts are the same: I shall succeed in calling out only if *TC* is on. But that does not show that *TC*'s being on is a necessary condition of my ability to do so. For whether or not *TC* is on is (thanks to GA) under my control. When the phone system was less automated, it was actually rather like that. Another agent, upon 'divining' my intentions from certain signals at a switchboard, thereupon activated certain switches.

As it is with ringing up the pizza parlour, so it is with moving my hand. When *C* is a necessary condition of one's doing *M*, *C* is not a necessary condition of one's being able to *M* if the presence of *C* is reliably dependent on one's will. *A fortiori* for the case where *C* is willing. That may be a causally necessary condition of one's doing *M*, but it cannot be such a condition of one's being able to *M*. As these examples show, that much is ensured by the concept of 'is able to'.

(viii) Objections to the conditional analysis:
(b) Chisholm's argument

One gets a different argument when it is supposed that I am somehow prevented from willing. This supposition is pivotal to Roderick Chisholm's argument against conditional analyses. At least since Bishop Bramhall replied to Hobbes, conditional analyses have seemed inadequate because they seem endemically incapable of giving significance to questions about freedom of the will. This point could be developed in two different ways. It could be granted that freedom of action is adequately captured by some conditional analysis, but that freedom of will is not; and what we want is not (merely) the former but (mainly) the latter. Alternatively, it could be argued that since the conditional analysis is inadequate for freedom of will, it is inadequate for freedom of action. That is the thrust of Chisholm's argument.

Chisholm argues that the proposition that *S* would have acted otherwise if *S* had willed to act otherwise does not entail that *S* could have acted otherwise unless *S* could have willed otherwise. For suppose that *S* cannot choose otherwise and that she will do otherwise only if she chooses to do otherwise. Then it follows that *S* cannot do otherwise. These suppositions are consistent with the conditional analysis; thus that analysis does not entail that S could have done otherwise (Chisholm [2003]).

As Davidson points out, this argument shows 'that the antecedent of a causal conditional that attempts to analyse "can" or "could" or "free to" must not contain, as its dominant verb, a verb of action, or any verb which makes sense of the question, Can someone do *it*?' ([1980*b*], p. 68.) It shows that what the conditionalists are after, and must be after, is a notion of ability that is exercised only in intentional action. Any conditional analysis whose antecedent employs a verb of intentional action will thus fail. By the same token, Chisholm's objection will not hold against a conditional analysis whose verb is not a verb of intentional action. For the argument can then be blocked at the premise: '*S* cannot *v*'. For that premise will either make no sense, or involve a different notion of 'cannot'.[23]

As far as it goes, this point seems right; but it does not go far enough. For the very thing that protects the analysis—namely, restricting it to intentional action—guarantees that it is too narrow to answer to many philosophers' concerns about free agency, those concerns that are naturally expressed as concerns about free will. Davidson concedes as much: 'I do not want to suggest that the nature of an agent's beliefs and desires, and the question how he acquired them, are irrelevant to questions of how free he, or his actions, are. But these questions are on a different and more sophisticated level from that of our present discussion'.[24] It is precisely these more 'sophisticated' questions that Hobbes, and some other compatibilists, dismiss when they dismiss talk of free will as 'absurd speech'.

---

[23] See Aune [1982] for a similar point. Reid anticipates Chisholm's argument: '. . . to say that what depends upon the will is in a man's power, but the will is not in his power, is to say that the end is in his power, but the means necessary to that end are not in his power, which is a contradiction' ([1788] p. 266). The mistake is to think that willing something is a *means*.

[24] This concession is in tension with the passage quoted from Davidson at the beginning of this Part. Have the 'hosts' of writers Davidson mentions really done all that is needed to deal with these more 'sophisticated' questions? Many do not even raise them.

The parties to this dispute are both partly right and partly wrong. Both parties have tended, in different ways, to conflate questions of free will and free action. Incompatibilists have done so by insisting that without free will there is no significant freedom at all. In that respect they are wrong. They are wrong to dismiss the notion picked out by conditionalists as a mere contrivance in the service of a compatibilist programme. For that notion is (one of) *our* notion(s). Clinging to this insight, conditionalists have rightly resisted the attempted collapse. But conditionalists have gone wrong in their characteristic claim that that notion is the only significant one, and that libertarian worries about free will can be dismissed as confusions. The incompatibilists should concede this notion, for one can be a libertarian about free will and a conditionalist about ability to act. For their part, conditionalists should concede, as Davidson has, that there are questions about free agency that cannot be put in these terms.

What these questions are is the topic of Part III.

III Libertarianism and free will

(ix) 'Free will'?

Both in ordinary language and in current philosophical literature, the use of the phrase 'free will' is a curious one. In common parlance, the phrase is either encumbered with a lot of nonsense learned at Sunday School, or irrelevant to traditional concerns. As an example of the former, I happened to share a table some time ago with a high-ranking official of the Orange County (California) Republican Party. During the conversation, his companion bemoaned her unsuccessful campaign to get the City Council of Santa Ana to take action to ameliorate the plight of homeless people in that city. With a sense of bewilderment and exasperation, she noted that the City had been willing to fund shelters for dogs and cats while it did nothing for people. The party official was untroubled. 'The difference', he said, 'is that people have free will'. If free will can explain and justify the myriad plagues and miseries that mark human history, thereby justifying God's ways to mortals, surely it can handle a bit of destitution in Santa Ana, California.

Ordinary language has more innocent usages. We speak of 'acting of one's own free will' in connection with coercion. If someone shows up for induction into the army only to avoid a jail term, that is a paradigm instance of not acting of one's own free will. But this usage has little if any connection with traditional concerns for free will. What happens in these paradigm cases is not that the person has no options, but that certain options are made prohibitively expensive. But we do not speak of restrictions on free will when such costs are consequences of natural, rather than human, forces. It is doubtful that the source of the cost should matter to the question of free will. So it is doubtful that one can find in these ordinary locutions a serious use for the phrase 'free will'.[25]

Turning to the current philosophical literature, one might expect the phrase to spring most readily to the lips of libertarian philosophers, as it once did. But, currently, the most common practice, by both parties, is either to ignore the term or to define it in terms of ability (or possibility) to act, as though the word 'will' had no particular importance. (See van Inwagen [1982] and [1983], and Richard Taylor: 'The question whether men have "free will" is really only the question whether men ever act freely. No special concept of the will is in any way needed to understand that question' ([1960] p. 264).)

This usage is curious, I say, because, despite it, no one thinks that being unable to travel to distant galaxies is a restriction on free will; or conversely, that the greater abilities of Superman in these respects correspond to a greater freedom of will. This anomaly may be explained in part by the preoccupation of much of this literature with determinism. If determinism is incompatible with alternative possibilities generally, there may seem to be little reason to discuss the

---

[25] But see Slote [1980] and Frankfurt [1973] on coercion.

specific case of alternatives for the will. Perhaps, as well, there is a prevalent distrust of talk about the will at all.

Is there, then, a distinctive question about free will? And what is it? Notoriously, Hobbes [1969] denied that there is any such question. Along with many compatibilists, I had supposed that what made Hobbes's answer notorious was the superficiality of his conception of impediments; for, again, that conception overlooked the fact that one can find one's own desires and emotions as impediments. It is easy to suppose that this neglect explains why a Hobbesean approach can account at most for freedom of action, and not for freedom of will; for it is easy to think that free will can be explained in terms of the absence of these more 'internal' obstacles. But this thought is mistaken in an important way.[26]

To see this, recall the point in Part I that this Hobbesean superficiality can also be construed as a superficiality about the will. One could satisfy the Hobbesean criteria and still be acting contrary to one's will. Hence, we concluded, we should not think of the will in terms of appetite and desire. It follows, however, that the recognition of such 'internal' impediments as cruder compatibilism overlooked will not help us formulate a distinctive question of free will. For, however internal, these obstacles are still obstacles in virtue of their (potentially) getting in the way of *implementing* one's will. Therefore, however internal in other respects, they are still external to the will. They are impediments in virtue of their limitations on the capacity to effect one's will. In this respect, their status is no different from boulders and chains. They are not themselves constraints on *willing*; they affect your ability to get what you will, but not your willing of it. It is only this last point that raises a distinctive question about free will.

The question about free will is a question, as Bramhall put it, about 'the elective power of the rational will' ([1962], p. 42); that is, the power of rational beings to will one way rather than another, as

---

[26] It was Rogers Albritton's [1985] paper that first made me see this point.

alternatives present themselves.[27] No subtle discussion of internal obstacles will help us with this question (though it will help us to understand the relevant notion of the will). Even Frankfurt's discussion, which is unusual among compatibilist writing in its insistence on distinguishing freedom of action from freedom of will, is unhelpful here. For if we set aside his technical notion of will as effective first-order desire (which is after all thoroughly Hobbesean), and think of the will as one's higher-order motivations, then we can say that Frankfurt gives us a better understanding than Hobbes of the *efficacy* of will, but not of its freedom.

At the end of Part II, I suggested that it is a mistake for the incompatibilists to deny that the conditionalists succeed in identifying a notion that is important in our practice, and does not depend upon this distinct notion of freedom. That denial detracts attention from what to them must be the most important issue: what this power is, and whether we have it. They can grant a distinct notion of freedom of action and still insist that that is not all the freedom we want, or the most important freedom. Freedom of action is important enough, they may grant, but they want to tie what is special about human beings to this further power; that is what underwrites the sense of human dignity. (Note Bramhall's umbrage at the Hobbesean picture in the passage quoted at the beginning of this part; that picture is not merely wrong but demeaning.)

It is far from obvious what this further power is. What is obvious, however, is that, whatever it is, it is not something which can be captured by an impediment model. It is this fact about it, I suspect, that leads such an otherwise uncartesian philosopher as Rogers Albritton to endorse Descartes's view that we enjoy *perfect* freedom of will.[28] This breathtaking opinion is widespread among defenders

---

[27] Cp. Reid: 'By the liberty of a moral agent, I understand a power over the determinations of his own will' ([1788] p. 259). See Kane [1985 and 1996] for the insistence on separating questions of free will from questions of free action.

[28] This thought rests on a consideration we have already seen: that, while there are all too many obstacles to implementing or effecting our wills, there can be no obstacle

of free will, even though it is hard to understand (as Albritton himself emphasizes) how a real power in the world could be unlimited. Bernard Williams [1985] also notes that, on the traditional conception, free will is supposed to be an all or nothing affair. And Aurel Kolnai [1966–7] points out that the notion in question is not the notion of a virtue, but a presupposition of both virtue and vice (which are consequences of the exercise of this power). Unlike what we can say of self-control, we do not say: 'So-and-so is a person of surpassing freedom of will'. It is something that comes simply with consciousness and the possession of a rational will. Nor is it simply a matter of responsiveness to considerations of practical reason, since it is in virtue of free will that we can reject as well as comply with its dictates. (Hence many of the considerations we mentioned earlier in connection with Brave New World cases are not directly relevant to this notion.)

If free will means the capacity to act *ir*rationally, some will say, it is not a power so much as a liability, and it is far from clear that we should want it; it seems instead a weakness that we would be well rid of. Now, some of us do not want it, perhaps. But whether it is a source of dignity or dread (and why not both?), perhaps we have it just the same. In any case, many of us have the notion.

to willing itself. In this sense, the will cannot be blocked. (Compare O'Shaughnessy: 'the will itself cannot be paralysed', [1980] vol. 2, p. 42.) The truth behind this thought is I think this. The concept of willing is such that there is no such thing as failing to will; willing is necessarily successful. But an obstacle is such that it blocks the path to success. In the case of willing, there is no path. Rather willing is 'going for something', starting on the path. There is room for an obstacle between willing and its object, but no obstacle to willing itself.

Whether or not one thinks this to be true, trivially, because willing just is trying, it does not follow that one cannot be prevented from willing, not by having obstacles placed in the path, but by having one's will pushed as it were toward one path or another. So it might seem in cases of brainwashing or hypnotism. Albritton finds the idea of unfreedom of the will 'inconceivable', and suspects he could handle any examples to the contrary; but it is significant that he does not consider these examples. Perhaps he would say in such cases the will is not forced but bypassed (as in his examples of automatism). But I don't see why.

Thomas Reid disagrees with the purists. He finds that free will is 'impaired or lost' by vicious habits, melancholy, madness, divine intervention . . . ([1788] p. 262).

As for dignity, it is arguable that moral conceptions of a serious Kantian bent require powers which answer to this description. If we have a use for the idea that what is morally significant about people is that they are 'ends-in-themselves', where that is interpreted to mean that we have the capacity to define ('set') and pursue our own ends, then moral significance seems to require a serious notion of free will.

(x) Vagaries of libertarianism

That libertarian conceptions of free agency are obscure is news to no one.[29] Rather than simply repeating that charge here, I want instead to explore why that obscurity seems ineliminable, and to locate it within the scheme I introduced at the beginning. What is the characteristic libertarian conception of the two features of freedom we have been discussing?

To be a libertarian is to interpret the condition of alternative possibilities indeterministically. Different varieties of libertarianism result from different ways of relating this condition to that of self-determination. One variety stems from the thought that in a deterministic world there is no room for (true) *self*-determination. If the will is the product of culture and physiology, then there is no room for the idea that the agent is the author of his or her will. On this account, the interpretation of the condition of alternative possibilities (the negative condition) results from the interpretation of self-determination. The problem for this account is to make sense of the positive condition without metaphysical extravagance. This type is represented by agent-causation theories.

Another variety treats the indeterministic interpretation of alternative possibilities as independent of the feature of self-determination, and attempts to interpret the latter in metaphysically innocent ways. In the end this type of libertarianism leaves it obscure how the

---

[29] See Broad [1962], and also BonJour [1976], Goldman [1978], Nagel [1986], and Thalberg [1976]. For a partial defence of 'immanent causation', see van Inwagen [1978b].

addition of that negative condition to the metaphysically innocent condition can be the source of the special value that libertarians are after, or how both could add up [to] a positive notion of power. It appears, then, that that value and that kind of control can be secured only at the cost of metaphysical extravagance.

Let me explain this point in connection with an important essay by David Wiggins [1973]. Wiggins argues for the indeterministic interpretation of alternative possibilities on modal grounds (the Consequence Argument). Noting (as all agree) that mere indetermination is insufficient for ascriptions of free agency or responsibility, he suggests that all that is needed in addition is that our biographies unfold 'non-deterministically but intelligibly' in terms of our purposes, ends, and choices, that our behaviour be 'coherent and intelligible in the low-level terms of practical deliberation'.

> . . . maybe all we really need to imagine or conceive is a world in which (a) there is some macroscopic indeterminacy founded in microscopic indeterminacy, and (b) an appreciable number of the free actions or policies or deliberations of individual agents, although they are not even in principle hypothetico-deductively derivable from antecedent conditions, can be such as to persuade us to fit them into meaningful sequences. ([Wiggins 1973] p. 52.)

This interpretation of the positive condition seems insufficient. If the condition of self-determination—namely, on this interpretation, teleological intelligibility—is not by itself sufficient for the especially valuable form of power, then the addition of indetermination will not bring that value back in. If we know of two agents, A and B, that both their behaviour is teleologically intelligible, and so on, then it is incredible to suppose that the additional information that determinism holds in A's world but not in B's confers some special value or dignity to B's life. For it implies no special *powers* for B. In whatever way A is supposed to be powerless, B is as well, if that is the only difference between them. [For further discussion, see chapter 7, this volume.]

The only way to meet this difficulty, it would seem, is to strengthen the condition of self-determination. But no strengthening of that condition which is itself compatible with determinism will do. Hence, the structure of an adequate libertarian account of freedom must be such that the condition of self-determination itself entails indeterminism. And then the burden will be to provide an intelligible interpretation of that condition.[30]

(As for condition (a), does it matter how much macroscopic indeterminacy we have? Is our freedom in direct proportion to the extent of this indeterminacy, or is just a bit of it sufficient for all the freedom we want?)

(xi) The prerogatives of prime movers unmoved

This structural condition is satisfied by agent-causation theories. These theories are responses to the familiar dilemma: mere indetermination seems to conflict with free agency and responsibility because no one is responsible for 'random' events; and pre-determination also conflicts with these things for familiar reasons. To avoid this dilemma, Roderick Chisholm says, 'we must make somewhat far-reaching assumptions about the self or the agent' ([1982], p. 26), namely that

we have a prerogative which some would attribute only to God: each of us, when we act, is a prime mover unmoved. In doing what we do, we cause certain events to happen, and nothing—or no one—causes us to cause those events to happen. ([2003], p. 34.)

Hence: 'in one very strict sense of the term, there can be no science of man' (ibid., p. 35).

To be a free and responsible agent, I must, in acting on a purpose, determine what purpose, if any, I act on (that is, my will), and that precludes pre-determination by events and states of affairs. That, at least,

---

[30] This condition would be met by Wiggins's account if teleological intelligibility itself required indetermination. See Watson [1982b], 'Introduction'.

is the impression one gets from Chisholm's earlier work. His later work suggests a different line. The remarks quoted above—'In doing what we do, we cause certain events to happen, and nothing . . . causes us to cause those events to happen'—can be interpreted in two different ways. Agent-causation could be identified with the relation indicated in the first part of the sentence—persons causing certain events to happen—whereas a second, independent condition is expressed by the second. That would be to say that agent-causation does not itself imply indetermination.

This view has been explicitly adopted by Richard Taylor, who thinks that an irreducible notion of agent-causation is involved in the very idea of acting. Action involves a relation between an individual and an event such that the individual causes the event. To say, then, that I moved my hand is to say that I caused my hand to move. And this cannot be understood solely in terms of event-causation. For 'if I caused something to happen, this would seem to entail that it is *false* that any event, process, or state not identical with myself should be the cause of it' ([1960] p. 111).

Taylor hastens to add that more is needed for *free* action. That I moved my hand entails that the motion of my hand cannot be completely explained by antecedent events and states of affairs. But that fact is consistent with pre-determination, Taylor says, for I might be caused to move my hand—that is, caused to cause my hand to move—by antecedent circumstances and events. So while action itself implies event-indetermination, it does not imply that the action itself is undetermined. I am a free agent just in case I was not caused to cause my arm to move.

The roots of this idea of agent-causation are different from the roots of the idea first introduced. Both require a break in event-causation (or at least event-necessitation—see Anscombe [1981*a*]. But this idea derives from the thought that if *I* move my hand, no events can (completely) cause my hand to move (since I am not identical with any set of such events). The other idea comes instead from a problem about freedom and autonomy. If the former idea were sufficient for the latter, then all action would be free action, and spiders, if they are agents at all, would have to be free agents. (Might we be prime movers without being prime movers unmoved?)

Chisholm seems to run these two notions together in the following passage:

> . . . if those beliefs and desires in the particular situation in which he happened to have found himself caused him to do just what it was that we say he did do, then, since *they* caused it, he was unable to do anything other than just what it was that he did do. It makes no difference whether the cause of the deed was internal or external; if the cause was some state or event for which the man himself was not responsible, then he was not responsible for what we have been mistakenly calling his act. ([2003], p. 27.)

On Taylor's [1960] view, this passage confuses the question of whether someone acts (that is, is a cause of something) with the question of whether someone acted in freedom (that is, was caused to act). And on any view, we want to distinguish between action and free action; we want to allow for the agency of spiders. It is of course baffling how instances of agent-causation could be necessitated by events and states of affairs,[31] but that is just a special case of the general problem of how agent-causes can interact with events at all (without doing so via changes within the agent). If we could make sense of the idea of agents determining events, we could make sense of them being determined by them.

My purpose here is not to call attention to these mysteries, which are again no news to anyone, but to press the question about the relation between the two features of freedom on a libertarian account. If the condition of alternative possibilities is held to be independent of the condition of self-determination, then the account seems bound to fail. Whether agent-causation is defined in terms of the latter

---

[31] Cp. M. Zimmerman: 'Suppose that determinism is true. On such a supposition it would seem that any special type of causation that might be effected by agents would be wholly superfluous and hence it would seem that there is no reason to believe that such causation ever takes place' ([1984] p. 211).

condition alone (as Taylor [1960] does it) or in terms of the conjunction of independent conditions of indeterminacy and self-determination, the resulting view will not accommodate the intuitions that motivate the account.

Consider spiders. As we normally think of them, spiders are agents. Their legs do not merely move; they move their legs in certain ways, say, in the pursuit of a fly (see Frankfurt [1978]). However their agency is to be analysed, it is ridiculous to suppose that spiders would be free agents merely on account of satisfying the indeterminacy condition. (And for all we know, they *do* satisfy this condition.) What (else) then is lacking?

Chisholm connects agent-causation with the concept(s) of 'undertaking' or 'endeavoring'. Agent-causation occurs when an individual causally contributes to something. That occurs if the individual's undertaking to do something contributes causally to something. But it also occurs merely if an individual undertakes something. For Chisholm stipulates that 'If a person undertakes something, then he contributes causally to his undertaking that something' ([1976], p. 205), though not in this case *by* undertaking something else.

Is a spider an agent-cause? Perhaps 'it lacks the equipment necessary for undertaking or endeavoring' ([1976] p. 201, said of 'sub-atomic particles', not spiders). No doubt 'undertaking' and 'endeavoring' seem not quite the right words for spiders. But we do think of spiders as *trying* to get to a fly. And I think that where a serious notion of action is applicable, so is that of trying.[32] And the 'concept in question', Chisholm says, 'is sometimes expressed by means of the word "trying"' (ibid., p. 201).

So might spiders be agent-causes in Chisholm's sense? Perhaps we find it absurd to think that spiders causally contribute to their

---

[32] On 'trying', see O'Shaughnessy [1980], and Hornsby [1980]. O'Shaughnessy links trying with the 'will'. One of the more egregious omissions of the present essay is its lack of an examination of the notion of the will, as well as of the general topic of teleological explanation. [See Chapter 5, this volume, for an attempt to rectify the former omission.]

'tryings'. But even if they did, that is not sufficient for free agency. Free agency requires, for Chisholm, that the agent be 'free to undertake' what the agent does undertake, and this means that 'there are no sufficient causal conditions' for undertaking something or not (ibid., p. 202). Perhaps spiders fail (ever) to meet this condition.

I am quite prepared to entertain the thought that we might be wrong about spiders, to entertain the thought that spiders are free agents. After all, quite generally our ordinary conceptions of the other animals are ill-founded. And I don't know whether spiders meet this condition or not. (I doubt whether even entomologists know this.) But what I am not prepared to entertain is the claim that indetermination would suffice to make the exercise of such agency as spiders enjoy free agency. If the difference between an agent-cause in the narrower (Taylorean) sense, and a prime mover unmoved is that the latter's movings are undetermined, then this difference will not itself be a difference in the agents' powers. This is the old problem again.

Ordinarily we think that free agency (and 'having a choice') requires a psychological complexity of the kind that the spider is not presumed to possess. What is required is at least, in Bramhall's [1962] phrase, the 'rational will'. While the spider moves its limbs about here and there, and guides those movements, it has no choice whether and whither to guide them. Having such a choice requires being a chooser, and that requires certain cognitive capacities, at a minimum, the capacity to entertain, and be presented with, alternatives for selection. This much is neutral with respect to libertarianism. The distinctively libertarian thought is that I must have the power to determine which, among the alternatives I have the capacity to entertain, I shall will (undertake, try for, . . .). All that is clear about this power is that it cannot be secured merely by the indeterminist interpretation of alternative possibilities.

Libertarianism *is* obscure. But as Wiggins [1973] suggests, that charge may be as much a charge against some central features of our self-conception as it is a charge against the philosophies that go by this name.

(xii) Conclusion

Although the terms of the debate have been considerably sharpened, it is fair to say that the basic issue between Hobbes and Bramhall still lives. That is discouraging, but not altogether surprising. The issue intersects with issues about the mind, about explanation, about naturalism, about morality; and controversy in these areas is controversy about a proper and defensible self-image. It is hard to say where this argument will go, or even where it should go. Yet through the dust of three centuries of debate, we can see at least one point clearly: if no amount or kind of cognitive and volitional capacity and complexity that could obtain in a deterministic world will suffice for free agency, then simply adding the requirement of indetermination will not suffice either. That means that either naturalism is inadequate, free agency (or some significant part of our conception of free agency) is illusory, or compatibilism is true. Take your pick (if you can).[33]

[33] I am indebted to Lorraine Rapp for bibliographical assistance in the preparation of this paper. I am also very grateful, in different ways, to Gerry Santas, and to Sara Lundquist, for providing me with some freedom of opportunity (though not freedom of will) to write this paper.

7 Soft Libertarianism and Hard Compatibilism

Both compatibilism and its denial are in some respects unappealing; that's why the issue remains a classical philosophical problem. The cost of incompatibilism seems to be a choice between skepticism or a metaphysically and morally problematic (if not incoherent) picture of free agency. But compatibilists have their own troubles explaining how human beings can be products of nature and at the same time authors of their actions, how freedom as they see it can amount to anything more than what Kant contemptuously called the "freedom of the turnspit."[1]

Some recent libertarian and compatibilist sympathizers have tried to minimize the costs of their respective commitments by qualifying them in certain ways.[2] In this paper, I will speak against some of these attempts. In the first part of the paper, I criticize the most well developed version of what I will call "soft libertarianism," Robert Kane's *The Significance of Free Will*.[3] Then I take up the corresponding temptation to qualify compatibilism. I conclude by endorsing

This paper began as a contribution to a symposium on Robert Kane's *The Significance of Free Will* at the University of Arkansas in September 1997. I profited from discussion with the participants on that occasion, especially Kane.

[1] Immanuel Kant, *Critique of Practical Reason*, translated by Lewis White Beck, The Liberal Arts Press (1956), pp. 100–1.

[2] We lack a term that stands to "compatibilism" as "libertarianism" stands to "incompatibilism," so this opposition is admittedly awkward.

[3] Oxford University Press (New York, 1996). Parenthetical page references to Kane in the text will be to this work.

Harry Frankfurt's uncompromising refusal to soften his position in the face of the familiar objections. Soft compatibilism,[4] I argue, is not a real alternative.

I. Soft Libertarianism[5]

The burdens of libertarianism are three-fold. First, it must explain why there can be no free will in a deterministic world. This is the negative, incompatibilist part of the project. Second, it must make it reasonable to believe that we live in an indeterministic world. Third, in contrast to skeptical incompatibilists, it must explain how free will and responsibility can be realized in such a world.[6] Here I will be concerned exclusively with some general reasons for thinking that libertarianism cannot successfully carry out this third part of the project.

This project presumes a point that is conceded by everyone, namely, that free agency cannot be understood solely in terms of the negative condition of indetermination or indeterminacy. The question is what more is needed.

Libertarians have answered this question in two ways. The first answer is that free agency involves the exercise of a distinct and *sui generis* form of causality. I call this "hard" libertarianism because it is widely thought to have unpalatable philosophical and empirical

---

[4] I borrow the term from Kane, *The Significance of Free Will*, pp. 67 ff. This usage obviously adapts William James' distinction between *hard and soft determinism*, roughly, between incompatibilists and compatibilists. Just as "soft determinists" say, "Don't worry. Determinism is not threatening to freedom, correctly qualified," so soft libertarians and soft compatibilists soften what is taken to be the harsher implications of their views.

Alfred R. Mele uses the term "soft libertarianism" in a different sense in "Soft Libertarianism and Frankfurt-Style Scenarios," in *Philosophical Topics* 24(2) (1996).

[5] The central points of this section are familiar, and Kane in particular addresses versions of this point in his own way. But at the end of the day, after a close reading of the book, I fail to see how those responses add up to an effective rejoinder. So I want to try to make the case once again, as forcefully as I can, in the hope that, if nothing else, the issues will be clearer.   [6] This is what Kane calls the "intelligibility issue."

implications. The second (softer) answer tries to articulate a meta-physically less demanding position.

It will be useful to recall an old objection to libertarianism. The objection is by now discredited, but it opens up an instructive dialectic. No one can be a free and responsible agent with respect to undetermined events or indeterministic processes, the argument goes, because such events would be merely random or accidental—hence, under no one's control. This accusation is meant to show that libertarian freedom is unintelligible; the incompatibilist half of the doctrine rules out the possibility of a positive account. It follows that incompatibilism leads to skepticism.

The problem with this complaint, to begin with, is that it would prove more than most compatibilists would want to accept; free agency would not only be compatible with causal determination, but would require it. More importantly, its central claim is false or anyway question-begging. To assume that undetermined events are random or accidental is to preclude libertarian agency from the start. To say these things is to say that the event is inexplicable or contrary to human purposes or control. But indetermination doesn't imply any of these things. It implies only that what I do is not explained by reference to deterministic laws and antecedent conditions. That leaves open the possibility of other sorts of explanation, for example, the sort of account that is after all characteristic of human behavior, explanation by reasons, intentions and purposes. So indeterministic behavior need be neither inexplicable nor "accidental" in any ordinary sense.

Although the objection fails as it stands, it brings out something helpful to the discussion.[7] It shows that the conditions needed beyond indeterminacy must work specifically by revealing how the indeterministic behavior is not "random" but can be attributable to the agent as its author. The objection can be construed as a challenge.

---

[7] David Wiggins makes this point in "Towards a Reasonable Libertarianism," repr. in Watson 2003, p. 112.

The reply, that not all forms of explanation are deterministic, indicates the space in which the challenge might be met.

In view of the foregoing exchange, then, we can assume the following as a part of the framework for current discussion: *By itself, the assumption of indeterminacy in choice or behavior neither entails nor conflicts with ascriptions of free will and responsibility.*

Libertarianism is committed, then, to identifying certain conditions, C, which, in addition to libertarianism, must obtain if that behavior is to be attributed to the subject as a free and responsible agent. Attempts to carry out this commitment are of two kinds, depending on how they suppose the assumption of indeterminacy (I) to be related to the further conditions (C). On one version of the theory, free agency will be explained in terms of a conjunction of conditions, $I, C_1 \ldots, C_n$, I being the incompatibilist conjunct. What is crucial here is that I is independent of the other conditions. In contrast, the second version of libertarianism sees I not as an independent condition, but as implicated in some way in one or more of the other conditions.

In "Towards a Reasonable Libertarianism," David Wiggins sketches a conjunctive view of this kind. In addition to indeterminacy, Wiggins suggests, what must obtain in the libertarian world are

patterns that are coherent and intelligible in the low level terms of practical deliberation, even if they are not amenable to the kind of generalisation or necessity that is the stuff of rigorous theory. On this conception, [a free agent's] possible peculiarity as a natural thing among things in nature is simply that his biography unfolds not only non-deterministically but also intelligibly; non-deterministically in that personality and character are never something complete and need not be the deterministic origin of action; intelligibly in that each new action or episode constitutes a comprehensible phase in the unfolding of character, a further specification of what the man has by now *become* (ibid., p. 114).

What more is needed, in short, is the condition of practical intelligibility. This is a conjunctive view, I say, if practical intelligibility does not by itself imply indeterminacy. That seems to be Wiggins's own view.[8]

Non-conjunctive versions of libertarianism can be illustrated by so-called agent-causation theories. The indeterministic processes in which free agency is involved are not "random" if they result from, or are exercises of, a distinctive form of causation by the agent. These processes are uniquely attributable to the agent as their source. This form of causation cannot in principle exist in a deterministic world. Hence, if the negative condition of indeterminacy is not met, necessarily, the positive condition of agent-causation is not met.[9]

Non-conjunctive views like agent-causation are generally thought to be metaphysically problematic. I have nothing to add to this discussion here. For my purposes, the important point is that many libertarians (among them Wiggins and Kane) have felt the force of that charge. This accounts for the appeal of conjunctive views like Wiggins's. In addition to indeterminacy, which is in any case in harmony with current scientific understanding, the positive conditions are no more problematic than the ordinary framework of intentional explanation in which we conduct our lives and define what's important in human life. We need not be panicked by our concern for freedom into metaphysical extravagance.

This response is developed more recently by Robert Kane, who makes it a constraint on any satisfactory theory of freedom that the theory satisfy the "Free Agency Principle." This principle is laid down precisely to avoid the intelligibility problem. The principle denies any "appeal to categories or kinds of entities . . . that are *not also needed by non-libertarian (compatibilist or determinist) accounts of free agency* . . . " (116). By definition, libertarians posit

---

[8] Some might disagree, arguing that practical intelligibility itself precludes determinism. I discuss this briefly in the introductory essay to *Free Will*, ed. Gary Watson (Oxford: Oxford University Press, 1982).

[9] Richard Taylor is an exception here; see his *Action and Purpose* (Prentice Hall, 1960).

indeterminacy, but

these undetermined events or processes will not otherwise be of categories or ontological kinds that do not also play roles in non-libertarian accounts of free agency (such as choices, decisions, efforts, practical judgments, and the like)—the difference being that in nonlibertarian theories, these events or processes need not be undetermined (116).

I shall call any libertarian view that submits to the strictures of the Free Agency Principle *soft libertarianism*. In contrast, "hard" libertarians admit or insist that the metaphysical implications of free agency are far-reaching.

My thesis is that libertarianism cannot be so easily domesticated.[10] I want to say about libertarianism something parallel to what James Joyce said somewhere about Christianity. If you are going to be a Christian at all, he said, you should go all the way to Catholicism. Nothing in between makes sense. Similarly, if you are going to be a libertarian, you are going to have to pay the costs. It is hard libertarianism or nothing.

Soft libertarianism is vulnerable to an objection common to all conjunctive views. In contrast to the hard version, the problem is not that it sets out conditions that are empty, incoherent, or unintelligible; the problem is that soft libertarian views cannot give a proper account of the *significance* of indeterminacy.

Any version of soft libertarianism will analyze free agency in terms of a conjunction of indeterminacy and some further conditions, C, which could obtain in a deterministic world. Hence, compatibilists can consistently accept C as a sufficient account of free agency. Let us call a world that meets these further conditions a *C-world*. The compatibilist says: any C-world includes free agency. Incompatibilists say: only C-worlds that are also indeterministic in

[10] As I said earlier, the considerations I develop below are familiar from the history of the subject. Here I draw upon some of my own earlier presentations, including "Free Action and Free Will," *Mind*, 1987 [Ch. 6, this volume]. See more recently, Richard Double, *The Non-Reality of Free Will* (Oxford: Oxford University Press, 1991), p. 58.

certain ways include free agency. What is incredible, I submit, is that the mere addition of indeterminacy to the C-world could have the significance libertarians attribute to it.

The basic incompatibilist intuition is something like this: determinism is inconsistent with the existence of certain human capacities and powers, say autonomy or self-determination, that are central to the meaning and dignity of human life. The knowledge that something is a C-world is not enough to determine whether or not the individuals in this world enjoy this possibility or are doomed to utter impotence and emptiness. What is incredible is to suppose that these values are secured by the mere truth that some of the relevant events and processes are indeterminate. If C is not enough to ground those values, introducing the negative condition of indeterminacy will not do it either.

Let's return to Wiggins's soft libertarian view for illustration. If having a practically intelligible life is not enough for autonomy in a deterministic world, how can indeterminacy restore that vaunted power? Adding the fact that my conduct is *not* determined by antecedent conditions does not transform practical intelligibility into self-determination or autonomy. Therefore, the difference between two agents, one of whom meets condition C only, and the other of whom meets C + I, is not a difference between someone who lacks and someone who has that special capacity; mere indeterminacy could not make that kind of difference.

To put it slightly differently, incompatibilism arises from a worry about the *sources* of human action. On a conjunctive view, those who meet C-conditions might still fail altogether to be sources of their own conduct or wills. But adding to C the negative fact that our conduct lacks certain sources (indeterminacy) cannot make one any more of a source than one would be in a mere C-world.

This conclusion is quite general. The relative metaphysical modesty of soft libertarianism is not after all an advantage; for it cannot get what libertarians want without a kind of alchemy. Any theory that is adequate to explain the significance of indeterminacy must have a non-conjunctive structure—the absence of indeterminacy must imply that something else will be missing in the biographies of individuals. This condition is met, for example, by classical agent-causation theories. The negative requirement that the will not be causally necessitated by antecedent events is dictated, on those views, by the positive requirement that the will be determined by the agent.

Hence, this argument is not against libertarianism as such. The standard objection to what I am calling hard libertarianism is that it appeals to empty or incoherent or irredeemably obscure conditions. In contrast, soft libertarian conditions might well be perfectly clear and satisfiable. The problem is that the satisfaction of the conditions that it lays down do not add up to a distinctively libertarian free agency. From the perspective of hard libertarianism, they do not add up to true freedom at all; from a compatibilist perspective, if they add up to free agency at all, the indeterminacy condition is redundant. If the positive conditions are such that they might obtain in a deterministic world, then they will be too weak to answer to the incompatibilist demands of the doctrine.

Let me press this objection further in connection with Kane's more complex analysis. Here I can only highlight the features of the view that are most relevant to the issue. On Kane's account, the indeterminacy in free will must be located in the relation between desire and choice, or reason and intention (27). But again, as everyone admits, mere indeterminacy is not enough. Free agency requires what Kane calls 'ultimate responsibility'. He makes a good case for saying that it is this notion that underlies incompatibilism. It is this requirement that no compatibilist treatment of alternative possibilities can satisfy. It is therefore important to our assessment of Kane's version of libertarianism to see how it is met in his account.

His account of ultimate responsibility depends on a notion of personal responsibility, which he defines in this way:

An agent is *personally responsible* for an occurrence of an event or process E just in case the agent voluntarily did or omitted to do something (call this action or omission A); the agent could have avoided voluntarily Aing; and the agent's Aing either causally contributed to or was E's occurrence.

He then characterizes ultimate responsibility as follows:

An agent is *ultimately responsible* for the occurrence of E only if (R) the agent is personally responsible for E's occurrence, and (U) for any X, if X is a sufficient cause or ground or explanation of A, the agent is personally responsible for X.[11]

Note several points. First, Kane emphasizes that clause R is to be interpreted in a way that doesn't require incompatibilism; agents can be personally responsible for events in a deterministic world. Note also that this is only a partial characterization of UR by way of a necessary condition. It says roughly that you are ultimately responsible for something only if it has no sufficient causes for which you are not personally responsible.[12]

From UR (and the assumption that there can be no infinite regress of voluntary actions), Kane infers that some of the voluntary actions for which a free agent is personally responsible must be undetermined. "Let us call these," he stipulates, "self-forming actions" (74; he eventually identifies this activity with *willing*). This stipulation reflects a central theme of the book: that, in virtue of such undetermined actions, we determine and thereby bear responsibility for what kind of people we become (for our characters).[13]

While Kane might by this stipulation be restricting the term 'self-forming actions' to indeterminate or undetermined actions, the Free Agency Principle requires that these self-forming activities be in

[11] To make it clearer to myself, I deviate slightly from Kane's own formulation of UR on p. 35. I hope I do not thereby distort his meaning.

[12] One reason why it is not sufficient is that the characterization of personal responsibility is much too weak for moral responsibility, as Kane acknowledges (180). For example, it ignores questions of foreseeability. If someone voluntarily flipped a light switch that initiated a complicated causal chain culminating in an explosion in a distant city, she would be personally responsible on Kane's account, but we would never hold her responsible unless she knew what she was doing, or ought to have known. Perhaps Kane thinks of himself as setting out all the non-normative criteria for responsibility. But I suggest below that there are non-normative issues as well: the conditions are insufficient in virtue of their failure to guarantee uniqueness.

[13] This stipulation is somewhat presumptuous at this point of the argument. UR does *not* entail that any of the actions for which we are responsible have this self-forming property. I'll return to the issue of responsibility for character below.

themselves compatible with determinism. What is undetermined here (willing this or that) is part of the C-world. (In his gloss on the Free Agency Principle, Kane explicitly says that choices, acts of will and the like "might be undetermined, but we are not to assume that they cannot be determined in principle," 118.) Free agency, on this account, consists in a conjunction of indeterminacy plus activity of a kind that might exist in a deterministic world. To put it another way, on Kane's account, ultimate responsibility is non-ultimate responsibility plus indeterminacy.

Consider two worlds, both of which are full of folks who are personally responsible for a great deal of what they do. The lives of those in the first world will nonetheless be altogether empty of dignity, autonomy, creativity, objective value, praise and blameworthiness, in short *true* responsibility, whereas the lives of those in the second world will have all of these things—not because of any differences at all in the difficulty or nature of their struggles and opportunities, or the content of their choices and aspirations, or the character of their achievements and failures, but solely because the second world is subject to indeterminacy. This difference alone invests human beings in the second world with what Kane calls the "power . . . to be ultimate creators . . . of their own ends and purposes" (32). Then and only then can they possess "a worth for their existence that transcends transitory satisfactions" (101).

This view seems to me to be open to something very close to the original objection. That objection was indeed mistaken to claim that indeterminacy implied randomness in a sense that precludes responsibility and control. But a correct point underlies this worry: that if meeting conditions C (practical intelligibility, the possession of full plural voluntary control over one's willings, or whatever else is supposed to be constitutive of free agency besides indeterminacy) is not enough to give creatures the power to be "ultimate creators," merely adding indeterminacy will not suffice. The mere absence of causation (which is consistent with randomness) could not transform a compatibilist personal responsibility into something that has this significance.

Again, unlike the original objection, this argument is directed only against conjunctive views. Hard libertarians can themselves press this point against their cousins. For them, it is not indeterminacy by itself that makes the difference: indeterminacy is a corollary of the powers in which free agency consists.

II. Ultimacy and Uniqueness

I want now to take up, briefly, another puzzling feature of Kane's treatment of ultimate responsibility: namely, that as it stands, it doesn't guarantee uniqueness. This is troubling for a number of reasons.

To illustrate, consider Kane's example of the woman who is in conflict about whether to stop to help a victim of assault or to push on to a business meeting that's very important to her. Suppose she decides to help, and that this decision meets the conditions for personal responsibility and is moreover undetermined. Her decision is therefore a self-forming activity for which she is ultimately responsible. But suppose her mother's moral teachings about the importance of altruism made a "causal contribution" to the daughter's decision. They were an input that increased the probability that the daughter would choose altruistically; they inclined without necessitating. Suppose these teachings were undetermined activities for which her mother was ultimately responsible. Then the mother's teachings satisfy UR. On this account, the mother is ultimately responsible for the daughter's decision for the same reason the daughter is.

In general, any agent whose undetermined voluntary actions make a causal contribution to an event satisfies this condition for ultimate responsibility. Typically, these will be numerous. Perhaps this failure to guarantee uniqueness is one reason why Kane thinks of UR as only a necessary condition. But it is an important gap in the theory.

To be sure, it is not implausible to suppose that the mother shares some responsibility for her daughter's choice. Indeed, responsibility here might be widely distributed throughout the moral culture. But I don't think this gives Kane what he wants: the sense in which the daughter is not only directly responsible for the decision, but responsible in a primary way that no one else could be. Whether or not the concept of ultimacy itself implies uniqueness, Kane seems to require it. He speaks of "a personal responsibility that is also ultimate in a strong sense: the agent and no one and nothing else has ultimate responsibility for the resolution of the conflict in his or her will" (180).

To be sure, only the daughter is *directly* responsible for her decision. But on Kane's account, ultimacy is not always direct. This point plays a very large role in his account of responsibility for character. His reply, for example, to the example of Luther's "I can do no other" is to say that Luther is ultimately responsible for his stand, even if his character leaves no alternatives, because he is ultimately responsible for his character-forming acts. Perhaps so. However, this reply places the character-forming acts of the young Luther on the par with the moral training by his elders. We may suppose that all of these are voluntary acts that influence the voluntary acts of the mature Luther.

It is true that we bear some responsibility for the next generation. The difficulty is that Luther is responsible for his mature acts, and his acts in character, in a way that his elders never could be. As it stands, Kane's theory cannot account for this. One wonders whether any soft libertarian account of ultimate responsibility could do so.

This points to a general limitation of the common "tracing" strategy to explain responsibility for acts done in character. The best that can be done on such a view will be to appeal to an influence on an agent's character that she shared to some degree with many other people. Even if a person's vicious character can be traced in part to an earlier pattern of heedless activity, she will then be blameworthy for a kind of negligence or recklessness, a charge that applies equally perhaps to her parents.[14] The tracing strategy is simply too weak to yield all we want.

[14] I make this point in "Responsibility and the Limits of Evil," in F. Schoeman (ed.), *Responsibility, Character, and the Emotions* (Cambridge: Cambridge University Press, 1987) [Ch. 8, this volume].

III. Hard Compatibilism

Because of their disagreement about what Kane calls ultimate responsibility, compatibilists believe, whereas incompatibilists deny, that free agency can emerge by causal necessitation from conditions of non-responsibility. For the compatibilist, the constitutive conditions of free agency do not conceptually depend on their origins. In this sense, free and responsible agency is not an historical notion. Consequently, compatibilism is committed to the conceptual possibility that free and responsible agents, and free and responsible exercises of their agency, are products of super-powerful designers. For consider any compatibilist account of the conditions of free agency, C. It is possible for C to obtain in a causally deterministic world. If that is possible, then it is possible that a super-powerful being intentionally creates a C-world, by bringing about the relevant antecedent conditions in accordance with the relevant laws. This possibility follows from the general point that the conditions of responsibility do not necessarily depend upon their causal origins.

From the incompatibilist point of view, this implication is of course a *reductio ad absurdum*. It is a premise in what I call the *robot argument*. If we define a robot as a creature whose existence and detailed "program" were brought about by design, then the foregoing reasoning commits compatibilists to the possibility that free agents are robots. And surely that is absurd, incompatibilists say. For being completely the product of design in this way is surely a responsibility-undermining factor.[15]

Some writers seem to be tempted to accommodate this complaint by acknowledging a distinction between determination by natural causes and purposeful determination. They want to be compatibilists about the former but not about the latter. Following Kane, let's call them "soft compatibilists." Kane rightly complains that this distinction seems arbitrary. For it is hard to see what differences there could be

---

[15] In one form or another, this reasoning is common. The "nefarious neurosurgeon" objection is a familiar instance.

between the natural and purposeful forms of determination that would be relevant to freedom and control. The argument of the first section reinforces this conclusion. If purposeful determination of one's actions by another agent undermines freedom, so does determination by the natural world. Soft compatibilism isn't really a viable option.

We can put this in the form of a dilemma. One alternative is to "bite the bullet," as Kane puts it, insisting that free agents might indeed be the products of manipulation by designers. Many would agree with Kane that this is "a hard line indeed, and one that . . . is also hard to accept" (67). Or else free agency must be admitted to be at least partly an historical concept: agents are free if and only if they meet conditions C . . . (perhaps *inter alia*) and C is not determined by the design of another agent. But this admission is the thin edge of a wedge that inevitably makes way for the full force of historical considerations. So this option is theoretically unstable. The intuition to which it responds is incompatibilist. The only good reason for thinking that purposeful determination undermines freedom is a reason for thinking the same in the natural case—that it violates something like the principle of ultimate responsibility.

In "Three Concepts of Free Action I,"[16] Don Locke uses something like the robot argument against Frankfurt's position. The idea of a "devil/neurologist" who ensures our every action and desire is clearly inconsistent, Locke urges, with

the idea that it is up to the agent, within his control, not merely what he does but also which wants, and in particular which second-order volitions, he has.[17]

In his response, Frankfurt indeed bites the bullet:

There is no paradox in the supposition that a [devil/neurologist] might create a morally free agent. It might be reasonable, to be sure, to hold the

[16] *Proceedings of the Aristotelian Society*, Supplementary Volume XLIX (1975), pp. 95–112 [reprinted in John Martin Fischer, *Moral Responsibility* (Ithaca: Cornell University Press, 1986), pp. 97–112].

[17] "Three Concepts of Free Action I," pp. 106–7 of the Fischer reprinting.

d/n too morally responsible for what his free subject does, at least insofar as he can fairly be held responsible for anticipating the subject's actions. This does not imply, however, that full moral responsibility for those actions may not also be ascribable to the subject.[18]

What determines the application of the concepts of what is up to or within the control of the agent "is not so much a matter of the causal origins of the states of affairs in question, but [one's] activity or passivity with respect to those states of affairs" (p. 54).

John Fischer also criticizes the views of Frankfurt and some others for failing to be sensitive to historical considerations.[19] Fischer thinks the problem is that Frankfurt's hierarchical view defines responsibility as a "mesh" between behavior and volitional elements and is therefore purely structural. For this reason it is inescapably vulnerable to certain counterexamples. In defining responsibility in terms of some features of a "current time-slice" of the agent, it ignores how those features come about. But some ways of bringing those about, say by manipulation of the agent's brain, or indoctrination, are plainly incompatible with attributions of responsibility. An adequate theory of responsibility, he thinks, must be historical—keeping one eye on the past, to ensure that the actual sequence does not include any responsibility-undermining causes.[20]

To take the measure of this criticism, it is crucial to distinguish two senses in which a theory of free agency and responsibility might be said to be 'historical.' In one sense, I've been stressing, any compatibilist theory must be non-historical. But another sense is

[18] "Three Concepts of Freedom," reprinted in *The Importance of What We Care About* (Cambridge: Cambridge University Press, 1988), p. 54. Parenthetical page references to Frankfurt in the text are to this reprinting.

[19] The following pages make use of some passages from my "Some Worries about Semi-Compatibilism," *Journal of Social Philosophy*, 29: 135–43.

[20] See "Responsiveness and Moral Responsibility," in F. Schoeman (ed.), *Responsibility, Character, and the Emotions* (Cambridge: Cambridge University Press, 1987), pp. 103–5; and *The Metaphysics of Free Will* (Cambridge, MA: Blackwell, 1994), pp. 208–9.

suggested by the contrast between structural (or "mesh") theories and their rivals.

First of all, I don't think Frankfurt's view is best understood as a "current time-slice" theory. Frankfurt has an *origin* or *authorship* theory, according to which conduct for which the individual is responsible originates in volitional processes of a certain character. This is an account of responsibility in terms of processes, not in terms of static structural relations. Consider Frankfurt's use of the example of the willing addict, an example that's supposed to show the possibility of responsibility without alternative possibility. "What the willing addict's action reveals about him is the same as what is revealed by the action of the non-addict [who takes the drug]. It is not the same as what the action of the unwilling addict reveals" (p. 51). On Fischer's construal of Frankfurt, what is common to the willing addict and the non-addicted drug user is something about the structure of the time-slice. I interpret the remarks differently. What is revealed is the *endorsement* of the action. And this is not merely a structural notion.[21]

If the intervention of the devil/neurologist is continuous and total, Frankfurt thinks "the subject is not a person at all. His history is utterly episodic and without inherent connectedness [like a marionette]." On the other hand, he goes on to say, if the manipulator "provides his subject with a stable character or program," then the being "may *become* morally responsible assuming he is suitably programmed" by taking responsibility for his desires:

In virtue of a person's identification of himself with one of his own second-order desires, that desire becomes a 2nd-order volition. And the person

---

[21] In "The Faintest Passion" (*Proceedings and Addresses of the American Philosophical Association* 66 (1992), pp. 5–16), Frankfurt suggests that in certain cases "identification" may consist in no more than being satisfied with (not being dissatisfied with) one's desires. This may seem to be a static, structural condition, but I suggest that satisfaction in this negative sense can amount to identification only against a background of active endorsement. I do not take Frankfurt to mean a being who merely meets this negative condition would therefore be a free and responsible agent.

thereby *takes* responsibility for the pertinent first- and 2nd order desires and for the actions to which these desires lead him.[22]

These notions have no application to a "time-slice."

Perhaps Fischer is right to think that the processes Frankfurt takes to constitute taking responsibility are insufficiently diachronic to do the job.[23] But that does not impugn Frankfurt's insistence upon ahistoricity in his response to Locke. The point here, to which all compatibilists must assent, is that the responsibility-conferring features of the actual processes are identifiable without any *further* reference to the history (the causal story) regarding the features so identified. And if it makes sense to imagine that the C-conditions might be brought about by design, it makes sense to think that the life of a free and responsible agent can be the product of design on the part of another agent.

A hard compatibilist, I conclude, is the only kind of compatibilist to be. How hard is that? It is in many ways puzzling. To think of oneself as at once a full fledged free agent and as a creature whose every move, every hope and scheme is a part of another's plan is certainly vertiginous. To begin with, the presuppositions of this thought might not be fully coherent. It presupposes, for one thing, a tight unity among what are for us disparate conceptual schemes. There would have to be a blueprint detailing the relation between the hardware, the software, and the social/normative contexts in which human beings dwell. And the designer would have to have a detailed

---

[22] "Three Concepts of Free Action," p. 53. Frankfurt speaks of taking responsibility elsewhere:

> . . . there is an important sense in which he takes responsibility for the fact of having the desire . . . when he identifies himself with it. Through his action in deciding, he is responsible for the fact that the desire has become his own in a way in which it was not unequivocally his own before ("Identification and Wholeheartedness," in *The Importance of What We Care About*, p. 170).

[23] For Fischer's most recent discussion of this point, see (with Mark Ravizza) *Responsibility and Control* (Cambridge: Cambridge University Press, 1997). I touch on this discussion in Chapter 10, this volume.

command of these schemes. All of this is not obviously intelligible. Here is one of many places where the dispute turns on deeply contested points in philosophy of mind. Furthermore, one's relation to the designer is also puzzling. Should a fully free moral agent think of herself as a moral equal of her maker? Should she in fairness share blame and credit with the designer for her merits and faults? But how can that be compatible with the free agent's view of herself as the author of her deeds?

The issues, as I say, are unsettling. But unless there are difficulties with the coherence of the idea of designing a free agent that don't apply to the very idea of a deterministic world (in which case, *both* compatibilism and incompatibilism are misconceived), the compatibilists are stuck with it. Is this a decisive reason for rejecting their philosophy?

This problem is made more difficult to think about by the rhetorical strategies of the critics of hard compatibilism. Although his discussion is generally marked by an admirable fairness to opposing points of view, Kane's exemplars of hard compatibilists—Hobbes and Skinner—seem to have been chosen for their shock value. The rhetorical strategy here is to insinuate that hard compatibilists must have a view of human beings like theirs, which is of course bad.

Moreover, speaking of the "robot argument," as I have, tends to activate all kinds of irrelevant "intuition pumps," to use Daniel Dennett's phrase. Think of what is conjured up by speaking of human beings as "robotic." In the passage quoted above, Frankfurt cautions against seeing the creature as a marionette which is directly (or indirectly) manipulated by its maker. A more appropriate image (minus the assumption of benevolence) seems to me to be that of a Leibnizian God actualizing a C-world. On this image, God doesn't manipulate or control his creatures at all. He *creates* them by instantiating a world of a specific character, a world containing free and responsible agents.[24] This picture has always provoked theological,

---

[24] Indeed, it is hard to see how a designer could determine a creature's every thought and action without designing a whole world.

moral and metaphysical controversy, but it has never as far as I know been widely taken as a *reductio*.

What seems in the abstract like a responsibility-undermining history might seem so only because it abstracts from the constitutive properties of what is supposed to emerge (by design or not) from that history. If we fill out these histories, according to compatibilism, some will be responsibility-undermining, some not. If so, that will be because the design fails to realize some of the C-conditions, not because it is deterministic.

That at any rate is the compatibilist's burden. I haven't tried to add to the arguments for thinking it can be discharged. But I do hope to have made it plausible that neither soft libertarianism nor soft compatibilism are credible options. The philosophical alternatives for those who take freedom seriously (as I think we all must, in practice) are hard.

Part III
Responsibility and Answerability

8 Responsibility and the Limits of Evil: Variations on a Strawsonian Theme

Responsibility is . . . one aspect of the identity of character and conduct. We are responsible for our conduct because that conduct is ourselves objectified in actions.

—John Dewey, *Outlines of a Critical Theory of Ethics*

There is nothing regrettable about finding oneself, in the last analysis, left with something which one cannot choose to accept or reject. What one is left with is probably just oneself, a core without which there could be no choice belonging to the person at all. Some unchosen restrictions on choice are among the conditions of its possibility.

—Thomas Nagel, *The Possibility of Altruism*

Our practices do not merely exploit our natures, they express them.

—Peter Strawson, "Freedom and Resentment"

Introduction

Regarding people as responsible agents is evidently not just a matter of belief. So regarding them means something in practice. It is shown

To Sally Haslanger and Brian Skyrms, I am grateful for discussing bits and pieces of this material with me; to Ferdinand Schoeman, for comments on an earlier draft.

in an embrace or a thank you, in an act of reprisal or obscene gesture, in a feeling of resentment or sense of obligation, in an apology or demand for an apology. To regard people as responsible agents is to be ready to treat them in certain ways.

In "Freedom and Resentment,"[1] Peter Strawson is concerned to describe these forms of treatment and their presuppositions. As his title suggests, Strawson's focus is on such attitudes and responses as gratitude and resentment, indignation, approbation, guilt, shame, (some kinds of) pride, hurt feeling, (asking and granting) forgiveness, and (some kinds of) love. All traditional theories of moral responsibility acknowledge connections between these attitudes and holding one another responsible. What is original to Strawson is the way in which they are linked. Whereas traditional views have taken these attitudes to be secondary to seeing others as responsible, to be practical corollaries or emotional side effects of some independently comprehensible belief in responsibility, Strawson's radical claim is that these "reactive attitudes" (as he calls them) are *constitutive* of moral responsibility; to regard oneself or another as responsible just is the proneness to react to them in these kinds of ways under certain conditions. There is no more basic belief which provides the justification or rationale for these reactions. The practice does not rest on a theory at all, but rather on certain needs and aversions that are basic to our conception of being human. The idea that there is or needs to be such an independent basis is where traditional views, in Strawson's opinion, have gone badly astray.

For a long time, I have found Strawson's approach salutary and appealing. Here my aim is not to defend it as superior to its alternatives, but to do something more preliminary. A comparative assessment is not possible without a better grasp of what Strawson's theory (or a Strawsonian theory)[2] *is*. As Strawson presents it, the theory

---

[1] *Proceedings of the British Academy*, 1962, reprinted in *Free Will*, edited by Gary Watson, Oxford University Press, 2003; pp. 72–93. Hereafter, page references in the text will be to the latter edition.

[2] My interpretation of Strawson's essay will be in many places very conjectural, and I will sometimes signal this fact by speaking of a "Strawsonian" theory.

is incomplete in important respects. I will investigate whether and how the incompleteness can be remedied in Strawsonian ways. In the end, I find that certain features of our practice of holding responsible are rather resistant to such remedies, and that the practice is less philosophically innocent than Strawson supposes. I hope that the issues uncovered by this investigation will be of sufficient importance to interest even those who are not as initially sympathetic to Strawson's approach as I am.[3]

Strawson's theory

Strawson presents the rivals to his view as responses to a prima facie problem posed by determinism. One rival—consequentialism—holds that blaming and praising judgments and acts are to be understood, and justified, as forms of social regulation. Apart from the question of its extensional adequacy, consequentialism seems to many to leave out something vital to our practice. By emphasizing their instrumental efficacy, it distorts the fact that our responses are typically personal reactions to the individuals in question that we sometimes think of as eminently appropriate reactions quite aside from concern for effects. Rightly "recoiling" from the consequentialist picture, some philosophers have supposed that responsibility requires a libertarian foundation, that to bring the "vital thing" back in, we must embrace a certain metaphysics of human agency. This is the other rival.

What these otherwise very different views share is the assumption that our reactive attitudes commit us to the truth of some independently apprehensible proposition which gives the content of the belief in responsibility; and so either the search is on for the formulation of this proposition, or we must rest content with an intuition of its

---

[3] I have learned much from the penetrating exploration of Strawson's essay by Jonathan Bennett: "Accountability," in *Philosophical Subjects*, edited by Zak van Straaten, Oxford: Clarendon Press, 1980, pp. 14–47.

content. For the social-regulation theorist, this is a proposition about the standard effects of having and expressing reactive attitudes. For the libertarian, it is a proposition concerning metaphysical freedom. Since the truth of the former is consistent with the thesis of determinism, the consequentialist is a compatibilist; since the truth of the latter is shown or seen not to be, the libertarian is an incompatibilist.

In Strawson's view, there is no such independent notion of responsibility that explains the propriety of the reactive attitudes. The explanatory priority is the other way around: It is not that we hold people responsible because they *are* responsible; rather, the idea (*our* idea) that we are responsible is to be understood by the practice, which itself is not a matter of holding some propositions to be true, but of expressing our concerns and demands about our treatment of one another. These stances and responses are expressions of certain rudimentary needs and aversions: "it matters to us . . . whether the actions of other people . . . reflect attitudes toward us of good will, affection, or esteem on the one hand or contempt, indifference, or malevolence on the other" (p. 76). Accordingly, the reactive attitudes are "natural human reactions to the good or ill will or indifference of others toward us [or toward those we care about] as displayed in *their* attitudes and actions" (p. 80). Taken together, they express "the demand for the manifestation of a reasonable degree of good will or regard, on the part of others, not simply towards oneself, but towards all those on whose behalf moral indignation may be felt . . . " (p. 84).

Hence, Strawson accuses rival conceptions of "overintellectualizing" our practices. In their emphasis on social regulation, consequentialists lose sight of sentiments these practices directly express, without which the notion of moral responsibility cannot be understood. Libertarians see the gaping hole in the consequentialist account, but rather than acknowledging that "it is just these attitudes themselves which fill the gap" (p. 92), they seek to ground these attitudes in a metaphysical intuition—"a pitiful intellectualist trinket for a philosopher to wear as a charm against the recognition of his own humanity" (p. 92). Holding responsible is as natural and primitive in human life as friendship and animosity, sympathy and antipathy. It rests on needs and concerns that are not so much to be justified as acknowledged.

Excusing and exempting

To say that holding responsible is to be explained by the range of reactive attitudes, rather than by a commitment to some independently comprehensible proposition about responsibility, is not to deny that these reactions depend on a context of belief and perceptions in particular contexts. They are not mere effusions of feeling, unaffected by facts. In one way, Strawson is anxious to insist that these attitudes have no "rationale," that they neither require nor permit a "rational justification" of some general sort. Nevertheless, Strawson has a good deal to say about the particular perceptions that elicit and inhibit them. Reactive attitudes do have internal criteria, since they are reactions to the moral qualities exemplified by an individual's attitudes and conduct.[4]

Thus, reactive attitudes depend upon an interpretation of conduct. If you are resentful when jostled in a crowd, you will see the other's behavior as rude, contemptuous, disrespectful, self-preoccupied, or heedless: in short, as manifesting attitudes contrary to the basic demand for reasonable regard. Your resentment might be inhibited

---

[4] Reactive attitudes thus permit a threefold classification. Personal reactive attitudes regarding others' treatment of one (resentment, gratitude, etc.); vicarious analogues of these, regarding others' treatment of others (indignation and approbation); self-reactive attitudes regarding one's own treatment of others (and oneself?) (guilt, shame, moral self-esteem, feeling obligated). Many of the reactive attitudes reflect the basic demand (on oneself and others, for oneself and others), whereas some (for example, gratitude) directly express the basic concern.

Contrary to some of Strawson's discussion, responsibility does not concern only other-regarding attitudes. You can hold yourself responsible for failing to live up to an ideal that has no particular bearing on the interests or feelings of others. It may be said that others cannot *blame* you for this failure; but that would be a moral claim.

if you are too tired, or busy, or fearful, or simply inured to life in the big city. These are causal inhibitors. In contrast, you might think the other was pushed, didn't realize, didn't mean to. . . . These thoughts would provide reasons for the inhibition of resentment. What makes them reasons is, roughly, that they cancel or qualify the appearance of noncompliance with the basic demand.[5]

In this way, Strawson offers a plausible account of many of the "pleas" that in practice inhibit or modify negative reactive attitudes. One type of plea is exemplified by the aforementioned reasons for inhibited sentiments. This type of plea corresponds to standardly acknowledged *excusing* conditions. It works by denying the appearance that the other failed to fulfill the basic demand; when a valid excuse obtains, the internal criteria of the negative reactive attitudes are not satisfied. Of course, justification does this as well, but in a different way. "He realized what he was doing, but it was an emergency." In general, an excuse shows that *one* was not to blame, whereas a justification shows that one was not to *blame*.

Strawson distinguishes a second type of plea. These correspond roughly to standard *exempting* conditions. They show that the agent, temporarily or permanently, globally or locally, is appropriately exempted from the basic demand in the first place. Strawson's examples are being psychotic, being a child, being under great strain, being hypnotized, being a sociopath ("moral idiot"), and being "unfortunate in formative circumstances." His general characterization of pleas of type 2 is that they present the other either as acting uncharacteristically due to extraordinary circumstances, or as psychologically abnormal or morally undeveloped in such a way as to be incapacitated in some or all respects for "ordinary adult interpersonal relationships."

In sum, type-2 pleas bear upon the question of whether the agent is an appropriate "object of that kind of demand for goodwill or regard which is reflected in ordinary reactive attitudes" (p. 65).

---

[5] Below, this remark is qualified significantly.

If so, he or she is seen as a responsible agent, as a potential term in moral relationships, as a member (albeit, perhaps, in less than good standing) of the moral community. Assuming the absence of such exemptions, type-1 pleas bear upon the question of whether the basic demand has been met. These inhibit negative reactive attitudes because they give evidence that their internal criteria are not satisfied. In contrast, type-2 pleas inhibit reactive attitudes because they inhibit the demand those attitudes express (p. 73).

When reactive attitudes are suspended on type-2 grounds, we tend to take what Strawson calls an "objective view." We see individuals not as ones to be resented or esteemed but as ones to be controlled, managed, manipulated, trained. . . . The objective view does not preclude all emotions: "It may include repulsion and fear, it may include pity or even love," though not reciprocal adult love. We have the capacity to adopt an objective view toward capable agents as well; for certain kinds of therapeutic relationship, or simply to relieve the "strains of involvement," we sometimes call upon this resource.

As we have seen, one of Strawson's concerns is to deny the relevance of any theoretical issue about determinism to moral responsibility. In effect, incompatibilists insist that the truth of determinism would require us to take the objective attitude universally. But in Strawson's view, when we adopt the objective attitude, it is never a result of a theoretical conviction in determinism, but either because one of the exempting pleas is accepted, or for external reasons— fatigue, for example, or relief from the strain of involvement. No coherent thesis of determinism entails that one or more of the pleas is always valid, that disrespect is never meant, or that we are all abnormal or undeveloped in the relevant ways. Holding responsible is an expression of the basic concern and the basic demand, whose "legitimacy" requires neither metaphysical freedom nor efficacy. The practice does not involve a commitment to anything with which determinism could conflict, or which considerations of utility could challenge.

Blaming and finding fault

This is the basic view as Strawson presents it. For convenience, we may call it the expressive theory of responsibility. With certain caveats,[6] the expressive theory may be called a nonconsequentialist form of compatibilism; but it is not the only such form. It can be clarified by contrasting it with another.

Consider the following common view of blame and praise: To blame someone morally for something is to attribute it to a moral fault, or "shortcoming," or defect of character, or vice,[7] and similarly for praise. Responsibility could be construed in terms of the propriety conditions of such judgments: that is, judgments to the effect that an action or attitude manifests a virtue or vice.[8]

As I understand the Strawsonian theory, such judgments are only part of the story. They indicate what reactive attitudes are reactions *to* (namely, to the quality of the other's moral self as exemplified in action and attitude), but they are not themselves such reactions. Merely to cite such judgments is to leave out something integral to the practice of holding responsible and to the concept of moral responsibility (of being one to whom it is appropriate to respond in certain ways). It is as though in blaming we were mainly moral clerks, recording moral faults, for whatever purposes

[6] The term "compatibilism" denotes the view that determinism is compatible with responsibility. Hence it may presuppose that determinism is an intelligible thesis. Since Strawson seems skeptical about this presupposition, he might refuse this appellation.

[7] See Robert Nozick, *Philosophical Explanations* (Harvard University Press, 1981, p. 396).

[8] Such a view is hinted at by James Wallace: "Answers to [the question of when an action is fully characteristic of an excellence or a vice] are fundamental for an account of the conditions for the appropriateness of praise, blame, reward and punishment and for an account of the derivative notion of responsibility" (*Virtues and Vices*, Cornell University Press, p. 43). This also seems to be R. Milo's view in *Immorality* (Princeton University Press, 1984). I don't say that such a view is necessarily compatibilist—it could be insisted that conduct fully exemplifies a virtue or a vice only if determinism is false (this is clearly the Abélardian view, discussed below)—but it is clear how a compatibilist version would go.

(the Last Assizes?).[9] In a Strawsonian view, blaming is not merely a fault-finding appraisal—which could be made from a detached and austerely "objective" standpoint—but a range of responses to the agent on the basis of such appraisals.[10] These nonpropositional responses are constitutive of the practice of holding responsible.

I will have something to say later about the nature of these responses. Clearly they make up a wide spectrum. Negative reactions range from bombing Tripoli to thinking poorly of a person. But even those at the more covert and less retributive end of the spectrum involve more than attributions of defects or shortcomings of moral character. Thinking poorly (less well) of a person is a way of regarding him or her in view of those faults. It has subtle implications for one's way of treating and interacting with the other. (Where the other is dead or otherwise out of reach, these implications will be only dispositional or potential.) It is the sort of attitude that is forsworn by forgiveness, which itself presupposes the attribution of (former) fault.

Some critical questions

I turn now to certain hard questions for the expressive theory. It accounts nicely for "excusing conditions," pleas of type 1; but exactly—or even roughly—what is its account of type-2 pleas? The "participant" reactive attitudes are said to be "natural human

---

[9] Consider Jonathan Glover's remark: "Involved in our present practice of blame is a kind of moral accounting, where a person's actions are recorded in an informal balance sheet, with the object of assessing his moral worth" (*Responsibility*, Routledge and Kegan Paul, 1970, p. 64).

[10] "Blaming is a type of response to faults in oneself or in others," Robert Adams, "Involuntary Sin," *Philosophical Review*, January 1985, p. 21. Adams does not tell us what kind of response it is. Since he thinks that thinking poorly of someone *is* a form of unspoken blame (ibid.), he must think that thinking poorly of is more than noting a moral fault. I think this is correct.

reactions to the good or ill-will or indifference of others as displayed in their attitudes and actions" (p. 80); but this characterization must be incomplete, for some agents who display such attitudes are nevertheless exempted. A child can be malicious, a psychotic can be hostile, a sociopath indifferent, a person under great strain can be rude, a woman or man "unfortunate in formative circumstances" can be cruel. Evidently reactive attitudes are sensitive not only to the quality of others' wills, but depend as well upon a background of beliefs about the objects of those attitudes. What are those beliefs, and can they be accommodated without appealing to the rival accounts of responsibility that Strawson sets out to avoid?

Strawson says that type-2 pleas inhibit reactive attitudes not by providing an interpretation which shows that the other does not display the pertinent attitudes, but by "inhibiting" the basic demand. It would seem that many of the exemption conditions involve *explanations* of why the individuals display qualities to which the reactive attitudes are otherwise sensitive. So on the face of it, the reactive attitudes are also affected by these explanations. Strawson's essay does not provide an account of how this works or what kinds of explanations exempt.

The problem is not just that the theory is incomplete, but that what will be necessary to complete it might undermine the theory. Strawsonian rivals will rush to fill the gap with their own notions. So it will be said that what makes some of these explanations exempting is that they are deterministic; or it will be said that these conditions are exempting because they indicate conditions in which making the basic demand is inefficacious. To the extent that some such account seems necessary, our enterprise is doomed.

In the following sections, I investigate a Strawsonian alternative. Following Strawson's idea that type-2 pleas inhibit reactive attitudes *by* inhibiting the basic demand, I propose to construe the exempting conditions as indications of the constraints on intelligible moral demand or, put another way, of the constraints on moral address.

I shall not attempt anything like a comprehensive treatment of the type-2 pleas mentioned by Strawson. I discuss, first and rather briefly, the cases of being a child and being under great strain. I then turn to a more extended discussion of "being unfortunate in formative circumstances," for this looks to be entirely beyond the resources of the expressive theory.

Demanding and understanding

As Strawson is fully aware, being a child is not simply exempting. Children "are potentially and increasingly capable both of holding, and being objects of, the full range of human and moral attitudes, but are not yet fully capable of either" (p. 88). Children are gradually becoming responsible agents; but in virtue of what are they potentially and increasingly these things? A plausible partial answer to this question is "moral understanding." They do not yet (fully) grasp the moral concepts in such a way that they can (fully) engage in moral communication, and so be unqualified members of the moral community.

The relevance of moral understanding to the expressive theory is this: The negative reactive attitudes express a *moral* demand, a demand for reasonable regard. Now a very young child does not even have a clear sense of the reality of others; but even with this cognitive capacity, children may lack an understanding of the effects of their behavior on others. Even when they understand what it is to hurt another physically, they may lack a sense of what it is to hurt another's feelings, or of the various subtle ways in which that may be done; and even when these things are more or less mastered, they may lack the notion of *reasonable* regard, or of justification. The basic demand is, once more, a moral demand, a demand for reasonable regard, a demand addressed to a moral agent, to one who is capable of understanding the demand. Since the negative reactive attitudes involve this demand, they are not (as fully) appropriately directed to those who do not fully grasp the terms of the demand.

To be intelligible, demanding presumes understanding on the part of the object of the demand. The reactive attitudes are incipiently forms of communication, which make sense only on the assumption that the other can comprehend the message.

No doubt common views about the moral capacities of children are open to challenge, and the appeal to the notion of understanding itself raises important issues.[11] However, what is important here is whether these views can be understood by the Strawsonian theory, and it seems the ordinary view that reactive attitudes make less sense in the case of children is intelligible in Strawsonian terms; this exemption condition reflects constraints arising from the notion of moral demand.

In a certain sense, blaming and praising those with diminished moral understanding loses its "point." This way of putting it smacks of consequentialism, but our discussion suggests a different construction. The reactive attitudes are incipient forms of communication, though not in the sense that resentment et al. are usually communicated; very often, in fact, they are not. Rather, the most appropriate and direct expression of resentment is to address the other with a complaint and a demand. Being a child exempts, when it does, not because expressing

[11] Do *we adults* fully comprehend the notions of justification and reasonable regard? Does understanding presuppose a disputable cognitive view of morality? Certainly conceptions of children are subject to cultural variation. William Blackstone discusses the case of an 8-year old boy who was tried for setting fire to some barns. Because he was found to exhibit "malice, revenge, and cunning, he was found guilty, condemned and hanged accordingly." (In *Commentaries on the Laws of England* (1765–7), as quoted by Jennifer Radden, *Madness and Reason*, George Allen and Unwin, 1985, p. 136.)

It is doubtful that diminished moral understanding is the only relevant factor here. Surely various capacities of concentration and "volitional" control are relevant as well. I do not know how the expressive theory could take these into account.

resentment has no desirable effects; in fact, it often does. Rather the reactive attitudes lose their point as forms of moral address.[12]

Not being oneself

Let's consider whether this kind of explanation can be extended to another of Strawson's type-2 pleas: "being under great strain." Strawson includes this plea in a subgroup of exemptions that include "he wasn't himself" and "he was acting under posthypnotic suggestion." His statement of the rationale in the case of stress is somewhat cryptic:

> We shall not feel resentment against the man he is for the action done by the man he is not; or at least we shall feel less. We normally have to deal with him under normal stresses; so we shall not feel towards him, when he acts under abnormal stresses, as we should have felt towards him had he acted as he did under normal stresses. (p. 78)

I take it that what leads Strawson to group these cases together is that in each case the agent, due to special circumstances, acts *uncharacteristically*.

When you learn that someone who has treated you extremely rudely has been under great strain lately, has lost a job, say, or is going through a divorce, you may reinterpret the behavior in such

---

[12] Reactive attitudes are even more clearly pointless in the case of a radically disintegrated personality, one that has no coherent moral self to be addressed. The case of the sociopath is much more complicated, but arguably something similar may be said here. Those who deal with sociopaths often lose the sense that such characters have a moral self at all; despite appearances, there is "no one home."

For case studies and psychiatric commentary, see Hervey Cleckley, *The Mask of Sanity*, C. V. Mosby, 1941. For philosophical discussion, see Herbert Fingarette, *On Responsibility*, Chap. 2; Vinit Haksar, "The Responsibility of Psychopaths," *The Philosophical Quarterly*, Vol. 15 (1965); M. S. Pritchard, *On Becoming Responsible* (Lawrence, Kan.: University Press of Kansas, 1991); Antony Duff, "Psychopathy and Moral Understanding," *American Philosophical Quarterly*, Vol. 14 (1977); and Jeffrie Murphy, "Moral Death: A Kantian Essay on Psychopathy," *Ethics*, Vol. 82 (1972).

a way that your erstwhile resentment or hurt feelings are inhibited and now seem inappropriate. How does this reinterpretation work? Notice, again, that unlike type-1 pleas, the new interpretation does not contradict the *judgment* that the person treated you rudely; rather, it provides an explanation of the rudeness.

What Strawson says about this case seems plausible. What seems to affect your reactive attitudes is the thought that she's not herself, that the behavior does not reflect or fully reflect the person's moral "personality." The following remark indicates the same phenomenon: "He was drunk when he said that; I wouldn't hold it against him." (There is room here for disagreement about the bounds of the moral self. Some parts of folk wisdom have it that one's "true self" is revealed when drunk. To my knowledge, this has never been claimed about stress.) Again, what is the Strawsonian rationale?

Perhaps this type of case can also be understood in terms of the conditions of intelligible moral address. Insofar as resentment is a form of reproach addressed to an agent, such an attitude loses much of its point here—not, as before, because the other does not fully understand the reproach, but because *he* or *she* (the true self) repudiates such conduct as well. Unlike the case in which the agent acts rudely in the absence of "strain," here the target of your resentment is not one who "really" endorses the behavior you are opposing. You see the behavior as not issuing from that person's moral self, and yet it is the person, qua moral self, that your resentment would address.

The point can be put more generally in this way: Insofar as the negative reactive attitudes express demands (or in some cases appeals) addressed to another moral self, they are conceptually conditioned in various ways. One condition is that, to be fully a moral self, the other must possess sufficient (for what?) moral understanding; another is that the conduct in question be seen as reflecting the moral self. Insofar as the person is subject to great stress, his or her conduct and attitudes fail to meet this latter condition.

I am unsure to what extent these remarks accord with Strawson's own views. They are in any case exceedingly sketchy, and raise problems I am unable to take up here. For one thing, the notion of moral address seems essentially interpersonal, and so would be unavailing in the self-reflexive case. We have negative reactive attitudes toward and make moral demands upon ourselves. To determine whether this is a fatal asymmetry, we would have to investigate the reflexive cases in detail. For another thing, the notion of moral self is certainly not altogether transparent. Why are our responses under stress not reflections of our moral selves—namely, reflections of the moral self under stress? Clearly then, the explanation requires development.

It will be recalled, however, that I am not trying to determine whether a Strawsonian account of the exemption conditions is the *best* account, but to indicate what such an account might be. It will be enough for my purposes here if we can be satisfied that a Strawsonian theory has the resources to provide *some* explanation.

To recapitulate, then, the thesis is this: First, type-2 pleas indicate in different ways limiting conditions on moral address. These are relevant to reactive attitudes because those attitudes are incipiently forms of moral address. This thesis makes sense of Strawson's remark that pleas of this type inhibit reactive attitudes by inhibiting moral demand. Second, given that those conditions are satisfied, type-1 pleas indicate that the basic demand has not been flouted, contrary to appearances (though here again, we must distinguish excuse from justification).

On this account, the practice of holding responsible does indeed seem metaphysically modest, in that it involves no commitments to which issues about determinism are relevant. In a subsequent section I will consider some more bothersome features of our practice; but first I want to call attention to some general issues raised by the account given so far.

Evil and the limits of moral community

To understand certain exempting and extenuating considerations, I have appealed to the notion of the conditions in which it makes

234 · RESPONSIBILITY AND ANSWERABILITY

sense morally to address another. I suggested that in different ways these conditions are not (fully) satisfied by the child and the person under severe stress. In the case of children, it seemed plausible to speak of a lack of understanding. What is involved in such understanding is a complex question. Obviously we do not want to make *compliance* with the basic demand a condition of moral understanding. (After all, for the most part, children *do* "comply," but without full understanding.) For the negative reactive attitudes come into play only when the basic demand has been flouted or rejected; and flouting and rejecting, strictly speaking, require understanding.

These remarks raise a very general issue about the limits of responsibility and the limits of evil. It is tempting to think that understanding requires a shared framework of values. At any rate, some of Strawson's remarks hint at such a requirement on moral address. He writes that the reactive attitudes essentially involve regarding the other as "a morally responsible agent, as a term of moral relationships, as a member of the moral community" (p. 73). This last phrase suggests shared ends, at some level, or a shared framework for practical reasoning. Thus, comembers of the moral community are potential interlocutors. In his discussion of Strawson's essay, Lawrence Stern suggests this point:

. . . when one morally disapproves of another person, it is normal to believe that he is susceptible to the appeal of the principles from the standpoint of which one disapproves. He either shares these principles or can come to share them.[13]

Does morally addressing another make sense unless we suppose that the other can see some reason to take us seriously, to acknowledge our claims? Can we be in a moral community with those who reject the basic terms of moral community? Are the enemies of moral community themselves members? If we suppose that moral address requires moral community, then some forms of evil will be exempting

[13] "Freedom, Blame, and Moral Community," *Journal of Philosophy*, February 14, 1974, p. 78.

conditions. If holding responsible requires the intelligibility of moral address, and if a condition of such address is that the other be seen as a potential moral interlocutor, then the paradox results that extreme evil disqualifies one for blame.

Consider the case of Robert Harris.

On the south tier of Death Row, in a section called "Peckerwood Flats" where the white inmates are housed, there will be a small celebration the day Robert Alton Harris dies.

A group of inmates on the row have pledged several dollars for candy, cookies and soda. At the moment they estimate that Harris has been executed, they will eat, drink and toast to his passing.

"The guy's a misery, a total scumbag; we're going to party when he goes," said Richard (Chic) Mroczko, who lived in the cell next to Harris on San Quentin Prison's Death Row for more than a year. "He doesn't care about life, he doesn't care about others, he doesn't care about himself.

"We're not a bunch of Boy Scouts around here, and you might think we're pretty cold-blooded about the whole thing. But then, you just don't know the dude."

San Diego County Assistant Dist. Atty. Richard Huffman, who prosecuted Harris, said, "If a person like Harris can't be executed under California law and federal procedure, then we should be honest and say we're incapable of handling capital punishment."

State Deputy Atty. Gen. Michael D. Wellington asked the court during an appeal hearing for Harris, "If this isn't the kind of defendant that justifies the death penalty, is there ever going to be one?"

What crime did Robert Harris commit to be considered the archetypal candidate for the death penalty? And what kind of man provokes such enmity that even those on Death Row . . . call for his execution?

On July 5, 1978, John Mayeski and Michael Baker had just driven through [a] fast-food restaurant and were sitting in the parking lot eating lunch. Mayeski and Baker . . . lived on the same street and were best friends. They were on their way to a nearby lake for a day of fishing.

At the other end of the parking lot, Robert Harris, 25, and his brother Daniel, 18, were trying to hotwire a [car] when they spotted the two boys. The Harris brothers were planning to rob a bank that afternoon and did not want to use their own car. When Robert Harris could not start the car, he pointed to the [car] where the 16-year-olds were eating and said to Daniel, "We'll take this one."

He pointed a . . . Luger at Mayeski, crawled into the back seat, and told him to drive east. . . .

Daniel Harris followed in the Harrises' car. When they reached a canyon area . . . , Robert Harris told the youths he was going to use their car in a bank robbery and assured them that they would not be hurt. Robert Harris yelled to Daniel to get the .22 caliber rifle out of the back seat of their car.

"When I caught up," Daniel said in a recent interview, Robert was telling them about the bank robbery we were going to do. He was telling them that he would leave them some money in the car and all, for us using it. Both of them said that they would wait on top of this little hill until we were gone, and then walk into town and report the car stolen. Robert Harris agreed.

"Michael turned and went through some bushes. John said, 'Good luck,' and turned to leave."

As the two boys walked away, Harris slowly raised the Luger and shot Mayeski in the back, Daniel said. Mayeski yelled: "Oh, God," and slumped to the ground. Harris chased Baker down a hill into a little valley and shot him four times.

Mayeski was still alive when Harris climbed back up the hill, Daniel said. Harris walked over to the boy, knelt down, put the Luger to his head and fired.

"God, everything started to spin," Daniel said. "It was like slow motion. I saw the gun, and then his head exploded like a balloon, . . . I just started running and running. . . . But I heard Robert and turned around.

"He was swinging the rifle and pistol in the air and laughing. God, that laugh made blood and bone freeze in me."

Harris drove [the] car to a friend's house where he and Daniel were staying. Harris walked into the house, carrying the weapons and the bag [containing] the remainder of the slain youths' lunch. Then, about 15 minutes after he had killed the two 16-year-old boys, Harris took the food out of the bag . . . and began eating a hamburger. He offered his brother an apple turnover, and Daniel became nauseated and ran to the bathroom.

"Robert laughed at me," Daniel said. "He said I was weak; he called me a sissy and said I didn't have the stomach for it."

Harris was in an almost lighthearted mood. He smiled and told Daniel that it would be amusing if the two of them were to pose as police officers and inform the parents that their sons were killed. Then, for the first time, he turned serious. He thought that somebody might have heard the shots and that police could be searching for the bodies. He told Daniel that they should begin cruising the street near the bodies, and possibly kill some police in the area.

[Later, as they prepared to rob the bank,] Harris pulled out the Luger, noticed blood stains and remnants of flesh on the barrel as a result of the point-blank shot, and said, "I really blew that guy's brains out." And then, again, he started laughing.

. . . Harris was given the death penalty. He has refused all requests for interviews since the conviction.

"He just doesn't see the point of talking," said a sister, . . . who has visited him three times since he has been on Death Row. "He told me he had his chance, he took the road to hell and there's nothing more to say."

. . . Few of Harris' friends or family were surprised that he ended up on Death Row. He had spent seven of the previous 10 years behind bars. Harris, who has an eighth-grade education, was convicted of car theft at 15 and was sentenced to a federal youth center. After being released, he was arrested twice for torturing animals and was convicted of manslaughter for beating a neighbor to death after a dispute.

Barbara Harris, another sister, talked to her brother at a family picnic on July 4, 1978. He had been out of prison less than six months, and his sister had not seen him in several years.

. . . Barbara Harris noticed his eyes, and she began to shudder. . . . "I thought, 'My God, what have they done to him?' He smiled, but his eyes were so cold, totally flat. It was like looking at a rattlesnake or a cobra ready to strike. They were hooded eyes, with nothing but meanness in them.

"He had the eyes of a killer. I told a friend that I knew someone else would die by his hand."

The next day, Robert Harris killed the two youths. Those familiar with the case were as mystified as they were outraged by Harris' actions. Most found it incomprehensible that a man could be so devoid of compassion and conscience that he could kill two youths, laugh about their deaths and then casually eat their hamburgers. . . .

. . . Harris is a dangerous man on the streets and a dangerous man behind bars, said Mroczko, who spent more than a year in the cell next to Harris'. . . .

"You don't want to deal with him out there," said Mroczko, ..."We don't want to deal with him in here."

During his first year on the row, Mroczko said, Harris was involved in several fights on the yard and was caught trying to supply a prisoner in an adjacent yard with a knife. During one fight, Harris was stabbed and the other prisoner was shot by a guard. He grated on people's nerves and one night he kept the whole cell block awake by banging his shoe on a steel water basin and laughing hysterically.

An encounter with Harris always resulted in a confrontation. If an inmate had cigarettes, or something else Harris wanted, and he did not think "you could hold your mud," Mroczko said, he would try to take them.

Harris was a man who just did not know "when to be cool," he said. He was an obnoxious presence in the yard and in his cell, and his behavior precipitated unwanted attention from the guards. . . .

He acted like a man who did not care about anything. His cell was filthy, Mroczko said, and clothes, trash, tobacco and magazines were scattered on the floor. He wore the same clothes every day and had little interest in showers. Harris spent his days watching television in his cell, occasionally reading a Western novel.[14]

On the face of it, Harris is an "archetypal candidate" for blame. We respond to his heartlessness and viciousness with moral outrage and loathing. Yet if reactive attitudes were implicitly "invitations to dialogue" (as Stern puts it), then Harris would be an inappropriate object of such attitudes. For he is hardly a potential moral interlocutor, "susceptible to the appeal of the principles from the standpoint of which one disapproves." In this instance, an invitation to dialogue would be met with icy silence (he has "nothing more to say") or murderous contempt.

[14] From Miles Corwin, "Icy Killer's Life Steeped in Violence," *Los Angeles Times*, May 16, 1982. Copyright, 1982, *Los Angeles Times*. Reprinted by permission. For the length of this and the next quotation, I ask for the reader's patience. It is very important here to work with realistic and detailed examples.

However, not all communication is dialogue. Harris refuses dialogue, and this refusal is meant to make a point. It is in effect a repudiation of the moral community; he thereby declares himself a moral outlaw. Unlike the small child, or in a different way the psychopath, he exhibits an inversion of moral concern, not a lack of understanding. His ears are not deaf, but his heart is frozen. This characteristic, which makes him utterly unsuitable as a moral interlocutor, intensifies rather than inhibits the reactive attitudes. Harris's form of evil *consists* in part in being beyond the boundaries of moral community. Hence, if we are to appeal to the constraints on moral address to explain certain type-2 pleas, we must not include among these constraints comembership in the moral community or the significant possibility of dialogue—unless, that is, evil is to be its own exemption. At these outer limits, our reactive attitudes can be nothing more (or less) than a denunciation forlorn of the hope of an adequate reply.

The roots of evil

I said that Harris is an archetypal candidate for blame—so, at least, we react to him. Does it matter to our reactions how he came to be so? Strawson thinks so, for, among type-2 pleas, he includes "being unfortunate in formative circumstances." We must now investigate the relevance of such historical considerations to the reactive attitudes. As it happens, the case of Robert Harris is again a vivid illustration.

[During the interview] Barbara Harris put her palms over her eyes and said softly, "I saw every grain of sweetness, pity and goodness in him destroyed. . . . It was a long and ugly journey before he reached that point."

Robert Harris' 29 years . . . have been dominated by incessant cruelty and profound suffering that he has both experienced and provoked. Violence presaged his birth, and a violent act is expected to end his life.

Harris was born Jan. 15, 1953, several hours after his mother was kicked in the stomach. She was 6½ months pregnant and her husband, an insanely jealous man, . . . came home drunk and accused her of infidelity. He claimed that the child was not his, threw her down and kicked her. She began hemorrhaging, and he took her to the hospital.

Robert was born that night. His heartbeat stopped at one point . . . but labor was induced and he was saved. Because of the premature birth, he was a tiny baby; he was kept alive in an incubator and spent months at the hospital.

His father was an alcoholic who was twice convicted of sexually molesting his daughters. He frequently beat his children . . . and often caused serious injury. Their mother also became an alcoholic and was arrested several times, once for bank robbery.

All of the children had monstrous childhoods. But even in the Harris family, . . . the abuse Robert was subjected to was unusual.

Before their mother died last year, Barbara Harris said, she talked incessantly about Robert's early years. She felt guilty that she was never able to love him; she felt partly responsible that he ended up on Death Row.

When Robert's father visited his wife in the hospital and saw his son for the first time, . . . the first thing he said was, "Who is the father of that bastard?" When his mother picked him up from the hospital . . . she said it was like taking a stranger's baby home.

The pain and permanent injury Robert's mother suffered as a result of the birth, . . . and the constant abuse she was subjected to by her husband, turned her against her son. Money was tight, she was overworked and he was her fifth child in just a few years. She began to blame all of her problems on Robert, and she grew to hate the child.

"I remember one time we were in the car and Mother was in the back seat with Robbie in her arms. He was crying and my father threw a glass bottle at him, but it hit my mother in the face. The glass shattered and Robbie started screaming. I'll never forget it," she said. . . .

"Her face was all pink, from the mixture of blood and milk. She ended up blaming Robbie for all the hurt, all the things like that. She felt helpless and he was someone to vent her anger on."

. . . Harris had a learning disability and a speech problem, but there was no money for therapy. When he was at school he felt stupid and classmates teased him, his sister said, and when he was at home he was abused.

"He was the most beautiful of all my mother's children; he was an angel," she said. "He would just break your heart. He wanted love so bad he would beg for any kind of physical contact.

"He'd come up to my mother and just try to rub his little hands on her leg or her arm. He just never got touched at all. She'd just push him away or kick him. One time she bloodied his nose when he was trying to get close to her."

Barbara Harris put her head in her hands and cried softly. "One killer out of nine kids. . . . The sad thing is he was the most sensitive of all of us. When he was 10 and we all saw 'Bambi,' he cried and cried when Bambi's mother was shot. Everything was pretty to him as a child; he loved animals. But all that changed; it all changed so much."

. . . All nine children are psychologically crippled as a result of their father, she said, but most have been able to lead useful lives. But Robert was too young, and the abuse lasted too long, she said, for him ever to have had a chance to recover.

[At age 14] Harris was sentenced to a federal youth detention center [for car theft]. He was one of the youngest inmates there, Barbara Harris said, and he grew up "hard and fast."

. . . Harris was raped several times, his sister said, and he slashed his wrists twice in suicide attempts. He spent more than four years behind bars as a result of an escape, an attempted escape and a parole violation.

The centers were "gladiator schools," Barbara Harris said, and Harris learned to fight and be mean. By the time he was released from federal prison at 19, all his problems were accentuated. Everyone in the family knew that he needed psychiatric help.

The child who had cried at the movies when Bambi's mother dies had evolved into a man who was arrested several times for abusing animals. He killed cats and dogs, Daniel said, and laughed while torturing them with mop handles, darts and pellet guns. Once he stabbed a prize pig more than 1,000 times.

"The only way he could vent his feelings was to break or kill something," Barbara Harris said. "He took out all the frustrations of his life on animals. He had no feeling for life, no sense of remorse. He reached the point where there wasn't that much left of him."

. . . Harris' family is ambivalent about his death sentence. [Another sister said that] if she did not know her brother's past so intimately, she would support his execution without hesitation. Barbara has a 16-year-old son; she often imagines the horror of the slain boys' parents.

"If anyone killed my son, I'd try my damnedest, no matter what it took, to have my child revenged," Barbara Harris said. "I know how those parents must suffer every day.

"But Robbie in the gas chamber. . . ." She broke off in mid-sentence and stared out a window. "Well, I still remember the little boy who used to beg for love, for just one pat or word of kindness. . . . No I can't say I want my brother to die."

. . . Since Harris has been on Death Row, he has made no demands of time or money on his family. Harris has made only one request; he wants a dignified and serene ceremony after he dies—a ceremony in marked contrast to his life.

He has asked his oldest brother to take his ashes, to drive to the Sierra, hike to a secluded spot and scatter his remains in the trees.[15]

No doubt this history gives pause to the reactive attitudes. Why does it do so? "No wonder Harris is as he is!" we think. What is the relevance of this thought?

Note, to begin with, that the story in no way undermines the judgments that he is brutal, vicious, heartless, mean.[16] Rather, it provides a kind of explanation for his being so. Can the expressive theory explain why the reactive attitudes should be sensitive to such an explanation?

Strawson's general rubric for type-2 pleas (or the subgroup in which this plea is classified) is "being incapacitated for ordinary interpersonal relationships." Does Harris have some independently identifiable incapacity for which his biography provides evidence? Apparently, he *is* incapacitated for such relationships—for example, for friendship, for sympathy, for being affected by moral considerations. To be

---

[15] Miles Corwin, op. cit. Copyright, 1982, *Los Angeles Times*. Reprinted by permission.

[16] Although, significantly, when his past is in focus, we are less inclined to use certain *reactive* epithets, such as "scumbag." This term is used to express an attitude about the appropriate treatment of the individual (that he is to be thrown in the garbage, flushed down the toilet, etc.). Some other reactive terms are "jerk," "creep," "son of a bitch."

homicidally hateful and callous in Harris's way is to lack moral concern, and to lack moral concern is to be incapacitated for moral community. However, to exempt Harris on these grounds is problematic. For then everyone who is evil in Harris's way will be exempt, independently of facts about their background. But we had ample evidence about *this* incapacity before we learned of his childhood misfortunes, and that did not affect the reactive attitudes. Those misfortunes affect our responses in a special and nonevidential way. The question is why this should be so.

This would seem to be a hard question for compatibilist views generally. What matters is whether, in one version, the practice of holding responsible can be efficacious as a means of social regulation, or whether, using the expressive theory, the conditions of moral address are met. These questions would seem to be settled by how individuals *are*, not by how they came to be. Facts about background would be, at most, evidence that some other plea is satisfied. In themselves, they would not seem to matter.

A plea of this kind is, on the other hand, grist for the incompatibilists' mill. For they will insist on an essential historical dimension to the concept of responsibility. Harris's history reveals him to be an inevitable product of his formative circumstances. And seeing him as a product is inconsistent with seeing him as a responsible agent. If his cruel attitudes and conduct are the inevitable result of his circumstances, then he is not responsible for them, unless he was responsible for those circumstances. It is this principle that gives the historical dimension of responsibility and of course entails the incompatibility of determinism and responsibility.

In this instance, however, an incompatibilist diagnosis seems doubtful. In the first place, our response to the case is not the simple suspension of reactive attitudes that this diagnosis would lead one to expect, but ambivalence. In the second place, the force of the example does not depend on a belief in the *inevitability* of the upshot. Nothing in the story supports such a belief. The thought is not "It had to be!" but, again, "No wonder!"

Sympathy and antipathy

How and why, then, does this larger view of Harris's life in fact affect us? It is too simple to say that it leads us to suspend our reactive attitudes. Our response is too complicated and conflicted for that. What appears to happen is that we are unable to command an overall view of his life that permits the reactive attitudes to be sustained without ambivalence. That is because the biography forces us to see him as a *victim*, and so seeing him does not sit well with the reactive attitudes that are so strongly elicited by Harris's character and conduct. Seeing him as a victim does not totally dispel those attitudes. Rather, in light of the "whole" story, conflicting responses are evoked. The sympathy toward the boy he was is at odds with outrage toward the man he is. These responses conflict not in the way that fear dispels anger, but in the way that sympathy is opposed to antipathy. In fact, each of these responses is appropriate, but taken together they do not enable us to respond overall in a coherent way.

Harris both satisfies and violates the criteria of victimhood. His childhood abuse was a misfortune inflicted upon him against his will. But at the same time (and this is part of his very misfortune) he unambivalently endorses suffering, death, and destruction, and that is what (one form of) evil is. With this in focus, we see him as a victimizer and respond to him accordingly. The ambivalence results from the fact that an overall view simultaneously demands and precludes regarding him as a victim.

What we have here is not exactly a clash between what Thomas Nagel has called the objective and subjective standpoints.[17] It is not that from the more comprehensive viewpoint that reveals Harris as a victim, his responsibility is indiscernible. Rather, the clash occurs within a single point of view that reveals Harris as evil (and hence calling for enmity and moral opposition) and as one who is a victim (calling for sympathy and understanding). Harris's misfortune is

[17] In *The View from Nowhere*, Oxford University Press, 1986.

such that scarcely a vestige remains of his earlier sensibilities. Hence, unless one knew Harris as a child or keeps his earlier self vividly in mind, sympathy can scarcely find a purchase.

Moral luck and moral equality

However, what is arresting about the Harris case is not just the clash between sympathy and antipathy. The case is troubling in a more personal way. The fact that Harris's cruelty is an intelligible response to his circumstances gives a foothold not only for sympathy, but for the thought that if I had been subjected to such circumstances, I might well have become as vile. What is unsettling is the thought that one's moral self is such a fragile thing. One tends to think of one's moral sensibilities as going deeper than that (though it is not clear what this means). This thought induces not only an ontological shudder, but a sense of equality with the other: I too am a potential sinner.[18]

This point is merely the obverse of the point about sympathy. Whereas the point about sympathy focuses on our empathetic response to the other, the thought about moral luck turns one's gaze inward. It makes one feel less in a position to cast blame. The fact that my potential for evil has not been nearly so fully actualized is, for all I know, something for which I cannot take credit. The awareness that, in this respect, the others are or may be like oneself clashes with the distancing effect of enmity.

Admittedly, it is hard to know what to do with this conclusion. Equality of moral potential does not, of course, mean that Harris is not actually a vile man; on the contrary, it means that in similar circumstances I would have become vile as well. Since he is an evil

---

[18] In "Determinism and Moral Perspectives," *Philosophy and Phenomenological Research*, September 1960, Elizabeth Beardsley calls attention to the perspective evoked by such cases as Harris, though she links this perspective too closely, in my opinion, to the notion of determinism.

man, we cannot and should not treat him as we would a rabid dog. The awareness of moral luck, however, taints one's own view of one's moral self as an achievement, and infuses one's reactive attitudes with a sense of irony. Only those who have survived circumstances such as those that ravaged Harris are in a good position to know what they would have done. We lucky ones can only wonder. As a product of reflection, this attitude is, of course, easily lost when the knife is at one's own throat.

Determinism and ignorance

Nothing in the foregoing reflections is necessarily inconsistent with the expressive theory. The ways in which reactive attitudes are affected by sympathy and moral luck are intelligible without appealing to any of the conceptions of responsibility that Strawson eschews. Nevertheless, our attitudes remain puzzling in a number of respects.

Earlier we questioned an incompatibilist diagnosis of our example on the grounds that the historical explanation need not be construed as deterministic. Horrid backgrounds do not inevitably give rise to horrid people. Some manage somehow to survive a similar magnitude of misfortune, if not unscathed, at least as minimally decent human beings. Conversely, people are sometimes malicious despite a benign upbringing. What do we suppose makes the difference?

Strictly speaking, no one who is vicious in *just* the way we have interpreted Harris to be could fail to have had an abusive childhood. For our interpretation of who Harris is depends upon his biography, upon our interpretation of his life. Harris's cruelty is a response to the shattering abuse he suffered during the process of socialization. The objects of his hatred were not just the boys he so exultantly murdered, but the "moral order" that mauled and rejected him. (It is significant that Harris wanted to go out and kill some cops after the murder; he wanted not just to reject authority, but to confront it.)

He defies the demand for human consideration because he has been denied this consideration himself. The mistreatment he received becomes a ground as well as a cause of the mistreatment he gives. It becomes part of the content of his "project."

Thus, someone who had a supportive and loving environment as a child, but who was devoted to dominating others, who killed for enjoyment, would not be vicious in the way Harris is, since he or she could not be seen as striking back at "society"; but such a person could be just *as* vicious. In common parlance, we sometimes call such people "bad apples," a phrase that marks a blank in our understanding. In contrast to Harris, whose malice is motivated, the conduct of "bad apples" seems inexplicable. So far, we cannot see them as victims, and there is no application for thoughts about sympathy and moral luck.

However, do we not suppose that *something* must have gone wrong in the developmental histories of these individuals, if not in their socialization, then "in them"—in their genes or brains? (Suppose a certain kind of tumor is such that its onset at an early age is known to be strongly correlated with the development of a malicious character. This supposition is no doubt bad science fiction; that a complex and articulated psychological structure could be caused by gross brain defect seems antecedently implausible.) Whatever "nonenvironmental" factors make the difference, will they not play the same role as Harris's bad upbringing—that is, will they not have victimized these individuals so that thoughts about sympathy and moral luck come into play? Or can evil be the object of unequivocal reactive attitudes only when it is inexplicable?

If determinism is true, then evil is a joint product of nature and nurture. If so, the difference between any evil person and oneself would seem to be a matter of moral luck. For determinism seems to entail that if one had been subjected to the internal and external conditions of some evil person, then one would have been evil as well. If that is so, then the reflections about moral luck seem to entail that the acceptance of determinism should affect our reactive attitudes in the same way as they are affected in Harris's case. In the account we have suggested, then, determinism seems to be relevant to reactive attitudes after all.

Actually, this conclusion does not follow without special metaphysical assumptions. For the counterfactuals that underlie thoughts about moral luck must be constrained by the conditions of personal identity. It may be that no one who had been exposed to just the internal and external conditions of some given individual could have been me. To make sense of a counterfactual of the form, "If i had been in C, then i would have become a person of type t," C must be supposed to be compatible with i's existence as an individual (i must exist in the possible world in which C obtains). For example, it is widely held that genetic origin is essential to an individual's identity. In that case, the counterfactual, "If I had had Harris's genetic origin and his upbringing, then I would have been as evil as he," will not make sense. Now it might be that Harris's genetic origins are among the determinants of his moral development. Thus, even if this is a deterministic world, there may be no true counterfactual that would support the thought that the difference between Harris and me is a matter of moral luck. There is room for the thought that there is something "in me" by virtue of which I would not have become a vicious person in Harris's circumstances. And if that factor were among my essential properties, so to speak, then that difference between Harris and me would not be a matter of moral luck on my part, but a matter of who we essentially were. That would not, of course, mean that I was essentially good or Harris essentially evil, but that I would not have been corrupted by the same circumstances as those that defeated Harris. To be sure, to suppose that this difference is in itself to my moral credit would be odd. To congratulate me on these grounds would be to congratulate me on being myself. Nevertheless, this difference still might explain what is to my credit, such moral virtues as I may possess. This will seem paradoxical only if we suppose that whatever is a ground of my moral credit must itself be to my credit. But I see no compelling reason to suppose this.

Historical responsibility

Libertarians believe that evil is the product neither of nature nor of nurture, but of free will. Do we understand what this might mean?

It is noteworthy that libertarians will be able to agree with much of what we have said about moral luck. Harris's history affects us because it makes us wonder how *we* would have responded, and thus shakes our confidence that we would have avoided a pernicious path in those circumstances. But this effect is perfectly compatible with Harris's responsibility for how he did respond, just as we would have been responsible for how we would have responded. The biography affects us not because it is deterministic, libertarians can say, but because it shakes our confidence that we would have exercised that freedom rightly in more dire straits. We are not, of course, responsible for our formative circumstances—and in this respect we are morally lucky and Harris is unlucky—but those circumstances do not determine our responses to them. It is the individual's own response that distinguishes those who become evil from those who do not.

This idea is nicely captured by Peter Abélard: "Nothing taints the soul but what belongs to it, namely consent."[19] The idea is that one cannot simply be caused to be morally bad by the environment. So either Harris's soul is not (morally) marred, or he has been a willing accomplice to the malformation of the self. His evil means that he has consented to what he has become—namely, one who consents to cruelty. Thus, Abélardians try to fill the statistical cracks with the will. The development of the moral self, they will say, is mediated by consent.

We should be struck here by the a priori character of libertarian convictions. How is Harris's consent to be construed, and why *must* it have occurred? What evidence is there that it occurred? Why

---

[19] Peter Abélard, *Ethics* (c. 1139), in *Ethical Writings* (Indianapolis: Hackett, 1995), p. 10.

couldn't Harris just have become that way? What is the difference
between his having acquiesced to what he became and his simply
having become that way? The libertarian faces the following difficulty: If there is no such difference, then the view is vacuous, for
consent was supposed to explain his becoming that way. If there is
a difference, what evidence is there that it obtains in a particular
case? Isn't there room for considerable doubt about this, and
shouldn't libertarians, or we, insofar as we are libertarians, be very
doubtful about Harris's responsibility—and indeed, on the
Abélardian thesis, even about whether Harris is an evil man,
whether his soul is morally marred? (Notice that the tumor case is
a priori impossible on that thesis, unless we think of the tumor
somehow as merely presenting an occasion for consent—as inclin-
ing without necessitating.) One suspects that the libertarian confidence in their attributions of historical responsibility is rooted in
a picture according to which the fact that Harris became that way
proves that he consented. Then, of course, the appeal to consent is
explanatorily vacuous.

Epistemology apart, the attempt to trace the evil self to consent
at an earlier stage is faced with familiar difficulties. If we suppose
(fancifully) that Harris, earlier on, with full knowledge and deliberation, launched himself on his iniquitous career,[20] we would be
merely postponing the inquiry, for the will which could fully and
deliberately consent to such a career would have to have its roots
in a self which is already morally marred—a self, therefore, which
cannot itself be seen simply as a product of consent. Are we instead
to suppose that at some earlier stage Harris slipped heedlessly
or recklessly into patterns of thought and action which he ought to
have known would eventuate in an evil character? (This seems
to have been Aristotle's view in *Nicomachean Ethics*, Book III.5.)

[20] If such a thing ever occurred, it must have occurred at a stage when Harris clearly
would have fallen under the exemption condition of "being a child."

In that case, we would be tracing his present ways to the much less egregious faults of negligence.[21]

Responsibility for the self

Strawson and others often charge libertarians with a metaphysically dubious conception of the self. The foregoing reflections indicate a basis for this charge. Libertarianism combines the Abélardian view about consent (or something like it) with the principle (or something like it) that to be responsible for anything, one must be responsible for (some of) what produces it. If we think of agents as consenting to this or that *because* they are (or have?) selves of a certain character, then it looks as though they are responsible for so consenting only if they are responsible for the self in which that consent is rooted. To establish this in each case, we have to trace the character of the self to earlier acts of consent. This enterprise seems hopeless, since the trace continues interminably or leads to a self to which the individual did not consent. The libertarian seems committed, then, to bearing the unbearable burden of showing how we can be responsible for ourselves. This burden can seem bearable only in a view of the self as an entity that mysteriously both transcends and intervenes in the "causal nexus," because it is both product and author of its actions and attitudes.

Must libertarians try to bear this burden? Perhaps the idea that they must rests upon a view of the self to which libertarians need not be committed. Perhaps the trouble arises in the first place from viewing the self as a thing standing in causal relation to acts of consent. The libertarian might say that to talk about the (moral) self is not to talk about an entity which necessitates specific acts of consent, but to talk about the sorts of things to which an individual

---

[21] Adams makes this point; op. cit.

tends to consent. To speak of Harris's moral self is not to explain his conduct, but to indicate the way he is morally. What we are responsible for are the particular things we consent to. We need not consider whether we are responsible for the genesis of the entity whose characteristics necessitate those acts of consent, for there is no such entity. In a way, of course, one is derivatively responsible for one's self, since one's moral self is constituted by the character of what one consents to, and one is responsible for what one consents to.[22]

The historical dimension of the concept of responsibility results from the principle that one is not responsible for one's conduct if that is necessitated by causes for which one is not responsible. This leads to a problematic requirement that one be responsible for one's self only if one thinks of the self as an entity that causes one's (its) actions and willings. Libertarians can reject this view. What they must affirm is that we are responsible for what we consent to, that consent is not necessitated by causes internal or external to the agent, and that if it were, we could not properly hold the individual responsible for what he or she consents to. These claims are far from self-evident. But they hardly amount to a "panicky metaphysics" (p. 93).[23]

In the end, however, I do not think that libertarianism can be so readily domesticated. The idea that one is responsible for and only for what one consents to is not of course distinctive of libertarianism; that idea has no historical implications. What is distinctive is the further requirement that consent be undetermined. I do not think the idea that consent is undetermined is in itself particularly problematic. The trouble begins only when we ask why this is *required*. The ground of this requirement is the intuition that unless consent were undetermined, we would not truly be *originators* of our deeds. We

---

[22] It is noteworthy that Harris himself seems to accept responsibility for his life: "He told me he had his chance, he took the road to hell and there's nothing more to say." (From the end of the first excerpt from the Corwin article.)

[23] For an attempt at libertarianism without metaphysics, see David Wiggins, "Towards a Reasonable Form of Libertarianism," in Watson 2003. Wiggins responds specifically to Strawson at pp. 117–20.

would be merely products, and not, as it were, producers. It is this intuition to which the libertarian finds it so difficult to give content. "Being an originator" does not mean just "consenting to," for that is already covered by the first thesis. Nor is this notion captured simply by adding the requirement of indeterminism; that is a merely negative condition. Attempts to specify the condition in positive terms either cite something that could obtain in a deterministic world, or something obscurely transcendent.

I suspect, then, that any metaphysically innocuous version of libertarianism must leave its incompatibilist component unmotivated. [For more on this point, see Chapter 7, this volume.]

Ignorance and skepticism

I have been exploring some ways in which the expressive theory might explain the relevance of certain historical considerations. Whatever the best explanation may be, the remarkable fact is that we are, for the most part, quite ignorant of these considerations. Why does our ignorance not give us more pause? If, for whatever reason, reactive attitudes are sensitive to historical considerations, as Strawson acknowledges, and we are largely ignorant of these matters, then it would seem that most of our reactive attitudes are hasty, perhaps even benighted, as skeptics have long maintained. In this respect, our ordinary practices are not as unproblematic as Strawson supposes.

It might be thought that these suspicions about reactive attitudes have no bearing on responsibility, but with the expressive theory, that point cannot be easily maintained. As we normally think of the matter, not all considerations that affect reactive attitudes are strictly relevant to responsibility. For example, if one shares a moral fault with another, one may feel it inappropriate to blame the other. Here the point is not that the other is not responsible or blameworthy, but that it is not *one's* business to blame. One should tend to one's own faults first.[24] Thoughts about moral luck seem to be continuous with this ordinary phenomenon. The thought is not that the other is not blameworthy, but that one may be no better, and that indignation on one's part would be self-righteous and indulgent. By calling our attention to our general ignorance of historical considerations, the skepticism we have just been considering is merely an extension of these reflections.

With an expressive theory, however, it is not clear that a general skepticism about the propriety of the reactive attitudes can be separated from skepticism about responsibility. For the latter concept *is* the concept of the conditions in which it is appropriate to respond to one another in reactive ways. In a Strawsonian view, there is no room for a wedge between the practices that evince the reactive attitudes and the belief in responsibility. In a particular case, one may believe another to be responsible without actually responding to him or her in reactive ways (due to strains of commitment and so on), because one may regard the other as blameworthy, as an appropriate object of the reactive attitudes by others in the moral community. But if one thinks that *none* of us mortals is in a position to blame, then it is doubtful that any sense can be given to the belief that the other is nonetheless blameworthy. One can still attribute cowardice, thoughtlessness, cruelty, and so on, to others; but as we have seen, these judgments are not sufficient in a Strawsonian view to characterize the practice of holding responsible. We might try to appeal to the reactive attitudes of a select group of actual or hypothetical judges, but then the connection to reactive attitudes becomes so tenuous or hypothetical that the attitudes lose the central role they are given in "Freedom and Resentment," and the expressive theory loses its distinctive character. It then collapses into the view discussed in the section called "Blaming and finding fault."

---

[24] Montaigne would not agree: "To censure my own faults in some other person seems to me no more incongruous than to censure, as I often do, another's in myself. They must be denounced everywhere, and be allowed no place of sanctuary." ("On the Education of Children," in *Essays*, Penguin Classics, 1971, p. 51.)

Objectivity and isolation

It remains unclear to what extent our ordinary practices involve dubious beliefs about ourselves and our histories. To acknowledge the relevance of historical considerations is, on any account, to acknowledge a potential source of skepticism about those practices; moreover, in a Strawsonian account (though not in a libertarian account), such skepticism cannot be readily separated from skepticism about responsibility itself. In this respect, Strawson is inordinately optimistic about our common ways.

However, these practices are vulnerable to a different kind of suspicion. This suspicion is related to Strawson's conception of the place of "retributive" sentiments in those practices, and to his claim that that practice, so conceived, is not something that is optional and open to radical criticism, but rather is part of the "framework" of our conception of human society. One could agree that the expressive theory best gives the basis and content of the practice of holding responsible and still maintain that abandoning this practice is not only conceivable but desirable, for what it expresses is itself destructive of human community. I conclude with some comments on this further issue.

Consider some remarks by Albert Einstein:

I do not at all believe in human freedom in the philosophical sense. Everybody acts not only under external compulsion but also in accordance with inner necessity. Schopenhauer's saying, "A man can do what he wants, but not want what he wants," has been a very real inspiration to me since my youth; it has been a continual consolation in the face of life's hardships, my own and others', and an unfailing well-spring of tolerance. This realization mercifully mitigates the easily paralysing sense of responsibility and prevents us from taking ourselves and other people all too seriously; it is conducive to a view of life which, in particular, gives humor its due.[25]

---

[25] Albert Einstein. *Ideas and Opinions*, Crown Publishers, 1982, pp. 8–9.

Significantly, in the same place Einstein speaks of himself as a "lone traveler," with a "pronounced lack of need for direct contact with other human beings and human communities," who has

never belonged to my country, my home, my friends, or even my immediate family, with my whole heart; in the face of all these ties, I have never lost a sense of distance and a need for solitude—feelings which increase with the years.

The point that interests me here is not that these remarks confute Strawson's claim that reactive attitudes are never in practice affected by an acceptance of determinism, but that they corroborate his central claim about the alternative to the reactive, participant stance. The "distance" of which Einstein speaks is just an aspect of the "detachment" Strawson thinks characterizes the objective stance. At its extremes, it takes the form of human isolation. What is absent from Einstein's outlook is something that, I suspect, Strawson cherishes: the attachment or commitment to the personal, as it might be called.[26]

Whatever its grounds, Einstein's outlook is not without its appeal. Perhaps part of its appeal can be attributed to a fear of the personal, but it is also appealing precisely on account of its repudiation of the retributive sentiments. In another place, Einstein salutes the person "to whom aggressiveness and resentment are alien."[27] Can such an ideal of the person be pursued only at the cost of the attachment to the personal? Must we choose between isolation and animosity?

Some of Strawson's remarks imply that we must:

Indignation, disapprobation, like resentment, tend to inhibit or at least to limit our goodwill towards the object of these attitudes, tend to promote

---

[26] To what extent Einstein lived up to this outlook, I am not prepared to say. Some other writings suggest a different view: "External compulsion can . . . reduce but never cancel the responsibility of the individual. In the Nuremberg trials, this idea was considered to be self-evident. . . . Institutions are in a moral sense impotent unless they are supported by the sense of responsibility of living individuals. An effort to arouse and strengthen this sense of responsibility of the individual is an important service to mankind" (op. cit., p. 27). Is Einstein taking a consequentialist stance here?

[27] Ibid.

at least partial and temporary withdrawal of goodwill. . . . (These are not contingent connections.) But these attitudes . . . are precisely the correlates of the moral demand in the case where the demand is felt to be disregarded. The making of the demand *is* the proneness to such attitudes. . . . The holding of them does not . . . involve . . . viewing their object other than as a member of the moral community. The partial withdrawal of goodwill which these attitudes entail, the modification they entail of the general demand that another should if possible be spared suffering, is . . . the consequence of *continuing* to view him as a member of the moral community: only as one who has offended against its demands. So the preparedness to acquiesce in that infliction of suffering on the offender which is an essential part of punishment is all of a piece with this whole range of attitudes. . . . (p. 90)

This passage is troubling. Some have aspired to rid themselves of the readiness to limit goodwill and to acquiesce in the suffering of others not in order to relieve the strains of involvement, nor out of a conviction in determinism, but out of a certain ideal of human relationships, which they see as poisoned by the retributive sentiments. It is an ideal of human fellowship or love which embodies values that are arguably as historically important to our civilization as the notion of moral responsibility itself. The question here is not whether this aspiration is finally commendable, but whether it is compatible with holding one another morally responsible. The passage implies that it is not.

If holding one another responsible involves making the moral demand, and if the making of the demand *is* the proneness to such attitudes, and if such attitudes involve retributive sentiments and hence[28] a limitation of goodwill, then skepticism about retribution is skepticism about responsibility, and holding one another responsible is at odds with one historically important ideal of love.

Many who have this ideal, such as Gandhi or King,[29] do not seem to adopt an objective attitude in Strawson's sense. Unlike Einstein's,

---

[28] Rather than attempting to separate retribution from responsibility, one might try to harmonize retribution and goodwill. This possibility seems to me worth exploring.

[29] For these examples, and the discussion in this section, I am indebted to Stern (op. cit.).

their lives do not seem characterized by human isolation: They are often intensely involved in the "fray" of interpersonal relations. Nor does it seem plausible to suppose that they do not hold themselves and others morally responsible: They *stand up* for themselves and others against their oppressors; they *confront* their oppressors with the fact of their misconduct, *urging* and even *demanding* consideration for themselves and others; but they manage, or come much closer than others to managing, to do such things without vindictiveness or malice.

Hence, Strawson's claims about the interpenetration of responsibility and the retributive sentiments must not be confused with the expressive theory itself. As these lives suggest, the retributive sentiments can in principle be stripped away from holding responsible and the demands and appeals in which this consists. What is left are various forms of reaction and appeal to others as moral agents. The boundaries of moral responsibility are the boundaries of intelligible moral address. To regard another as morally responsible is to react to him or her as a moral self.[30]

POSTSCRIPT TO 'RESPONSIBILITY AND THE LIMITS OF EVIL' (ADDED 2004)

Robert Harris, often described in the media as the 'laughing killer', didn't get the last laugh. That went to some of the witnesses of his execution at San Quentin Prison on 21 April 1992. Michael Kroll described what he saw that morning for *The Nation* magazine (6 July, 1992). Calling himself 'a close friend [of Harris] for nearly a decade', Kroll records that as Harris was finally fastened to the chair in the gas chamber, he looked around and, recognizing the father of one of his victims, mouthed the words, 'I'm sorry.' Sixteen minutes after the cynanide was released, an official pronounced Harris dead. The scene that prompted the laughter, according to Kroll, was this: for seven minutes, Harris 'writhed . . . , his head falling on his

---

[30] We have, of course, seen reasons why these boundaries require further delineation.

chest. . . . He lifted his head again and again. . . . His heart . . . kept pumping for nine more minutes.' In this way, the state of California enacted the reactive attitudes of its citizens.

Kroll writes:

> We were in the middle of something indescribably ugly. Not just the fact of the cold-blooded killing of a human being, and not even the fact that we happened to love him—but the ritual of it, the witnessing itself of this most private and personal act. It was nakedly barbaric. Nobody could say this had anything to do with justice, I thought. Yet this medieval torture chamber is what a larger majority of my fellow Californians . . . believe in. The implications of this filled me with fear . . . while my friend was being strangled slowly to death in front of me.

One thing is clear from this report that was not obvious at the time of the killings: in his last years Harris either remained, or became once again, capable of friendship and remorse. His crimes were monstrous, but he was not a monster. He was one of us.

9   Two Faces of Responsibility[1]

1. Responsibility as Self-Disclosure

In an early work, John Dewey wrote:

[W]hen any result has been foreseen and adopted as foreseen [by the agent], such result is the outcome not of any external circumstances, not of mere desires and impulses, but of the agent's conception of his own end. Now because the result thus flows from the agent's own conception of an end, he feels himself responsible for it. . . . The result is simply an expression of himself; a manifestation of what he would have himself to be. Responsibility is thus one aspect of the identity of character and conduct. *We are responsible for our conduct because that conduct is ourselves objectified in actions.*[2]

This passage indicates a conception of responsibility that has appealed in various versions to many writers, including me. This conception goes naturally with a view of free action and free will as autonomy. Actions which "express" ourselves in the required sense are free actions, whatever their farther causes may be. To be a responsible

[1] This paper originated in an Author Meets Critic session on Susan Wolf's *Freedom within Reason* at the Pacific Meeting of the American Philosophical Association in 1992. A number of audiences have heard versions of this material since that occasion. I am grateful for their comments. I have profited especially from discussions with the members of the Moral and Political Philosophy Society of Southern California, and with Richard Arneson, Michael Bratman, John Fischer, Janet Levin, Michael Martin, and Dion Scott-Kakures.

[2] John Dewey, *Outlines of a Critical Theory of Ethics* (1891; reprint, New York: Hillary House, 1957), 160–1.

agent is to have what Dewey calls "moral capacity," which is the power to "put various ends before the self" and "to be governed in action by the thought of some end to be reached." This capacity entails "freedom from the appetites and desires"; it is "the power of self-government."[3]

For obvious reasons, I shall call this conception of responsibility the *self-disclosure*[4] *view*. This view, along with its companion conception of freedom as autonomy, has been vigorously criticized on a number of grounds. One problem is that its paradigm of free and responsible action—namely, action that expresses self-adopted ends—is not obviously applicable to cases of negligent conduct or to "weak-willed" or to self-deceptive behavior. Another problem is that individuals' "conceptions of their own ends" might be due to "brainwashing" or indoctrination of a kind that significantly undermines or compromises responsibility and freedom.

Whether or not the self-disclosure view can effectively respond to these criticisms. I shall not discuss here. Instead, I want to take up a different charge and to explore a distinction between two perspectives on responsibility to which this criticism gives rise. The criticism is articulated in Susan Wolf's book. *Freedom within Reason*.[5] Views of the type that I am here calling self-disclosure views Wolf calls "real self views," by which she means the idea that freedom is controlled by one's "deepest" values or commitments and that responsibility is defined in terms of the relationship between one's conduct and those values. One of her complaints is that "real self views" ignore the importance of *normative competence*;[6] a person's status as a responsible agent requires not only the capacity to conform her desires and conduct to her deepest values ("self-government," in Dewey's phrase) but also the capacity to acquire the *right* values—that is, those we hold her responsible for having.

---

[3] Ibid., 158–9.

[4] For this term, I am indebted to Paul Benson's insightful discussion in "Freedom and Value," *The Journal of Philosophy* 84 (1987): 465–86.

[5] Susan Wolf, *Freedom within Reason* (Oxford: Oxford University Press, 1990).

[6] For a helpful discussion of normative competence, see Benson, op. cit.

A second complaint is that the real self view[7] can at best account for a "superficial" kind of responsibility. We want an account of responsible agency, she thinks, which explains why individuals have a special status

in virtue of which the good and bad things they do can resound [*sic*] to their respective credit or discredit while lower animals and objects cannot be so deeply evaluated for the good and bad traits they display.[8]

She goes on:

[W]hen we hold an agent morally responsible for some event, we are doing more than identifying her particularly crucial role in the causal series. . . . [W]e are not merely judging the moral quality of the event with which the individual is so intimately associated; we are judging the moral quality of the individual herself in some focused, noninstrumental, and seemingly more serious way. We may refer to the latter sense of responsibility as deep responsibility, and we may speak in connection with this of deep praise and blame.[9]

To capture "deep" responsibility, she argues, we must turn from real self views to what she calls the "reason view": responsible agency consists in "the ability to form, assess, and revise those values on the basis of a recognition and appreciation of . . . the True and the Good."[10]

The question of normative competence is a very important one. Self-disclosure views have said too little about it. Holding people responsible is not just a matter of the relation of an individual to her behavior; it also involves a social setting in which we demand (require) certain conduct from one another and respond adversely to one another's failures to comply with these demands. Self-disclosure views have largely ignored this context. Typically, they are silent about the content of the ends of responsible agents, about the capacity

---

[7] My use of this phrase should not conceal significant differences among views of this kind, differences that might effect the force of Wolf's criticisms. Nor will the ontological overtones of talk of "real selves" be appropriate for some members of this class.

[8] Wolf, op. cit., 63.   [9] Ibid., 41.   [10] Ibid., 117.

of self-governing agents to comprehend the grounds on which moral requirements rest, and about our authority to hold one another to these. (This itself is a kind of normative competence.) Even though Dewey calls it our "moral" capacity, the "power of self-government" is too abstractly characterized to explain the kind of responsibility that is involved in the practice of holding one another morally accountable. The self-governing agent as described so far might be morally dead (or "insane" as Wolf puts it elsewhere).[11]

But I do not agree that the self-disclosure view accounts at best for a "superficial" notion of responsibility. Moral accountability is only part, and not necessarily the most important part, of our idea of responsibility. The self-disclosure view describes a core notion of responsibility that is central to ethical life and ethical appraisal. In virtue of the capacities identified by the self-disclosure view, conduct can be attributable or imputable to an individual as its agent and is open to appraisal that is therefore appraisal of the individual as an adopter of ends. Attributability in this sense *is* a kind of responsibility. In virtue of the capacities in question, the individual is an agent in a strong sense, an author of her conduct, and is in an important sense answerable for what she does. While (strict liability aside) attributability in this sense is crucial to the practices of moral accountability, it does not all by itself underwrite them.

Attributability has an importance to ethical life that is distinct from concerns about accountability. Responsibility is important to issues about what it is to lead a life, indeed about what it is to have a life in the biographical sense, and about the quality and character

---

[11] See Susan Wolf, "Sanity and the Metaphysics of Responsibility," in *Responsibility, Character, and the Emotions*, ed. F. Schoeman (Cambridge: Cambridge University Press, 1987), 46–62.

Wolf's defense of the reason view, here and in her book, does not seem to me sufficiently attentive to the interpersonal contexts of accountability, either. To develop an understanding of normative competence of the kind that she justly finds lacking in self-disclosure views, we must investigate these contexts in detail. For the relevant conditions of normative competence depend on these.

of that life. These issues reflect one face of responsibility (what I will call its *aretaic* face). Concerns about accountability reflect another.[12]

While there is room for philosophical skepticism about both perspectives, the skeptical doubts are distinct. In particular, the pressure for some kind of problematic principle of avoidability comes entirely, I would argue, from accountability and its corresponding notion of blame.

I will develop these points in the remainder of the essay.

2. *Two Perspectives*

Some remarks by Peter van Inwagen might help me to develop the distinction between these two perspectives on responsibility. Van Inwagen speaks of a colleague

who has written a paper in which he denies the reality of moral responsibility. And yet this same philosopher when certain of his books were stolen, said, "That was a shoddy thing to do." But no one can consistently say that a certain act was a shoddy thing to do *and* say that its agent was not morally responsible when he performed it. . . . [13]

---

[12] Harry Frankfurt's work on responsibility, for example, comes largely from the perspective of attributability rather than accountability.

> My philosophical attention has for the most part been guided less by an interest in questions about [how we ought to conduct ourselves in relation to others] than by a concern with issues belonging more properly to metaphysics or the philosophy of mind. . . . (Harry Frankfurt, *The Importance of What We Care About* [Cambridge: Cambridge University Press, 1988], vii).

I do not take Frankfurt's point here to be that his concern has been metaphysics and philosophy of mind *rather than* morality or ethics in a broad sense. It is clear from the beginning of his work on these subjects that the "metaphysical" notions he focuses on are understood to be crucial to our sense of what is important in human life, to our sense of ourselves as persons.

[13] Peter van Inwagen, *An Essay on Free Will* (Oxford: Oxford University Press, 1983), 207.

To blame, to remonstrate, to hate, van Inwagen claims, "is to demonstrate more than any high-minded speech ever could that we believe in moral responsibility."[14] But "believing in moral responsibility," I want to say, is a complex thing. While it would be idle to speculate about what van Inwagen's colleague meant, this case can help us to see some of that complexity.

To say (or judge) that stealing the books was a shoddy thing to do implies that the thief behaved shoddily, and hence that the act was attributable to the agent. To call the conduct "shoddy" is to see it as "inferior goods," as a poor exercise of human evaluative capacities, as characteristic of someone who cares little about standards of excellence in human affairs. It is right to see this judgment as imputing shoddy behavior to the subject, in virtue of which he is in a way answerable as its agent. However, such attributions should not be too quickly grouped with other judgments which the colleague allegedly wishes to eschew.

"Those who are not morally responsible for what they do may perhaps deserve our pity," van Inwagen goes on to say, "they certainly do not deserve our censure."[15] But 'shoddy' need not express "censure." That implies a public forum, in which the subject is liable to formal sanction. To speak of conduct as deserving of "censure," or "remonstration," as "outrageous," "unconscionable" (and on some views, even as "wrong"), is to suggest that some *further response* to the agent is (in principle) appropriate. It is to invoke the practice of holding people morally accountable, in which (typically) the judge (or if not the judge, other members of the moral community) is entitled (in principle) to react in various ways.

To return to my earlier point: the judgments by van Inwagen's colleague do commit him to attributability of the kind identified by the self-disclosure view. But nothing in this view explains or justifies any such reactive entitlement. What the colleague rejects, we may conjecture, are further features of the practice of moral accountability.

---

[14] Ibid.   [15] Ibid.

He might or might not be right to do so, but he is not, I think, therefore inconsistent.

This point can be put in terms of the concept of blame. In one way, to blame (morally) is to attribute something to a (moral) fault in the agent; therefore, to call conduct shoddy *is* to blame the agent. But judgments of moral blameworthiness are also thought to involve the idea that agents deserve adverse treatment or "negative attitudes" in response to their faulty conduct.[16] The former kinds of blaming and praising judgments are independent of what I am calling the practices of moral accountability. They invoke only the attributability conditions, on which certain appraisals of the individual as an agent are grounded. Because many of these appraisals concern the agent's excellences and faults—or virtues and vices—as manifested in thought and action, I shall say that such judgments are made from the *aretaic perspective*.[17]

If we think of the aretaic perspective as concerned with the question of what activities and ways of life are most choiceworthy, then some aretaic appraisal, for example, van Inwagen's colleague's, is what we would call moral. But even if one takes all such appraisals to be moral in a broad sense, they are independent of the particular moral norms that are invoked in accountability. This becomes clearer by taking a different example. If someone betrays her ideals by choosing a dull but secure occupation in favor of a riskier but potentially more enriching one, or endangers something of deep importance to her life for trivial ends (by sleeping too little and drinking too much before important performances, for example), then she has acted badly—cowardly, self-indulgently, at least

---

[16] For the first conception of blame, see Ronald Milo, *Immorality* (Princeton, N.J.: Princeton University Press, 1984). The second sort of account is expressed by Richard Brandt, "Blameworthiness and Obligation," in *Essays in Moral Philosophy*, ed. A. I. Melden (Seattle: University of Washington Press, 1958), and Jonathan Glover, *Responsibility* (New York: Humanities Press, 1970).

[17] A related distinction between moral credit and moral worth is usefully developed in E. L. Beardsley, "Determinism and Moral Perspectives," *Philosophy and Phenomenological Research* 17 (1960): 1–20.

unwisely. But by these assessments we are not thereby *holding* her responsible, as distinct from holding her to be responsible. To do that, we would have to think that she is accountable to us or to others, whereas in many cases we suppose that such behavior is "nobody's business." Unless we think she is responsible to us or to others to live the best life she can—and that is a moral question—we do not think she is accountable here. If her timid or foolish behavior also harms others, and thereby violates requirements of interpersonal relations, that is a different matter.

It is no contradiction, then, to respond to the aretaic face of responsibility while denying the legitimacy of moral accountability. For all that I will argue here, that denial may or may not be defensible. But van Inwagen's colleague *is* mistaken, I am trying to show, to think that he can speak from the aretaic perspective without committing himself to responsibility in any way at all. It is this core notion of responsibility with which the self-disclosure view is concerned.

3. *Deep Responsibility and Practical Identity*

I turn now to Wolf's complaint that this notion is, after all, "shallow." Real self views cannot provide for "deep responsibility," she argues, because they cannot explain "how . . . persons [can] deserve a distinctive and more serious kind of blame for being deceitful or petty than pigs deserve for being sloppy or books for being frayed."[18] She presses this point against the following remark by R. E. Hobart:

He did not make his character; no, but he made his acts. Nobody blames him for making such a character, but only for making such acts. And to blame him for that is simply to say that he is a bad act-maker.[19]

[18] Wolf, *Freedom within Reason*, 64.

[19] R. E. Hobart, "Free Will as Involving Determinism and Inconceivable without It," in *Free Will and Determinism*, ed. Bernard Berofsky (New York: Harper and Row, 1966), 83. Hobart should have said: "to blame him for making an act is to say he made a bad act"; one bad act doesn't make a bad act-maker.

Hobart's claim is untrue, Wolf thinks, of "the particular kind of blame that is associated with the philosophical question of responsibility."[20] Wolf develops her point in this way:

When we say that an individual is responsible for an event in the superficial sense, we identify the individual as playing a causal role that, relative to the interests and expectations provided by the context, is of special importance to the explanation of that event. And when we praise or blame an individual in the superficial sense, we acknowledge that the individual has good or bad qualities, or has performed good or bad acts. But when we hold an individual morally responsible for some event, we are doing more than identifying her particularly crucial role in the causal series that brings about the event in question. We are regarding her as a fit subject for credit or discredit on the basis of the role she plays.[21]

Wolf's distinction here is long-standing. In 1744, Christian Crucius argued that free will

should make a man responsible for his activity, so that one does not only ascribe it to him as the efficient cause but also can think him open to praise or blame or to charges of guilt and can hold him worthy of punishment or reward because he acted this way rather than that.[22]

Crucius goes on to distinguish "two sorts of praise and blame,"

first the nonmoral, which is nothing but a judgment of the perfection or imperfection of the thing, and second, the moral, when we hold someone to be the free cause of a characteristic that we recognize as worthy of praise or blame.[23]

Two separate points are asserted in these passages—first, that so-called responsibility on real self views is merely causal (and therefore ethically superficial); second, that what I am calling aretaic

---

[20] Wolf, *Freedom within Reason*, 40.   [21] Ibid., 40–1.

[22] Christian Crucius, *Guide to Rational Living*, in *Moral Philosophy from Montaigne to Kant*. vol. 2, ed. J. B. Schneewind (Cambridge: Cambridge University Press, 1990), 570–1. I am grateful to Schneewind for calling my attention to these passages.   [23] Ibid., 571.

appraisals are simply descriptions of a thing's qualities and differ in kind from moral blame in the strict (deep?) sense.[24] On the self-disclosure view, to blame someone for an outcome is to trace this effect to some fault (imperfection) in the thing. I want to dispute both of these points.

The first claim depends, I suspect, upon taking real self views as more or less sophisticated variants of a basically Hobbesian picture. In the simplest form of this view, an agent is taken to be responsible for an event when and because it is caused by his desires. Thus all "voluntary actions" (roughly, bodily motion caused by desires and expectations) are such that the agent is responsible for them. In this stripped-down version, the real self is the will (that is, the strongest desire).

In this form, the defects of the real self view (so construed) are conspicuous. It obscures the relevant distinctions between animals and human beings, between persons and automata, between voluntary conduct and operant conditioning, between structural defects and virtues. More sophisticated versions can be seen as attempts to avoid these embarrassments by distinguishing between "mere desires" and something psychologically and motivationally more complex: as the case may be, values, reason, higher-order volitions, identifications.

On the diagnosis I have in mind, the common defect of views of this kind is that they flout the *control principle*: we can't be rightly blamed unless we have control over the causes of our conduct. If we

---

[24] On this point, Wolf and Crucius would be joined by Galen Strawson:

[I]f determinism is true, then to pass moral judgements on people, and to say that they acted morally rightly or wrongly, is, in a crucial respect, exactly like saying they are beautiful or ugly—something for which they are not responsible (Galen Strawson, *Freedom and Belief* [Oxford: Oxford University Press, 1986], 92).

And, as we say, beauty is only skin deep. I do not object to treating aretaic judgments as aesthetic. What I object to is the opposition between these and moral judgments. As I go on to insist, the beauty and ugliness in question here are qualities of people *as agents*.

lack control of our desires, as no Hobbesian view can preclude, we lack control of our wills, thereby violating the control principle. (This diagnosis is that of Crucius,[25] and probably also that of Wolf.) Real self views are clearly hopeless as responses to this problem. Wolf puts the point well: "The kind of control . . . that we feel to be lacking cannot be supplied by another loop to the internal structure of the agent."[26]

But I think we should take real self views to have a different focus. They are prompted by a concern with agency or attributability, rather than with control and accountability. The significant relation between behavior and the "real self" is not (just)[27] causal but *execut-ive* and *expressive*. When thought or behavior are exercises of what Dewey calls an agent's moral capacity, they and their results are open to distinctive kinds of evaluation. These evaluations are inescapably evaluations of the agent because the conduct in question expresses the agent's own evaluative commitments, her adoption of some ends among others. To adopt some ends among others is to declare what one stands for.

Aretaic evaluations thus differ significantly from other forms of appraisal. If I dance clumsily, it is inescapably true of me that I was (on that occasion) a clumsy dancer. But if what I do flows from my values and ends, there is a stronger sense in which my activities are inescapably my own: I am committed to them. As declarations of my adopted ends, they express what I'm about, my identity as an agent. They can be evaluated in distinctive ways (not just as welcome or

[25] The importance of control in Crucius's critique is evident:

> [A]n act to which the efficient substance were determined through its own ideas and desires which one calls spontaneity or spiritual self-activity . . . would not cease to be necessary. . . . In such a case, all our virtue would be turned into a mere piece of luck (Crucius, op. cit., 570–1).

[26] Wolf, *Freedom within Reason*, 44.

[27] A proper account of the relationship might well involve a causal analysis; but the crucial point is not that adopting an end caused a result but that the conduct in some way *realizes* or executes the intention.

unwelcome) because they themselves are exercises of my evaluative capacities.

We are now in a position to respond to a challenge issued by Wolf:

Why should the distinctive kind of complexity that is constituted by the possession of a real self make a creature subject to a different kind of accountability from that to which other creatures and objects are subject?[28]

The point of speaking of the "real self" is not metaphysical, to penetrate to one's ontological center; what is in question is an individual's fundamental evaluative orientation. Because aretaic appraisals implicate one's practical identity, they have ethical depth in an obvious sense.

This brings out the way in which aretaic appraisal involves an attribution of responsibility. To adopt an end, to commit oneself to a conception of value in this way, is a way of taking responsibility. To stand for something is to take a stand, to be ready to stand up for, to defend, to affirm, to answer for. Hence one notion of responsibility—*responsibility as attributability*—belongs to the very notion of practical identity.[29]

4. Control and Responsibility for One's Ends

I do not mean to say that the notion of control is irrelevant to responsibility on the self-disclosure view. Rather, issues of control are

---

[28] Wolf, *Freedom within Reason*, 43.

[29] Here I am indebted to Charles Taylor's suggestive remarks in *Sources of the Self* (Cambridge, Mass.: Harvard University Press, 1989), esp. ch. 2. I agree with Taylor that the notion of identity is a social notion. One has an identity, a self, only within a "web of interlocution." "I am a self only in relation to certain [actual or potential or hypothetical] interlocutors" (ibid., 36). See also Cheshire Calhoun, "Standing for Something," *Journal of Philosophy* 92 (1995): 235–60.

In speaking of *adopting* ends, I take very seriously the performative and social connotations of the word 'adopt': "to take as one's own in affection and law" (*Webster's Unabridged Dictionary*).

subsidiary to issues of attributability. Control bears on responsibility only so far as its absence indicates that the conduct was not attributable to the agent.[30] "I couldn't help it" negates responsibility, for example, only by indicating that the individual's behavior (or omission) was not after all an exercise of "moral capacity."

The focus on attributability explains why "responsibility for ends" is a very different issue for a self-disclosure view than for a control-centered view. From the latter standpoint, any account of control in terms of the relation between the agent's conduct and her ends will seem incomplete and superficial unless the agent also is "responsible for her ends," that is, has control over what ends she has. On self-disclosure views, responsibility for ends is the limiting case; ends in the relevant sense are necessarily self-disclosing, since they are direct exercises of moral capacity.[31] The primary issue for self-disclosure views is not control but how to specify the relevant sense of "adopting ends." Consider the way in which hypnosis and brain-washing are thought to engender "motivation" for which the agent is not responsible. Whereas other views would explain this by appealing to the absence of control, the problem on the self-disclosure view is to explain how these processes undercut attributability.

5. Holding Accountable

Against the charge of superficiality, I have been arguing that the self-disclosure view identifies a core notion of responsibility. Aretaic

---

[30] As Harry Frankfurt has shown, in his "Alternate Possibilities and Moral Responsibility," sec. 5, in *The Importance of What We Care About*.

[31] Consider Frankfurt's remarks in "Identification and Wholeheartedness" (in *The Importance of What We Care About*): In virtue of an agent's identification with a desire, "there is an important sense in which he takes responsibility for the fact of having the desire." "The question," he goes on to say, "of whether the person is responsible for his own character has to do with whether he has taken responsibility for his characteristics" (ibid., 170–1). I would go further: taking responsibility for one's characteristics is necessary for having a character.

appraisals are not merely attributions of "causal responsibility" that for this reason lack depth. I have conceded, however, that the self-disclosure view does not suffice for an understanding (or defense) of the practices of holding accountable. Arguably, control is a central issue for those practices. If so, the issue of responsibility for one's ends might reemerge in that context.

This conjecture is borne out by Aristotle's influential but difficult discussion of responsibility in *Nicomachean Ethics*, book 3, chapters 1–5. Early on, in his discussion of the "voluntary," Aristotle observes that mistakes about what is choiceworthy in human life do not render conduct involuntary; on the contrary, "that is a cause of blame." After all, on his view, "every vicious person is ignorant of the actions he must do or avoid."[32] In book 3, chapter 5, rather abruptly, Aristotle raises a worry of a different order, namely, whether the kind of people we are is in our power. These two discussions answer to two goals he announces at the outset of book 3: to clarify the nature of virtue and to say something useful to those who assign honors and punishments. It is plausible to see his discussion of the voluntary as a delineation of the attributability conditions for virtues and vices. These conditions are not affected by issues about control of one's character, which are driven by concerns about accountability (reward and punishment).[33]

I return to the question of responsibility for ends below. Let's turn now to the general idea of accountability.

The practice or practices of holding one another accountable are too varied and complex to investigate in detail here, but I hope to bring out some of this variety and describe some general features. Because some of these practices—and notably the practice of moral accountability—involve the imposition of demands on people, I shall argue, they raise issues of fairness that do not arise for aretaic appraisal. It is these concerns about fairness that underlie the

---

[32] Aristotle, *Nicomachean Ethics*, trans. Terence Irwin (Indianapolis, Ind.: Hackett, 1985), 57. [33] I say more about aretaic judgments in the appendix.

requirement of control (or avoidability) as a condition of moral accountability.

Putting the important self-reflexive case to one side, holding responsible is a three-term relationship in which one individual or group is held by another to certain expectations or demands or requirements. The party who is subject to these demands, etc., is said to be responsible *to* the other *for* complying with the demands. 'Holding responsible' can be taken as equivalent to 'holding accountable'. But the notion of 'holding' here is not to be confused with the attitude of *believing* (as in, 'I hold that she is responsible for *x*'). Holding people responsible involves a readiness to respond to them in certain ways.

Talk of responsibility is sometimes ambiguous between contexts in which we refer to someone's responsibilities and contexts in which we refer to someone's failures to meet her responsibilities.[34] The department chair is responsible for conducting personnel actions; it is her responsibility—that is, duty. She is also held responsible for failing to do so. In either case (again, the self-reflexive case aside), holding responsible is a triadic relation involving two people and a requirement (task, responsibility).

As these examples show, holding responsible is not always a moral or legal matter. If I hold the president (partly) responsible for worsening the economy, then I judge that he failed in his job (responsibility) to promote economic prosperity. (Perhaps I also judge that the president ruined the decor of the White House, but I will not hold him responsible for that unless I take it to be contrary to one of his responsibilities.) What is in question here is not necessarily a moral failure. In the same way, the building custodian is held responsible for neglecting the furnace. Another nonmoral example is given in the following (imaginary) sports-page article:

The Slugger fans booed Jim Takayama last night, after the rookie was tagged out at the plate. Takayama would have scored the tying run on

---

[34] A helpful discussion of this and related distinctions is to be found in H. L. A. Hart, *Punishment and Responsibility* (Oxford: Oxford University Press, 1968), ch. 9.

Jaime Benevides' single, but he hesitated as he rounded third. Manager Tom Forster told reporters that Takayama shouldn't be held responsible for the loss, because the runner received mixed signals from the third base coach.

The failure need not be something that is within the control of the agent. Certain ways of completing the phrase, 'He shouldn't be held responsible because . . . ' will not do, even though they cite factors beyond the player's control which explain his poor performance: for example, 'because he's an incompetent ball player (or gets confused easily, or lacks experience)'. Unlike the manager's explanation, or the fact that a bee stung him in the thigh as he rounded the corner, these do not get him off the hook. What gets him off the hook is what shows that he performed his role as a baseball player competently. Ineptitude does not get the president or the building custodian off the hook, either.

Clearly, then, it is not a general requirement that one be able to comply with the standards to which one is held responsible. Under what conditions does this requirement hold?

6. Liability and Authority

To be "on the hook" in these and other cases is to be liable to certain reactions as a result of failing to do what one is required. To require or demand certain behavior of an agent is to lay it down that unless the agent so behaves she will be liable to certain adverse or unwelcome treatment. For convenience, I shall call the diverse forms of adverse treatment "sanctions." Holding accountable thus involves the idea of liability to sanctions. To be entitled to make demands, then, is to be entitled to impose conditions of liability.

Practices of holding accountable give rise to two questions. First, by what authority do we subject one another to sanctions? And, second, what kind or kinds of sanction are involved in a particular practice? Obviously, sanctions take various forms: in the case of job responsibilities, the sanction will be the loss of one's position or earnings (or an increase in the probability that one of these will occur in the future). The nature of sanctions in the moral case is not so clear. That is one of the obscurities of moral accountability. I'll return to this second question later.

Suppose a hijacker says to one of his captives: "I'm holding you responsible for keeping the others in line. If they try anything, you'll answer to me." The demand is, of course, illegitimate ("unreasonable") in two ways. The captive might well be unable to control the others, to comply with the demand. Furthermore, the hijacker has no authority to make such a demand.

But we have just seen that it is not always unfair to hold people responsible for what is not under their control. To take another case, if you hire people to keep order in your dance hall, you hold them responsible for failing to do so. Perhaps they are no more able to control the crowd than the captive is. Yet there we suppose the sanction is fair enough. For we are supposing that the employees have agreed to the requirements and that the terms of the agreement were not unjust.

These examples suggest the following rough generalization. *It is unfair to impose sanctions upon people unless they have a reasonable opportunity to avoid incurring them.* If one had a fair opportunity to avoid being subject to the demand in the first place, or if, once subjected, one has the capacity to comply with it, then this condition is met. If one is subject to a requirement as part of a noncoercive and nonexploitative agreement, then one might be fairly held responsible for failing to satisfy it even if (as above) one is quite unable to do so. So 'demand' does not imply 'can'. The connection is rather a moral one: *just* demands require the opportunity to avoid the concomitant sanctions in one of these ways.

But just demands require more than this; they imply the legitimacy of the authority to make the demands. The hijackers' demands would still be unjust even if, scrupulously, they only made demands that could be satisfied.[35]

Since morality involves the authorization to make various demands on one another, the question of authority is an independent source of obscurity about distinctively moral accountability. In the case of special rights, the ground of authority seems relatively clear. If you make a promise to me, you thereby authorize me to hold you responsible in certain respects; you undertake certain responsibilities.[36] However, nothing like this seems to be true of general moral requirements.[37]

There is, then, an important connection between moral and political theory and the theory of moral responsibility. Moral theory must explain not only the content of morality but the source of the authority to impose moral requirements.[38]

7. Blame and Moral Sanctions

Let's return to the question of "sanctions." If holding responsible goes beyond aretaic appraisal, what more is involved in the moral case?

[35] Coercive political agencies are bands of thugs, we are inclined to think, unless they derive their authority from the consent of those who are subject to its demands. One of the main appeals of democracy is that it alone promises to meet this condition. Parental authority, however, is an acknowledged source of coercive demands that violates this principle.

[36] To be a thoroughgoing skeptic about moral responsibility, one would have to deny the possibility of valid promises.

[37] It would be a misconception about contractualism to suppose that it attempts to do just this. The fact that we *would have* agreed to be governed by certain principles has force only because we are required to look at interpersonal relations in these hypothetical terms. It is the authority to demand this of one another that is in question here.

[38] The question of authority seems especially difficult for moral theories such as emotivism and prescriptivism (as Gilbert Harman observes in his "Morality and Politics," *Midwest Studies in Philosophy*, vol. 3, ed. Peter A. French, Theodore E. Uehling, Jr., and Howard K. Wettstein [Minneapolis: University of Minnesota Press, 1978]). These theories give no basis for supposing that those who are subject to moral prescriptions have the slightest reason to pay attention to what others prescribe.

Recall our earlier discussion of blame. As we have already seen, the aretaic perspective is a source of blaming judgments in one plain sense: judgments that the agent's conduct was faulty in some way. If the fault is moral, so is the blame. But accountability blame is a response to the faults identified in aretaic blame.

The aretaic sense seems to collapse any distinction between blaming and judgments of blame. In this sense, one is worthy of blame just in case the attribution of fault is warranted. 'S is blameworthy for C' stands to 'S's conduct is faulty' as ' "P" is true' stands to 'P'; judging blameworthy is virtually blaming. In the accountability sense, however, there is a difference.

On one common view, to blame S for C is to have an unfavorable attitude toward S on account of C. Since it is one thing to think that someone deserves to be an object of such attitudes and another actually to have these attitudes, on this view one can judge someone to be blameworthy without blaming him or her oneself.

Some writers identify the blaming response with indignation, resentment, and disapprobation. Others, such as Jonathan Glover,[39] are content to speak simply of an undifferentiated "disapproval." On this view, the sanctions involved in being held morally accountable consist in being subject to these attitudes. One is blameworthy, and holding one responsible is warranted, just in case those attitudes are warranted.

But how is being subject to blaming attitudes a *sanction*? To most of us, it is disagreeable, as Glover says, to be disapproved of.[40] But how far will this take us? It is disagreeable only when the disapproval is felt. And some may be indifferent to others' disapproval altogether; can't they too be unfairly blamed? Now even unexpressed disapproval can result in adverse (for instance, less friendly) treatment; perhaps the targets of this disapproval tend to receive fewer of the benefits of human society. Let us assume, then, that blaming attitudes are not only disagreeable when directly expressed but

[39] See Glover, op. cit.   [40] Ibid.

that they involve dispositions to treat others in other generally unwelcome ways.

Yet we blame the dead and the otherwise inaccessible. Can we make sense of this in the accountability sense? Of course the dead can be wrongly accused or charged. But we are considering blame as a response to faulty conduct. That response cannot be disagreeable for the dead; blaming attitudes cannot therefore be sanctions in those cases.

It does not follow that blaming the dead for their faulty conduct could not be unfair. For we must distinguish the unfairness of the attitudes from the unfairness of the corresponding treatment. If it *would be* unfair to impose certain penalties on someone, then it *is* unfair to be ready (however impotently) to do so. If, as I have said, blaming attitudes involve a readiness to adverse treatment, then they might be unjust even when the exercise of this disposition is impossible. One's blaming attitudes are unfair if it would be unfair for whatever reason to subject others to the adverse treatment to which one's attitudes dispose one.[41]

8. Avoidability

Our earlier discussion led to the thought that people can be fairly subject to demands and their concomitant sanctions only if they had reasonable opportunities to comply. Indeed, Glover suggests that an appeal to justice of this kind can explain "all the excuses" relevant to responsibility: "We think it unfair to adopt an attitude of disapproval towards someone on account of an act or omission, where this

---

[41] This discussion raises issues about what counts as a penalty. If the dead can be harmed, and if being judged (or at least publicly proclaimed) to have acted wrongly counts as a harm, then the dead can be subject to sanctions. (I owe this point to David Sosa.) Clearly, the idea that a private negative judgment can in itself be a harm to an individual (dead or alive) makes sanctions inseparable from aretaic judgment.

was something outside his control." Assuming, again, that "it is disagreeable to be disapproved of," Glover takes this thought to derive from the principle that *we do not deserve to suffer what we cannot avoid*.[42] Whether or not this generalization about excusing conditions is entirely defensible, it brings out something that many wish to say in particular cases.

These remarks on sanctions are no more than a crude beginning to a real exploration of this territory. They treat moral accountability as a legal-like practice, an informal institution serving the ends of social regulation and/or of retributive and compensatory justice. No doubt this treatment leaves out crucial features of moral blame, and taken by itself it would give a very distorted view.[43] Yet it seems to me an important truth that blame *does*, among other things, serve these functions. In any case, my thesis is that it is only insofar as and because blaming responses (at least potentially) affect the interests of their objects adversely that moral accountability raises the issues of avoidability that have been central to the traditional topic of moral responsibility.[44]

9. Blaming the Victim

The distinction between aretaic and accountability blame helps to explain our ambivalence toward the vicious criminal who is himself a victim of an abusive childhood. His deliberate and remorseless

[42] Glover, op. cit., 73.

[43] For illuminating discussions of these ideas, see H. L. A. Hart, "Legal Responsibility and Excuses," in his *Punishment and Responsibility*; and T. M. Scanlon, "The Significance of Choice," in *The Tanner Lectures on Human Values*, vol. 8 (Salt Lake City: University of Utah Press, 1988).

As Scanlon says, to treat morality as "a social institution set up to serve certain extrinsic purposes" leaves out "the distinctive content of moral blame" (ibid., 212).

[44] Connections among the notions of accountability, fairness, and sanctions are developed in an important recent book by R. Jay Wallace, *Responsibility and the Moral Sentiments* (Cambridge, Mass.: Harvard University Press, 1994).

murders characterize him as malicious and cruel in a sense that no nonreflective being could be. The fact that life gave him a rotten deal, that his squalid circumstances made it overwhelmingly difficult to develop a respect for the standards to which we would hold him accountable, does not impugn these aretaic appraisals. His conduct is attributable to him as an exercise of his "moral capacities." It expresses and constitutes his practical identity, what he stands for, what he has made of his life as he found it.

At the same time, there is an inclination to doubt that such a person can rightly be held accountable, at least fully, that while he might "deserve pity," as Wolf says, he "does not deserve blame."[45] This ambivalence mirrors the two faces of responsibility. What gives rise to our "pity" are concerns about fairness. Facts about his formative years give rise to the thought that the individual has already suffered too much and that we too would probably have been morally ruined by such a childhood.[46] What is inhibited by these concerns is accountability blame.[47]

To be sure, this inhibition does not shield victim-criminals from legal sanctions. We still protect ourselves against their murderous assaults; we hunt them down, lock them up, shoot them. Hence our scruples about fairness are of no consolation (or compensation) to them. Nevertheless, these concerns affect our sense of what we're doing. Seeing the criminal as himself a victim will not prevent us from shutting the cage or pulling the trigger. But these responses will then tend to seem regulative rather than retributive. In a disconcerting way, they lose their normal expressive function.

[45] Wolf, *Freedom within Reason*, 81.

[46] I discuss cases of this kind at more length in my "Responsibility and the Limits of Evil," in *Responsibility, Character, and the Emotions* [Ch. 8, this volume].

[47] I do not mean to suggest that facts about the individual's formative years are irrelevant from the aretaic perspective. The fact that his conduct was a response to that wretched background should be a salient part of an understanding of what his life comes to and what he makes of it. To feature the cruelty would be misleading and inappropriate; that is only part of the story.

This discussion suggests that the standards for normative competence might be different for accountability than for attributability. Aretaic appraisal clearly requires some normative competence on the part of the subjects of that appraisal. The subjects of moral appraisal in particular must have the capacity to apply moral predicates to their deliberations. In general, aretaic appraisal requires the intelligence and sensibility to comprehend at least the normative concepts in terms of which the relevant forms of appraisal are conceived. (For example, one is open to appraisal as cruel only if one has the concept of cruelty.) There is no reason to think that this competence must include "the ability to acquire the right values."

However, since moral and legal accountability raises issues of fair opportunity, there is at least a prima facie case for something like this stronger criterion in those contexts. The answer depends on a detailed account of these practices and their rationales and upon a fuller understanding of what "acquiring the right values" comes to. It might make a difference whether someone is unable to know what is morally required or is unable to care in the right way. This brings us back to our discussion of "responsibility for ends and character" (see section 4). These concerns have a natural purchase from the perspective of accountability and must be taken seriously.

10. Asymmetries

The distinctions I have been exploring help us to understand the appeal of Susan Wolf's asymmetry thesis: that blameworthiness requires avoidability, while praiseworthiness does not. This proposition falls out of her conception of responsibility in the following way. Responsible agency is the capacity to respond to relevant reasons. If you do respond to relevant reasons (thereby acting well), you will have exercised that capacity, and be praiseworthy, even if you could not (say, psychologically) have done otherwise. But if you (psychologically) cannot respond to relevant reasons, you thus lack the capacity in question and are not blameworthy.[48] Incapacity therefore undercuts blame but not praise.

Wolf takes her thesis to be supported by common judgment. If someone acts well because of a moral clarity and commitment so strong that she could not have done otherwise, then we still think her praiseworthy. But if she acts badly because her deprived childhood has rendered her unable to care about the moral considerations in question, then she is not thought to be blameworthy.

The appeal of Wolf's thesis depends, I think, on a shift between the perspectives of accountability and aretaic appraisal. It is from the aretaic perspective that the agent in Wolf's example is plainly praiseworthy despite her supposed inability to do otherwise. For she conducts herself well, and that *is* to be praiseworthy. However, whether she deserves praise in the sense of some further favorable treatment in response to her virtuous conduct is more doubtful. Similarly, if we remain within the same perspective, the victim of the deprived childhood is blameworthy as well, since his conduct reflects badly upon him as a moral agent. From within this outlook, there is no difference. The sense of asymmetry results from a shift to the perspective of accountability.

However, an asymmetry of a different kind might seem to result from the negative and positive values of blame and praise. Like most writers on this subject, I began by talking about the connections between responsibility and praise and blame but became preoccupied with the negative case. We seem to have a richer vocabulary of blame than of praise. This slant is not due solely to mean-spiritedness. At least part of the explanation is that blaming tends to be a much more serious affair; reputation, liberty, and even life can be at stake, and understandably we are more concerned with the conditions of adverse treatment than with those of favorable treatment.

---

[48] Wolf, *Freedom within Reason*, 79 f.

The fact that 'holding responsible' has, strictly speaking, no positive counterpart reinforces the asymmetry. To be held liable is to be on the hook, and we lack a ready phrase for the positive counterpart to the "hook." But clearly we do have a counterpart notion; just as (moral) blame is sometimes called for as a response to the flouting of (moral) requirements, so praise is an appropriate response to respect for moral requirements or moral ends. We express praise by recognition: bestowing a medal or, more commonly, remarking on the person's merits. ("It was good of you [him] to help.")[49]

Hence, considerations of fairness might still support an asymmetry solely within the perspective of accountability. For if the requirement of avoidability derives from the idea that we should not be made to suffer from sanctions which we had no reasonable opportunity to avoid, then the requirement will have no relevance to the conditions of appropriate praise. The special objection to responding adversely to those who could not do otherwise simply does not apply to the case of favorable treatment.

If so, Wolf is partly right about asymmetry. While blame requires avoidability only from the perspective of accountability, praise requires avoidability from neither perspective. This would mean that asymmetry would hold in the one perspective but not the other.

But I think even this putative asymmetry is disputable. For praise also raises issues of fairness when considered comparatively. If Rosa is praised (or otherwise favorably treated) for her unavoidable conduct, *she* cannot complain that she is being treated unjustly. But if Joan's unavoidable negative conduct disqualifies her from this

---

[49] This point is connected to a further asymmetry. By the nature of the case, we do not hold people responsible for failing to behave in ways in which we do not require or expect them to behave. But there is more to morality than what is required. There are moral failures that are not failures to live up to requirements—that are failures to respect further moral ends. We praise people, and think well of them, for respecting these further moral ends. We think less well of people for failing to do so. At this point, the distinction between the perspectives blurs. Is this a kind of blame? Is it a "natural" concomitant of aretaic appraisal, or is it a judgment that some further negative response is (in principle) in order?

favorable treatment, can't *she* (or anyone from a perspective of justice) complain that a system that benefits Rosa rather than her, when neither can do otherwise, is unfair? Of course, Joan cannot put this point coherently by saying she *deserves* the benefit as much as Rosa, for she didn't act well. But she might well complain that Rosa deserves it no more than she herself.

I do not say that this complaint would be right. My point is that once we view praise and blame in terms of the fairness of assigning rewards and sanctions, as it seems we must from the perspective of accountability, we cannot dismiss this complaint out of hand.

11. *Conclusion*

I return, in conclusion, to van Inwagen's colleague. Van Inwagen is right to say that his colleague's appraisals implied an ascription of responsibility. But since the colleague is skeptical about moral accountability (I conjectured), to say that his judgments commit him to responsibility *sans phrase* is also misleading. For accountability is a central part of the notion of responsibility. I have pointed to two possible sources of this skepticism: that the authority of moral requirements, and therewith our entitlement to make demands upon one another, is illusory or that the conditions for fairly blaming others cannot be met. When one is skeptical—for one or both of these reasons—about accountability, one might be said to be skeptical about the ordinary full-fledged concept of moral responsibility. When the two perspectives are held apart, as we have done, and one of them is affirmed and the other is denied, the least misleading answer to the question of whether one believes in moral responsibility is: "In part yes, in part no."

Underlying these distinguishable perspectives are two sets of overlapping interests, both central to the ethical life. One set of interests hinges on our concern with living a good human life, with models and ideals of human possibility. The second set of interests pertains to social regulation and (more obscurely) to retributive and compensatory justice.[50] In the end, I doubt that these interests can be fully held apart. But it is important to see, as I have tried to show, that they have distinct sources.

APPENDIX: VIRTUE AND SKILL

Let me say more about the kind of evaluations I have called "aretaic."

(I)

Wolf observes that "deep responsibility" need not be moral. We appraise people's "intellectual, physical and artistic achievements," and these appraisals are "not reducible to an acknowledgement of these individuals' causal roles."[51] For example, she suggests, "one would not credit a child who, in playing with fingerpaints, produced a beautiful picture in the same way that one would credit a more mature artist who produced an equally beautiful painting."[52]

These examples are insightful. Such achievements are self-disclosing. It is natural to see the painting case as involving a difference in skill and sensibility. The artist's painting is a product (expression) of these, whereas it is more or less accidental that the child's play issued in an equally striking result. The aesthetic character of the artist's work is a realization of her conception, and hence its merits are hers. Similarly in the case of intellectual work. The excellences of *Freedom within Reason* are its author's. Imagine, instead, that the "text" had been produced inadvertently. In the course of conducting an experiment, say, Wolf had turned a dozen chimpanzees loose in a computer lab at Johns Hopkins, and astonishingly, the work under discussion ensued. In that case, the philosophical interest of the book would not have reflected *Wolf's* philosophical virtues.

But the notions of self-disclosure or deep appraisal are richer than the notion of a skill. For beings without self-reflective capacities can be more or less skillful, as dogs can be good at catching Frisbees. The appraisal of skills or talents is importantly different from aretaic evaluation in a way identified by Aristotle. Knowledge of an agent's ends, intentions, and

---

[50] I have profited from discussing this and other points in this essay with Greg Kavka.
[51] Wolf, *Freedom within Reason*, 41.   [52] Ibid.

efforts has a different effect on aretaic appraisals than on the others. Indifference in a performance doesn't count against one's skill, whereas a less than wholehearted effort to save someone's life does impugn my moral character. Talent and skill are fully displayed only in wholehearted performances, whereas the aretaic perspective is also concerned with the "will,"[53] that is, with one's purposes, ends, choices, concerns, cares, attachments, and commitments. Not trying can be a failure of virtue but not of skill.

What these nonmoral examples have in common is that the performances in question are exemplifications of what I would call *disciplines*.[54] Insofar as evaluations of athletic, aesthetic, and intellectual performances are concerned with character as well as technique, they involve aretaic appraisals. To this extent, they have an ethical dimension. Standards for disciplinary performances are concerned not only with skills (that is, the capacity to overcome technical difficulties) but also with virtues (such things as boldness, devotion to the discipline, originality, sensibility, etc.). My half-hearted effort on the tennis court would not support a negative evaluation of my proficiencies at that sport. Nevertheless, it might bear negatively on me as a tennis player. One can be "good at" playing tennis without being overall a good tennis player. A good tennis player, overall, possesses not only a high level of skill but, among other things, a commitment to the game, a responsibility to its distinctive demands. (In this way, 'good tennis player' functions rather like 'good human being'.)

(II)

In a recent essay, "Ethics without Free Will," Michael Slote attempts to distinguish an ethics of virtue from an ethics of blame.[55] By this title, Slote

---

[53] Contemporary discussions of Aristotle's point occur in the title essay of Philippa Foot's *Virtues and Vices and Other Essays in Moral Philosophy* (Berkeley: University of California Press, 1978), as well as in James Wallace's *Virtues and Vices* (Ithaca, N.Y.: Cornell University Press, 1978). Wallace's book contains a useful extended discussion of differences among excellences.
As Wallace points out, Aristotle used the term 'arete' to cover both skills and what we would call virtues.

[54] The notion of a discipline is similar in important ways to the notion of *practices* that Alasdair MacIntyre defines in *After Virtue* (Notre Dame, Ind.: University of Notre Dame Press, 1981).

[55] Michael Slote, "Ethics without Free Will," *Social Theory and Practice* 16 (1990): 369–83.

means moral or ethical appraisal without any commitment to judgments of blameworthiness or responsibility. Since the "ethics" he has in mind is supposed to be an ethics of virtue, Slote too wishes to separate aretaic judgments from accountability: "The mere or pure judgment/claim that someone relates poorly to other people (or has a vicious streak . . .) commits us to nothing in the line of blame or blameworthiness. . . . "[56]

But his defense of this position is grist for the mills of Wolf and Crucius. It depends upon the "shallow" conception of virtue appraisal that I have been at pains to avoid. For he argues that "in the case of dogs, the judgment of viciousness in no way commits anyone to a judgment of reprehensibility or blameworthiness, and there is absolutely no reason to think viciousness as described above would be conceived any differently."[57] But Slote had earlier described viciousness as "something important to do with character,"[58] and this is a decisive reason for setting the human case sharply apart from the case of the dog. In the case of people, but not dogs, it presupposes moral capacity, the capacity for adopting and pursuing ends. This capacity is crucial to aretaic judgment.

In the end, Slote manages to eliminate blame only by eliminating virtue.

[56] Michael Slote, "Ethics without Free Will," *Social Theory and Practice* 16 (1990): 378. [57] Ibid., 377.
[58] Ibid., 371.

10   Reasons and Responsibility

The idea that moral responsibility is crucially connected to the capacity to respond to reasons is a natural one. It is not an accident that the "age of reason" appears to coincide with the age of responsibility. But this connection has been defended and developed in very different ways. The most detailed and widely known recent formulation of the idea is due, jointly and individually, to John Martin Fischer and Mark Ravizza.[1] In *Responsibility and Control*, Fischer and Ravizza gather together and extend many of their earlier arguments in an effort to present a comprehensive theory that is informed by criticisms of their previous publications. Although many of the notions and strategies employed in the book are familiar from these previous publications, *Responsibility and Control* is an important contribution to the subject for several reasons. For one thing, it is good to have the ideas set out systematically. Whereas most discussions are confined to responsibility for actions, for example, this work presents a framework for analyzing responsibility for consequences, responsibility for omissions, and responsibility

A review of John Martin Fischer and Mark Ravizza, *Responsibility and Control: A Theory of Moral Responsibility* (Cambridge: Cambridge University Press, 1998). I am grateful to John Fischer for stimulating discussions of this material. I have also been helped by the comments of Dan Speak, and the editors of *Ethics*.

[1] Among other articles, see John Martin Fischer, "Responsiveness and Moral Responsibility," in *Responsibility, Character and the Emotions*, ed. F. Schoeman (New York: Cambridge University Press, 1987); and John Martin Fischer and Mark Ravizza, "Responsibility and Inevitability," *Ethics* 101 (1991): 258–78; and Mark Ravizza, "Semi-compatibilism and the Transfer of Non-responsibility," *Philosophical Studies* 75 (1994): 61–93.

for character as well. More important, *Responsibility and Control* moves beyond the previous theory in two significant ways. First, it provides a more nuanced and multidimensional account of "reasons-responsiveness" than before. Second, the authors no longer take reasons-responsiveness, however refined, to be sufficient, for actions with that property still might not "belong" to the individual in the right way. Chapters 7 and 8 argue that responsibility is a "historical" notion precisely because of the requirement of ownership. My aim here is to assess these two foundational developments.

I. Reasons-Responsiveness

A. Fischer and Ravizza employ the idea of reasons-responsiveness in defense of two basic theses: first, that (moral) responsibility involves a certain kind of control ("guidance control"); second, that this control does not require "alternative possibilities," or the ability to do otherwise ("regulative control"). An individual's responsibility for an action, say, depends only upon features of the actual sequence issuing in the action, rather than upon the possibility of alternative sequences. (The authors thus identify themselves as compatibilists about moral responsibility.) According to Fischer and Ravizza, the feature of the actual sequence on which responsibility, and hence guidance control, hinge is responsiveness to reasons. The central thesis, then, is that someone "exhibits guidance control of an action insofar as the mechanism that actually issues in the action is his own, reasons-responsive mechanism" (p. 39).

B. In one sense, being responsive to reasons is just what it is to be a reasonable creature. This points to the most immediate problem for any view that links responsibility tightly to reasons-responsiveness. We blame people precisely for their insensitivity to reasons, so reasonableness and responsibility are not to be equated. One obvious way to mark the difference is to treat responsibility as the capacity to respond to reasons. But this places the burden on the notion of capacity, and by itself leaves open the traditional modal issues raised by causal determinism. Some philosophers—including Fischer and Ravizza—have aimed to explicate the relevant capacity precisely in terms of responsiveness to reasons. The problem for these philosophers, therefore, is to specify the sense in which people who sometimes and perhaps even regularly fail to respond to reasons can nevertheless be said to be responsive.

In their earlier work, Fischer and Ravizza took the requirements for reasons-responsiveness to be minimal: the "mechanism"[2] must be sensitive to reasons only in the sense (roughly) that the presence of at least some sufficient reasons to do otherwise would have led the agent to act accordingly. But this requirement is too weak. It might suffice to rule out cases of "direct neurophysiological manipulation," brainwashing, and so on, but it accounts poorly for the limited responsibility of creatures whose moral understanding is severely stunted or absent altogether. By itself, the minimal position would include "wantons" and very small children among those who are responsible for their behavior.[3] On the other hand, while the condition of responsiveness to *any* sufficient counter-reason ("strong" reasons-responsiveness) escapes this objection,[4] it is clearly not a necessary condition, since (as the authors observe) it would rule out most (if not all) blameworthy conduct, including weakness of will.

This problem leads Fischer and Ravizza to stipulate a condition of moral competence: "The kind of responsiveness required for moral responsibility ought to be characterized not merely as a responsiveness to reason, but rather as a responsiveness to a range of reasons that

[2] I'll say more about 'mechanism' later; for now, just note that this term is meant to refer to "the process that leads to the action, or the way the action comes about."

[3] R. Jay Wallace makes this criticism in *Responsibility and the Moral Sentiments* (Cambridge, Mass.: Harvard University Press, 1994), p. 190.

[4] On some interpretations of counterfactuals, even this formulation is problematic as a sufficient condition. Toddlers and wantons might vacuously satisfy it because they could not meet the conditions of the antecedent.

include *moral* reasons" (p. 81).[5] This supplement is part of a broader revision of the authors' conception of reasons-responsiveness, in which they distinguish "reactivity" from "recognition or receptivity" to reasons, that is, from the "capacity to recognize the reasons that exist" (p. 69). The requirement of moral competence, then, is the requirement that an agent have at least the capacity to recognize, if not react to, moral considerations.

But the distinction between reactivity and receptivity is recommended not only by concerns about moral competence. The authors are worried more generally about the "sanity" of the agent. Someone might be weakly reactive to reasons, they think, but in such a bizarre way that their behavior is merely "further evidence of his insanity and consequent lack of responsibility" (p. 65). In these cases, the agent's motivation is rationally unintelligible to us. Fischer and Ravizza give the example of a mass murderer who would be deterred from his slaughter only if the would-be victim were smoking a certain kind of pipe. Reason-receptivity adds to weak reactivity the requirement that one's responsiveness exhibit "an understandable pattern of reasons-recognition, minimally grounded in reality" (p. 73).[6]

---

[5] Naturally, moral competence of some kind is a condition for moral responsibility, and that is the avowed concern of the book. However, in many passages Fischer and Ravizza seem equally concerned with attributions of responsibility in nonmoral contexts, for example, in the context of assessments of prudence. Thus, the capacity to recognize moral reasons should not be taken without argument to be necessary for responsibility *simpliciter*. If responsibility is responsiveness to reasons, and individuals can be sensitive to nonmoral reasons without being morally competent, then individuals can be responsible agents in these other respects. Perhaps this reasoning is objectionable, but it deserves an answer. (I take up a related point at the end of this article.)

[6] The appeal to the criteria of an intelligible pattern of reason recognition, and of "minimal groundedness in reality," brings Fischer and Ravizza's view somewhat closer to Susan Wolf's "reason view"; see Susan Wolf, *Freedom within Reason* (New York: Oxford University Press, 1990). But as it stands, it introduces a large measure of vagueness into the theory: *how* intelligible and *how* minimal? Does the reality requirement mean that the individual cannot be substantially deluded about that part of her circumstances that is relevant to the context of appraisal? Or can she be deluded about this so long as she is in touch with a good bit of the "background world"? The

Fischer and Ravizza call this revised condition "moderate reasons-responsiveness." Agents exhibit guidance control in acting only if their actions are moderately responsive to reasons. This condition reflects, the authors argue, an asymmetry between reactivity and receptivity: "Whereas moral responsibility requires that an agent act on a mechanism that shows *regularity* in recognizing reasons, this same demand cannot be made with respect to reactivity. . . . For an agent to be responsible, . . . he must act on a mechanism that is regularly receptive to reasons and at least weakly reactive to them" (p. 81).

C. The revised view gives rise to a number of difficult questions. Let me begin with a smaller concern about the aforementioned asymmetry thesis. It will lead to more central issues. Consider another case that the authors use to illustrate the asymmetry thesis. Suppose that Brown is weakly reactive to reasons because he would be led to refrain from purchasing a ticket to the basketball game if it cost significantly more than he actually pays—if, say, the price were a thousand dollars. Now the condition of weak reactivity is satisfied even if this price is the *only* counterincentive to which Brown would respond—if Brown would refrain just in case the ticket price were exactly $1,000. Fischer and Ravizza rightly think that this minimal reactivity is insufficient for responsibility because it evinces an unintelligible pattern of reason-recognition. They infer that a stronger condition is required for receptivity or recognitional capacity than for reactivity—hence, the asymmetry.

But this inference is hasty. For the failure to find an intelligible general pattern of reason-recognition must affect the understanding of what reason the agent is reacting to as well. By hypothesis, he is reacting to something about the price. The initial impression that

former reading seems too strong, if 'deluded' just means mistaken. One can be terribly and innocently wrong about one's circumstances and still be appropriately responsive to the reasons as they present themselves. On the other hand, the second reading lays down a standard that is never violated, if Davidson is right that we can attribute delusion or mistake to an agent only against a background of presumed agreement. It is often unclear to me what overall picture of responsibility influences the decisions that the authors make.

this is a reaction to the expense of the ticket is called into question by his subsequent willingness to pay higher prices. So we are left without an intelligible interpretation of what reason (if any) he was reacting to. Perhaps it was something else about the price besides the monetary value that moved him—an obscure superstition, perhaps. But that interpretation will constrain what we say about the overall pattern of reason-receptivity as well. The same point applies to the case of the mass murderer who would be deterred only by the sight of a certain pipe. Without an understanding of what moves the killer, there is no telling what reason he is reacting to, or even whether he is moved by a reason (as distinct from a brute urge) at all.

In sum, it is not clear to me that the reactivity and recognition conditions can be held apart in the way that is necessary for the claim of asymmetry. Any interpretation of an individual's behavior on which he or she is even weakly reactive to reasons will place at least some constraints on our interpretation of the agent's pattern of reason-recognition. So cases in which the condition of recognitional intelligibility is altogether flouted will not be cases in which there is an asymmetry between reactivity and receptivity but cases which cast doubt on how and even whether the condition of weak reasons-reactivity is met at all.

D. There is another reason for thinking that weak reactivity is too weak as a condition of moral responsibility: it is arguably consistent with motivational compulsion. Fischer and Ravizza would reject this claim because they define motivational compulsion as a failure of weak receptivity. Consider their remarks about addiction: "When a [drug addict] acts from a literally irresistible urge, he is undergoing a kind of physical process that is not reasons-responsive, and it is this lack of reasons-responsiveness of the actual physical process that rules out guidance control and moral responsibility" (p. 48). A drug is said to be nonaddictive if it "does *not* issue in *irresistible* urges to take it" (p. 69).

This account of resistibility makes it doubtful that compulsion and addiction occur at all; if they do, they are surely not common even among the cases of severe drug dependency that prompt us to speak of compulsion. Few, if any, are the addicts who would respond to no counterincentive whatever, say, to the prospect of immediate agonizing physical suffering. To take another example of apparent compulsion, it is well known that severely phobic individuals are virtually always susceptible to counterincentives of the right kind. However housebound, the agoraphobic will somehow manage to muster the strength to leave when the building is ablaze.[7]

Now these implications are not decisive objections, since the concepts of compulsion and addiction are highly contested. Perhaps the thrust of the authors' account is just this: "here is what compulsion and irresistibility has to be if it exists. It is up to others to decide whether and when it occurs." Nonetheless, weak reactivity seems to me suspect as a mark of responsibility and control. Suppose that the only thing that would deter me from taking my heroin is to link my behavior to a consequence that utterly terrifies me—say, by placing my supply in a cage of hungry rats, of which I am profoundly phobic. Here my susceptibility to counterincentives is not evidence that my heroin ingestion is under my control but rather suggests that I am in the grip of competing compulsions.

What this objection shows is that control can't be identified with susceptibility to counterincentives. If motivated behavior—that is, behavior that is contingent on incentives—can fail to be under the control of the agent, as it might be in cases of compulsion or irresistibility, then the existence of a possible scenario in which the individual is moved by a counterincentive proves nothing about control unless the incentive is noncompulsive in that scenario. One needs, it seems, an independent account of compulsion.[8]

<hr/>

[7] Isaac Marks, *Fears, Phobias, and Rituals* (New York: Oxford University Press, 1987), p. 344.

[8] I press this difficulty against reasons-responsiveness views in "Disordered Appetites: Addiction, Compulsion, and Dependence," in *Addiction: Entries and Exits*, ed. Jon Elster (New York: Russell Sage Foundation, 1999), pp. 3–28 [Ch. 3, this volume]. These cases indicate the need to distinguish reasons from incentives. The susceptibility to counterincentives (which are indeed reasons) might not, after all, be responsiveness to them qua reasons. One's response to what is in fact a reason might not be an instance of sensitivity to reasons.

E. However, Fischer and Ravizza suggest a reply to this objection. The authors do not explicitly or systematically discuss the kinds of examples I have raised, but they do consider in general terms cases in which an "agent somehow gets considerably more energy or focus if he is presented with a *strong* reason to do otherwise" (p. 74). They think that the exposure to certain alternative incentives might "give rise to a *different mechanism* from the actual mechanism." Therefore, control, for them, is not just a matter of a person's susceptibility to counterincentives but requires that the actual sequence mechanism be capable of responding to contrary considerations. The reply to the countercompulsion objection, then, is that the alternative scenarios in which the individual is exposed to the dreadful consequences do not "hold fixed the actual mechanism." The theory is that the actual mechanism that motivates the action must be reasons-responsive. In our example, the mechanism that operates to keep the man inside the house until the fire alarm goes off (the phobia) is not the same kind of mechanism that is operating in the emergency (the fear of fire). Similarly, the mechanism that would operate when my heroin is put in the rat cage—my dread of rats—is different from the mechanism in the actual scenario (my addiction to heroin). So it is not enough for reasons-responsiveness, and hence for guidance control, that there be alternative scenarios in which different mechanisms lead me to act otherwise. Guidance control requires that the actual mechanism be such that *it* would respond differently in the presence of some different reasons.

F. This reply is hard to assess because it depends on obscure issues about the identity of mechanisms. The authors candidly admit that they "cannot specify in a general way how to determine which mechanism is 'the' mechanism that is relevant to assessment of responsibility" (p. 47). But they are confident that in most specific cases this determination is intuitively clear. I am not so sure. Let's consider some examples.

1. To update one of the cases in the book, Goldie votes for Nader for the good reason that the other candidates are corrupt or mediocre.

Here, apparently, the "mechanism" is the process of deliberating about which politician to support. Fischer and Ravizza's test for whether that process is reasons-reactive is whether there is an alternative scenario in which (a) the actual mechanism operates, and (b) there is sufficient reason to do otherwise, and (c) the agent does otherwise for this reason (see p. 86). It is easy enough to see how Goldie's voting behavior meets this test. Suppose the last minute news that the Green Party is a front for a Christian Identity group (news supplied by a trusted friend as Goldie enters the polling place) would have influenced her to vote against Nader. In this "alternative scenario," it is plausible to say that the same mechanism, namely, the deliberation regarding whom to vote for, results in different behavior. This process is thus reasons-responsive.

2. A second example begins to raise worries, however. Fischer and Ravizza imagine a case in which the self-indulgent Brown wastes his days in an euphoric haze induced by Plezu, a "non-addictive" but highly pleasurable drug. Although "he recognizes that there are strong reasons *not* to take the drug every morning . . . , the only scenario in which Brown would not take Plezu is one in which he is told that injecting the drug once more would have an extremely grave consequence—death" (pp. 69–70).

The authors conclude that Brown is responsible for his drug taking in so far as his behavior is weakly reactive. But it is not at all clear to me that this example satisfies condition *a* of the foregoing test. The process that explains his drug taking is the craving for the drug or his desire to get high. In what way is *that* process operative in the counterfactual circumstance in which Brown refrains on account of his fear of sudden death? Surely this fear displaces, renders inoperative, the desire to take the drug in the same way in which the dread of rats overcomes the craving for heroin in our example of countercompulsions. The desire to get high could not be the "process" that leads to the refusal to get high. (This desire might still exist in the alternative scenario but would not be "operative.")

Of course, we might imagine that the mechanism that operates in both the actual and alternative scenarios is the reflection on reasons, to which the fear of death is an input. Then the Plezu case would be just like the voting case. But Fischer and Ravizza rightly want to account for responsibility for weak-willed behavior and offer this case as an instance of acting contrary to practical reason.

3. Fischer and Ravizza also want to explain responsibility for habitual or routine behavior, such as taking a certain freeway exit to work. In other words, again, they do not want to say that deliberation or practical reflection, defective or otherwise, is the only reasons-responsive mechanism. Suppose I see the sign for University Avenue and take the exit, as I do everyday, out of habit or routine. The authors imagine that "the University Avenue exit is blocked because of road construction and we hold fixed the fact that the agent does not deliberate about what to do; presumably, there are scenarios in which he simply automatically . . . responds by taking the next exit from the freeway. This fact helps to show that the agent's actual-sequence action (from a non-reflective mechanism) is moderately reasons-responsive" (p. 86). As it stands, this case is puzzling. The operative mechanism in the actual sequence is my habit of exiting at University. The test requires that we hold this fixed. But obviously my habit of taking that off-ramp is not what leads me in the alternative scenario to pass on by.

These worries indicate some of the difficulties regarding the individuation of mechanisms, but they are not conclusive. Various replies are available in the authors' defense. In case 2, for example, they can plausibly deny that the deliberative process is bypassed in cases of weakness. Instead, when the agent knowingly gives too much weight to some considerations over others, his deliberative mechanisms are indeed operating, albeit defectively. The same deliberative mechanism that operates defectively when Brown takes the drug would be in effect when he refused to get high for fear of death. This is not an implausible way to think of weakness of will.[9]

Similarly, in case 3, the authors' conclusion can be made more plausible by redescribing the process that explains the behavior. What is operative in the actual and alternative sequences is not, as they say, the habit of taking a certain exit but a kind of monitoring capacity that is governed by my goal of getting to campus. When events unfold according to routine, my daily habits take their usual course. Otherwise, my readiness to make adjustments as needed is triggered. All of this is consistent with minimal or no reflection.

G. Perhaps, then, these and other concerns about mechanism individuation can be effectively answered, though I remain unconvinced. I worry that the notion of a mechanism, of "a process resulting in behavior," is too amorphous to do the refined work needed by the theory. Let me conclude my discussion of this part of the theory with three observations.

1. Fischer and Ravizza take up the following objection to their thesis that weak reactivity is all the reactivity necessary for moral responsibility. Return to the case of Brown's devotion to Plezu. Someone might worry that the mechanism on which Brown acts could not have responded differently to the actual incentive to do otherwise. So it is unfair to hold him responsible for his response to that incentive. The authors' reply to that objection is that "reactivity is all of a piece": "That is, . . . if an agent's mechanism reacts to *some* incentive to . . . do other than he actually does, this shows that the mechanism *can* react to *any* incentive to do otherwise. . . . Reactivity is all of a piece: if the mechanism can react to any reason to do otherwise, it can react to all such reasons" (pp. 73–4). This modal

---

[9] Once we think of it in this way, however, it becomes unclear how we can distinguish cases of compulsion in which the actually operative mechanism would be replaced in the alternative scenario from cases of weakness. On what possible grounds could we distinguish between Brown's situation and that of the aforementioned heroin addict or phobic whose actual mechanism is alleged to be bypassed in the alternative scenario?

claim is very puzzling. In general, dispositional properties don't behave in this way. That a substance is soluble in one kind of liquid does not indicate that it will respond this way to other kinds. Solubility is not "all of a piece." Why would reasons-reactivity be any different? The mechanism that animates Brown (his defective practical reason, we have been supposing)[10] *never* responds to the incentive to go to work when he has a chance to get high. Isn't that excellent evidence that the process can't respond under those circumstances?

2. It is also somewhat curious that Fischer and Ravizza feel the need to make this modal claim. The objection regarding fairness seems to arise from intuitions supporting a principle of alternative possibilities (holding people responsible is unfair unless they could have done otherwise). Fischer and Ravizza reject this principle because of so-called Frankfurt cases, in which some fail-safe device stands by to ensure that an individual behaves in a certain way. For example, suppose that if Goldie were to change her mind at the last moment about voting for the Green candidate, the fail-safe device would ensure that she punched the "Nader" tab anyway. So, there is no possibility that she would not punch that tab. Fischer and Ravizza reasonably conclude that this modal fact does not entail that her actual voting behavior is not reasons-responsive. This leads them to reject the idea that to be responsible, the agent must have alternatives to what she does. In Frankfurt cases, Fischer and Ravizza like to say, the agents could not have responded differently in the face of contrary incentives, but the actually operative mechanisms could have (see, e.g., p. 38).

What is curious, then, is that Fischer and Ravizza seem to feel the need to employ a notion of alternative possibilities at the level of mechanisms. They seem to be conceding that there is a sense in which the fairness of holding someone responsible depends upon the capacity

---

[10] If, as the text seems to suggest, the mechanism in the Brown case is the desire to get high, how does it even make sense to say that it responds to the incentive to go to work?

of the mechanism in question to respond otherwise, a capacity that must be compatible with causal determinism, on their view. But it is hard to see how this move can answer the concern about fairness, unless we can translate talk about the capacities of mechanisms into talk about what persons can do. And if we can do that, we should endorse a compatibilistic version of the principle of alternative possibilities rather than rejecting the relevance of alternative possibilities altogether.

3. Let me pose a final question about reasons-responsiveness in Frankfurt cases. We have been supposing that the fail-safe mechanism works by displacing one's reason-responsive mechanism. Suppose instead that the activated device decisively influenced Goldie's reasoning (by affecting how she weighs the reasons and evidence, etc.). Wouldn't her "actual mechanism" then be operative in the alternative scenario? Although this form of counterfactual intervention seems no less threatening than the other, it should be significantly different, on Fischer and Ravizza's theory. For in the alternative scenario, Goldie is acting on a moderately reasons-responsive mechanism.

As we'll see below, Fischer and Ravizza will try to explain what is threatening to responsibility in both types of intervention by appealing to a feature of mechanisms that is supposed to be independent of reasons-responsiveness: "ownership."

II. History and Ownership

A. I have been focusing so far on reasons-responsiveness, the first part of the theory of guidance control. Fischer and Ravizza think that reasons-responsiveness is not all there is to responsibility. An individual might be animated by a mechanism that is indeed responsive to reasons, they think, but one that is not the individual's own. This problem can be illustrated by the case we just sketched, in which Goldie is made to vote for Nader by a device that affects her deliberative processes. Even though the behavior manifests a reasons-responsive process, it is not *her* process: she is not in this case voting on her own. This worry doesn't depend in any way on the limited reactivity of that process. Perhaps the device is more sensitive to the "reasons there are" than her own unaided efforts would have been. The problem is that the intervention undermines her agency, not her rationality (though one might say that it undermines *her* rationality).

Here is how Fischer and Ravizza state the challenge: "It seems that the operation of a moderately reasons-responsive mechanism just prior to the action can *itself* be the product of a process that intuitively rules out moral responsibility. . . . What seems relevant is not only the fact that the mechanism issuing in the action is suitably reasons-responsive; what also matters is *how* that mechanism has been put in place" (pp. 230–1). This challenge leads the authors to conclude that an account of reasons-responsiveness must be supplemented by an account of ownership, which they sketch in chapter 8. But they also draw another important conclusion: because it matters how a mechanism has been put in place, any satisfactory theory of responsibility must be historical. The first conclusion seems to me true and important, but I have serious doubts about the second. Let me begin with those.

B. Fischer and Ravizza think that the idea of responsibility is historical in somewhat the same sense as the ideas of a fair distribution of gambling winnings and of being an authentic Picasso are historical. The fairness of the distribution of winnings cannot be determined merely by a description of who has what at a particular time; it matters whether it came about by cheating or playing by the rules. Nor does a complete description of the physical properties of a painting at a given time settle the question of whether it was a real Picasso; you have to be able to trace the work back to that artist's hand. The properties of being a fair distribution and of being a Picasso are historical in the sense that they cannot be instantiated by a state of affairs or of an object just in virtue of the "time-slice" properties of the state of affairs or object.

The thesis, then, is that responsibility is an historical phenomenon. The "snapshot properties of the agent and the mechanism that leads to certain behavior do not suffice to specify an agent's moral responsibility" (p. 195). On the basis of this claim, Fischer and Ravizza argue against what they call mesh or structural theories, according to which "an agent is responsible for an action insofar as" a structural conformity obtains between various components leading to the behavior.[11] Such theories must be ahistorical, they think, in a sense that makes them inescapably vulnerable to certain counterexamples.

To take the measure of this claim, it is important to distinguish two features of mesh theories that the authors tend to run together. First, obviously any view of this kind is ahistorical in the sense that it doesn't matter how the mesh comes to obtain. For it is the obtaining of this mesh in which responsibility is alleged to consist. But this feature does not entail that all such views must be what the authors call current time-slice or snapshot theories. Whether or not a mesh theory has this feature depends on the nature of the components of the mesh and their structural relations. They may include processes, which take time. More contentiously, they may include states, such as beliefs and values, which are only sensibly attributable to individuals on the basis of a narrative interpretation of some significant portion of their lives.[12]

---

[11] The book takes (pp. 184 ff.) Harry Frankfurt's "Freedom of the Will and the Concept of a Person," *Journal of Philosophy* 68 (1971): 5–20, and my "Free Agency," *Journal of Philosophy* 72 (1975): 205–20 [Ch. 1, this volume] to be defenses of mesh theories.

[12] I pursue these points in "Soft Libertarianism and Hard Compatibilism," *Journal of Ethics* 3 (1999): 351–65 [Ch. 7, this volume]. There I also suggest that we should reject a "current time-slice" interpretation of Frankfurt's view, since that view could not make sense of the phenomenon of identification (pp. 363–4). But Fischer and Ravizza's take on Frankfurt seems to be correct after all. For, in his contribution to the volume just cited, Frankfurt confirms the time-slice interpretation: "What would seem to count is just the outcome of the process, or the state of affairs that prevails once the process has been completed. In that case, the endorsement condition can be satisfied within a structural account" ("Responses," p. 372).

For instance, take George Vuoso's assertion that "an agent can properly be held morally responsible for his actions to the extent and only to the extent that they reflect badly on his character. . . . The sort of character a person has is relevant to assessing his moral responsibility for an action, but not how he came to have that character."[13] Although Fischer and Ravizza count this as a mesh theory, having a certain character is an especially unpromising candidate for a "snapshot" property. This account might be wrong, but it need not be faulted because it is a current time-slice theory.

C. We should not assume, then, that theories that are ahistorical in the sense just indicated above are necessarily beset with the special problems of time-slice views. The question is, what reasons are there for thinking that mesh theories must be ahistorical in an objectionable sense? In chapter 7, the authors develop two considerations in favor of this conclusion. First, the authors note that any plausible theory of responsibility must accommodate the phenomenon of "tracing," where, roughly, an individual is responsible for less than fully voluntary behavior at one time in virtue of her earlier negligent or voluntary conduct (driving incompetently while drunk, for example; pp. 195 f.).

While the phenomenon of tracing shows that any plausible theory of responsibility must be partly historical, it does not, I think, present any real problems for mesh theories. To accommodate tracing, a theory must endorse something like N: No full description of a person's behavior, dispositions, and capacities at time T entail that she should *not* be held responsible for how she behaves or for what happens at T.[14] For a person might be responsible in virtue of her earlier behavior for what happens later, no matter in what

---

[13] George Vuoso, "Background, Responsibility, and Excuse." *Yale Law Journal* 96 (1987): 1680–1 (quoted in Fischer and Ravizza, p. 186).

[14] In speaking of the "full description" of the behavior, etc., I am ignoring the issues raised about "snapshot" properties, which we agreed to set aside. N remains true when formulated in terms of "snapshot" properties, but I want to emphasize that the assessment of mesh theories should not turn on this.

condition she may then find herself. But a mesh theory can and should accept N. For it will hold that an agent is responsible for some behavior or state of affairs just in case it is suitably related to the mesh, m, in which responsibility is taken to consist—for example, to the agent's higher-order volitions, or reflective evaluations, or character. Such views will accept N because a full description at a time may leave out relevant information about the relation between the behavior or state of affairs and m (the agent's volitions, or values or character).

Since such a view accommodates N, it is to that extent historical. But this is consistent with its being ahistorical in the sense in which it is obvious that any mesh theory must be. For it need not hold that m itself, the primary feature on which tracing ascriptions are based, is a historical phenomenon. The theory can be ahistorical in the sense specified earlier because N doesn't entail its positive counterpart, P: No full description of a person's behavior, dispositions, and capacities at time T entails that she should be held responsible for how she behaves or for what happens at T. ('P' is 'N' without the 'not'.) P will be false on a mesh theory because any description that entails that M obtains (e.g., that the behavior or state of affairs reflects badly on the agent's character) entails that the agent is responsible, no matter how m came to obtain.

D. The question, again, is this: should this feature of mesh theories count against them, independently of the content of those theories? The authors argue that it should. Their argument is this. Take any theory according to which responsibility consists primarily in the obtaining of some m. Since this is a nonhistorical fact, it could have been produced by hypnosis, or subliminal advertising, or direct neurophysiological manipulation. But these are clearly "responsibility-undermining" processes. Therefore, responsibility cannot consist in the obtaining of m. So any adequate theory of responsibility must be historical in a sense in which mesh theories cannot be. (Note that this objection does not depend on m being specifiable in "snapshot" terms.)

This argument is powerful if one accepts the so-called transfer principle, according to which an individual's responsibility cannot be derived by causal necessitation from processes for which the individual is not responsible. Then the processes listed above would indeed seem to preclude responsibility (unless, of course, they themselves are suitably "traceable"). But the authors firmly deny this principle, on which arguments for incompatibilism pivot. Why, then, should we think that such processes are necessarily responsibility-undermining? Of course, they normally are. However, that is arguably because in the normal cases such processes prevent the realization of m—as for example, "manipulation" undermines one's capacity for reflective evaluation.

The authors' appeal to an open-ended list of "intuitively responsibility-undermining factors" leaves their argument philosophically ungrounded in a worrisome way (p. 202). To be sure, the appeal to intuitive plausibility in philosophy is inevitable and not to be deplored. But the foregoing argument against mesh theories can be extended to apply to any compatibilist position, including Fischer and Ravizza's. To be a compatibilist is to hold that certain conditions, c, are both sufficient for responsibility and realizable in a completely deterministic world. The claim that c obtains is consistent with the claim that c has been produced by one or more of the factors on the pretheoretical list of processes that seem, paradigmatically, to defeat responsibility. Why isn't this just as good a reason for rejecting compatibilism as for rejecting the subset of compatibilist theories that identify c with m? In particular, why doesn't the foregoing argument tell against *their* version of compatibilism?

III. Ownership and Taking Responsibility

A. I will take up this question in the context of the theory of ownership advanced in chapter 8. This theory explains ownership in terms of "taking responsibility": "Taking responsibility is part of the process by which a mechanism leading (say) to an action becomes *one's own*" (p. 206). The main "ingredients" of taking responsibility are first, that "an individual must see himself as an agent; he must see that his choices and actions are efficacious in the world" (p. 210). Second, he "must accept that he is a fair target of the reactive attitudes as a result of how he exercises this agency in certain contexts" (p. 211).[15] The process by which an individual comes to satisfy these two conditions is a process of "coming to have a certain cluster of beliefs (in a certain way)."[16] The set of beliefs in which this process culminates is not typically reflective or explicit. On the basis of this account, Fischer and Ravizza conclude that "an agent's being morally responsible is genuinely historical in the sense that it requires that the agent have previously taken responsibility" (p. 214).

So there are two ways in which the process leading to an action could undermine responsibility. It could prevent reasons-responsiveness, or it could subvert ownership, or both. Suppose Judith is seized by an urge to punch Jane (p. 232). If the process is totally unreactive to reasons, then she is not responsible, but even if it is weakly reactive, she will not be responsible if the urge is induced by a process for which she has not taken responsibility. So weakly reactive or not, if the strong desire to punch Jane has been directly induced by the manipulations of Martian scientists, when she is animated by this urge she is acting on a mechanism that is not her own. For if someone "has had his brain manipulated in certain ways, and has not had the opportunity to become aware of the manipulation and reflect on it, then he has *not* taken responsibility for the kind of mechanism that issues in his

[15] There appears to be an overlap between these requirements and the condition of moral competence laid down in the account of reasons-responsiveness. It is not clear to me how an agent could recognize that moral reasons apply to him or her without meeting both conditions 1 and 2. So it is not clear to me that an individual could be reasons-responsive on Fischer and Ravizza's account without satisfying these conditions of ownership.

[16] This parenthetical clause reflects a third condition on ownership: that the agent comes to have the set of beliefs required by these two conditions in the right way (see p. 213). We'll see later how this condition comes into play.

behavior" (p. 243). It is in this way, presumably, that Fischer and Ravizza would respond to the challenge issued in the last section. They think they can account for the relevance of manipulation cases by appealing to the conditions for taking responsibility, conditions that nonhistorical theories do not require.

I think that Fischer and Ravizza are right to claim that their earlier account of responsibility, as well as that of mesh theories, needs to be supplemented by some kind of ownership condition. For whether the crucial theoretical notion is reasons-responsiveness, conformity with higher-order volitions, or expressiveness of the agent's critical values, the states or processes must be attributable to the agent, rather than to someone else, or rather than merely happening to or in or around him. Of course, counterexamples regarding ownership can be ruled out notionally by the stipulation that the agent's behavior results from *his* reasons-responsive mechanism, or higher-order volitions, or reflective evaluations. But obviously that just leaves the difficulty in place. I am also sympathetic to their view that taking responsibility, in something like the way they explicate it, is indeed crucial to the practice of holding one another responsible. But I am not persuaded that this idea of taking responsibility solves the problem of ownership or that the problem of ownership requires a theory that is historical in some contentious sense. I will develop these doubts in what follows.

B. First of all, I don't think that Fischer and Ravizza's attempt to explain the worries about manipulation cases in terms of the failures to take responsibility succeeds. Furthermore, it is not clear why the process of taking responsibility cannot itself be induced by "manipulative mechanisms" of the worrisome kind. If it can, won't their account be open to the same objection they make to nonhistorical theories after all?

Let's begin with the claim that if someone "has had his brain manipulated in certain ways, and has not had the opportunity to become aware of the manipulation and reflect on it, then he has *not* taken responsibility for the kind of mechanism that issues in his behavior" (p. 243). It is not obvious to me that this is true, even on the authors' own criteria.[17] As Fischer and Ravizza acknowledge, there is much about the springs of action that we do not know, and such ignorance doesn't in general mean that the conditions of taking responsibility have not been met. They say that "in taking responsibility for the actions that flow from a kind of mechanism, [one] takes responsibility for acting from the mechanism in all its details" (p. 216) and emphasize that taking responsibility for a certain mechanism doesn't require knowing "all the details," for example, "the details of the neural states that underlie the mental states that constitute his practical reasoning" (p. 216). My question is, Why couldn't the details about the exotic origins of the process be among those that one needn't know? According to Fischer and Ravizza, an important feature of the processes that lead to the actions of which we might be ignorant is their "deterministic character." As compatibilists, they think that this ignorance does not rule out our rightly taking responsibility for some of them. Why isn't it just as plausible to think that those meddlesome Martians might have initiated some of the processes for which we rightly take responsibility?

We are sometimes subject to strong hostile desires, like Judith's, whose origins are obscure. That doesn't prevent our taking responsibility for our responses. Unless their origins bear upon how hard it is for one to resist enacting them, why should it matter to responsibility whether these desires are induced by fatigue, stress, low blood sugar, repressed memory, native irascibility, or by those pesky aliens? To rule out the latter, it is not enough to cite the absence of the opportunity for reflective awareness.

C. In everyday life, we do not accept the idea that we are responsible for our behavior only insofar as we act on mechanisms for which we

---

[17] The book is vague about how and why we come to take responsibility for some mechanisms and not others. We are told that individuals typically take responsibility for actions resulting from the "mechanism of practical reason" (p. 215), as well as certain "non-reflective mechanisms" (p. 216). The latter are said to include habits of driving an automobile, but not epileptic seizures, though the principle of selection is unclear.

have taken responsibility. What would concern us about Judith's desire to punch Jane is not how she acquired the urge but whether she could reasonably be expected to have controlled herself. How an urge is induced is irrelevant to how difficult it is to control. Whatever its etiology, unless a desire is somehow "irresistible," we hold ourselves responsible for resisting it or not. The reason why Judith's case, as presented in the text, is bothersome is that what is "implanted" is not just a single desire, leaving untouched the rest of the agent's preferences and commitments: what is implanted is a desire that is to be inhibited only by the consideration that punching Jane would result in the deaths of innocent people. To induce a desire with this character, to get Judith to act on this desire in this wide range of circumstances, the manipulators must manage the woman's intentions and her hitherto formed character in fairly extensive ways (if not by altering then by suspending them for a time). The manipulators are not just implanting a mechanism and leaving intact her normal capacities of resistance and her other preferences; they are taking control of her agency.

Her responsibility for punching Judy is in question in this case not because she hasn't taken responsibility for a mechanism covertly installed by external agents. Rather, the intervention is incompatible with the integrity of her agency. In this case, the depth and breadth of the intervention indicates that she is not the locus of action here. Indeed, such behavior would not become Judith's own in the relevant sense even if she *had* reflectively authorized the intervention.[18] Taking responsibility is not sufficient to make certain processes attributable to one agent rather than another; otherwise my authorizing a process which I know will culminate in my loss of agency, for instance, my undergoing an epileptic seizure, would make that seizure my own. This brings out the fact that not everything for which one is rightly held responsible can helpfully be considered one's own.

---

[18] Reflective authorization is certainly not necessary for taking responsibility on the authors' account, but it is, I think, meant to be sufficient, so long as the third condition is met.

D. Fischer and Ravizza argue that responsibility depends "not only on the fact that the mechanism issuing in the action is suitably reasons-responsive; what also matters is *how* that mechanism has been put in place" (pp. 230–1). Consider three ways in which my reasons-responsiveness might be affected.

1. Owing to a periodic problem with my neurotransmitters, I am abnormally susceptible to certain faulty reasoning, say, to the gambler's fallacy or to discounting the future in faulty ways. Fortunately, I am able to eliminate this vulnerability by a pill that regulates the production of this transmitter. Since I take the pill deliberately, and for this purpose, there is no reason to deny that the resultant reasoning process is my own.

2. Suppose instead that, unbeknownst to me, carrot juice has the same effect on me as this pill would. When I drink carrot juice regularly, for other reasons, I am not (as) susceptible to these failures of reasoning. That the process is influenced by carrot juice without my knowledge doesn't make those processes less my own. This seems to be a case like the one imagined by Fischer and Ravizza in which I am ignorant of the ways my ordinary reasoning is physically realized (or even that it is physically realized).

3. Substitute for the carrot juice the benign interventions of the Martian monitors, who are able to stimulate the production of the requisite chemicals whenever the natural processes begin to falter. This seems no different in principle from the carrot juice.

Again, this example casts doubt on the claim that if someone "has had his brain manipulated in certain ways, and has not had the opportunity to become aware of the manipulation and reflect on it, then he has *not* taken responsibility for the kind of mechanism that issues in his behavior" (p. 243). I don't see any way of excluding 3 without excluding 2 and other more normal cases of ignorance. And we shouldn't want to exclude 3. It can make no difference to my agency whether the necessary physical conditions of my competence are induced by natural causes or by other agents; the only difference it makes is whether other agents, too, share some responsibility for the outcome.

On reflection, it seems, none of these unknown processes interferes with my ownership of my reasoning; rather they enable me to restore or maintain my normal capacities. The case of Goldie in the voting booth seems different. When the Frankfurt intervener causes her to vote for the better candidate for the better reason, this seems like a subversion of her agency because it is not a case of returning her to her normal capabilities, but bypassing them in order to exercise the intervener's deliberations. And yet the criteria of ownership remain obscure. Perhaps Goldie's normal mediocre deliberative skills are due to a deficiency of neurochemicals. Suppose she eats a nutrition bar just prior to entering the booth, which happens to remedy the deficiency temporarily. As a result, her vote reflects a level of analytic skill that she had never displayed before, and would never attain again. Should we say that her vote doesn't reflect her capacity or that her capacities were enhanced momentarily? Perhaps it is not clear what to say, but on reflection the case doesn't seem significantly different from the Frankfurt intervener case. For these reasons, it is problematic to put a great deal of weight in exotic contexts on the paradigm list. We need a better framework for discussing questions of ownership.

E. I turn now, more briefly, to the question I raised before: why isn't the reasoning that Fischer and Ravizza take to be fatal to mesh theories also fatal to any compatibilist position, including theirs? Specifically, couldn't the process of taking responsibility be induced by "electronic manipulation of the brain" or some other paradigm responsibility-defeating condition? Recall that to take responsibility is to acquire a set of beliefs. The question, then, is whether the acquisition of such a set might be induced by manipulation, or direct stimulation of the brain. Here is where Fischer and Ravizza put the third condition to work. They claim that "an individual who has been electronically induced to have the relevant view of himself (and thus satisfy the first two conditions on taking responsibility) has *not* formed his view of himself in the appropriate way" (p. 236). The basic thought here is that, to be appropriate, a belief must have an appropriate relation to the world; it must track evidence. But if one's beliefs were electronically stimulated, they would not be appropriately grounded. In contrast, they think, there is no incompatibility between a belief's being causally determined and its being appropriately related to the environment.

We should be careful to distinguish two issues here. One is whether any state of mind that could be directly stimulated in this way could be properly called a belief at all. To classify a state as a belief is to place restrictions on its origins. This is a contested question in the philosophy of mind. (We touched on this above in discussing "current time-slice" views.) But the issue Fischer and Ravizza are addressing is whether any state that originates in this way can "track evidence" in the right kind of way. They are confident that none could, but I am not so sure. Perhaps what Fischer and Ravizza are thinking is that for a state to be caused in this way is for it to be sustained by the same process. This indeed would rule out its being a state that answers to the evidence (unless the stimulation itself was so responsive). I have no idea, of course, what process 'electrical stimulation' might refer to; the phrase functions here merely as a gesture at some science fictional procedure. But I see no philosophical reasons to think that something of this description couldn't give rise to a state that is indeed responsive to evidence in the way that beliefs are supposed to be; that is exactly what this wonderful technology is supposed to do. If someone's attitudes were responsive to relevant considerations, then that would seem to me to settle the question of their appropriateness.

But it is not clear whether it should settle the authors' question about ownership. Even if it is possible for reasons-responsive states to be induced in this way, what makes them the individual's own? If taking responsibility is a set of attitudes that is needed to ensure ownership of other reason-responsive processes, what ensures that those attitudes belong to the individual? If reasons-responsiveness is not enough for responsibility because it is not enough for ownership, the appropriateness of that individual's having those attitudes does not suffice to ensure that they are his. For appropriateness is just a kind of reasons-responsiveness. And if they are not guaranteed to be his, how can they guarantee that the mechanisms for which he takes responsibility are his?

Perhaps, however, the problem of ownership doesn't arise for taking responsibility in the way in which, according to the authors, it arises for the mechanisms for which we take responsibility. Perhaps the appropriateness of the set of attitudes in which taking responsibility consists does ensure ownership in virtue of the content of those attitudes. To say that they are appropriate is to say that the agent is right to take responsibility for acting on certain mechanisms. And if she is right to take responsibility, then she is responsible for so acting. Her being responsible is constituted by her appropriately holding those attitudes. So if those attitudes are sound, no further question of ownership arises.

IV. Concluding Remarks

A. Let me take up two more points by way of conclusion.

1. I said earlier that I am sympathetic to Fischer and Ravizza's suggestion that mesh theories are missing something when they ignore the set of attitudes that they call 'taking responsibility'. But I am inclined to give a different significance to these attitudes. Fischer and Ravizza use the notion of taking responsibility to ensure ownership and hence guidance control. They sketch their picture in this way: "Lacking the required view of himself, he is essentially passive, buffeted by forces that assail him. . . . An individual who fails to take responsibility (in our sense) is a bit like a sailor who does not believe his rudder is working; he allows the boat to be buffeted by the strong winds. He does not guide the boat" (p. 221). This might be an apt metaphor for someone who has the reflective belief that he is not an agent and who therefore submits passively to the various

stimulations and pressures to which he is subjected. But it is not applicable to every creature who fails to take responsibility in the authors' sense. For example, someone who failed to meet the second condition, that is, who doesn't see himself as someone who others can properly hold responsible, need not see himself as lacking any kind of control; nor is there any reason to think he would in truth lack control.[19]

What is missing here, it seems to me, is a set of beliefs and (I would add) concerns and skills in virtue of which individuals are capable of reflective critical reason and are therefore capable of participating in the practices of critical evaluation. It is not relevant, as far as I can see, how, or even whether (if this supposition is coherent) they acquired them. What is crucial is not a kind of control but the competence required for meaningful response to the norms to which we hold one another responsible.

2. Finally, I want to raise a question about the relation among various parts of the theory. Clearly, the foundational concepts of the book are reasons-responsiveness, ownership, and guidance control. But Fischer and Ravizza also endorse a Strawsonian conception of moral responsibility, according to which "moral responsibility requires that the agent be an apt candidate for" a range of reactions such as resentment, indignation, and gratitude (see p. 8). The notion of reactive attitudes also plays an important part in the account of taking responsibility, which is said to involve the belief that one

---

[19] Just following the passage quoted above, Fischer and Ravizza align themselves with the views of Galen Strawson, who argues that seeing oneself as free and responsible is a condition of being so. They cite Strawson's example of "natural Epictetans" who have no use for the notions of freedom and responsibility because they live in such a congenial environment and are so naturally wise that they are never in doubt about what to do (Galen Strawson, *Freedom and Belief* [Oxford: Clarendon Press, 1986], pp. 249 ff.). But the moral of Strawson's story doesn't support Fischer and Ravizza's theme. What the natural Epictetans are missing, according to Strawson, is not control or agency (he calls them a race of "gifted and active creatures"). The better analogy is not with the sailor whose boat is not under his control but with unreflective but master navigators—with the salmon, say.

is a fair object of the reactive attitudes. It is not clear to me how this Strawsonian conception is to be integrated into the rest of the doctrine.

Although Fischer and Ravizza sometimes appear to treat the connection between reactive attitudes and moral responsibility as definitional or conceptual (as when they say that moral responsibility requires that one be seen as an apt target of those attitudes), that doesn't seem to be the best way to think of the connection. Reasons-responsiveness (however analyzed) extends way beyond the purview of indignation and gratitude, to contexts of prudential and theoretical reason. It would be peculiar if there were not, on this theory, a generic notion of responsibility with a correspondingly broad extension. Of course, the reactive attitudes are naturally seen as markers of moral responsibility. But I think it would be a mistake to take them as definitional even of this "species" of responsibility, rather than as reactions to the exercise of the capacities in which morally responsible agency consists. Those who think on moral grounds that we should never feel resentment or indignation toward others need not be skeptics about moral responsibility. They can still see and respond to others as morally competent, reasons-responsive agents. And this can be understood only by applying the broader notion of reasons-responsiveness and acknowledging that reactive attitudes have at most a secondary status in a satisfactory account of responsibility.

B. Clearly, I have found much to dispute in *Responsibility and Control*. Fischer and Ravizza stake out a definite and distinctive position on a wide array of controversial issues. So they stick their necks out in ways that invite dispute. I have accepted that invitation with the hope that a close critical examination of the main theses will contribute to the next stage of their project.

But I do not want this critical focus to conceal my admiration for what Fischer and Ravizza have done. *Responsibility and Control* is at once an ambitious and painstaking work. It is scrupulously attentive to traditional and current scholarly contributions to the intersecting topics with which it is concerned. It is subtle, systematic, and sympathetic in its treatment of opposing arguments. For this reason alone, there is much to be learned from its chapters. Furthermore, Fischer and Ravizza's responses to their critics are invariably respectful and generous rather than defensive. By its tone, the book also teaches us how to do philosophy in a way that is at once tough-minded but noncombative.

11   Excusing Addiction

One of the main objections to criminalizing the use of certain addictive (as well as non-addictive "psychoactive") substances is that doing so is illiberal: it interferes unduly with the liberty of citizens to govern their own lives as they will. Another objection is that the "criminals" in this case are typically not in control of their "drug" consumption; they are therefore inappropriate subjects for punishment. (Here the slogan is: "drugs are a medical problem, not a criminal problem".) These arguments are in tension because the first affirms a capacity for individual autonomy on the part of users which the second denies.

What interests me here is an issue raised by the second argument: under what circumstances, and by what rationale, can or should the criminal law treat addictive behavior as less than fully responsible?[1] This issue arises even when drug use itself is not criminal, for example, when a penniless alcoholic steals the money for drink. And certain crimes (say, assault, "peace breaching", or recklessness) often

I want to thank Michael Corrado and Gerald Postema for organizing the stimulating Carolina Workshop in Law and Philosophy, September, 1998, for which this paper was originally prepared. I learned a great deal from the participants on that occasion.

[1] In what follows, I will be exploring the possible rationale for an addiction-based defense, rather than mitigation. (But see the Conclusion.) This distinction is very important for many purposes, but much of what I say will be relevant to both issues. For the proposal that many addicts should be eligible for an "excuse of partial responsibility" (though on the basis of impaired rationality rather than control), see Stephen J. Morse, "Hooked on Hype" [Law and Philosophy 19/1 (2000), 3–49]. Morse argues against duress interpretations of impaired control excuses in "Culpability and Control", *The University of Pennsylvania Law Review*, Vol. 142 (1994), pp. 1587–1660.

result from the psychological effects of using drugs—from getting drunk or high—rather than from the addictive need to use them. If one were not responsible for getting drunk, and if one were not then responsible for certain behavioral effects of intoxication, criminal responsibility would be an issue even if substance-use itself were legal.[2]

Big "ifs", to be sure. As it stands, the law has been understandably resistant to defenses based on addiction. For one thing, experts continue to disagree substantially about the nature and effects of addictions and indeed about what conditions to include in that category. The courts tend to be conservative in the face of such disagreement. In addition, it is not clear how to interpret the impairments identified by leading theories of addiction in terms of the standard categories of legal exculpation. But the biggest obstacle to an addiction-based defense might be this: almost always, individuals become addicted by their voluntary behavior. Even if addictive conditions are in some (not yet well understood) way responsibility-undermining, addicts are complicit in their own impairment.[3]

Despite this resistance, the law remains under significant moral and theoretical pressure to extend well-established excuses to addictive crimes—by which I mean, illegal behavior that is predominantly motivated (or in some other way explained)[4] by addictive needs and cravings. It seems to me that the most plausible way of understanding this pressure is to see addictions as creating circumstances of duress. That, in any case, is the idea I want, eventually, to explore. While the practical prospects of a successful defense along these lines are admittedly dim, the investigation is still theoretically worthwhile. For legal doctrine in this area seems to me especially

---

[2] The issue of responsibility for addiction arises in civil law too. For example, it is central to recent litigation involving the tobacco industry.

[3] See Sanford Kadish, "Excusing Crime", *California Law Review*, vol. 75 (1987), pp. 257–89.

[4] Again, if being intoxicated were to result in a tendency to criminal violence, say, then the addictive need that leads to the intoxication would not *motivate* the crime.

undeveloped and ambivalent; it will be of interest to articulate some of these weaknesses.

I. Some Assumptions about Addiction

Let's begin with the commonplace that addictions involve *compulsion*. Certainly, popular and technical work on addiction has tended to construe addiction in these terms. In its influential formulation of 1969, the World Health Organization defined 'dependence' (a term that replaced the use of 'addiction' in its earlier declarations) as

a state, psychic and sometimes also physical, resulting from the interaction between a living organism and a drug, characterized by behavioral and other responses that always include a compulsion to take the drug on a continuous or periodic basis in order to experience its psychic effects, and sometimes to avoid the discomfort of its absence.[5]

Recent writers tend to be more guarded. Prompted by the goal of appealing only to "patterns of pathological use that can be objectively quantified", the authors of the Third Edition of the *Diagnostic and Statistical Manual of Mental Disorders of the American Psychiatric Association* departed from previous editions by omitting the phrase 'compelling desire to use a substance' in their *definition* of 'dependency'. Yet this goal does not prevent them from relying upon the "ability to cut down or stop use" as a diagnostic *criterion*.[6] And it is still common to find 'addiction' or 'dependency' defined in terms of 'irresistibility'. For example, James Halikas *et al.* define 'craving', which is taken to be a central

---

[5] Quoted in Grinspoon and Bakular, *Cocaine: A Drug and its Social Evolution* (New York: Basic Books, 1976), p. 177.

[6] See John Kuehule and Robert Spitzer, "DSM III Classification of Substance Use Disorders", in J. H. Lowinson and P. Ruiz (eds.), *Substance Abuse: A Comprehensive Textbook* (Baltimore: Williams and Wilkins, 2nd edn., 1992), pp. 22–3.

component of addiction, as "an irresistible urge to use a substance that compels drug seeking behavior."[7]

This way of defining addiction or dependency has given rise to a certain amount of skepticism, which has in turn affected legal opinion.[8] Nevertheless, there is a substantial body of research, from different quarters, in support of George Loewenstein's claim that

drug-craving limits the scope for volitional control of behavior. Once the addict is "hooked", and subject to intermittent craving, the scope for volition narrows to the point where it may not be useful, either theoretically or practically, to view the addict's behavior as a matter of choice. . . . As an individual becomes addicted to a drug, . . . there is a progressive loss of volitional control over drug taking.[9]

---

[7] "The Measurement of Craving in Cocaine Patients Using the Minnesota Cocaine Craving Scale", *Comprehensive Psychiatry*, 32(1), pp. 22–7. In "Acute and Chronic Pain" (in J. H. Lowinson, P. Ruiz, R. B. Millman, and J. G. Langrod (eds.), *Substance Abuse: A Comprehensive Textbook* (Baltimore: Williams and Wilkins, 3rd edn., 1996), pp. 563–89), Russell K. Portenoy and Richard Payne insist upon a distinction between physical dependence and addiction, defining addiction as a condition in which one is unable to abstain: "Use of the term 'addiction' to describe patients who are merely physically dependent reinforces the stigma associated with opioid therapy and should be abandoned. If the clinician wishes to describe a patient who is believed to have the capacity for abstinence, the term physical dependence must be used" (p. 564).

[8] The skeptics include Herbert Fingarette, *Heavy Drinking: the Myth of Alcoholism as a Disease* (Berkeley: University of California Press, 1988); Grinspoon and Bakular, supra note 5, and Stanton Peele, *The Meaning of Addiction* (New York: Health, 1985), and *The Diseasing of America* (Lexington, Mass.: Lexington Books, 1989). For judicial expressions of skepticism that addictions involve volitional impairments of the legally relevant kind, see Justice Leventhal's concurring opinion in *U.S. v. Moore*: "Drug addiction of varying degrees may or may not result in loss of self-control, depending on the strength of character opposed to the drug craving. . . . the difficulty is sharpened by the appreciable number of narcotic 'addicts' who do abandon their habits permanently, and much larger number who reflect their capacity to refrain by ceasing use for varying periods of time. The reasons are not clear but the phenomenon is indisputable . . . " Sanford H. Kadish and Stephen J. Schulhofer, *Criminal Law and its Processes* (Boston: Little, Brown, 5th edn., 1989), pp. 1071 and 1074. (All references to this edition are hereafter cited as "Kadish and Schulhofer".)

[9] George Loewenstein, "A Visceral Account of Addiction", in Jon Elster and O. J. Skog (eds.), *Getting Hooked: Rationality and Addiction* (Cambridge and New York: Cambridge University Press, 1999). See also Loewenstein's "Out of Control: Visceral

Loewenstein adds: "Once addicted, behavior is periodically driven by craving, which overwhelms rational deliberations concerning self-interest."[10] Surely these claims are *prima facie* relevant to moral and criminal responsibility. If the law excludes considerations of addiction altogether, it does so despite substantial evidence that addictive behavior can be out of control and hence less than fully morally responsible.

II. Addiction and the Law

For the purposes of philosophical argument, I will assume that Loewenstein and others are right to claim that addiction, at least in advanced stages, leads to "loss of volitional control over drug taking". Consider then the following case for exculpating (some) addictive crimes.[11]

Suppose there is a law against drinking alcohol in public. Imagine an alcoholic defendant, D, who is homeless, that is, who has no legal access to anything but "public space". Thus:

1. D is a severe alcoholic.
2. Severe alcoholics lack control over their alcohol consumption.
3. Therefore, D lacks control over his alcohol consumption.
4. Criminal sanctions should not be imposed for behavior over which an individual has no control.
5. Therefore, criminal sanctions should not be imposed on D for drinking in public.

Influences on Behaviour", *Organizational Behavior and Human Decision Processes*, 65(3) (1996), pp. 272–92. For a judicious overview of this issue, see Jon Elster, "Rationality and Addiction": ". . . most addictive behavior can be traced back to irrationality in the choice, the belief formation, or the information acquisition of the agent", typescript, p. 1.

[10] "Out of Control", p. 40.

[11] I do not here attribute to Loewenstein any particular view about the implications of his work for legal responsibility. I am using his theories, which I find plausible, to fix ideas for the purposes of my argument. See note 21 below.

What's wrong with this argument? The example partially parallels *Powell v. Texas* which came before the U.S. Supreme Court in 1968. The constitutional issue was whether punishing for alcoholic behavior is "cruel and unusual", hence prohibited by the Eighth and Fourteenth Amendments. That punishing addiction *per se* was unconstitutional for this reason had been found in *Robinson v. California*, 1962. In the actual case, Powell was not homeless, and his appeal was rejected partly on this ground. But what is interesting here is the reasoning accepted by both Justice White, who concurred in the denial of the appeal, and by Justice Fortas *et al.*, who dissented. "If it cannot be a crime to have an irresistible compulsion to use narcotics", White argued, "I do not see how it can constitutionally be a crime to yield to such a compulsion. Punishing an addict for using drugs convicts for addiction under a different name."[12] Thus, White accepts premise 2 of the above argument,[13] and contends that if Powell had been "unable to stay off the streets on the night in question", the rationale in *Robinson* would have applied.[14]

Fortas *et al.* formulate this rationale in this way: "Criminal penalties may not be inflicted upon a person for being in a condition he is powerless to change", a principle they take to be "the foundation of individual liberty and the cornerstone of the relations between a civilized state and its citizens."[15] Of course, this is, more or less, the fourth premise of the argument under consideration.

However, the majority opinion in *Powell* construes the thrust of *Robinson* much more narrowly. The constitutional defect in the California law was simply that it criminalized a *status* rather than an act. Whatever the merits of premise 4 as a substantive principle of criminal responsibility, the court was not willing to find it or any other doctrine of accountability in the Constitution.

[12] Kadish and Schulhofer, p. 1066.

[13] For a challenge to the conception of alcoholism employed in this reasoning, see Herbert Fingarette, "The Perils of *Powell*: In Search of a Factual Foundation for the 'Disease Concept of Alcoholism' ", *Harvard Law Review* 83 (1970).

[14] It should be noted that White himself had dissented from the majority in *Robinson*.   [15] Kadish and Schulhofer, p. 1068.

It is doubtful that the implications of *Robinson* can be so narrowly contained. The court there likens criminalizing addiction to making leprosy or mental illness a crime, something that would "be universally thought to be an infliction of cruel and unusual punishment in violation of the Eighth and Fourteenth Amendments."[16] The court leaves the basis of this thought unexplained. An obvious explanation is that punishing people for leprosy is punishing them for something over which they have no control, and that looks cruel. Without an alternative story, we are led back to the very principle cited by Fortas *et al.*

III. Obstacles to an Addiction-Based Defense

We have seen that the idea that addiction might diminish criminal responsibility is far from absurd. Nevertheless, apart from doubts about our assumptions about addiction, the law's reluctance to recognize such a defense has two sources: equity, and the needs for social regulation.

(i) The second need is practical. The criminal law aims to protect citizens against certain harms and aggressions by means of a fair system of prohibitions and punishments. This seems to require that citizens not be punished unless they are responsible for violating legal requirements. Thus one constitutive aim of the law is to track the responsibility of defendants. But the pursuit of this aim must be balanced against protective concerns. In legal practice, the law tends to be conservative, recognizing a defense only when, as Meir Dan-Cohen puts it, it "is both of a rare kind and is generally perceived to be clearly convincing. By insisting on these two conditions, the law affirms its commitment to fairness (or justice) without significantly

---

[16] Kadish and Schulhofer, p. 1056.

diminishing its effectiveness."[17] The defense of addiction is not thought to meet these conditions.

These considerations are clearly to the fore in *U.S. v. Moore* (U.S. Court of Appeals, District of Columbia, 1973), where the Court considers the appellant's contention that his "overpowering need to use heroin" resulted in "substantial impairment of his behavior controls . . . relevant to his criminal responsibility for unlawful possession. . . ."[18] In his concurring opinion, Justice Leventhal concludes (contrary to the claims of Fortas *et al.* in *Powell*) that

> there is no broad common law principle of exculpation on ground of lack of control but rather a series of particular defenses staked out in manageable areas, with the call for justice to the individual confined to ascertainable and verifiable conditions, and limited by the interest of society in control of conduct. . . .

Leventhal goes on to insist that many people are held responsible despite

> substantial impairment and lack of capacity due, say, to weakness of intellect that establishes susceptibility to suggestion; or . . . loss of control of the mind as a result of passion, whether the passion is of an amorous nature or the result of hate, prejudice or vengeance; or . . . a depravity that blocks out conscience as an influence on conduct.[19]

Any acceptable defense on the basis of impairment of control would have to "discern a demarcation . . . that keeps the defense within verifiable bounds that do not tear the fabric of the criminal law as an instrument of social control. . . ."[20] Thus Leventhal rejects premise 4 of the argument with which we began the last section.

Something like this point is made again and again in legal discussions of addiction and related defenses. Perhaps addictions *are* sources of volitional impairments, the courts seem to grant. Nevertheless,

---

[17] "Actus Reus", Sanford Kadish (ed.), *Encyclopedia of Criminal Justice* (New York: Free Press, 1983). Quoted in Kadish and Schulhofer, p. 1077.

[18] Kadish and Schulhofer, p. 1071.   [19] Kadish and Schulhofer, p. 1074.

[20] Kadish and Schulhofer, p. 1073.

unless there is a way to "demarcate" the kind of impairment involved in addiction from the ways in which passions, prejudices, undue influenceability, weakness of will, *etc*. diminish control (impairments that may well affect the "vast bulk of the population"), acknowledging this defense "threatens to tear the fabric of the criminal law as an instrument of social control". So it is not that claims of addiction do not draw upon powerful legally relevant principles; it is that the law cannot see a way of keeping this defense within predictable and reasonable bounds.

This worry is aggravated by George Loewenstein's theory, according to which addiction is only one among a number of other prevalent "visceral" factors that diminish volitional control, including cravings arising from "extreme hunger, thirst, pain, anger, sleepiness . . . ", as well as sexual desire.[21] Granted that the addict is in some sense out of control, so are the hot tempered and the horny. Lord Cooper gave voice to the same concern regarding a general diminished responsibility defense as it was developing in England in 1945:

. . . it will not suffice in law, for the purpose of this defence of diminished responsibility, merely to show that an accused person has a very short temper, or is unusually excitable and lacking in self-control. *The world would be a very convenient place for criminals, and a very dangerous place for other people, if that were the law.*[22]

Here Lord Cooper was anticipating the kind of worry created by the English Homicide Bill of 1957, which reduced a charge of murder to manslaughter if the accused

was suffering from such abnormality of mind (whether arising from a condition of arrested or retarded development of mind or any inherent

---

[21] "A Visceral Account of Addiction", p. 3. Again, I should say that Loewenstein himself does not address the legal implications of his position. In "Out of Control", he acknowledges the issue about policy. "Although we hold people accountable for their behavior as a matter of policy", he thinks that "sexually motivated behaviour often seems to fall into 'the gray region' between pure volition and pure compulsion" (p. 286).

[22] Quoted in Nigel Walker, *Crime and Insanity in England* (Edinburgh: Edinburgh University Press, 1968), p. 156 (my emphasis).

causes or induced by disease or injury) as substantially impaired his mental responsibility for his acts or omissions in doing or being a party to the killing.[23]

Under this law in 1959, Patrick Byrne pled diminished responsibility to a charge of rape/murder, claiming to suffer from an "abnormal sexual impulse . . . so strong that he found it difficult or impossible to control", a claim that nowadays would be cast in terms of sexual addiction.[24]

(ii) Often, then, the aim of fair treatment of individuals, of tracking individual responsibility, gives way to the goal of maintaining an effective protective apparatus. However, these last remarks point to a consideration that is more than strategic. That someone's behavior is "out of control" is more often an accusation than an exculpation. The concern is not just that the plea itself becomes widely available, but that it wrongly lets some of us off the hook. Citizens have a standing legal duty to develop and maintain sufficient capacities of self-control to enable them to conform to the law. As a 19th century American court put it: "It is the duty of men who are not insane . . . to control their evil passions and violent tempers or brutal instincts and if they do not do so, it is their own fault, and their moral and legal responsibility will not be destroyed or avoided by the existence of such passions. . . . "[25] Even if addicted defendants were in a demonstrably responsibility-impaired state, it seems wrong to excuse them just for

---

[23] Walker, *Crime and Insanity in England,* p. 150.

[24] See *Crime and Insanity in England,* p. 155. According to Ariel Goodman ("Sexual Addiction", in *Substance Abuse,* pp. 340–54), "Sexual addiction is defined as a condition . . . characterized by two key features: (a) recurrent failure to control sexual behavior and (b) continuation of the behavior despite significant harmful consequences" (p. 342). As it turns out, the majority of sexual addicts are men, who experience the "onset" of the affliction "prior to age 18"; the condition "typically peaks between the ages of 20 and 30, and then gradually declines" (Goodman, p. 342). In other words, sexual addiction is the condition of prolonged male adolescence that is so familiar from frat house to White House, a condition known to our moral traditions as philandering, intemperance, promiscuity, or debauchery, as the case may be.

[25] *Fitzpatrik v. Commonwealth of Kentucky* (1883).

this reason. The legal duty to maintain self-control means that we allow ourselves to become addicted at our own peril.

To be sure, the idea that people become addicted knowingly and willingly is somewhat simplistic. As Loewenstein brings out, people systematically underestimate "the force of the craving they will experience if they try to stop taking the drug, [and] . . . overestimate their own future ability to stop taking the drug. Early drug-taking behavior, therefore, results from a decision that is distorted by biased expectations."[26] Moreover, these misestimates often occur in adolescence when prudential skills are poorly developed. But these sorts of limitations of rationality are hardly grounds for exculpation in our legal and moral tradition.

But aren't there circumstances in which the law should allow that a person's lack of self-control was not her fault, that she could not reasonably have been expected to become a fully law-abiding citizen?[27] At least one case (*U.S. v. Lyons* (1984)) involved evidence attributing the defendant's addiction to the innocent use of pre-scribed pain medication. The *Robinson* court had acknowledged this possibility: "not only may addiction innocently result from the use of medically prescribed narcotics, but a person may even be a nar-cotics addict from the moment of his birth. . . . "[28] The position that addicts are responsible for their diminished control should be a rebuttable assumption.

That the assumption is generally true has been challenged by recent research on the "Reward Deficiency Syndrome". Certain individuals are born, according to these studies, with genetic abnormalities affect-ing the dopamine system in such a way that the individual cannot find

---

[26] "A Visceral Account . . . ", p. 3.

[27] The so-called "rotten social background" defense suggests one attempt to define a class of exceptions to the standing obligation to conform to the law. For a sympathetic consideration of this issue, see Richard Delgado, " 'Rotten Social Background': Should the Criminal Law Recognize a Defense of Severe Environmental Deprivation?", in *Law and Equality* 3, 1985. [28] Quoted in Kadish and Schulhofer, p. 1057, note 9.

enjoyment, satisfaction, "positive reinforcement", without resorting to the kind of stimulation provided by the use of addictive substances.[29] This would be an instance of what Paul Robinson calls a "chromosomal abnormality defense". No such defense has ever succeeded, Robinson notes. He sketches a defense along these lines in this way:

... An actor is excused for his conduct constituting an offense if, as a result of (1) chromosomal abnormality, (2) the actor ... is not sufficiently able to control his conduct so as to be held accountable for it.[30]

As I understand them, some RDS theorists claim that these conditions are met by many individuals involved in substance abuse.

It is an understatement to say that at this point these claims have not been made out to the satisfaction of the scientific community. Furthermore, whatever the chromosomal findings, the difficulty is to justify claims such as (2).[31] It will not suffice to show that the probability of substance abuse is significantly higher for those with the abnormality in question. For higher probability does not entail or even suggest diminished control in the sense relevant to accountability. Even where there is good reason to believe that individuals with the abnormality have a harder time of it than those without it (again, this is not entailed by the probabilities), this on its own would not place

---

[29] See Kenneth Blum et al., "Reward Deficiency Syndrome", American Scientist 84 (1996), pp. 132–45. For a popular report, see J. Madeleine Nash, "Addicts", Time 149(18) (1997), pp. 69–77.

[30] Criminal Law Defenses, Vol. 2 (St. Paul: West Publishing Co., 1984), pp. 444–5.

[31] According to Nash, "Americans tend to think of drug addiction as a failure of character. But this stereotype is beginning to give way to the recognition that drug dependence has a clear biological basis" ("Addicts", p. 70). The fact that addiction has a biological basis is neither surprising nor clearly relevant to our question. What should strike us here is the crudity of the contrasts, as though having a "biological basis" precludes failure of character; as though we must think that the natural appetites cannot have a "biological basis", if we think they can be implicated in vice. In "Disordered Appetites" [Ch. 3, this volume], I argue that there is nothing about the ways in which addictions impair agency to distinguish them in kind from natural appetites. I think this is also a feature of Loewenstein's visceral theory.

them in a category calling for special legal consideration.[32] It would not distinguish them, for example, from those whose environments, or natural appetites, made it abnormally hard to attain temperance.

As a general matter, then, the prospect of excusing addiction raises serious practical and moral qualms. Nevertheless, in particular instances, the intuitive case for special consideration can seem quite powerful. As I have said, this case can best be understood in terms of the category of *duress*. But before we take up this point, it will be instructive to consider the possibility of a defense on grounds of insanity.

IV. Addiction as Insanity

Some addicted defendants have attempted to present an insanity defense.[33] At least on those versions of the defense that depart from M'Naughton in allowing for "irresistible impulse" or "volitional incapacity", the case is *prima facie* plausible. The Model Penal Code's version is perhaps the most commonly cited of these:

A person is not responsible for criminal conduct if at the time of such conduct as a result of mental disease or defect he lacks substantial capacity either to appreciate the criminality [wrongfulness] of his conduct or to conform his conduct to the requirements of law. . . . [34]

[32] For a good discussion of this point, see Christopher Boorse, "Premenstrual Syndrome and Criminal Responsibility", in *Premenstrual Syndrome: Ethical and Legal Implications in a Biomedical Perspective* (New York: Plenum Press, 1987), pp. 81–124. As Boorse points out, that one (probably) wouldn't have committed robbery if one had been middle-aged, or committed murder if one had not been male is not taken to be extenuating. "Causal influence of a factor, even when mediated by an endocrine process, does not negate and may not even limit criminal responsibility. On the contrary, criminal law expects everyone to meet stress with increased self-control, and it must take more, not less, care to punish anti-social acts where typical temptation to them is strong" (p. 102).

[33] See *U.S. v. Freeman* (1966), and *U.S. v. Lyons* (1984).

[34] Section 4.01 of the 1985 Model Penal Code, quoted in Kadish and Schulhofer. p. 981.

The failure of these attempts reflects a loss of confidence during the last several decades in MPC-type rules generally. The attitude of the *Lyons* Court, quoting from the *American Psychiatric Association's* "Statement on the Insanity Defense", is typical:

There is . . . no objective basis for distinguishing between . . . the impulse that was irresistible and the impulse not resisted, or between substantial impairment of capacity and some lesser impairment. . . . We see no prudent course for the law to follow but to treat all criminal impulses—including those not resisted—as resistible. To do otherwise in the present state of medical knowledge would be to cast the insanity defense adrift upon a sea of unfounded scientific speculation. . . . [35]

This conclusion reflects an understandable general concern about the obscurity of the notion of volitional impairment.[36] And as we've seen, some opinions in particular are suspicious of addiction-based insanity pleas. But of more theoretical interest is Leventhal's point in *Moore*[37] that an addiction defense does not meet the requirement that the incapacity result from a disease or defect. Whether or not one takes addiction to be a "disease", the important lesson to me is that the disease-requirement is not really cogent. Imagine that someone satisfies the M'Naughton cognitive test, say, but without any showing of disease. It is morally absurd to differentiate between two equally incapacitated individuals solely on the grounds that one of the conditions could be traced to a disease. Surely it is that condition itself, not

[35] Kadish and Schulhofer, pp. 998–9.

[36] I think the Court's confidence in the comparative clarity and objectivity of the "cognitive" part of the insanity standard is misplaced; the claim that " . . . psychiatric testimony about volition is more likely to produce confusion for jurors than is psychiatric testimony concerning a defendant's appreciation of the wrongfulness of his act" (Kadish and Schulhofer, p. 998) seems to me highly doubtful.

[37] Although the defendant in *Moore* did not officially offer an insanity defense, he claimed his addiction resulted in substantial impairment of his "behavior controls" (specifically a loss of self-control over the use of heroin) that is sufficient in common law for exculpation.

its causes, that constitutes the individual's incompetence from a legal standpoint.[38]

The problem with the disease-requirement then is that it is either unnecessary or insufficient. Any formulations of the conditions for legal insanity, say the M-test or the MPC-test, *sans* requirement, either identifies sufficient conditions for legal incompetence or it does not. If so, their causal origins do not matter. If these conditions are not sufficient, then requiring that they be caused by disease will not ensure incompetence, and we have an inadequate test.

Causal origins *do* matter, it might be replied, because it matters whether the individual is responsible for his impairment. Very well—but the disease-clause does not answer to this concern. For someone might be responsible for incurring the disease. In any case, as far as I know, the law has never been open to evidence bearing on this question in the case of the insanity defense.[39]

Hence I disagree with Justice Leventhal when he denies (in the *Moore* case, cited above) that "because one condition (mental

[38] Admittedly, the foregoing may be hard to imagine. But that is because to meet the M-test *is* to be "defective" or "diseased" in an important sense. In that case, the requirement of "caused by a disease" is superfluous. Compare the gloss on "mental disease" in *McDonald v. United States*: " . . . a mental disease or defect includes any abnormal condition of the mind which substantially affects mental or emotional processes and substantially impairs behaviour controls" (Kadish and Schulhofer, p. 1010). Again, any impairment of mental, emotional, or volitional processes is bound to be abnormal in *some* sense, thus obviating a causal inquiry. (But consider adolescence!)

[39] Note the recommended standard of the American Psychiatric Association, which not only excludes a defense of volitional incapacity, and narrows the understanding of cognitive impairment, but explicitly excludes any conditions that result from voluntary drug-use: "A person charged with a criminal offense should be found not guilty by reason of insanity if it is shown that as a result of mental disease or mental retardation he was unable to appreciate the wrongfulness of his conduct at the time of the offense. As used in this standard, the terms mental disease or mental retardation include only those severely abnormal mental conditions that grossly and demonstrably impair a person's perception or understanding of reality and that are not attributable primarily to the voluntary ingestion of alcohol or other psychoactive substances." (Kadish and Schulhofer, p. 1003.)

disease) yields an exculpatory defense if it results in impairment of and lack of behavioral controls the same result follows when some other condition impairs behavior controls."[40] I think it *does* follow—unless (unlike other causes) a "mental disease" is something by its nature for which the individual could not be responsible. But it is not.

I suspect that the disease-clause of the insanity tests is a flat-footed attempt to honor some considerations of justice—namely, to exculpate dramatically impaired moral actors—while screening out countless further pleas too difficult to substantiate and too widely available. But the resulting doctrine is incoherent, for it reflects a lack of confidence in the criteria of competence identified in those tests. If those criteria are not indeed sufficiently clear to identify those whom it would be wrong to hold criminally responsible, then it does not advance this aim at all to tie them to a requirement that they be brought about in a certain way.

I conclude that an addiction-based insanity defense should not be ruled out by the disease-requirement. For that requirement is unreasonable. Nonetheless, 'insanity' is not, in my view, the proper category in which to understand the exculpating tendency of addiction. Indeed, I think in general it was a moral and conceptual error to attempt to fashion a single plea out of the disjunction of volitional and M'Naughton-type impairments. These considerations are simply too disparate. Instead, volitional impairments are better understood as grounding a defense of duress.[41]

---

[40] Kadish and Schulhofer, p. 1072.

[41] I should say that what I have in mind by volitional impairments are not merely defects of something called the will, as distinct from reason or intellect. As I see them, impairments of the kind typified by addictions characteristically involve cognitive distortions of various kinds. The ability to see things straight, and in focus, is not entirely separable from the ability to respond to the reasons one knows one has. In contrast, in "Addiction as Defect of the Will: Some Philosophical Reflections", *Law and Philosophy*, 18/6 (1999), R. Jay Wallace wishes to isolate defects of will from defects of reason. I am not sure this can be done. Otherwise, I find Wallace's account congenial and insightful.

V. Addiction and Compulsion

Let's return to the initial thought that addictions diminish responsibility (when they do) because they are sources of compulsive motivation. In what sense can desires be "compulsive" and how is that sense relevant to moral and legal culpability?

Aristotle's discussion of "voluntary" action in *Nicomachean Ethics* is a helpful starting point. Here Aristotle distinguishes different ways (or senses) in which "force" might negate voluntariness. He defines voluntary action, that is, behavior for which individuals are open to praise or blame, as behavior which is neither forced nor done in ignorance. "What is forced", he says, "has an external origin, the sort of origin in which the agent or victim contributes nothing— e.g. if a wind or human being who controls him were to carry him off."[42] He goes on to consider a different kind of force, namely what we would call duress or coercion.

Suppose, e.g. a tyrant tells you to do something shameful, when he has control over your parents and children, and if you do it, they will live, and if not, they will die. . . . The same sort of thing . . . happens with throwing cargo overboard in storms; for no one willingly throws cargo overboard, unconditionally, but anyone with any sense throws it overboard . . . to save himself and the others.[43]

Such behavior resembles the first category of forced behavior because it is in a way unwilling. The agent is forced to do something "evil" whatever she does. But here what she does depends on her choice. Hence the "origin" is not just external. And she might choose well or badly, and consequently be open to praise or blame for what she does. Aristotle notes, however, that "In some cases there is no praise, but there is pardon, whenever someone does a wrong action because of conditions of a sort that overstrain human nature, and that no one would endure."[44]

---

[42] *Nicomachean Ethics*, Book 3.1, 1110a1–4, translated by Terence Irwin (Indianapolis: Hackett, 1985). [43] *Nicomachean Ethics*, 3.1, a4–12. [44] 1110a25 f.

Inquiry into whether you are blameworthy for having caused harm or violated a law therefore might have three types of conclusion.

1. *Literal Force*   There is no choice or agency exercised at all. You are blameless because you did nothing.

The wind or some hooligan literally forces you into others, knocking them down.

2. *Choice Among Evils*   In an emergency, you are faced with terrible options, and choose what you judge to be the lesser evil.

Here again there are two cases, depending on whether or not the difficult choice-situation is created by human design. (We normally speak of "coercion" only in the first type of case, but I will ignore this distinction in speaking of "coercive predicaments".)

2a. Hooligans threaten you: "unless you knock the other into the ditch, we'll kill this child".

2b. A runaway truck is heading directly toward another, creating the following circumstance: unless you knock the other down, he will be crushed.

You cannot be blamed for causing harm *per se*, but you will be blamed if you choose badly—that is, do not choose to knock the other down.

3. *Duress:*[45] One chooses wrongly but in circumstances in which choosing the right thing is too difficult to expect of one another. One is therefore not blameworthy (or not as blameworthy).

For example, a battered woman participates in a bank robbery, under the command of her abusive lover who threatens to kill her unless she goes along.[46] (There are undesigned examples here as well.)

Whether or not behavior falls into the category of literal force is normally fairly straightforward. The categories of duress and

---

[45] I use 'duress' here in a non-technical sense. The legal usage is much more restrictive, as we'll see.

[46] See *People of California v. Romer* (1992), in which the defendant pleaded duress to charges of robbery and attempted robbery on the grounds that she was threatened with death unless she participated. I discuss this case further in the next section.

justification, however, raise more complicated conceptual and normative questions. Some might think that the woman's participation in the bank robbery was justifiable in the circumstances. Further, the categories might overlap as follows: apart from the question of whether participating in the robbery in those circumstances is the right thing to do, it would "overstrain" human nature to expect people to withstand the threat. Now the idea of being too difficult to expect of one another is not easy to explain. In the remainder of the essay, I want to explore the proposal that addiction compromises responsibility in just this way, by creating circumstances of duress.

To begin with, one thing is clear: the sense that addictions can be overpowering forces should not mislead us into locating the excuse in Aristotle's first category, as though our defendant were like the man blown about by the wind. The problem with this idea is not that Aristotle restricts the first category to forces *external* to the body. (After all, behavior that results from epileptic seizures has, in some sense, "internal" origins.) The relevant notion of 'external', for this category, is independence from the will. If we could stand to our desires as to external forces, then to be compelled by a desire would not be a case of volitional incapacity, any more than being blown about by the wind would. It would not be to act at all.[47] Compulsive desire is not a force that moves me independently of my will; it is a "force" that leads me to make certain choices.[48] The appropriate interpersonal counterpart is not the thug who literally tosses me out of the room, but the one who *threatens* to beat me up unless I leave.

[47] On a conception of irresistible impulse as a force that overpowers the agent's will, it would be especially wrong-headed to think of that notion of compulsion as the non-cognitive prong of an insanity test. On this conception, the person's moral agency is not in that case undermined but bypassed; he is a passive bystander to internal forces. There is then no *actus reus*. It belongs again in Aristotle's first category.

[48] I elaborate this argument in "Disordered Appetites" [Ch. 3, this volume]. Robert Schopp also questions this conception of addictive desire in *Automatism, Insanity, and the Psychology of Criminal Responsibility* (Cambridge and New York: Cambridge University Press, 1991), p. 249.

(Or is it, in the case of addiction, rather like someone who seduces me to stay?)

This notion of compulsion is a normative one. Those who are subject to compulsive desires (in contrast to those who are merely weak of will) are those who could not reasonably be expected to hold out.[49] But this thought is subject to significantly different interpretations, as we'll now see.

VI. Two Interpretations of Duress

The legal category of duress is fraught with confusion and controversy. Duress is commonly thought to have a peculiarly dual character, appearing both excuse-like and justification-like. I think this appearance is due in part to a conflation under one heading of two distinct grounds of exculpation. This has given rise to two interpretations of the plea.

On the most common conception, duress is an excuse because coercive circumstances limit or compromise one's capacities for self-control. But a quite different idea is that circumstances of duress create special reasons in virtue of which criminal sanctions are inappropriate. On both defenses, it is unreasonable or unfair to expect a person to comply with the law under certain situations, and

---

[49] I suggest a normative account in "Skepticism about Weakness of Will", *The Philosophical Review*, April, 1977 [Ch. 2, this volume]. The idea is that weakness is the manifestation of a vice; someone is a victim of compulsion if she is subject to motivation that even a person of exemplary self-control could not resist.

See also Patricia Greenspan, who argues that the victim of motivational compulsion is "unfree because he is faced with a kind of threat, like a robbery victim coerced at gunpoint, with intense discomfort as his only option to compliance." "Behavior Control and Freedom of Action", *The Philosophical Review* 87 (1978), pp. 225–40, reprinted in John Fischer (ed.), *Moral Responsibility* (Ithaca: Cornell University Press, 1986), p. 196 of the reprinting. Greenspan's discussion focuses on those who are subjected to aversive behavioral control (such as the character Alex, in Anthony Burgess's *A Clockwork Orange*).

this makes it difficult to tell in some contexts which interpretation is at work. On the idea of duress as diminished capacity, the dire circumstances of the lawbreaker make it too difficult for even the decent citizen to comply with the law. On the second conception, those circumstances make it reasonable for one to act illegally. In the second case, the accused might well be responding fully and appropriately to the reasons he has, whereas in the other, the predicament makes it too difficult to expect even a person of good character to think straight or to act well.

The tendency to conflate these grounds is reinforced by technical features of the legal notion of justification. Take again the case of *People of California v. Romer,* in which the defendant pleaded duress to charges of robbery and attempted robbery on the grounds that she was threatened with death unless she participated. Suppose we think she has a defense on the second ground just mentioned. Still, this would not be a justification in the legal sense. As that defense is standardly defined, the illegal conduct must serve a greater good or avoid a greater harm, *from the standpoint of the law's general aims,* than that involved in the violation.[50]

Self-defense law illustrates this point. From a public policy point of view, it is better for the aggressor to be killed than the intended victim. The same point holds when you seek shelter from a deadly storm by trespassing on my property. Although you have technically broken the law, you are not a wrongdoer. As Joshua Dressler puts it, "Justification defenses amend the law. . . ."[51]

However, this condition is not clearly satisfied by the coerced participation in a bank robbery which exposes a number of citizens

---

[50] Section 3.02 of the MPC (1985) formulates the defense in this way: ". . . conduct which the actor believes to be necessary to avoid a harm or evil to himself or to another is justifiable, provided that the harm or evil to be avoided by the conduct is greater than that sought to be prevented by the law defining the offense charged [and the actor's choice situation isn't due to her own negligence or recklessness]".

[51] "Exegesis and the Law of Duress: Justifying the Excuse and Searching for its Proper Limits", *Southern California Law Review* 62(5) (1989), p. 1374.

to grave risks. As Dan Kahan and Martha Nussbaum[52] explain, a woman (as in the *Romer* case)

may be morally entitled (perhaps even morally obliged) to prefer her or her family's welfare to that of strangers, and may thus have a defense of duress. But given the risk that her actions create for innocent third parties, it cannot necessarily be said, from a consequentialist point of view, that her participation in the robbery results in a preferred state of affairs.[53]

The point turns on a distinction between justification from a legal/public point of view, and justification from a personal/private point of view. Thus, those who violate the law in these circumstances are, in one plain sense, justified in doing so: they act for sufficient reasons. But their conduct is not justifiable from the point of view of the general aims and values of the law. It would not be unreasonable for an individual in this predicament to refuse to subordinate her fundamental interests to that of the public. In effect, to recognize the defense of duress, on this conception, is to recognize a space in which compliance with the law is optional; it is to affirm the legal significance of what Samuel Scheffler[54] calls in other contexts *agent-centered prerogatives*.[55]

[52] "Two Conceptions of Emotion in Criminal Law", *Columbia Law Review* 96(2) (1996), pp. 269–374, p. 337. I have learned a lot from this perceptive essay, which I discuss further below.

[53] But this explanation doesn't explain why cases such as *State of New Jersey v. Toscano* (1977) would not be tried under a justification defense. Would it really be preferable or ideal from a public/legal point of view for the defendant to allow himself and his family to suffer death or severe injury rather than to falsify a medical report? I doubt it. This rationale needs more work.

[54] *The Rejection of Consequentialism* (Oxford: Clarendon Press, 1982). The idea is that morality permits us to act in a less than "optimisic" way when certain "personal" concerns are at stake. We recognize in morality that the standpoint of what is preferable from a moral point of view might be something the morally decent person has no overriding reason to adopt in a particular case.

[55] In their paper, Kahan and Nussbaum note that agent-centered reasons are important to their idea of duress as distinct from both justification and excuse. Dressler also notes that coercive predicaments might create a distinctive justification based on "self-interested" reasons ("Exegesis of the Law of Duress", p. 1356), though

Potentially, then, coercive predicaments provide three distinct bases for defence: an *impairment defense*, a *prerogative defense*, and a full justification (in the legal sense). The latter two are sometimes grouped under the heading of 'necessity'. Prerogative defenses, like legal justifications, raise the issue of whether the defendant's choice was reasonable, rationally defensible. A successful defense must show that it was. The impairment defense grants that this exercise of agency was defective, but argues that it was compatible with the commitments and virtues of the law-abiding citizen. The choice may have been faulty,[56] but that shouldn't be held against him. Therefore, both defenses require normative judgments at different points.

A particular predicament might ground all three defenses at once. The exigency of self-defense might plausibly provide a legal justification, create an agent-centered prerogative, and diminish a person's capacity to respond rationally at the same time.[57] A prerogative defense is neither a legal justification nor an excuse because it cites neither a legally sufficient reason nor an impairment.

Thus I agree in part with Kahan and Nussbaum, who argue that " . . . duress exculpates not because (and when) threats vitiate a person's moral agency, but because (and when) a person's fear expresses a rational and morally appropriate assessment of her circumstances. . . . "[58] The authors make a convincing case for the conclusion that the law often exculpates defendants in coercive

he argues that in legal practice, the defense of duress is best understood as an excuse. Alan Wertheimer argues that "duress is best understood as an agent-relative justification" (*Coercion* (Princeton, N.J.: Princeton University Press, 1987), p. 168).

[56] In saying this, I want to distinguish faulty conduct from innocent conduct that (accidentally, say) has bad consequences. Faulty conduct in my sense is open to criticism.

[57] However, for arcane reasons, self-defense could not in law ground a duress defense (on either interpretation). For one thing, in most jurisdictions, a defense of duress is not available in homicide cases. (I discuss this below.) For another thing, the defense is usually available only where the crime is a fulfillment of the coercive threat. For example, someone who escapes prison to avoid rape or other forms of brutality might have a justification defense rather than a duress defense; whereas the latter might be available if his tormentors threatened to kill him unless he escaped. See *People of Illinois v. Unger* (1977), discussed in Kadish and Schulhofer, pp. 903 ff.   [58] "Two Conceptions of Emotion in Criminal Law", p. 336.

situations out of respect for their reasons. But it doesn't follow that coercive circumstances cannot also be destructive of self-control in a way that is properly registered by the criminal law.[59]

The impression that duress is at once justification and excuse-like thus reflects these different overlapping conceptions. Clearly, the view of addictions that is most relevant to our topic is the impairment conception. But it is worth dwelling on the relatively neglected prerogative defense because it exhibits a principle of legal authority of the first importance: that the criminal law can be legitimate only if it is justifiable to those who are subject to its demands. And it can meet this condition only if its subjects have reason to comply. The recognition of the space of agent-centered prerogatives, I suggest, is the law's acknowledgment of the limits of its own moral jurisdiction. To punish in circumstances of duress (so interpreted) would be to treat the defendant in a way that could not be justified to him as a practical agent; it would be to treat him on grounds that he could reasonably reject. It would be a violation of his autonomy.

I am not claiming that this principle is explicitly and unequivocally endorsed by criminal law. But inasmuch as something like this ideal is arguably an axiom of modern liberal culture, it would be surprising if it failed to find significant (if guarded) expression, in one form or another, in Western European legal thought and practice.[60]

This ideal figures, I think, in the importance we attach to the criminal law as a distinct form of social regulation. We do not think of this system merely as the most effective way of regulating behavior.

[59] Their thesis reflects Kahan's and Nussbaum's larger argument on behalf of an "evaluative" rather than a "mechanistic" conception of emotions in understanding criminal law. The argument seems to me to rest on an overly simple contrast: emotions are either evaluations, and hence reasonable or unreasonable, or they are brute, nonrational forces that impede moral agency. In fact, emotions are both evaluative states and states that potentially interfere with rational control in various ways. It is therefore not surprising that coercive predicaments give rise to defenses expressing both of these truths.

[60] One could find expressions of this ideal in other parts of the law—for example, in making room for "conscientious objection". This ideal manifests itself, I suspect, only in relatively stable social contexts where concerns for justice as distinct from social control come to the fore.

As T. M. Scanlon puts it: "The law is not simply an organized system of threats. It also provides rules and standards which good citizens are supposed to 'respect', that is, to employ as a way of deciding what to do—not simply as a way of avoiding sanctions but as a set of norms which they accept as reason-giving."[61]

This conception bears upon the capacities that are presumed by the criminal law. To adapt a point that R. Jay Wallace makes about moral blame, since the criminal law is not purely strategic, legal obligations and corresponding sanctions are "fully intelligible only to people who are themselves capable of grasping the reasons that support those obligations."[62] So the non-strategic function of criminal law presumes that those subject to the law be capable of *appreciating* the validity of the norms to which they are being held accountable. This stronger requirement of normative competence is reflected in less conservative interpretations of the cognitive requirements of the M'Naughton rule.[63]

VII. Duress as Impairment

Let us focus on the idea of duress as impairment. The general standard by which incapacity is measured is what we can demand of

---

[61] *What We Owe to Each Other* (Cambridge: Harvard University Press, 1998), p. 266.

[62] *Responsibility and the Moral Sentiments* (Cambridge: Harvard University Press, 1994).

[63] For discussions of the notion of normative competence in general, see Wallace, *Responsibility and the Moral Sentiments*, as well as Paul Benson, "Freedom and Value", *Journal of Philosophy* 84(9) (1987). Normative competence, according to Benson, is "an ability to criticize courses of action competently by relevant normative standards" (p. 469). Susan Wolf uses this phrase to describe the kind of "sanity" that she takes to be presumed by our moral practices: "the minimally sufficient ability cognitively and normatively to recognize and appreciate the world for what it is." ("Sanity and the Metaphysics of Responsibility", in Ferdinand Schoeman (ed.), *Responsibility, Character, and the Emotions* (Cambridge and New York: Cambridge University Press, 1987), p. 56.)

the decent citizen of "reasonable firmness". The idea, as I've said, is that the kind of weakness manifested by conduct under duress is not weakness with respect to the law-abiding virtues, but weakness to which even the "resolute and well-disposed" are liable.[64] People who act illegally in coercive predicaments might well have satisfied all reasonable standards of self-control. To punish them would therefore be unfair.

However, in most jurisdictions, this excuse is sharply circumscribed in a number of ways. The restrictions that concern me are these: 1) The coercive predicament must be created by human design. That is, one's illegal conduct must be required by another's threat of grave harm to oneself or one's loved ones. 2) The defense is not valid in cases of murder. Section 2.09 of the MPC (1985) drops the second restriction but not the first:

It is an affirmative defense that the actor engaged in the conduct . . . because he was coerced to do so by the use of, or a threat to use, unlawful force against his person or the person of another, which a person of reasonable firmness in his situation would have been unable to resist.

Does it make sense to restrict the defense of duress to non-homicide crimes? Suppose we think that persons of ordinary fortitude will have steeled themselves against killing another under duress, that for a decent person such conduct will have become unthinkable. Then we will think, with Aristotle, that "there are some things we cannot be compelled to do, and rather than do them we should suffer the most terrible consequences and accept death."[65] The exclusion of a duress defense to homicide might reflect such a judgment in our community.[66] On the other hand (or also), it might reflect

---

[64] For this phrase, see the British case, *Lynch v. Director of Public Prosecutions*, quoted in Leo Katz, *Bad Acts and Guilty Minds* (Chicago and London: University of Chicago Press, 1987), p. 64.   [65] *Nicomachean Ethics*, 1110a27.

[66] Wertheimer points out that the exclusion would also make sense on the justification-interpretation of duress; it might reflect the judgment that nothing could justify taking the life of a non-aggressor. See *Coercion*, p. 155. This shows again how normative judgment is involved on both interpretations of the duress defense.

policy considerations of the kind that worried the British court in *Abbot v. the Queen*: a duress defense in murder cases looks like "a charter to terrorists, gangleaders and kidnappers. . . . Is there no limit to the number of people you may kill to save your life and that of your family?"[67]

When the coercive circumstances are created by design, the goal of discouraging the coercers might be thought to override the exculpatory force of the agent's plight. Note, however, that this rationale has no relevance in the case of duress by natural causes. The restriction of the defense to human coercion seems to me very difficult to justify on grounds either of deterrence or justice.[68]

VIII. Addiction as Duress

Assume, then, that what matters primarily in duress is that the defendant is subject to coercive circumstances sufficient to compromise her capacity for self-control. It shouldn't matter whether these circumstances result from human design or natural forces. Let's now ask whether it should matter whether the coercive circumstance is created by a peculiarity of the agent's psychology. Such conditions include not only addictions, but phobias and similar volitional impairments. Suppose someone threatens to lock another in a dark, rat-infested cellar unless he commits a certain crime, for example. Inasmuch as this prospect is as frightful to certain phobics as a life-threatening injury is to the rest of us, it seems that such individuals should be equally entitled to exculpation. Isn't it as plausible to think of the intensely felt compulsive needs of (some) addictions as capable

---

[67] Quoted in Katz, *Bad Acts and Guilty Minds*, p. 68.

[68] Here I agree with Dressler; Dressler rejects the blanket exclusion of defenses to murder as well—"Exegesis of the Law of Duress", p. 1071. Wertheimer, *Coercion*, also questions the rationale for the exclusion of homicide (pp. 155–6).

of creating coercive circumstances which an individual could not reasonably be expected to resist?[69]

The biggest obstacle to this defense is once again the issue of individual responsibility. A defense of duress presumes that the defendant is not responsible for his coercive predicament.[70] This issue distinguishes the case of addiction from phobias and other volitional deficiencies in that category; for addicts almost always play a role in their own impairment, whereas, I suppose, this is seldom true of these other afflictions.

To sharpen the issue, let's assume that a particular lawbreaker is indeed innocent in the initial process of getting hooked. Perhaps an abusive parent forces her to use heroin to the point of severe substance dependence. Suppose she has no legal access to money in the near future, and her intense cravings for heroin lead her to steal enough money to buy the drug. These admittedly artificial assumptions are at least imaginable. Would she now have a plausible duress defense to the charge of theft? It would be at least as plausible as a defense based on the claim that one was suffering from extreme deprivation of food or water, or under credible threat of serious harm by another.

[69] I know of no official attempt to offer an addiction-based defense of duress. But the defendant in *Moore* (cited above) claimed his addictive condition to be "on the same footing" as "a person forced under threat of death to inject heroin" (quoted in Kadish and Schulhofer, p. 1072).

Michael Moore seems to place addiction in the same category as other coercive circumstances, broadly conceived: "External threats, external but natural necessity, internal emotional turmoil, or passionate cravings [such as those of addiction] are different from one another, yet all make a choice difficult. Each at least mitigates the actor's responsibility because of the difficulty of refraining from doing what he ought not to do." *Law and Psychiatry* (Cambridge and New York: Cambridge University Press, 1984), p. 87.

[70] The MPC (1985) makes this explicit in the second clause of its codification of the defense: "The defense . . . is unavailable if the actor recklessly placed himself in a situation in which it was probable that he would be subject to duress. The defense is also unavailable if he was negligent in placing himself in such a situation, whenever negligence suffices to establish culpability for the offense charged."

Duress pleas require the defendant to show that she had no feasible alternative to breaking the law. In interpersonal coercion, for example, a defendant would have to show that he could not have avoided the threat by going to the police. (See *State of New Jersey v. Toscano* (1977), for opinions on this issue.) Here the addicted defendant would have to show that no alternative way of dealing with her addiction existed, or at least that she could not reasonably have been expected to have considered the alternatives under the circumstances.

This requirement suggests an important difference between addiction-based defenses and the legal paradigms of duress. To be addicted (on our assumptions) is to be disposed, perhaps episodically, to volitional impairment under certain circumstances, whereas in the standard case, the duress is a one-shot deal. And this difference complicates issues about responsibility even further. For the question is not just about the individual's responsibility for becoming addicted initially, that is, for becoming prone to coercive pressures; but about her responsibility for encountering these circumstances of duress in the future. The addict, on our assumptions, is like one who lives in a social/political environment in which one might expect to encounter coercive threats on a regular basis.[71] (Perhaps one should not have been hanging out in that neighborhood, or with that abusive character.) The question is to what extent one can reasonably be expected to change one's overall, long-term surroundings in the relevant ways. It is commonly supposed that the addict can with help do this. I am not sure what to say on this point; as far as I know, inexpensive and effective drug treatment programs are not available on every corner.

Now it might be thought that the fact that addiction is a standing disposition to episodes of diminished self-control creates problems for the application of the "reasonable firmness" standard. Does it make sense to ask whether the temperate and resolute citizen would have resisted an addictive craving for drugs of that intensity? Our

---

[71] But notice that this simile assumes a social climate in which the drug in question is liable to be in short supply. This factor is obviously affected by social policy.

assumption that our defendant is innocent in acquiring her affliction blocks the reply that a responsible man or woman would not have become addicted in the first place. Nevertheless, someone might argue that to be disposed to episodes of diminished self-control is incompatible with temperance and resolution; the well-disposed citizen is *ipso facto* not subject to such breakdowns.

However, this claim is very doubtful. A lot depends on what is meant by 'such breakdowns'. Addictions do not necessarily erode moral character in some general way.[72] And the likelihood that they will dispose one to loss of control is a contingent matter; whether and how often the addict's special vulnerability is indeed realized depends largely on social norms and her economic circumstances.[73] I'm told that it is possible for a well supplied and well regulated heroin addict to live an otherwise healthy and productive life. (Cocaine and amphetamines are another matter.)

In any case, imagine that this is so for a certain severely addictive substance, S, and that in a certain culture, otherwise similar to ours, the use of S is not only tolerated but respected as highly spiritually beneficial. This culture regards the dependency on this substance, which again entails a vulnerability to various kinds of diminished self-control in circumstances of deprivation, as a small price to pay for the enrichment of human life provided by S. Fortunately, S is readily obtainable, perhaps even socially subsidized by the society for religious reasons.

This fantasy makes it clear that the moral and legal significance of an individual's volitional weaknesses depends not only on judgments about individual responsibility and the limits of human endurance but on judgments about the meaning and value of those vulnerabilities. In our imagined society, both the use of and

---

[72] If George Ainslie is right, however, *some* addictive substances have the property of rendering individuals self-absorbed in a disturbing way. See "A Research-Based Theory of Addictive Motivation" [*Law and Philosophy*, 19/1 (1998), pp. 77–115]. Can't something similar be said of certain meditative/religious practices?

[73] The remarks in the next few paragraphs are adapted from my "Disordered Appetites" [Ch. 3, this volume].

dependency on S are regarded as entirely fitting and normal, on a par with the appetites for food and drink. Someone who acquires the addiction to S has not thereby run afoul of any social or legal obligation to maintain self-control. The threat of being deprived of one's S is here on a par with the coercive predicament created by the prospect of imminent starvation. This threat would provide as credible an excuse for certain kinds of legal wrongdoing as the fear of starvation could for us. Liability to such breakdowns would not be inconsistent with the standard of 'reasonable firmness'.

It will be noted that our legal tradition has not looked kindly upon pleas of starvation either. This might be due to a general prejudice against the poor; their plight is taken to be their own fault, either because they are responsible for their impoverishment or because there are thought to be legally available forms of relief. It has also been argued that recognizing this plea places the system of private property in jeopardy. Clearly the empirical plausibility of these points, as well as the social norms some of them invoke, are contestable. In any case it is surely possible that responsible citizens (by whatever standards) find themselves in dire straits with respect to the satisfaction of their natural appetites.[74] Many such cases would be grounds for justification; in other cases we might reasonably conclude that their capacities to conform to legal requirements have been impaired in a legally relevant way.

The reluctance to recognize an addiction-based excuse stems as much from norms about the value of addictive dependencies as from judgments about responsibility. We tend to see them as demeaning

---

[74] In a suggestive article, Gold, Johnson, and Stennie argue that the reward system activated by addictive drugs is the same system that responds to the "primitive species reinforcers" food, thirst, and sex. What happens is that these drugs come to "acquire the organismic significance attributed to food. They become an acquired primary drive equated with survival." See "Eating Disorders", in *Substance Abuse*, Third Edition, p. 320. As they put it, in addiction, "the fundamental processes of reward of primitive species survival drives" are "usurp[ed] . . . by exogenous agents" (p. 319). This conjecture accounts for the sense of urgency and alarm that is common to the experience of addictions and natural appetites.

rather than as conditions for meaningful human activity. We see them as impairments. For this reason, even if we don't favor criminalization, we expect people to avoid those conditions, and we see their plights as their own fault.

No substance in our culture has the role of S exactly, but there are instructive examples of parallel acquired dependencies which we encourage and honor. I have in mind the various relationship-attachments exemplified by having children, or being in love. Like addictions, to be attached in these ways is to be vulnerable to coercive predicaments that are sometimes the basis for paradigmatic pleas of duress (one was forced to falsify the document to protect one's child or lover from harm). We generally play some role in the acquisition of these attachments. But since there is no expectation that one is to avoid these relationships and their inherent liabilities, the issue of individual responsibility is of little or no importance here.

The judgment that one *impairs* oneself in cultivating some dependencies turns not only on the judgment that one has diminished one's autonomy in the abstract sense but on a conception of normal activity. Hence, if we deny the possibility of a plea on the grounds of addiction, it is not just because addicts have contributed to their own diminished self-control.

I am not arguing that addictions of any kind should be valued in the way we value the dependencies I just mentioned. Perhaps we are right as a culture to disrespect addiction. That deserves a separate discussion. My point is that the issue of excusing addiction turns as much on our sense of choiceworthy forms of human life as on questions of individual responsibility and the limits of human nature.

IX. Conclusion

I have done what I can to make a case for the moral and legal force of the duressful circumstances of some addicts. The law's resistance to addiction-based defenses runs counter to substantial evidence that addictive behavior can be less than fully responsible in legally pertinent ways. Nonetheless, the moral and practical reasons for resisting this defense are in the end probably decisive. Of course, this sort of conflict is not unusual; indeed it is inevitable. In order to do its job, the criminal law is severely limited in its capacity to respond to the merits of individual cases. We need legal institutions to be more or less heavy-handed.

But in this case, the heavy-handedness can be somewhat ameliorated by the compromise proposed in Stephen Morse's essay, "Hooked on Hype":[75] the introduction of a verdict of "guilty but partially responsible". This verdict would hold the defendant legally responsible but provide a systematic way to allow or require appropriate mitigation in sentencing. The details and implications of this proposal need to be developed. If it worked, it would allow us to record the defendant's complicity in her own plight and, at the same time, to do at least some justice to the special difficulties under which she labors.

[75] *Law and Philosophy*, 19/1 (2000). Once again, I do not follow Morse in construing the addict's "partial responsibility" as due to an impairment in rationality rather than in control.

Bibliography

Abélard, Peter (c.1139/1995), *Ethics*, in *Ethical Writings* (Indianapolis: Hackett), 1–58.

Adams, Robert (1985), 'Involuntary Sin', *Philosophical Review*, 94: 3–31.

Ainslie, George (1998), 'A Research-Based Theory of Addictive Motivation', *Law and Philosophy*, 19/1: 77–115.

Albritton, R.(1985), 'Freedom of Will and Freedom of Action', *Proceedings and Addresses of the American Philosophical Association*, 59: 239–51; repr. in Watson (2003), 408–23.

Allison, Henry (1990), *Kant's Theory of Freedom* (New York: Cambridge University Press).

Anscombe, G. E. M. (1963), *Intention*, 2nd edn. (Ithaca, NY: Cornell University Press).

—— (1981*a*), 'Causality and Determinism', in Anscombe (1981*b*), 133–47.

—— (1981*b*), *Metaphysics and the Philosophy of Mind: Collected Philosophical Papers*, vol. iii (Minneapolis: University of Minnesota Press).

—— (1981*c*), 'Soft Determinism', in Anscombe (1982*b*), 163–72.

Aristotle (1985), *Nicomachean Ethics*, trans. Terence Irwin (Indianapolis: Hackett).

—— (1954), *Nicomachean Ethics*, trans. David Ross, The World's Classics (London: Oxford University Press).

Aune, B. (1982), 'Hypotheticals and "Can" ', in Watson (1982), 36–41.

Austen, Jane (1932–54), *The Oxford Illustrated Jane Austen*, 3rd edn., ed. R. W. Chapman (Oxford: Oxford University Press).

Ayer, A. J. (1982), 'Freedom and Necessity', in Watson (1982), 15–23.

Beardsley, Elizabeth (1960), 'Determinism and Moral Perspectives', *Philosophy and Phenomenological Research*, 17: 1–20.

Bennett, Jonathan (1980), 'Accountability', in Zak van Straaten (ed.), *Philosophical Subjects* (Oxford: Clarendon Press), 14–47.

Benson, Paul (1987), 'Freedom and Value', *Journal of Philosophy*, 84: 465–86.

Berlin, Isaiah (1969), *Four Essays on Liberty* (New York: Oxford University Press).

Blackstone, William (1770), *Commentaries on the Laws of England (1765–7)* (Oxford: Clarendon Press).

Blum, Kenneth, *et al.* (1996), 'Reward Deficiency Syndrome', *American Scientist*, 84: 132–45.

Bok, Hilary (1999), *Freedom and Responsibility* (Princeton: Princeton University Press).

BonJour, L. (1976), 'Determinism, Libertarianism, and Agent Causation', *Southern Journal of Philosophy*, 14: 145–56.

Boorse, Christopher (1987), 'Premenstrual Syndrome and Criminal Responsibility', in *Premenstrual Syndrome: Ethical and Legal Implications in a Biomedical Perspective* (New York: Plenum Press), 81–124.

Bramhall, Bishop (1962), 'Questions Concerning Liberty, Necessity and Chance', repr. in Morgenbesser and Walsh (1962), 41–51.

Brand, M. and D. Walton (1976) (eds.), *Action Theory* (Dordrecht: Reidel).

Brandt, Richard (1958), 'Blameworthiness and Obligation', in A. I. Melden (ed.), *Essays in Moral Philosophy* (Seattle: University of Washington Press), 3–39.

Bratman, M. (1985), 'Davidson's Theory of Intention', in B. Vermazen and M. Hintikka (eds.), *Essays on Davidson: Actions and Events* (Oxford: Oxford University Press), 13–26.

—— (1986), 'Intention and Evaluation', in P. French *et al.* (eds.), *Midwest Studies in Philosophy*, vol. x (Minneapolis: University of Minnesota Press), 185–9.

—— (1987), *Intentions, Plans, and Practical Reason* (Cambridge, Mass.: Harvard University Press).

—— (1992), 'Practical Reasoning and Acceptance in a Context', repr. in Bratman (1999), 15–34.

—— (1996), 'Identification, Decision, and Treating as a Reason', *Philosophical Topics*, 24: 1–18; repr. in Bratman (1999), 185–206.

—— (1999), *Faces of Intention* (Cambridge: Cambridge University Press).

Broad, C. D. (1962), 'Determinism, Indeterminism, and Libertatianism', in Morgenbesser and Walsh (1962), 115–32.

Buss, Sarah (1999), 'What Practical Reasoning Must Be if We Act for our own Reasons', *Australasian Journal of Philosophy*, 77: 399–421.

—— and Overton, Lee (2002) (eds.), *Contours of Agency: Essays on Themes from Harry Frankfurt* (Cambridge, Mass.: MIT Press).

Calhoun, Cheshire (1995), 'Standing for Something', *Journal of Philosophy*, 92: 235–60.

Chisholm, R. (1964), 'Human Freedom and the Self', repr. in Watson (2003), 26–37.

—— (1976) 'The Agent as Cause', in Brand and Walton (1976), 199–212.

Cleckley, Hervey (1941), *The Mask of Sanity* (St Louis: C. V. Mosby).

Clifford, William Kingdon (1866), 'The Ethics of Belief', repr. in L. Stephen and F. Pollock (eds.), *Lectures and Essays by William Kingdon Clifford*, 2 vols. (London: Macmillan, 1879), ii. 177–211.

Code, Lorraine (1987), *Epistemic Responsibility* (Hanover, NH: University Press of New England).

Cohen, L. Jonathan (1989), 'Belief and Acceptance', *Mind*, 98: 367–89.

Corwin, Miles (1982), 'Icy Killer's Life Steeped in Violence', *Los Angeles Times*, 16 May.

Crucius, Christian (1990), *Guide to Rational Living*, in J. B. Schneewind (ed.), *Moral Philosophy from Montaigne to Kant*, vol. ii (Cambridge: Cambridge University Press), 569–85.

Cullity, Garrett, and Gaut, Berys (1997) (eds.), *Ethics and Practical Reason* (Oxford: Clarendon Press).

Dan-Cohen, Meir (1983), 'Actus Reus', in Sanford Kadish (ed.), *Encyclopedia of Crime and Justice* (New York: Free Press), 15–22.

Davidson, D. (1963), 'Actions, Reasons, and Causes', repr. in Davidson (1980), 3–19.

—— (1970), 'How is Weakness of the Will Possible?', repr. in Davidson (1980), 21–42.

—— (1973), 'Freedom to Act', repr. in Davidson (1980), 63–81.

—— (1978), 'Intending', repr. in Davidson (1980), 83–102.

—— (1980), *Essays on Actions and Events* (New York: Oxford University Press).

Delgado, Richard (1985), ' "Rotten Social Background": Should the Criminal Law Recognize a Defense of Severe Environmental Deprivation?', *Law and Equality*, 9.

Dennett, D. (1984), *Elbow Room* (Cambridge, Mass.: MIT Press).

Descartes, René (1641*a*/1967), 'Arguments Demonstrating the Existence of God and the Distinction between Soul and Body, drawn up in Geometrical Fashion', in *The Philosophical Works of Descartes*, trans. Elizabeth S. Haldane and G. R. T. Ross, 2 vols. (London: Cambridge University Press), ii. 52–9.

—— (1641*b*/1984), 'Author's Replies to the Sixth Set of Objections', in Descartes (1984), ii. 285–301.

—— (1641*c*/1984), *Meditations on First Philosophy*, in Descartes (1984), ii. 1–62.

—— (1649/1984), *The Passions of the Soul*, in Descartes (1984), i. 325–404.

—— (1984), *The Philosophical Writings of Descartes*, trans. John Cottingham, Robert Stoothoff, and Dugald Murdoch, 3 vols. (Cambridge: Cambridge University Press).

Dewey, John (1891/1957), *Outlines of a Critical Theory of Ethics* (New York: Hillary House).

Double, Richard (1991), *The Non-Reality of Free Will* (Oxford: Oxford University Press).

Dressler, Joshua (1989), 'Exegesis and the Law of Duress: Justifying the Excuse and Searching for its Proper Limits', *Southern California Law Review*, 62/5: 331–89.

Duff, Antony (1977), 'Psychopathy and Moral Understanding', *American Philosophical Quarterly*, 14: 189–200.

Dworkin, G. (1970), 'Acting Freely', *Nous*, 4: 367–83.

—— (1976) 'Autonomy and Behavior Control', *Hastings Center Report*, 6: 23–8.

Einstein, Albert (1982), *Ideas and Opinions* (New York: Crown Publishers).

Elster, Jon (1999*a*), 'Rationality and Addiction', unpublished typescript.

—— (1999*b*), *Ulysses Unbound* (Cambridge: Cambridge University Press).

Feinberg, Joel (1970), 'What is so Special about Mental Illness?', in *Doing and Deserving* (Princeton: Princeton University Press), 272–92.

Fine, G. (1981), 'Aristotle's Determinism', *Philosophical Review*, 90: 561–79.

Fingarette, Herbert (1967), *On Responsibility* (New York: Basic Books).

—— (1970), 'The Perils of *Powell*: In Search of a Factual Foundation for the "Disease Concept of Alcoholism" ', *Harvard Law Review*, 83: 793–812.

—— (1988), *Heavy Drinking: The Myth of Alcoholism as a Disease* (Berkeley: University of California Press).

Fischer, John Martin (1982), 'Responsibility and Control', *Journal of Philosophy*, 89: 24–40.

—— (1983), 'Incompatibilism', *Philosophical Studies*, 43: 127–37.

—— (1986), 'Van Inwagen on Free Will', *Philosophical Quarterly*, 36: 252–60.

—— (1987), 'Responsiveness and Moral Responsibility', in F. Schoeman (ed.), *Responsibility, Character, and the Emotions* (Cambridge: Cambridge University Press), 81–106.

—— (1994), *The Metaphysics of Free Will* (Cambridge, Mass.: Blackwell).

—— and Ravizza, Mark (1991), 'Responsibility and Inevitability', *Ethics*, 101: 258–78.

—— —— (1995), 'When the Will is Free', in Timothy O'Connor (ed.), *Agents, Causes, and Events* (New York: Oxford University Press), 239–69.

—— —— (1997), *Responsibility and Control* (New York: Cambridge University Press).

—— —— (1998), *Responsibility and Control: A Theory of Moral Responsibility* (Cambridge: Cambridge University Press).

Foley, R. (1979), 'Compatibilism and Control over the Past', *Analysis*, 39: 70–4.

Foot, Philippa (1978), *Virtues and Vices and Other Essays in Moral Philosophy* (Berkeley: University of California Press).

Frankfurt, H. (1969), 'Alternate Possibilities and Moral Responsibility', *Journal of Philosophy*, 89; repr. in Frankfurt (1988), 1–10.

—— (1971), 'Freedom of the Will and the Concept of a Person', *Journal of Philosophy*, 68/1; repr. in Frankfurt (1988), 11–25.

—— (1973), 'Coercion and Moral Responsibility', repr. in Frankfurt (1988), 24–46.

—— (1975), 'Three Concepts of Free Action', *Proceedings of the Aristotelian Society*, suppl. vol.; repr. in Frankfurt (1988), 47–57.

Frankfurt, H. (1976), 'Identification and Externality', repr. in Frankfurt (1988), 58–68.

—— (1978), 'The Problem of Action', *American Philosophical Quarterly*, 15; repr. in Frankfurt (1988), 69–79.

—— (1987), 'Identification and Wholeheartedness', repr. in Frankfurt (1988), 159–76.

—— (1988), *The Importance of What We Care About: Philosophical Essays* (Cambridge and New York: Cambridge University Press).

—— (1992), 'The Faintest Passion', *Proceedings and Addresses of the American Philosophical Association*, 66: 5–16; repr. in *Necessity, Volition, and Love* (New York: Cambridge University Press), 95–107.

—— (1999a), 'Autonomy, Necessity, and Love', in *Necessity, Volition, and Love* (New York: Cambridge University Press), 129–41.

—— (1999b), 'On Caring', in *Necessity, Volition, and Love* (New York: Cambridge University Press), 155–80.

—— (1999c), 'On the Necessity of Ideals', in *Necessity, Volition, and Love* (New York: Cambridge University Press), 108–16.

Gardner, Eliot L. (1997), 'Brain Reward Mechanisms', in Lowinson *et al.* (1997b), 51–85.

—— and Lowinson, Joyce H. (1993), 'Drug Craving and Positive/Negative Hedonic Brain Substrates Activated by Addicting Drugs', *The Neurosciences*, 5: 359–68.

Gert, B., and Duggan, T. (1979), 'Free Will as Ability to Will', *Nous*, 13: 197–217.

Ginet, C. (1966), 'Might We Have No Choice?', in Lehrer (1966), 87–104.

—— (1980), 'The Conditional Analysis of Freedom', in van Inwagen (1980), 171–86.

—— (1983), 'A Defense of Incompatibilism', *Philosophical Studies*, 44: 391–400.

Glover, J. (1970), *Responsibility* (London: Routledge and Kegan Paul).

Gold, Mark S., and Miller, Norman S. (1997), 'Cocaine (and Crack): Neurobiology', in Lowinson *et al.* (1997b), 167–80.

—— and Goodman, Ariel (1997), 'Sexual Addiction', in Lowinson *et al.* (1997b), 340–54.

—— Johnson, C., and Stennie, K. (1997), 'Eating Disorders', in Lowinson *et al.* (1997b), 319–30.

Goldman, A. (1970), *A Theory of Human Action* (Englewood Cliffs, NJ: Prentice-Hall).

—— (1978), 'Chisholm's Theory of Action', *Philosophia*, 8: 583–96.

Greenspan, P. S. (1978), 'Behavior Control and Freedom of Action', *Philosophical Review*, 87: 225–40; repr. in J. Fischer (ed.), *Moral Responsibility* (Ithaca, NY: Cornell University Press), 191–204.

Grinspoon, Lester, and Bakular, James (1976), *Cocaine: A Drug and its Social Evolution* (New York: Basic Books).

Haksar, Vinit (1965), 'The Responsibility of Psychopaths', *Philosophical Quarterly*, 15: 135–45.

Halikas, James, *et al.* (1997), 'Craving', in Lowinson *et al.* (1997*b*), 85–90.

—— (1991), 'The Measurement of Craving in Cocaine Patients using the Minnesota Cocaine Craving Scale', *Comprehensive Psychiatry*, 32/1: 22–7.

Hamill, Pete (1994), *A Drinking Life* (Boston: Little, Brown).

Hamilton, Edith, and Cairns, Huntington (1989) (eds.), *Plato: The Collected Dialogues* (Princeton: Princeton University Press).

Hampshire, S. (1959), *Thought and Action* (New York: Viking Press).

—— (1965), *Freedom of the Individual* (New York: Harper and Row).

—— (1983*a*), *Morality and Conflict* (Cambridge, Mass.: Harvard University Press).

—— (1983*b*), 'Two Kinds of Explanation', in Hampshire (1983*a*), 69–81.

—— (1983*c*), 'Two Kinds of Morality', in Hampshire (1983*a*), 10–68.

Harman, Gilbert (1978), 'Morality and Politics', in P. A. French, T. E. Uehling, and H. K. Wettstein (eds.), *Midwest Studies in Philosophy*, vol. iii (Minneapolis: University of Minnesota Press), 109–21.

Hart, H. L. A. (1968), *Punishment and Responsibility* (Oxford: Oxford University Press).

Heil, John (1983), 'Doxastic Agency', *Philosophical Studies*, 43: 355–64.

Herman, Barbara (2002), 'Bootstrapping', in Buss and Overton (2002), 253–74.

Hobart, R. E. (1966), 'Free Will as Involving Determinism and Inconceivable without it', in Bernard Berofsky (ed.), *Free Will and Determinism* (New York: Harper and Row), 63–95.

Hobbes, T. (1648/1969), 'Of Liberty and Necessity', in D. D. Raphael (ed.), *British Moralists, 1650–1800*, vol. i (Oxford: Oxford University Press), 61–70.

Hoffman, Paul (1995), 'Freedom and Strength of Will: Descartes and Albritton', *Philosophical Studies*, 77: 241–60.

Holstrom, N. (1977), 'Firming Up Soft Determinism', *The Personalist*.

Holton, Richard (1999), 'Intention and Weakness of Will', *Journal of Philosophy*, 96: 241–62.

—— (2003), 'How is strength of Will Possible?', in Strand and Taggolet (eds.), *Weakness of Will and Practical Irrationality* (Oxford: Oxford University Press, 2003).

Honderich, T. (1973) (ed.), *Essays on Freedom of Action* (London: Routledge and Kegan Paul).

Hornsby, J. (1980), *Actions* (London: Routledge and Kegan Paul).

Hurley, Susan (1989), *Natural Reasons* (New York: Oxford University Press).

Irwin, Terence H. (1992), 'Who Discovered the Will?', *Philosophical Perspectives*, 6: 453–73.

James, William (1896), 'The Will to Believe', repr. in F. H. Burkhardt, F. Bowers, and I. K. Skrupskelis (eds.), *The Will to Believe and Other Essays in Popular Philosophy* (Cambridge, Mass.: Harvard University Press, 1979), 13–33.

—— (1950), *The Principles of Psychology*, 2 vols. (New York: Dover).

Jeffrey, Richard C. (1974), 'Preferences among Preferences', *Journal of Philosophy*, 71/13: 377–91.

Kadish, Sanford H. (1987), 'Excusing Crime', in *California Law Review*, 75: 257–89.

—— and Schulhofer, Stephen J. (1989), *Criminal Law and its Processes*, 5th edn. (Boston: Little, Brown).

Kahan, Dan, and Nussbaum, Martha (1996), 'Two Conceptions of Emotion in Criminal Law', *Columbia Law Review*, 96/2: 269–374.

Kahn, Charles (1985), 'Discovering the Will: From Aristotle to Augustine', in J. M. Dillon and A. A. Long (eds.), *The Question of 'Eclecticism'* (Berkeley: University of California Press), 234–59.

Kane, Robert (1985), *Free Will and Values* (Albany, NY: State University of New York Press).

—— (1996), *The Significance of Free Will* (New York: Oxford University Press).

Kant, I. (1788/1956), *Critique of Practical Reason*, trans. Lewis White Beck (Indianapolis: Liberal Arts Press).

—— (1797/1991), *The Metaphysics of Morals*, trans. Mary Gregor (New York: Cambridge University Press).

Katz, Leo (1987), *Bad Acts and Guilty Minds* (Chicago and London: University of Chicago Press).

Kenny, A. (1976), *Freedom, Will and Power* (Oxford: Blackwell).

Kolnai, A. (1966–7), 'Freedom and Choice', in *The Human Self*, Royal Institute of Philosophy Lectures, I.

Korsgaard, Christine (1996*b*), *The Sources of Normativity* (Cambridge: Cambridge University Press).

—— (1997), 'The Normativity of Instrumental Reason', in Cullity and Gaut (1997), 215–54.

Kreek, Jeanne, and Reisinger, Marc (1997), 'The Addict as Patient', in Lowinson *et al.* (1997*b*), 997–1011.

Kuehule, John, and Spitzer, Robert (1992), 'DSM III Classification of Substance Use Disorders', in Joyce H. Lowinson and Pedro Ruiz (eds.), *Substance Abuse: A Comprehensive Textbook* (Baltimore: Williams and Wilkins, 1992; 2nd edn. 1997), 22–3.

Lamb, J. (1977), 'On a Proof of Incompatibilism', *Philosophical Review*, 86: 20–35.

Lehrer, K. (1966*a*), 'An Empirical Disproof of Determinism?', in Lehrer (1966*b*), 175–202.

—— (1966*b*), (ed.), *Freedom and Determinism* (New York: Random House).

—— (1980), 'Preferences, Conditionals, and Freedom', in van Inwagen (1980), 76–96.

—— (1982), 'Cans without Ifs', in Watson (1982), 41–5.

Lewis, D. (1981), 'Are We Free to Break the Laws?', *Theoria*; repr. in Watson (2003), 122–9.

Locke, Don (1975), 'Three Concepts of Free Action I', *Proceedings of the Aristotelian Society*, suppl. vol. 49: 95–112; repr. in John Martin Fischer, *Moral Responsibility* (Ithaca, NY: Cornell University Press), 97–112.

Locke, J. (1690/1975), *An Essay Concerning Human Understanding*, ed. P. Nidditch (Oxford: Clarendon Press).

Loewenstein, George (1996), 'Out of Control: Visceral Influences on Behaviour', *Organizational Behavior and Human Decision Processes*, 65/3: 272–92.

—— (1999), 'The Visceral Account of Addiction', in Jon Elster and Ole-Jorgen Skog (eds.), *Getting Hooked: Rationality and the Addictions* (Cambridge: Cambridge University Press), 235–64.

Lowinson, Joyce H., Marion, I. J., Joseph, H., and Dole V. P. (1997a), 'Methadone Maintenance', in Lowinson *et al.* (1997b), 550–61.

—— , Ruiz, Pedro, Millman, Robert B., and Langrod, John G. (1997b), *Substance Abuse: A Comprehensive Textbook*, 2nd edn. (Baltimore: Williams and Wilkins).

MacIntyre, Alasdair (1981), *After Virtue* (Notre Dame, Ind.: University of Notre Dame Press).

Magill, Kevin (1997), *Freedom and Experience* (Basingstoke: Macmillan).

Marks, Isaac (1969), *Fears and Phobias* (New York: Academic Press).

—— (1987), *Fears, Phobias, and Rituals* (New York: Oxford University Press).

McCann, Hugh (1974), 'Volition and Basic Action', repr. in McCann (1998), 75–93.

—— (1986), 'Intrinsic Intentionality', repr. in McCann (1998), 127–46.

—— (1998), *The Works of Agency: On Human Action, Will, and Freedom* (Ithaca, NY: Cornell University Press).

Melden, A. I. (1961), *Free Action* (London: Routledge and Kegan Paul).

Mele, Alfred R. (1996), 'Soft Libertarianism and Frankfurt-Style Scenarios', *Philosophical Topics*, 24/2: 123–41.

—— (2000), 'Deciding to Act', *Philosophical Studies*, 100: 81–108.

Melville, Joy (1977), *Phobias and Obsessions* (London: George Allen & Unwin Ltd.).

Milo, Ronald (1984), *Immorality* (Princeton: Princeton University Press).

Montaigne, Michel de (1971), *Essays* (London: Penguin).

Moore, Michael (1984), *Law and Psychiatry* (Cambridge and New York: Cambridge University Press).

Moran, Richard (2000), *Authority and Estrangement* (Princeton: Princeton University Press).

Morgenbesser, S., and J. Walsh (1962) (eds.), *Free Will* (Englewood Cliffs, NJ: Prentice-Hall).

Morse, Stephen J. (1994), 'Culpability and Control', *University of Pennsylvania Law Review*, 142: 1587–1660.

—— (2000), 'Hooked on Hype', *Law and Philosophy*, 19/1: 33–49.

Murphy, Jeffrie (1972), 'Moral Death: A Kantian Essay on Psychopathy', *Ethics*, 82: 284–98.

Nagel, T. (1970), *The Possibility of Altruism* (Oxford: Clarendon Press).

—— (1986), *The View from Nowhere* (New York: Oxford University Press).

Nash, J. Madeleine (1997), 'Addicts', *Time*, 149/18 (May 5): 69–77.

Neely, W. (1974), 'Freedom and Desire', *Philosophical Review*, 83/1: 32–54.

Nietzsche, Friedrich (1955), *Beyond Good and Evil*, trans. Marianne Cowan (Chicago: Gateway Editions).

Normore, Calvin (1998), 'Picking and Choosing: Anselm and Ockham on Choice', *Vivarium*, 36: 23–39.

Nozick, Robert (1981), *Philosophical Explanations* (Cambridge, Mass.: Harvard University Press).

O'Shaughnessy, B. (1980), *The Will: A Dual Aspect Theory*, 2 vols. (Cambridge: Cambridge University Press).

Owens, David (2000), *Reason without Freedom* (London: Routledge).

Peele, Stanton (1985), *The Meaning of Addiction* (New York: Heath).

—— (1989), *The Diseasing of America* (Lexington, Mass.: Lexington Books).

Penner, Terry (1971), 'Thought and Desire in Plato', in Vlastos (1971), ii: 96–118.

Perry, R. B. (1950), *General Theory of Value* (Cambridge, Mass.: Harvard University Press).

Pettit, Philip, and Smith, Michael (1996), 'Freedom in Belief and Desire', *Journal of Philosophy*, 93: 429–49.

Pink, Thomas (1996), *The Psychology of Freedom* (Cambridge: Cambridge University Press).

Piper, A. (1985), 'Two Conceptions of the Self', *Philosophical Studies*.

Plato, *Phaedrus*, trans. R. Hackforth, in Hamilton and Cairns (1989), 475–525.

—— *The Republic*, trans. Paul Shorey, in Hamilton and Cairns (1989), 575–844.

Portenoy, Russell K., and Payne, Richard (1997), 'Acute and Chronic Pain', in Lowinson *et al.* (1997b), 563–89.

Pritchard, M. S. (1991), *On Becoming Responsible* (Lawrence, Kan.: University Press of Kansas).

Radden, Jennifer (1985), *Madness and Reason* (London: George Allen and Unwin).

Ravizza, Mark (1994), 'Semi-compatibilism and the Transfer of Non-responsibility', *Philosophical Studies*, 75: 61–93.

Raz, Joseph (1999), 'When we are Ourselves: The Active and the Passive', in *Engaging Reason: On the Theory of Value and Action* (New York: Oxford University Press), 5–21.

Reid, T. (1788/1969), *Essays on the Active Powers*, ed. Baruch Brody (Cambridge, Mass.: MIT Press).

Roberts, Robert (1984), 'Will-Power and the Virtues', *Philosophical Review*, 93: 227–47.

Robinson, Paul (1984), *Criminal Law Defenses*, vol. ii (St Paul, Minn.: West Publishing).

Santas, G. (1966), 'Plato's *Protagoras*, and Explanations of Weakness', *Philosophical Review*, 75: 3–33.

Scanlon, T. M. (1988), 'The Significance of Choice', Lecture 1 in *The Tanner Lectures on Human Values*, vol. viii (Salt Lake City: University of Utah Press); repr. in Watson (2003), 352–71.

—— (1998), *What We Owe to Each Other* (Cambridge, Mass.: Harvard University Press).

—— (2002), 'Reasons and Passions', in Buss and Overton (2002), 165–83.

Scheffler, Samuel (1982), *The Rejection of Consequentialism* (Oxford: Clarendon Press).

Schopp, Robert (1991), *Automatism, Insanity, and the Psychology of Criminal Responsibility* (Cambridge and New York: Cambridge University Press).

Seeburger, F. (1993), *Responsibility and Addiction* (New York: Crossroads).

Shatz, D. (1986), 'Free Will and the Structure of Motivation', in P. French *et al.* (eds.), *Midwest Studies in Philosophy*, vol. x (Minneapolis: University of Minnesota Press).

Slote, M. (1980), 'Understanding Free Will', *Journal of Philosophy*, 77: 136–51.

—— (1982), 'Selective Necessity and Free Will', *Journal of Philosophy*, 79: 5–24.

—— (1990), 'Ethics without Free Will', *Social Theory and Practice*, 16: 369–83.

Solomon, Andrew (1998), 'Anatomy of Melancholy', *New Yorker*, Jan. 12: 46–58.

Sorabji, R. (1983), *Necessity, Cause, and Blame* (Ithaca, NY: Cornell University Press).

Stern, Lawrence (1974), 'Freedom, Blame, and Moral Community', *Journal of Philosophy*, 71: 72–84.

Strawson, Galen (1986), *Freedom and Belief* (Oxford: Oxford University Press).

Strawson, Peter (1962), 'Freedom and Resentment', *Proceedings of the British Academy*; repr. in Watson (2003), 72–93.

Stroud, Sarah, and Tappolet, Christine (2003) (eds.), *Weakness of Will and Practical Irrationality* (Oxford: Oxford University Press).

Taylor, C. (1985), *Human Agency and Language*, vol. i (Cambridge: Cambridge University Press).

—— (1989), *Sources of the Self* (Cambridge, Mass.: Harvard University Press).

Taylor, R. (1960), *Action and Purpose* (Englewood Cliffs, NJ: Prentice-Hall).

Thalberg, I. (1976), 'How Does Agent Causation Work?', in Brand and Walton (1976), 213–38.

—— (1978), 'Hierarchical Analyses of Unfree Action', *Canadian Journal of Philosophy*, 8: 211–26.

van Inwagen, P. (1978*a*), 'Ability and Responsibility', *Philosophical Review*, 87: 201–24.

—— (1978*b*), 'A Definition of Chisholm's Notion of Immanent Causation', *Philosophia*, 8: 567–80.

—— (1980), (ed.), *Time and Cause* (Dordrecht: Reidel).

—— (1982), 'The Incompatibility of Free Will and Determinism', repr. in Watson (1982), 46–58.

—— (1983), *An Essay on Free Will* (Oxford: Oxford University Press).

—— (1995), 'When is the Will Free?', repr. in Timothy O'Connor (ed.), *Agents, Causes, and Events* (New York: Oxford University Press), 219–36.

Velleman, J. David (1992), 'The Guise of the Good', repr. in Velleman (2000), 99–122.

—— (1996), 'The Possibility of Practical Reason', repr. in Velleman (2000), 170–99.

—— (2000), *The Possibility of Practical Reason* (Oxford: Clarendon Press).

Vlastos, Gregory (1971) (ed.), *Plato: A Collection of Critical Essays*, vol. ii (Garden City, NJ: Anchor).

Vuoso, George (1987), 'Background, Responsibility, and Excuse', *Yale Law Journal*, 96: 1680–1.

Walker, Nigel (1968), *Crime and Insanity in England* (Edinburgh: Edinburgh University Press).

Wallace, James (1978), *Virtues and Vices* (Ithaca, NY: Cornell University Press).

Wallace, R. Jay (1994), *Responsibility and the Moral Sentiments* (Cambridge, Mass.: Harvard University Press).

—— (1999), 'Addiction as Defect of the Will: Some Philosophical Reflections', *Law and Philosophy*, 18: 621–54.

—— (2001), 'Normativity, Commitment, and Instrumental Reason', *Philosophers' Imprint*, <www.philosophersimprint.org>, 1/3.

Warnock, G. (1963), 'Actions and Events', in D. Pears (ed.), *Freedom and the Will* (London: Macmillan and Co.), 69–79.

Watson, G. (1982) (ed.), *Free Will* (Oxford: Oxford University Press).

—— (1995), 'Freedom and Strength of Will in Hoffman and Albritton', *Philosophical Studies*, 77: 261–71.

—— (1998), 'Some Worries about Semi-Compatibilism', *Journal of Social Philosophy*. 29: 135–43.

—— (2003) (ed.), *Free Will*, 2nd edn. (Oxford: Oxford University Press).

Waugh, Evelyn (1945/67), *Brideshead Revisited* (New York: Dell).

Wertheimer, Alan (1987), *Coercion* (Princeton: Princeton University Press).

Wiggins, D. (1973), 'Towards a Reasonable Libertarianism', emended version in Watson (2003), 94–121.

Williams, B. (1978), *Descartes: The Project of Pure Inquiry* (London: Penguin).

—— (1981), 'Internal and External Reasons', in *Moral Luck* (Cambridge: Cambridge University Press), 101–13.

—— (1985), 'How Free Does the Will Need to Be?', Lindley Lecture, The University of Kansas.

—— (1995), 'Moral Incapacity', in *Making Sense of Humanity* (Cambridge: Cambridge University Press), 46–55.

Wolf, Susan (1987), 'Sanity and the Metaphysics of Responsibility', in F. Schoeman (ed.), *Responsibility, Character, and the Emotions* (Cambridge: Cambridge University Press), 46–62.

—— (1990), *Freedom within Reason* (Oxford and New York: Oxford University Press).

Wright, Larry (1995), 'Argument and Deliberation: A Plea for Understanding', *Journal of Philosophy*, 92: 565–85.

Yaffe, Gideon (2000), *Liberty Worth the Name: Locke on Free Agency* (Princeton: Princeton University Press).

Young, Robert (1979), 'Compatibilism and Conditioning', *Nous*, 1979: 361–78.

—— (1980), 'Autonomy and the "Inner Self" ', *American Philosophical Quarterly*: 35–43.

Youpa, Andrew (2002), 'Descartes and Spinoza on Freedom and Virtue' (Ph.D. dissertation, University of California, Irvine).

Zagzebski, Linda (1996), *Virtues of the Mind* (New York: Cambridge University Press).

—— (2001), 'Must Knowers be Agents?', in A. Fairweather and L. Zagzebski (eds.), *Virtue Epistemology: Essays on Epistemic Value and Responsibility* (New York: Oxford University Press), 142–57.

Zimmerman, D. (1981), 'Hierarchical Motivation and Freedom of the Will', *Pacific Philosophical Quarterly*, 62: 354–68.

Zimmerman, M. (1984), *An Essay on Human Action* (New York: Peter Lang).

Index

Abélard, Peter 226 n. 8, 249–50
ability and inability to act 69–72,
    89–100
    see also volitional necessity;
    conditional analysis of 'can'
accountability:
    as face of responsibility 10,
        263–7, 270, 272–84, 288
Adams, Robert 227 n. 10,
    251 n. 21
addiction 3–4, 13, 42–3, 59–61,
    65–87, 89, 117 n. 60, 294–5,
    318–34, 336, 341, 344–50
    as acquired appetite 74–7, 79
    as attachment 83, 85
    and compulsion 59–61, 320,
        334–6
    as devotion 61, 82–4
    and duress 319, 336, 344–50
    and insanity 330–3
    as legal defense 318 n. 1, 319,
        321 n. 8, 322–33, 344–50
    and responsibility 60, 294–300,
        318–37
    skepticism about 60, 321
agency:
    counter-normative 131–2, 134,
        137, 139, 147, 151, 153
    and deciding what to belief
        139–53
    and decision-making 124–8

desire/belief model of 89–90
internalist and externalist
    views of 129–37, 152–7
    see also belief: and the will;
    free agency
agoraphobics 97–100, 295
Ainslie, George 80 n. 34,
    347 n. 72
akrasia 3, 18 n. 3, 31 n. 12, 36–8,
    131–2, 134, 137–8, 153, 155
    theoretical 148
    see also incontinence; weakness
    of will
Albritton, R. 65 n., 102 n. 22,
    130–1, 133 n. 25, 164 n.,
    186 n., 187–8
alcoholism 82, 322–3
Allison, Henry 157
alternate possibilities 161–3,
    165, 173–84, 190, 195, 204,
    300–1
    see also indeterminism
Anscombe, G. E. M. 54 n. 20,
    153, 179–80, 192
appetites 21–2, 31, 40, 72, 74–81,
    86–7
    acquired 74–7, 79, 81, 83–4
    see also desires
Aristotle 48–9, 55, 129–30, 132,
    153–4, 250, 286–7, 343
    on *prohairesis* 153–4

Aristotle (*cont.*):
  on temperance 48, 84 n. 40
  on voluntariness 146–7, 161 n.,
    273, 334
attributability:
  and responsibility 10, 263–7,
    270–2
  see also self-disclosure view of
    responsibility
Audi, Robert 47 n.
Aune, B. 183 n. 23
Austen, Jane 106
autonomy 157, 161, 163, 172,
    174, 192–3, 203, 206,
    260–1
  see also self-determination
Ayer, A. J. 170, 176

Bakular, James 60, 321 n. 8
Bayesian model of
    deliberation 16
Beardsley, Elizabeth 245 n.,
    266 n. 17
belief:
  and the emotions 40 n.
  and Moore's Paradox 131,
    133, 149
  about objects of appetites
    75 n. 25
  and the will 5, 124–5, 128 n. 14,
    139–53
Bennett, Jonathan 221 n.
Benson, Paul 2 n., 261 n. 4,
    342 n. 63
Berlin, Isaiah 14, 31
Blackstone, William 230 n.

blame 9–10, 235, 238–9, 253–4,
    265–9, 277–85
  and finding fault 226–7
  and negligence 52–3, 208
  and weakness of will 51–3, 55
  see also moral sanctions;
    reactive attitudes
Blum, Kenneth 329 n. 29
Bok, Hilary 92 n.
BonJour, L. 189 n.
Boorse, Christopher 330 n. 32
Bramhall, Bishop 173, 182, 186,
    187, 195
Brandt, Richard 266 n. 16
Bratman, M. 1 n., 113 n. 45,
    117 n. 59, 135, 136 n. 32,
    148 n. 59, 149 n. 63, 169 n. 9
Brave New World cases 170–3
Broad, C. D. 189 n.
Burgess, Anthony 73 n., 337 n.
Burroughs, William 82 n. 35
Buss, Sarah 130

Calhoun, Cheshire 271 n. 29
can *see* ability and inability
caring *see* identification
causation 7, 170, 193 n. 31
  agent-causation 163, 189,
    191–6, 201, 204
  event-causation 192
  see also determinism;
    indeterminism
Chisholm, R. 163 n. 4, 166 n. 5,
    182–3, 191–5
choice:
  and addiction 321–2

as distinct from decision
  123 n. 2, 148 n. 61
and the will 55, 123–4, 153–4
Cleckley, Hervey 231 n.
Clifford, William Kingdon 148–9
A Clockwork Orange 73 n.,
  337 n.
Code, Lorraine 146 n. 53
coercion and coercive
  predicaments 334–50
as opposed to compulsion 43
cognitive agency 5, 130, 143–53
  see also belief: and the will
Cohen, L. Jonathan 128 n. 14,
  149 n. 63
compatibilism 6, 14–15, 161 n.,
  162–75, 186–7, 197–9,
  202–4, 222, 226, 243, 306
hard and soft forms of 209–15
  see also incompatibilism
compulsion 3, 14, 31, 59–76,
  165–6, 169, 294–5, 323
and addiction 59–61, 320,
  334–7
relativity of 50–1
and responsibility 52–3
skepticism about 63–6
and weakness of will 33–4, 39,
  41–54, 58, 72, 73 n.
  see also addiction; irresistibility
compulsive behavior 31, 41–2,
  53 n. 20, 73
  see also addiction; compulsion
conditional analysis of 'can'
  173–5, 177–84
consequence argument 175–9

continence 48, 50
  see also incontinence
contracausal freedom 14
  see also agent-causation
contractualism 277 n. 37
control 143–5, 150–2, 172–3,
  269–72, 273
and addiction 321–9
  see also guidance control;
    self-control
Corwin, Miles 238 n., 242 n. 15
courage 39–40
criminal responsibility 68, 319,
  322–50
critical evaluation:
  capacity for 2, 6, 9, 76
  see also normative competence
Crucius, Christian 268, 270 n. 25,
  288
current time-slice theory of
  agency 211–13, 302–4

Dan-Cohen, Meir 324
Davidson, Donald 54 n. 20,
  173, 174 n. 16, 179, 183–4,
  293 n.
belief/desire model of action
  89–90
on incontinence and weakness
  of will 34–6, 38, 46 n. 13,
  169 n. 9
decisions see agency; will;
  choice
decision theory 16, 39 n., 48
Delgado, Richard 328 n. 27
deliberative necessity 106–10

Dennett, D. 104–6, 108–9,
  171–2, 181
dependency 59–61, 77, 81–5,
  320–1
  existential 81–4
  levels of 74–5, 83
  physical 74–6, 77 n. 28, 81,
    321 n. 7
  see also addiction
Descartes, René 143 n. 50, 154–6,
  187
desires 15 n., 21, 71, 167–8
  acculturated 24–5
  effect on decisions 23–4
  estrangement from 19–20
  and Franfurt's hierarchical
    model 27–9
  irresistible and compulsive 4,
    41–51, 62 n. 5, 63–73, 77,
    320–3
  resisting 48–52, 63–5
  and valuing 14, 17–26, 35–9,
    168–9
  see also addiction; appetites;
    compulsion
determinism 6–7, 10, 31, 163,
  165 n., 170–8, 190–5,
  198–206, 209–10, 243, 246–8,
  255–8
  see also indeterminism
Dewey, John 219, 260–1, 263
Double, Richard 202 n.
doxastic agency see belief: and the
  will; cognitive agency
Dressler, Joshua 338, 344 n. 68
Duff, Antony 231 n.

Duggan, T. 67, 172 n. 14
duress 318 n., 319, 334–50
  as impairment 342–4
  see also: coercion and coercive
    predicaments
Dworkin, G. 166 n. 6, 172 n. 14

Einstein, Albert 255–8
Elster, Jon 72, 83 n. 37, 86 n. 42,
  322 n. 9
emotions 40
  see also reactive attitudes
enabling v. performance
  conditions 92–3, 98–100
endorsement see identification
English Homicide Bill 326–7
evaluational illusion 37
evaluational system (or
  standpoint) 26, 31, 167–9
evil 9, 39, 247–50
  limits of 234–5, 238–9, 243
expressive theory of
  responsibility 221–33, 242–8

Feinberg, Joel 46–7, 63–4, 66,
  68 n. 16
Fine, G. 162 n. 1
Fingarette, Herbert 60 n. 3, 82,
  231 n., 321 n. 8, 323 n. 13
Fischer, John Martin 105 n. 27,
  165 n., 171, 177 n. 20,
  211–13
  on reasons-responsiveness
    66–7, 70, 97 n. 13, 289–301
  on taking responsibility
    306–15

Foley, R. 177 n. 20
Foot, Philippa 287 n. 53
Frankfurt, H. 1 n., 5, 62 n. 5, 100,
    135 n. 31, 185 n., 187, 194,
    198, 210–14, 264 n. 12,
    272 n. 30, 303 n. 11
  on first-order desires and
    higher-order volitions
    27–30, 114, 165–8, 212–3
  on identification 28–30, 114–18,
    166–9, 212–3, 272 n. 31
  on volitional necessity 4,
    83 n. 38, 88–9, 100–6, 110–22
  on wantonness 28–30, 111–12
  on the will 27–8, 119 n. 64,
    123, 164–7
freedom:
  free action as distinct from
    free will 164–5, 182–4,
    186–7, 193
  free agency 2, 4–6, 9, 13–32,
    65 n., 68, 119 n. 64, 151,
    155–7, 161–96, 197–215,
    249–50
  see also causation;
    compatibilism; consequence
    argument; determinism;
    incompatibilism;
    indeterminism;
    libertarianism
  free will. see freedom: free agency
Freud, Sigmund (and Freudianism)
    24, 42 n. 11

Gandhi (Mahatma) 257–8
Gardner, Eliot 80 n. 34

Gert, B. 67, 172 n. 14
Ginet, C. 176 n.
Glover, J. 67, 69, 172 n. 14,
    266 n. 16, 278–80
God 31, 155–6, 214–15
Gold, Mark S. 81 n., 348 n.
Goldman, A. 179, 189 n.
Goodman, Ariel 327 n. 24
Greenspan, P. S. 73 n., 172 n. 14,
    337 n.
Grinspoon, Lester 60, 320 n. 5,
    321 n. 8
guidance control 66–7
  ownership component of
    301–14
  reasons-responsiveness
    component of 290–301

Haksar, Vinit 231 n.
Halikas, James 77 n. 26, 320
Hamill, Pete 82
Hampshire, Stuart 54 n. 21,
    64 n. 10, 93 n. 5, 96 n. 8, 172,
    175 n.
Harman, Gilbert 277 n. 38
Harris, Robert Alton 235–52,
    258–9
Hart, H. L. A. 274 n. 34,
    280 n. 43
Heil, John 144, 147 n. 56
Herman, Barbara 130 n., 157
hierarchical view of the
    self 27–30, 164–9,
    211–12
Hieronymi, Pamela 141 n. 41
Hobart, R. E. 267–8

Hobbes, T. 14, 161 n., 162 n. 2,
        166, 182, 183, 186–7
Hoffman, Paul 65 n. 11
Holstrom, N. 166 n. 6
Holton, Richard 124 n. 4,
        134 n. 28
Hume, David 143 n. 50
    on reason 15–18
    on desires 16–17, 168
Hurley, Susan 148 n. 62

identification 24, 101, 113–20,
        166–70, 173
    endorsement v. caring criterion
        of 116–22
    Frankfurt's account of 28–30,
        114–18, 166–9, 212–13,
        272 n. 31
incompatibilism 6–7, 10, 170,
        173–8, 197–207, 209–10,
        243, 253
incontinence 18 n. 3, 69, 70
    Davidson's account 34–6, 38,
        46 n. 13, 169 n. 9
    see also akrasia; weakness
        of will
indeterminism 198–207
intentions and intentional action
        90, 125–7, 129–33, 135–7,
        138, 140–2, 143 n. 49,
        144–6, 148, 150, 152–3,
        169 n. 9, 183
    see also Moore's Paradox
Irwin, Terence H. 153–4

James, William 70 n., 148–9,
        198 n. 4

Jeffrey, Richard C. 30 n. 11
Johnson, C. 348 n.

Kadish, Sanford 319 n. 3,
        325 n. 17, 340 n. 57
Kahan, Dan 339–41
Kahn, Charles 154
Kane, Robert 101–2, 103 n. 25,
        104, 131 n. 18, 132 n. 24,
        171 n., 187 n. 27, 197,
        198 n. 4, 214
    and libertarianism 201–2,
        204–10
    the Free Agency Principle
        201–2, 206
Kant, I. (and Kantianism) 123,
        130 n. 17, 138, 189
    on freedom 163 n. 4, 197
    wille as distinct from willkür
        157
Kenny, A. 177 n. 19
King, Martin Luther, Jr. 257–8
Kolnai, A. 188
Korsgaard, Christine 130 n.
Kreek, Jeanne 77 n. 27
Kuehule, John 60 n. 2, 320 n. 6

Lamb, J. 176 n.
laws of nature 175–8
Leaving Las Vegas 70–1
Lehrer, K. 166 n. 6, 174 n. 16,
        177 n. 20, 179–80
Lewis, D. 177
libertarianism 162–4, 184–96,
        249–53
    hard and soft forms of
        197–208, 215

liberty of indifference 161, 163
liberty of spontaneity 161
Locke, Don 210, 213
Locke, John 156, 161 n.,
    162 n. 2
Loewenstein, George 86 n. 41,
    321–2, 326, 328, 329 n. 31
Lowinson, Joyce H. 77 n. 27,
    80 n. 34

MacIntyre, Alasdair 287 n. 54
Magill, Kevin 142 n. 45
Marks, Isaac 42 n.11, 95 n. 7, 97,
    99 n. 17
McCann, Hugh 141 n. 43,
    146 n. 54
McDowell, John 139
Melden, A. I. 177 n. 19
Mele, Alfred R. 126 n. 7,
    142 n. 46, 198 n. 4
Melville, Joy 99 n. 17
mesh theories 211–12, 303–6
Miller, Norman S. 81 n.
Milo, Ronald 226 n. 8, 266 n. 16
M'Naughton rule 330–3, 342
Model Penal Code:
    duress defense 338 n. 50, 343,
        345 n. 70
    insanity defense 330–2
Montaigne, Michel de 254 n.
Moore, Michael 345 n. 69
Moore's Paradox 131–3, 149
moral incapacity see Williams, B.
moral luck 245–9
    and personal identity 248
moral sanctions 275–80, 283–5
    see also blame; punishment

Moran, Richard 127 n. 10,
    131 n. 20, 139
Morse, Stephen 318 n., 350
motivational system 15, 25–6, 31
Murphy, Jeffrie 231 n.

Nagel, T. 41, 164 n., 189 n.,
    219, 244
Nash, J. Madeleine 64 n. 9,
    329 n. 29, 329 n. 31
naturalism 162 n. 3, 164 n.
Neely, W. 31 n., 166 n. 6
negligence 52–3, 208, 261
Nietzsche, Friedrich 32, 46 n. 13
normative competence 2, 4, 5,
    71–2, 144, 147, 261–4,
    282, 342
normative necessity 102–4, 108
    see also volitional necessity
Normore, Calvin 154
Nozick, Robert 226 n. 7
Nussbaum, Martha 339–41

O'Connor, Timothy 105 n. 27
O'Shaughnessy, B. 123, 124 n. 3,
    125 n. 5, 133, 138 n. 36,
    141–3, 188 n., 194 n.
Owens, David 128 n. 13,
    135 n. 30, 136 n. 33, 140,
    144, 148 n. 60, 150

Payne, Richard 74 n. 24, 77 n. 28,
    321 n. 7
Peele, Stanton 60 n.3, 72 n. 20,
    321 n. 8
Penner, Terry 18 n. 3, 63 n. 7
Perry, R. B. 18 n. 5

Pettit, Philip 144 n.
phobias and manias 13, 42–3,
    68 n. 15, 89, 94–100, 165–6,
    344–5
    skepticism about 97–8
Pink, Thomas 123–4, 135,
    140 n. 39, 142 n. 48
Piper, A. 169 n. 10
Plato 15–18, 21 n. 6, 30, 34 n. 3,
    36–7, 62 n. 7
Portenoy, Russell K. 74 n. 24,
    77 n. 28, 321 n. 7
Powell v. Texas 323
practical irrationality 4, 46 n. 13,
    72, 136 n. 34
practical reason (deliberation)
    124–39, 148–9
Pride and Prejudice 106–10
Pritchard M. S. 231 n. 12
punishment 67–8, 324–5
    see also moral sanctions;
    retributivism

Ravizza, Mark 105 n. 27,
    213 n. 23
    on reasons-responsiveness
    66 n. 12, 97 n. 13, 289–301
    on taking responsibility
    306–15
Rawls, John 138
Raz, Joseph 149 n. 64
reactive attitudes 220–35, 238–9,
    242–8, 253–4, 259, 315–16
    and the objective view 225,
    227, 255–8
real-self view *see* self-disclosure
    view of responsibility

reasons-responsiveness 7–9,
    66–71, 97 n. 13, 151,
    289–301
    and addiction 67–71
    individuation of reasons-
    responsive mechanism
    296–301
    ownership of reasons-
    responsive mechanism
    301–14
    receptivity and reactivity to
    reasons 292–4
reason view of responsibility
    262–3, 292 n. 6
Reid, Thomas 183 n. 23,
    187 n. 27, 188 n.
Reisinger, Marc 77 n. 27
resistibility 48–52, 63–71
    conditional criterion of 64
    see also compulsion; desires
responsibility 6, 7–10, 67–8,
    91–2, 109, 150–3, 165,
    204–15, 219–59, 260–88,
    289–317, 318–50
    and addiction 60, 294–300,
    318–37, 344–50
    and avoidability 264, 274,
    276–7, 279–80, 282–5
    for belief 150–1
    for character 208, 251–3,
    271–3, 282
    of children 229–31
    and compulsion 52 n. 18, 52–6,
    294–300
    for ends 271–3, 282
    excusing and exempting
    conditions 223–5, 227–33

historical conditions of 209–15,
242–3, 249–54, 280–2, 301–14
holding responsible 267,
274–7, 284
and moral address 229–35,
238–9, 242–3
and moral luck 245–9
skepticism about 8, 253–8,
285–6
for uncharacteristic actions
231–33
for weakness of will 51–6,
132 n. 23, 298–9
see also accountability;
attributability; criminal
responsibility; expressive
theory of responsibility;
reason view of responsibility;
self-disclosure view of
responsibility; taking
responsibility; ultimate
responsibility
retributivism 151, 255–8, 280
see also moral sanctions;
punishment
Reward Deficiency Syndrome
328–9
Roberts, Robert 124 n. 4
Robinson, Paul 329
robot argument 209–15

Santas, G. 38 n.
Scanlon, T. M. 8 n., 107 n., 128, 147
n. 57, 148 n. 62, 280 n. 43, 342
Scheffler, Samuel 339
Schopp, Robert 336 n. 48
Schulhofer, Stephen J. 340 n. 57

Seeburger, F. 74 n. 23, 81,
82 n. 35, 84 n. 39
self-control 44 n., 48, 62, 66–7,
69, 72, 85, 327–8, 337, 341,
343–9
failure of 3, 41–2, 55
normal degree of 49–51, 53
as a virtue 40–1, 57
see also weakness of will
self-deception 24–5, 43–4
self-determination 161–6, 169,
172, 174, 189–91, 193–4, 203
see also autonomy
self-disclosure view of
responsibility 260–72,
280–8
shame 51–2, 66
Shatz, D. 166 n. 6
Slote, Michael 178 n., 185 n.,
287–8
Smart, J. J. C. 14
Smith, Michael 144 n.
Socrates 31 n. 2
on the virtues 39–40
on weakness of will 33–4,
36–8, 57
Solomon, Andrew 93–5,
97 n. 10
Sorabji, R. 162 n. 1
Spitzer, Robert 60 n. 2, 320 n. 6
Stennie, K. 348 n. 74
Stern, Lawrence 234, 257 n. 29
Strawson, Galen 269 n., 315 n.
Strawson, Peter 219–34, 239,
242, 253–8
strength of will 4, 63–4,
124 n. 4

taking responsibility 271,
272 n. 31, 277
see also Fischer, John Martin:
on taking responsibility
Taylor, C. 271 n. 29
Taylor, R. 163 n., 185, 192–4,
201 n. 9
temperance 18 n. 3, 48–50
temptation 61, 63–6, 69, 72, 77
see also compulsion; desire
Thalberg, I. 166 n. 6, 189 n.
tracing and responsibility 208,
304–5

ultimate responsibility 204–10
unalterable intentions 67–9

valuational system 25, 31
van Inwagen, Peter 105 n.,
165 n., 175–6, 185, 189 n.,
264–5, 285
Velleman, David 127 n. 12,
133 nn. 25–6
virtue 37, 39–41, 57
volitional disability 93–100
volitional necessity 4–5, 83 n. 38,
88–9, 100–22
and Luther cases 4, 100–7,
110, 208
voluntariness 53, 69, 161 n.,
269, 273
and belief 146–9
see also belief: and the will;
intentions
Vuoso, George 304

Wallace, James 226 n. 8, 287 n. 53
Wallace, R. Jay 8 n., 124, 131,
133, 136 n. 34, 138 n. 35,
143, 148 n. 62, 152,
280 n. 44, 291 n. 3, 333 n. 41,
342
wantonness 18 n. 3
Frankfurt's account of 28–30,
111–12
and second-order volitions 28–9
Warnock, G. 177 n. 19
Waugh, Evelyn 145 n.
weakness of will 2–3, 18 n. 3,
33–58, 69–72, 131–4, 137–8,
169, 337
and blame 51–3, 55
Davidson's account of 34–6,
38, 46 n. 13, 169 n. 9
skepticism about 33–9, 42,
44–8, 57
Socrates' account of 33–4,
36–8, 57
see also addiction; compulsion
Wertheimer, Alan 340 n. 55,
343 n. 66, 344 n. 68
Wiggins, D. 190, 191 n. 30, 195,
199 n., 200–1, 203, 252 n. 23
will 3–5, 123–57, 186–8, 287
ability and disability of 89–100
Aristotle's account of 153–4
and decision 123–8, 136, 140–7
Descartes' account of 154–6, 187
executive function of 135–6, 157
Frankfurt's account of 27–8,
119 n. 64, 123, 164–7, 168 n. 7

internalist and externalist
  views of 129–37, 152–7
Kant's account of 157
as practical judgment 44–5
see also weakness of will
Williams, B. 143 n. 50, 156,
  161 n., 188
on moral incapacity 89 n. 1,
  98, 100–6, 109–10, 111 n. 35,
  112–14, 118
Wolf, Susan 2 n., 72 n. 21,
  261–4, 267–71, 281, 286,
  288, 342 n. 63

and the asymmetry thesis 282–5
and the reason view 262–3,
  292 n. 6
Wright, Larry 125 n. 6

Yaffe, Gideon 156
Young, Robert 172 n. 14
Youpa, Andrew 156 n. 71

Zagzebski, Linda 146 n. 53,
  149 n. 64, 150 n. 66
Zimmerman D. 166 n. 6
Zimmerman M. 193 n. 31